ANALYZING THE PSALMS

ANALYZING THE PSALMS

With Exercises for Bible Students and Translators

Second Edition

Ernst R. Wendland

International

The Scripture quotations used in this publication, when not my own literal or concordant translation of the Hebrew text, are in the main taken from the following English versions: the *New International Version* (NIV) © 1984 by the New York International Bible Society; the *Revised Standard Version* (RSV) © 1973 by the Division of Christian Education of the National Council of Churches of Christ in the U.S.A.; the *New Revised Standard Version* (NRSV) © 1989 by the Division of Christian Education of the National Council of Churches of Christ in the U.S.A.; the *Today's English Version* (TEV) © 1976 by the American Bible Society; the *Contemporary English Version* (CEV) © 1995 by the American Bible Society; and *God's Word* (GW) © 1995 by God's Word to the Nations Bible Society. All these are used by permission, for which I am grateful.

Second edition
© 2002 by SIL International
ISBN: 1-55671-129-8
Library of Congress Control Number: 2002102979
Printed in the United States of America

First edition 1998

This volume is distributed by Eisenbrauns, Inc. in conjunction with
SIL International. Copies may be purchased from:

Eisenbrauns, Inc.
P. O. Box 275
Winona Lake, IN 46590-0275, USA

or

International Academic Bookstore
SIL International
7500 West Camp Wisdom Road
Dallas, TX 75236, U.S.A.
www.ethnologue.com

DEDICATION

To
Dr. Eugene A. Nida

Missionary, Translator, Scholar, Teacher, Friend—
whom I have had the privilege of knowing and learning from
throughout the years of my African service in Christian communication.

וְהָיָה כְּעֵץ שָׁתוּל עַל־פַּלְגֵי מָיִם
אֲשֶׁר פִּרְיוֹ יִתֵּן בְּעִתּוֹ
וְעָלֵהוּ לֹא־יִבּוֹל
וְכֹל אֲשֶׁר־יַעֲשֶׂה יַצְלִיחַ׃ (Ps. 1:3)

הַלְלוּ יָהּ
שִׁירוּ לַיהוָה שִׁיר חָדָשׁ
תְּהִלָּתוֹ בִּקְהַל חֲסִידִים׃ (Ps. 149:1)

TABLE OF CONTENTS

FOREWORD 11

PREFACE 13

1. INTRODUCTION TO THE BOOK OF PSALMS 17
1.1 The origin of the word *psalms* 17
1.2 A brief history of the Psalter 18
1.3 The numbering of the psalms 20
1.4 Text critical issues 20
1.5 "Books" and other groupings within the Psalter 21
1.6 Paired psalms 23
1.7 Hebrew titles of the psalms 24
    1.7.1 Information about the author, editor, or addressee 24
    1.7.2 Psalm types 25
    1.7.3 Musical notations 26
    1.7.4 Liturgical directions 28
    1.7.5 Historical references 29
1.8 Why "sing a new song to the LORD" in your language 29

2. CATEGORIZING THE PSALMS ACCORDING TO GENRE 32
2.1 The five major functions 34
    2.1.1 Petition 34
    2.1.2 Thanksgiving 38
    2.1.3 Praise 41
    2.1.4 Instruction 42
    2.1.5 Profession of trust 45
2.2 The five minor functions 46
    2.2.1 Repentance 46
    2.2.2 Remembrance 48
    2.2.3 Retribution 49
    2.2.4 Royalty 51
    2.2.5 Liturgy 53
2.3 Conclusion: The importance of genre in the study of the Psalms 54

3. CONNECTED PARALLELISM: THE INTERNAL AND EXTERNAL STRUCTURE OF PAIRED LINES IN THE PSALTER 61
3.1 Preparing to study the poetic devices of Hebrew 61
3.2 The nature of connected parallelism: Internal structure 62
3.3 The nature of near parallelism: External structure 66
    3.3.1 Similarity 67
    3.3.2 Contrast 74
    3.3.3 Addition 77
3.4 A summary of the semantic relations between parallel lines 98

4. DISTANT PARALLELISM: THE MARKING OF TEXT BOUNDARIES IN THE PSALTER 108
4.1 How separated parallelism reveals text boundaries 108
    4.1.1 Inclusion 108
    4.1.2 Junction 110
    4.1.3 Aperture 111
    4.1.4 Closure 113

4.2 How convergence and harmony reveal text boundaries 118
    4.2.1 Markers of a beginning 118
    4.2.2 Markers of an ending 120
4.3 Summary of the marking functions of separated parallels 122
4.4 Some extended patterns of parallelism 123
    4.4.1 The unfolding, step-by-step pattern 123
    4.4.2 The inverted pattern 125

5. LOWER-LEVEL STYLISTIC FEATURES OF HEBREW POETRY 135
5.1 Repetitive language 135
    5.1.1 Individual words 136
    5.1.2 Word pairs and related sets of terms 137
5.2 Figurative language 139
    5.2.1 Simile 140
    5.2.2 Metaphor 142
    5.2.3 Metonymy 147
    5.2.4 Synecdoche 148
    5.2.5 Personification 150
    5.2.6 Anthropomorphism 152
    5.2.7 Apostrophe 153
    5.2.8 Hyperbole 154
5.3 Rhetorical questions 157
5.4 Condensed language 159
    5.4.1 Contraction (condensing the form) 160
    5.4.2 Compaction (condensing the content) 162
5.5 Varied language 165
    5.5.1 Variation in word order 165
    5.5.2 Variation in verb usage (tense/aspect and voice) 167
    5.5.3 Pronoun shifting 169
    5.5.4 Other less frequent kinds of variation 171
5.6 Phonological resonance 171
5.7 Multifunctional language 175

6. CONTENT: WHAT THE PSALMISTS PRAY AND PRAISE ABOUT 180
6.1 The cast of psalmic participants 180
6.2 Topics and themes in the Psalter 183
    6.2.1 Kingship 183
    6.2.2 Covenant 184
    6.2.3 Community 184
    6.2.4 Peace 185
    6.2.5 Warfare 186
    6.2.6 Sin 186
    6.2.7 Faith and faithfulness 187
    6.2.8 Deliverance 188
    6.2.9 Judgment 189
    6.2.10 Worship 189
    6.2.11 Summary 190
6.3 Key terms of the Psalter 192
    6.3.1 Learning to distinguish components of lexical meaning 192
    6.3.2 Idiomatic expressions 199

7. A TEN-STEP METHOD FOR ANALYZING A COMPLETE PSALM 204
7.1 The ten steps 204
    7.1.1 Step one: Study the context 204
    7.1.2 Step two: Read and internalize the psalm 205

7.1.3 Step three: Determine the genre 205
7.1.4 Step four: Plot the patterns of repetition 206
7.1.5 Step five: Locate the major breaks and peaks 206
7.1.6 Step six: Sketch out the compositional structure 206
7.1.7 Step seven: Do a complete word study and a detailed thematic outline 207
7.1.8 Step eight: Analyze the poetic features of the individual verses 207
7.1.9 Step nine: Determine the main "speech acts" and the personal interaction 208
7.1.10 Step ten: Do a trial translation, comparing other versions 208
7.2 Sample analyses of selected psalms 209
   7.2.1 Psalm 1 210
   7.2.2 Psalm 2 216
   7.2.3 Psalm 6 219
   7.2.4 Psalm 16 221
   7.2.5 Psalm 24 224
   7.2.6 Psalm 30 226
   7.2.7 Psalm 98 229
   7.2.8 Psalm 19 231

APPENDIX: ORGANIZING A BIBLICAL POETRY WORKSHOP 237
  1. The nature and purpose of a poetry translation workshop 238
  2. Choosing a poet to be part of the translation team 239
  3. Form and function in poetic discourse 240
  4. The presentation of Hebrew poetry and its features 241
  5. Poetic composition in the workshop setting 245
  6. Final artistic touches 247
  7. Follow-up 249
  8. A short case study 250

RECOMMENDED READING 252

INDEX 254

FOREWORD

More translation of the Old Testament is in progress now than at any previous time in history. And the Book of Psalms is always one of the books most requested by churches worldwide. One of the greatest challenges facing Bible translators is that of translating Hebrew poetry—and about forty per cent of the Old Testament is in poetical form. Ernst Wendland's workbook provides essential training and help for those who are facing this challenge.

The workbook has already proved its worth in a number of locations in Africa where it has been used as a basic tool in translation workshops focusing on the Psalms. It stimulates the student to discover the wonder of the multifaceted patterns and intricacy of poetic forms in which the Psalms are expressed, and to relate these details of the form to the emotive feelings for which they are the vehicle of expression. Step-by-step guidance in analyzing individual Psalms, with accompanying practical exercises, ensures that translators internalize the insights shared and learns to apply them in their translation work.

Invaluable practical advice is offered in the appendix on how to organize a biblical poetry workshop. How to achieve a translation that is faithful both to the original content and to the original poetic expression is constantly in view, while recognizing the need for creative expression if this goal is to be achieved.

I commend this workbook to all who face the challenge and enjoy the privilege of translating the Psalms.

                                                          Katharine Barnwell
                                                          International Translation Coordinator
                                                          Summer Institute of Linguistics

PREFACE

The aim of this textbook is to introduce Bible students and translators to the basic compositional structure and literary style of Hebrew poetry, especially the lyric-liturgical poetry found in the Book of Psalms (the Psalter). It is also intended to give readers some idea of the functions of the different psalms, emphasizing the manner in which these texts were used, and are still being used, to carry out several important communicative purposes. We shall see how the psalmists constructed these beautiful prayer-songs so as to express their deepest spiritual needs, problems, thoughts, and emotions—to God first of all, but also to the great assembly of fellow believers. Although the basic principles that are learned here focus specifically on the Book of Psalms, they can also be applied in the many passages, both long and short, that have been written as poetry in the Old Testament, especially in the prophetic books.

The approach to be followed is known as "discourse analysis." This simply means that during the course of our study we will try to examine the different aspects of these poetic texts as an integrated whole. The focus will be upon the formal features of the psalms, on both the higher as well as the lower levels of discourse structure. But elements of content (e.g., key terms) and function (e.g., psalm types or genres) will also receive due consideration.

The method of translation recommended here is a meaning-based approach termed *literary* functional equivalence. This means that students or Bible translators are encouraged to find the closest natural functionally equivalent form in the target language (TL, also called the "receptor language") in order to render the particular source language feature under consideration in the Psalms. Generally this will turn out to be some type of poetic device or rhetorical technique that is commonly utilized in the traditional orature or popular literature of the local language.

A number of exercises in the form of questions on the different topics of analysis have been included, normally at the end of each major discussion. It is recommended that students actually write out their answers on a separate sheet of paper or in a notebook. In addition, as they progress through this text, students will analyze and translate a number of complete psalms according to the main types presented in chapter 2. This translation is to be done either from Hebrew into English (or some other language familiar to the student and then compared with various English and other language versions) and/or from English to the mother tongue of the student. It is hoped that this way of studying the Book of the Psalms will help exegetes and translators alike to make their own preliminary analysis of the overall structure and style of any one of these life-touching prayers and hymns.

Throughout the book many illustrative Scripture quotations are cited. These are from the NIV except where otherwise indicated. Certain key Hebrew terms are included in transliterated form; however, distinctions in the vowel sounds have not been made for the sake of simplicity.

In chapter 1 we begin by investigating some important background information on the Psalter in general: its history, internal arrangement, and introductory titles. Chapter 2 is an examination of the Psalter as groups of related psalms from the point of view of their form (structure), content (subject matter), and function (purpose). Here we will overview ten different psalm types, or "genres" (five general and five specific types), categorized according to why the writers wrote them and how they intended them to be used.

In chapter 3 the main characteristics of the style (manner of composing) of Hebrew poetry, are analyzed beginning with the most obvious and important feature: parallelism. Much of Hebrew poetry is written in pairs of lines closely related to each other in both form and meaning. There are three main categories of parallelism: parallels in which the second line repeats the basic sense of the first line in a *synonymous* way; parallel lines that are *contrastive*; and parallel lines that are *additive* (i.e., the second lines adds more specific information or extra emphasis to the meaning in the first line). Most commonly, the parallelism comprises two lines (a bicolon), but it sometimes comprises three or four related lines.

Normally parallel poetic lines follow one another; that is, they are adjacent or "connected" to each other in the text. But in certain instances they are "separated" from one another. Such separated parallel lines are treated in chapter 4, where we see how they serve to mark sectional boundaries, either a beginning (*aperture*) or ending (*closure*), or a point of special emphasis within the discourse in terms of theme (*peak*) or emotive tension (*climax*). An analysis of these and other types of linkage involving form, content, and function between two or more parallel lines helps us to better understand the structure of a given psalm. It also enables us to see more clearly how these different parts operate as a unit to give the main meaning of the entire psalm.

In chapter 5 we take a closer look at some of the other poetic devices that the psalmists used to convey their thoughts, feelings, attitudes, and intentions to a God whom they believed was holy and all-powerful, yet also close by and interested enough to listen to them. These features function together with the patterns of parallelism to mark the borders of poetic "paragraphs" (unequal/shorter = *strophes*, equal/longer = *stanzas*) and to emphasize the most important parts of the text. Among the main stylistic devices considered are repeated words, figures of speech, rhetorical questions, the use of condensed language, certain shifts from normal usage (word order, pronouns, tense), and "sound effects." This last feature shows that the psalms were obviously meant to be recited or sung—heard aloud rather than read silently.

In chapter 6 some of the principal religious themes and topics of the Psalter are briefly surveyed, and several ways of analyzing and translating its key terms, unfamiliar concepts, and idiomatic expressions are presented. The themes may be discovered by exploring the different relationships that exist among the three major participants referred to in the psalms: *God* (the primary focus of attention), the *psalmist* (or God's people), and the *enemies* (or some crisis or calamity). Other important notions become evident when consideration is given also to the secondary participants, namely, the "congregation" and the "nations."

In chapter 7 a ten-step methodology is suggested to help students analyze a complete psalm on their own in conjunction with a good practical commentary such as *A Translator's Handbook on the Book of Psalms* (THP) by Robert Bratcher and William Reyburn (United Bible Societies, 1991) or that of Broyles (1999) and a reliable Study Bible such as the NIV edition (NIV-SB, Zondervan, 1985). Several complete psalms are then examined in detail and then translated as a way of putting the analytical procedures into practice.

The discussion in the appendix may be helpful for organizers of a translation workshop that focuses on the Psalms. It gives an overview of one possible way in which the material of this book may be applied.

The students who use this textbook would find some knowledge of Biblical Hebrew useful, but if they do not know Hebrew, it would help to know how to use an interlinear version. Most of the exercises in this book can be done even without this, by using the standard versions of the Bible in English or whatever other languages the students know.

Before attempting the exercises, it is important for the students, Bible translators in particular, to make a careful study of the poetic types and features of their own literary tradition, whether oral or written. Once they have done this, they can compare the poetry of their own language to Hebrew poetry in terms of form and purpose, remembering always that it is the translator's aim to re-create the essential "meaning" (content + connotation + function) of a given Hebrew psalm by using the closest natural equivalents of poetic form in the target language.

After completing this course, further practice will be necessary so that the methodology and procedures become automatic. As experience is gained, translators will be better prepared to convey the central meaning of a Hebrew poetic text in a manner that evokes a similar esthetic, emotional, and volitional response from the people today for whom it is being translated as it did from the ancient people for whom it was first written—and recited or sung.

In closing I wish to acknowledge the many helpful comments of Mrs. Sheila Tuggy of the Summer Institute of Linguistics in Peru, who translated an initial draft of this workbook into Spanish and field-tested it. Dr. Murray Salisbury of Jerusalem reviewed the entire text and offered a number of valuable suggestions for improvement. I also benefited from the work of my colleague Dr. Lynell Zogbo, United Bible Societies' translation consultant in the Ivory Coast, who co-authored with me another book on the translation of biblical poetry (*Hebrew Poetry in the Bible: A Guide for Understanding and for Translating*, New York: United Bible Societies, 2000). Much encouragement and advice came along the way from Dr. Katharine Barnwell, International Translation Coordinator of the Summer Institute of Linguistics. A special word of thanks must be given to Mrs. Betty Eastman of the SIL Translation Department, who "translated" many of the technical expressions found in an earlier draft of this material into a more comprehensible style and to Mrs. Faith Blight who prepared the book for publication. Additional corrections, criticisms, and comments are always welcome. Please send these to:

> Ernst R. Wendland
> Lusaka Translation Centre (United Bible Societies)
> P.O. Box 310091 – Chelston 15301
> Lusaka, Zambia
>
> [E-mail: wendland@zamnet.zm; erwendland@hotmail.com]

PREFACE TO THE REVISED EDITION

This workbook has been in use now for several years, and during this time a number of errors has not surprisingly come to light, along with quite of few places in the text where some revision and/or addition would be helpful. I have profited from working through the book again with two more classes of students (Lutheran Seminary, Lusaka), and I have received some excellent suggestions for improvement from Dr. Lee Fields, who is using the text in a similar way at Roanoke Bible College (North Carolina), as well as from Dr. Andre Desnitsky, who is overseeing a translation and adaptation of the book into Russian (Institute for Bible Translation). This positive feedback plus several encouraging letters from individuals who are using the book in different parts of the world led me to review the entire text with a critical eye in order to prepare this revision. Many minor changes have been made throughout the text and a number of major ones as well. Undoubtedly even more needs to be undertaken, but this is the best I can do before the deadline for reprinting. Your continued critical suggestions are welcome and indeed appreciated. My thanks also go to Dr. Dick Blight of the SIL Production Department, who encouraged me to move ahead with the present revision.

The book of Psalms is a hymn on the entire Scripture.
Most beautifully and briefly it embraces everything in the entire Bible.

(Martin Luther)

E.W.—address as above, also:

Centre for Bible Translation in Africa

University of Stellenbosch
Stellenbosch, South Africa
November, 2001

1. INTRODUCTION TO THE BOOK OF PSALMS

In this opening section of our course we want to take a look at the Book of Psalms as a whole. Knowing some general background information will help prepare us to examine the Hebrew text in more detail later. What does the word *psalms* mean? What is the history of the Psalter? How is it organized and what is the significance of the various titles that head many of the individual psalms? Of what importance is the Book of Psalms to us today and why is it often one of the first books of the Old Testament to be translated in languages all over the world?

1.1 The origin of the word *psalms*

The Book of Psalms is a collection, or, to be more exact, several collections, of religious songs. "The English word 'Psalms' is a transliteration of the Greek term *psalmoi*, which is the title of the book in the Greek translation of the Old Testament, the Septuagint" (A Translator's Handbook on the Book of Psalms [hereafter THP], p. 1). The singular of this Greek noun was used to translate the Hebrew term *mizmor*, which means a song sung to the accompaniment of a musical instrument. It occurs fifty-seven times in the Book of Psalms (e.g., in Ps. 3). The Greek collective noun *psaltērion* refers to the entire book of 150 individual psalms. In some of the ancient Greek manuscripts it is seen as the book's title instead of *psalmoi*. The English word "Psalter" is a loanword from the Greek, just as "psalms" is.

The Hebrew title of this collection of God-centered poems is "The Book of Praises," or simply "Praises" (*təhillim*), a term which is also used to refer to a single "song of praise" like Psalm 145. This word is a fitting title because it calls attention to one of the main purposes of the book as a whole: all of the psalms in one way or another praise or proclaim the glory and majesty of God. Another appropriate designation is found in Psalm 72:20: *təpillot*, or "prayers." This, too, is a good name since the psalms are used to make known to the almighty and merciful Lord some of man's greatest needs and problems in life. Thus the Psalter is both the hymnbook and the prayer book of God's people throughout the ages. It enriches the public worship and private devotional life of believers today. For these reasons the Book of Psalms is usually one of the first Old Testament books to be translated into another language.

Exercise 1.1: Answer the following questions as fully as possible on a separate sheet of paper.

1. What word has been used to translate the name of the Book of Psalms in your language? See Luke 20:42 and Acts 1:20.

2. Could this word or phrase have some meaning other than "songs" in your language? Could it be confused with some similar-sounding word? If so, tell what this other word is and what it means.

3. If the word in your language is simply a transliteration from English or some other major language (e.g., in Chewa [CH], the word is *Masalimo*), what does this term really mean to most people, if anything? What do most English speakers understand by the word "Psalms"?

4. You have learned the meaning of the name used in the original Hebrew. Do you think that you could find a more fitting title for the Book of Psalms in your language? If so, write it down and tell what it means in your language. If not, explain why a more suitable term could not be found.

5. The title that the Chewa translation team first used was *Nyimbo za Mapemphero*, meaning "(the) songs of prayers." What do you think of this as a name for the Book of Psalms? Could it lead to

some confusion? Explain. Would this expression work in your language? Explain why or why not.

1.2 A brief history of the Psalter

Although it may not be evident at first reading, the 150 psalms in the Psalter were not all composed by the same person nor even in one person's lifetime. Rather, the book reflects a long religious and liturgical tradition which may span a thousand years or more. However, the greatest number of psalms were undoubtedly composed during the four centuries in which the dynasty of David ruled in Jerusalem, that is, about 1000–600 B.C. According to the historical records of Israel, it seems likely that most psalms were composed while David and Solomon were king, when the nation was strong and the "ministry of music" was especially encouraged (see 1 Chr. 25; 2 Chr. 5:12–13).

There are a number of psalms in the Old Testament in books other than the Psalter. For example, there are the ancient songs of Moses and Miriam which celebrate Yahweh's mighty deliverance of the people of Israel at the Red Sea (Exod. 15:1–18, 21). From the time of the Judges comes the ancient victory song of Deborah and Barak (Jdg. 5:2–31). Several beautiful psalms are found in the historical books of Samuel (e.g., 1 Sam. 2:1–10; 2 Sam. 1:19–27; 22; 23:1–7). There are also some psalms in the books of the pre-exilic prophets (e.g., Isa. 2:2–4; 12; 26:1–6; 27:2–5; 38:10–20; Jer. 14:7–9; Ezek. 19:1–14; Hos. 6:1–3; Hab. 3).

Around the time of the exile in Babylon and beyond, the poetic spirit of sacred music in Judah seemed to diminish greatly, no doubt because of the terrible things, both religious and secular, that the nation was experiencing. Thus it would appear that we have only a few psalms either from that disastrous period of history (e.g., Ps. 74; 78; 89:38–52; 137) or from the time of the restoration (e.g., Ps. 107:2–3; 147:2, 13). The difference in the style of composing Judah's "praises" after the exile can be seen in the long historical psalm-prayer found in Nehemiah 9:5–37.

Finally, we must remember that there are several important "psalms" in the New Testament, for example, the songs of Mary (Lk. 1:46–55) and Zechariah (Lk. 1:68–79). As it turns out, these compositions are collections of skillfully interwoven quotations from the Psalter.

On the basis of their studies of language and theme, many modern scholars date most of the psalms as coming from the post-exilic period. But more conservative commentators suggest that this is not necessarily the case. For one thing there was little to celebrate after the exile. True, the Jews were back in their own land again, but they certainly had very little else to sing about from a worldly point of view. Indeed, the period of God's special "inspiration" of chosen writers was rapidly drawing to a close. Therefore, it seems more likely that most psalms date from the earlier period of Israel's history—its "golden age" of power and influence in the Mediterranean region.

There is much archaeological evidence to bolster this view. Archeologists have discovered that similar musical traditions to the Psalms existed in both the oral and written literature of other peoples of Canaan (Palestine) even long before the time of Abraham (about 2100 B.C). The presence of certain alleged "late" Aramaic words in some of the psalms proves nothing since this language was already exerting its influence in the Middle East as a *lingua franca* during the time of David and Solomon (cf. 2 Kg. 18:26).

Another piece of indirect evidence for an early date comes from the Septuagint (LXX), the Greek translation of the Old Testament. Its translators, who were working in the third century B.C., seem to demonstrate some ignorance concerning the construction and content of ancient Hebrew poetry. This is especially true with regard to certain stylistic devices such as imagery and allusion. A somewhat different system of numbering, psalm arrangement, and occasionally also a variant Hebrew textual base is also in evidence. All this would suggest that the Septuagint translators carried out their work long after the psalms were originally composed.

Although the process of collecting, sorting, and arranging the psalms was probably a more or less continual one, especially during the Psalter's initial stages of development, it is likely that the main effort was concentrated in three major periods of activity. The first and most important of these was during the time of the "master singer-composer" himself, King David. In addition to his inspired work as the author of most of the psalms (2 Sam. 23:2-3), David probably also arranged for their collection and usage. For example, he assigned 4,000 Levites the task of attending to the musical aspect of temple worship, as we see in 1 Chronicles 23:5. This work surely continued during the reign of Solomon, at least during the years when Solomon was still completely devoted to the LORD (see 2 Chr. 5:11-14). Several hundred years later, when King Hezekiah reformed and revitalized the true worship of Yahweh in Jerusalem, he followed the guidelines of his famous ancestor David (see 2 Chr. 29:25-30). This reformation no doubt included renewed work on compiling and organizing the Psalter (2 Chr. 29:35b; 30:21; 31:2; cf. Prov. 25:1).

Finally, after the captivity in Babylon, proper religious worship was again instituted under the leadership of the Levites (Ezra 6:18; Neh. 12:27-30, 45-47). It may well be that Ezra the scribe, who "devoted himself to the study and observance of the Law of the LORD" (Ezra 7:10; cf. Neh. 7-10), was the person who played the major role in putting the Psalter into its present and final canonical form, a process that was probably completed in the third century B.C.

Exercise 1.2

1. Compare Nehemiah 9:5-37 with Psalms 78, 105, and 106. Mention several important *similarities* and *differences* that you find with respect to form or content.

2. Now compare 1 Chronicles 16:8-36 with Psalms 96, 105, and 106. Which verses correspond?

                                     1 Chronicles 16:8-36

    Psalm 105   _____   _____

    Psalm 96   _____   _____

    Psalm 106   _____   _____

3. Which psalm is exactly the same as 2 Samuel 22? This important passage gives us David's view of the Psalter as well as the Psalter's view of David. Explain why this is so.

4. Why is such correspondence important as far as our interpretation of the Psalter is concerned?

5. What was probably the most important spiritual event of David's life as recorded in 2 Samuel 7:1-17? How did David respond to this great revelation (see 2 Sam. 7:18-29 and 2 Sam. 23:5)? How does the LORD's covenant with David provide a central perspective on the entire Psalter? See Psalm 89, which revolves around vv. 3-4.

6. What are the major similarities between the thanksgiving songs of Hannah (1 Sam. 2:1-10) and Mary (Lk. 1:46-55)? What does this suggest about how Mary composed her song? Why is it necessary to compare similar and parallel passages *first* before attempting to translate any one of them?

7. How can you find out whether there are any parallel passages that apply to a text you are studying or wish to translate?

8. Use the cross reference section of your Bible to find at least three psalm passages that Mary may have used in her song.

9. Give the Scripture reference for three of the psalms that appear in the Books of Samuel. Then briefly describe the setting or occasion of each one.

10. Of what significance to Bible translation and the contemporary church of God is the fact that David established a special corps of Levites to oversee the music ministry of public worship at the tabernacle?

1.3 The numbering of the psalms

The earliest Hebrew manuscripts did not number the psalms in sequence. The convention of numbering was established later, and the total became fixed in the canon at 150. This system has been adopted by all Protestant Bible translations. The Greek Septuagint (LXX), however, which was followed by the Latin Vulgate, includes an additional psalm at the end (151). The Greek-Latin text (which is often followed by Catholic versions) also subdivides several of the psalms differently.

One must also keep in mind that the Hebrew Bible, known as the Masoretic text (MT), begins a numbering of the individual verses of a given psalm with its title, if one is present. This practice was not observed by the translators of most English versions. As a result, the verse numbers of such psalms are always one less than the numbers of the corresponding verses in the MT. There are several other differences in numbering between the ancient versions (the Hebrew, Greek, and Latin texts) and the modern versions such as the Revised Standard Version (RSV), New International Version (NIV), and Today's English Version (TEV). These differences are listed in the THP (pp. 1190–94).

Exercise 1.3

1. List one English version (or French, Spanish, etc.) that follows the verse numbering system of the psalms in Hebrew and two which do not number the title of the psalm.

2. Which numbering system does the major version of your region follow?

3. Which numbering system do you think is better to follow and why?

4. On page 12 in the THP is a table indicating the major differences in the way the Hebrew text numbers the psalms (followed by most English versions) and the way the Septuagint and Vulgate numbers them (followed by most Catholic translations). Examine this table and then fill in the spaces below:

    (a) Psalms _____ and _____ in the Hebrew text are combined as Psalm 9 in the _____ text.
    (b) Psalm _____ in the Greek text turns out to be Psalms _____ and 115 in the Hebrew text.
    (c) Psalm _____ in the Hebrew text is divided into Psalms 114 and _____ in the _____ text.
    (d) Psalm 147 in the Hebrew text is divided into Psalms _____ and _____ in the Greek text.

5. Why are the numbers of the psalms and verses important? Why do we not simply do away with the verse numbers?

1.4 Text critical issues

Textual criticism is the scholarly study that aims to determine the precise wording of the original text of Scripture, whether in Hebrew or Greek. The manuscripts that were written by the first authors are no longer in existence; only copies of these remain, and many of the earliest instances are either damaged or not complete. Textual critics compare the oldest manuscripts that we have, along with ancient translations like the Septuagint (LXX, Greek), the Vulgate (Latin), and the Syriac version, and using established techniques of comparative and intertextual analysis posit, with varying degrees of certainty, what the original texts must have been. Of course, there is a certain amount of speculation, doubt, and outright disagreement that is involved in such studies, but by and large a significant amount of consensus has been reached.

Due to the technical nature of these investigations and their basis in the original languages, we will not be able to explore this subject further. Several good reference works are available in case you wish to pursue some of these issues in more detail. For our purposes, we will simply depend on the advice and recommendations of reliable commentaries, such as the THP, as well as the textual notes that are provided in most English versions. Where such advice differs from one version to the next, students may follow the "majority opinion" (but giving THP three "votes" instead of one due to its importance for Bible translators).

Exercise 1.4

1. Read the NIV text note at Ps. 22:16. Write out the disputed portion of the passage as it stands and then below it the alternative text that is given in the note. Where does the difference lie and how significant is this to the meaning here? Now check the NRSV, GNB, and CEV to see how they handled this matter. What do you find—which reading has the "majority support"? What does the THP advise regarding this issue?

2. Check through the Psalms for another text note of this nature—one that does affect one's understanding as well as the translation of the verse. Compare the different versions as above, also the THP, and make your own recommendation concerning the problem that you have discovered.

1.5 "Books" and other groupings within the Psalter

The Book of Psalms appears at the beginning of the "Writings" (*kətubim*), which is the third principal division of the Hebrew Bible. This initial position may be an indication of its preeminence within this group of books. Thus the whole division was also sometimes referred to simply as "the Psalms." The first two of the Hebrew Bible's three divisions are "the Law" (*tōrâ*) and "the Prophets" (*nəbiʾim*), as noted in Luke 24:44. This prominence given to the Psalms shows how important they were to the religious faith and worship of the people of Israel.

There is a clear subdivision of the Psalter into five distinct sections. These sections are called "books." A clear marker of this structure is the special word of praise to God which concludes each of the five parts. In the first four books, this "doxology" consists of just a verse or two. But at the end of the fifth and final division, an entire psalm (i.e., 150—the "Great Hallelujah Hymn") performs this concluding function, no doubt because this marks the close of the liturgical collection as a whole. Many commentators think that this division into five books was an attempt to reflect the structure of the Torah, that is, the five books of Moses (the Pentateuch). This interpretation is supported by the placement of an obvious "Instruction of the LORD" psalm at the beginning of the Psalter (see Ps. 1).

A number of other distinct collections are found within the five major divisions. These collections are often indicated by similar expressions in the titles (headings) of certain groupings. (These titles will be examined more closely in the following exercise.) Other indications of separate groupings can be seen as well. In Books I, IV, and V, for example, the divine covenantal name *Yahweh* (*YHWH*) is stressed, while in Book II it is *Elohim* that occurs more frequently, the general term referring to the deity ("God"). In Book III, the middle grouping, the usage appears to be divided between the two names: in Psalms 73-83 it is *Elohim* and in Psalms 84-89 it is *Yahweh*. Furthermore, Book II ends with the statement "This concludes the prayers of David, son of Jesse" (72:20), suggesting that the first two sections at one time existed as a separate and independent unit. But then again there are two much smaller groups of "David" psalms that occur later in Book Five (108-110 and 138-145), thus extending David's "influence" throughout the entire Psalter. Other smaller sets of psalms can be seen grouped according to genre or content, such as the "kingship songs" of 93/96–99 and the "hallelujah psalms," 104–106, 111–117, and 146–150.

The Psalter as a whole has been organized carefully. It is not just a random, haphazard arrangement of unconnected items. Rather, important psalms are placed at key positions within the structural arrangement of the complete book. The occurrence of a teaching psalm at the very beginning of the Psalter is significant. It serves as the Psalter's motto or preface, indicating the importance of the LORD's "instruction" (*torah*) as the foundation for all proper worship and praise of him. Our faith is manifested in lives of faithful obedience to the "way" of his covenant (1:6). This teaching is closely connected with Psalm 2, a "royal" psalm, featuring the theme some scholars consider to be the principal one of the entire Psalter, namely, that of the supreme kingship of Yahweh, the covenant LORD, and of his "Anointed One," the Messiah. Our lives of righteous service (Ps. 1) and unbounded praise (Ps. 150) are to be focused and founded upon our glorious God and King (see Ps. 2 and Pss. 145–149). "Blessed" are all those people of his kingdom (Ps. 144:15) who recognize, value, and live according to these eternal principles (Ps. 1:1/2:12)!

Considering the Psalter in its entirety, we notice that there is a general movement from prayers of lament and petition to songs of thanksgiving and praise. This is a worshipful progression anchored by the three great teaching psalms (i.e., 1, 19, and 119), as well as by four key royal psalms (i.e., 2; 72 at the end of Book II; 89 at the end of Book III; and 145 near the end of Book V). Indeed, most individual psalms reflect this same development of theme from sadness to gladness, from sin and its consequences (as revealed by God's Law) to the results of salvation (as revealed in his gospel)—a point that will become clear in our study of the major psalm types. The "petitions," or prayers for help in the time of trouble, are concentrated especially in Books I–III, but "hymns," or songs of thanksgiving and praise, clearly predominate in Books IV and V. The Psalter culminates in a set of such joyful hymns, which summon all people to "Praise the LORD!" (note especially Ps. 150).

Exercise 1.5

1. Looking at your Bible or THP (p. 1), fill in the spaces below with the numbers of the psalms found in each of the five books and the numbers of the verse or verses that represent its concluding doxology ("word of praise"):

BOOK	Psalm Numbers	Verse(s) of the Doxology
I	_____	_____
II	_____	_____
III	_____	_____
IV	_____	_____
V	_____	_____

2. How do you think that these five major divisions ought to be indicated (if at all) in your Bible?

3. In what way would sectional headings help readers and students of the Psalms?

4. What is the theme of Psalm 150, and why is it an excellent way to end the Psalter?

5. Read the headings of the following groups of psalms and pick out the key word(s) that seem to link them together as a special collection.

   (a) 42–49, 84–88 =

   (b) 42–45, 52–55 =

   (c) 73–83   =

   (d) 120–134   =

(e) 138–145   =

6. What do Psalms 146–150 have in common, making them a distinct set? Why do you think that this group is placed where it is in the Psalter?

1.6 Paired psalms

It is interesting to observe how many pairs of psalms are linked to one another by means of the repetition of key ideas or similar words and phrases. It is almost as if the prominent Hebrew poetic feature of two parallel lines has been extended to the level of complete psalms. One of the clearest instances of "parallel psalms" is Psalms 42 and 43. First, we notice that Psalm 43 does not have a title as Psalm 42 does, and as the following psalms do. This would suggest that the title of Psalm 42 is meant to cover the contents of both Psalms 42 and 43. Second, we notice the same repeated "refrain" of both psalms in which the chorus, or congregation, encourages the singer with an exhortation to "put your hope in God!" (42:5, 11; 43:5). In addition, the two psalms are "framed" by synonymy. That is, they are enclosed by a strong expression of the desire to "meet with God" (42:1–2) and a corresponding vow to "go to the altar of God" (43:4). Because of these and other more detailed connections (e.g., the references to well-known mountains in 42:6 and 43:3), it is clear that this psalmic "parallel pair" was meant to be read, chanted, or sung *together*—and likewise interpreted together as a single composition.

There are many other examples of this important compositional feature in the Psalter as a whole. (Additional examples are mentioned in the exercises.) Some other psalms can be seen to be related, even though they do not occur right next to each other. Note, for example, that Psalms 14 and 53 are found in relatively similar positions in Books I and II. Such high-level "discourse parallelism" serves to give internal unity and structure to the entire Psalter. It also broadens the scope of one's interpretation of an individual psalm to include a much wider context.

Exercise 1.6

1. Psalms 9 and 10 are considered to be parallel psalms. Indeed, they form one psalm (9) in the Septuagint and Vulgate. Study these two psalms and then give at least one good piece of evidence to indicate their close connection. What is the common theme in 9:7 and 10:16?

2. What obvious piece of repetition joins Psalms 103 and 104? What is significant about the place where this repetition occurs? In general, what are the two great "works" of the LORD that each of these psalms speak about, in 103? In 104?

3. What common expression links Psalms 134 and 135? Here Yahweh's two great works are magnified. Which work is focused upon in 134 and which in 135?

4. What opening similarity calls attention to the fact that Psalms 105 and 106 may be interpreted as a unit? Which "wonderful/mighty acts of the LORD" do these two psalms remind us of?

5. Psalms 111 and 112 are joined at their border by an important thematic statement. What is it? What common subject also links these parallel psalms? Notice the connection also with Psalm 1. Write down the key words and phrases that are similar.

6. What common topic unites Psalms 127 and 128? What special "blessing" (127:3–5) comes to those who "fear the LORD" (cf. 128:1–4)?

7. Carefully compare Psalms 14 and 53. List the corresponding verses that are *exactly the same* and those that are somewhat *different*. Now observe the names that are used to refer to God. What do you notice here? (The many similarities and several differences would suggest that these two versions of the same psalm once belonged to separate "collections.")

8. Should such correspondences and contrasts be reflected in a Bible translation? Why?

9. List some of the major similarities and differences in how Psalms 1 and 73 view the righteous and the wicked in this life. A consideration of Psalm 1 seems to fit well between the two verses that mark the chief turning point of Psalm 73, that is, between verses ____ and ____.

10. Observe where Psalms 1 and 73 occur within the overall organization of the Psalter: 1 at the beginning of Book ____ and 73 at the beginning of Book ____. What does this suggest about the arrangement of psalms in the Psalter (cf. Ps. 72:20)? Psalm 73 is thus located at the midpoint of the book as a whole. Read through Ps. 73 and see if you can see any reason for its special placement. We should always be looking out for larger patterns and correspondences, whether exact or synonymous, wherever they occur in the Psalms. We must then try to determine the special contextual significance of these structures in terms of form-structure, content-theme, and/or purpose-function. (For a detailed study of this feature of Psalm 73, see "Introit 'into the sanctuary of God' (Psalm 73:13): Entering the theological 'heart' of the psalm at the centre of the Psalter," *Old Testament Essays* 11/1, 1998, 128-153.)

1.7 Hebrew titles of the psalms

Every psalm has a heading or title, also called a superscription, with the exception of the thirty-four known as "orphan" psalms. (In the Septuagint, half of these orphan psalms *are* given titles.) The title may have been included by the author-compiler of a given psalm at the time of its writing, or it may have been attached later by an editor.

The titles present various kinds of information concerning the nature and composition of the individual psalms they head. Unfortunately, much of this information is not very helpful to us today because scholars have not been able to determine the original meaning in many cases. Five major categories of information may be distinguished, though these are not neatly separated: (1) information about the author, editor, or addressee; (2) the genre type; (3) musical notations; (4) liturgical directions; and (5) the historical setting.

1.7.1 Information about the author, editor, or addressee

Preceding any proper name or official title in a heading, there appears the Hebrew preposition *l-*. This can mean "of," "to," "by," "about," or "for." Due to its wide area of meaning, it is sometimes difficult to determine whom the name following the preposition was intended to designate—the author (composer or collector/compiler), the addressee, or the sponsor of a particular psalm. The expression "to the (name)" could mean the person who wrote the psalm, the one to whom it was dedicated, the one who was commissioned to perform it, or the one who authorized and supported its composition. It might even indicate the person who selected the psalm for inclusion within a given collection.

Occasionally, the phrase "to/for + personal name" is found twice within a single title. For example, the title of Psalm 4 (literally) is "to/for-the-one-directing with-stringed-instruments a-song-of to/for-David." In this instance, the first name is probably a reference to the person who was responsible for seeing to it that the psalm was put into the proper musical collection or was sung correctly during public worship (the NIV has "the director of music"). The second name then refers to the author (the NIV has "a psalm of David"). Despite some uncertainty, it is perhaps best to conclude that whenever "to" is followed by a proper name, it refers to a psalm's author (THP, p. 9).

Seventy-three of the psalms are ascribed to King David: 3-9, 11-32, 34-41, 51-65, 68-70, 86, 103, 108-110, 122, 124, 131, and 138-145. As this list shows, David's psalms are found both individually and in groups throughout the Psalter, thus serving as an anchor or foundation for the whole collection. The tradition that King David was Israel's foremost "singer of songs" is strong in both testaments (see 2 Sam. 22:1; 1 Chr. 6:31; 16:7; Neh. 12:24; Amos 6:5; Acts 4:25; 13:36;

Rom. 4:6–8; Heb. 4:7). The Old Testament historical books bear witness to the fact that David did have considerable musical abilities (1 Sam. 16:18, 23; 2 Sam. 6:5) and was the founder of Israel's official "hymnal" (1 Chr. 15:16; 16:7; 23:2–6; 25:1; Ezra 3:10). Furthermore, a number of his songs are recorded outside the Psalter, in 2 Samuel, for example (1:19–27, a lament over the deaths of Saul and Jonathan; 3:33–34, a lament over Abner; 22:2–51, thanksgiving for deliverance from all his enemies; and 23:2–7, his farewell hymn). Therefore it is very likely that David did in fact compose—or at least personally select and adapt—many if not all of the psalms that bear his name. But other names referring to authors, choirmasters, or song collectors are also found.

Exercise 1.7.1

1. In your language what is the most natural way of translating the phrase "A psalm of David" (see Ps. 29, NIV)? Give a literal back-translation of this expression in English. Is there any possibility that some people might misunderstand this expression? For example, could it mean "a song about David"?

2. The song of David in 2 Samuel 22 is exactly the same as one of the psalms. Which psalm? How does this support the argument that David wrote this particular psalm as well as many others?

3. Which personal name is given in the heading of the following psalms and groups of psalms?
   (a) 42, 44–49, 84–85, 87 (see also 1 Chr. 6:31, 33, 39).
   (b) 50, 73–83 (see 1 Chr. 16:5; 25:1–2; 2 Chr. 29:30).
   (c) 72, 127.
   (d) 89 (see 1 Chr. 15:9; 2 Chr. 5:12).
   (e) 90 (see Exodus 15).
   (f) 88 (see 1 Kg. 4:31).

4. More than one person was involved in either composing, editing or revising the 150 psalms of the Psalter. Why is knowing this valuable for exegesis and translation?

1.7.2 Psalm types

In this section we will consider the main types, or *genres,* of psalm within the Hebrew musical tradition. This classification is "internal" (sometimes termed "emic"). It is different from the sort of "external" (or "etic") classification that is based upon the analyst's own view of the structure, content, and apparent purpose of a given psalm. (An external classification is given in chapter 2.) An internal classification is important because it gives us an "insider's" point of view on how the psalms correspond or differ from one another in terms of style or function. The great problem, however, is that we know so little about most of the Hebrew expressions used for the various categories. In addition, scholars and commentators differ with regard to what they see as the main significance of each of these terms. About all we can do here is survey this set of musical designations and offer a few tentative suggestions as to their possible meaning.

The most commonly used term is *mizmor*. It occurs fifty-seven times. It refers to a song accompanied by musical instruments. Such a "song" is a formal poem composed to be either sung (i.e., with a changing melody) or chanted (i.e., with many syllables uttered at the same pitch or tone), rather than simply recited (i.e., pronounced with a rhythmic beat). The most general Hebrew word for "song" is *šir*. This is a song of any kind, including secular ones (e.g., Gen. 31:27; Eccl. 7:5). The word occurs thirty times, often together with *mizmor* (e.g., Pss. 30 and 48). *Mizmor* occurs only in the Psalter. This fact, coupled with its frequency of usage, is the reason why most English versions render it by the specific term "psalm," while "song" is used for *šir*. There are other, more specific types of musical composition as well, as noted in the exercise below.

Exercise 1.7.2

1. Are there words in your language with which you can distinguish between "psalm" (*mizmor*) and "song" (*šir*)? If so, what are they? How do their meanings differ in popular usage?

2. What are the advantages and disadvantages of using an indigenous term rather than a loanword such as Chewa's *[ma]salimo* for the word "psalm(s)"?

3. Using a literal English version (e.g., NASB), look up the psalms listed below and write down the term that is used for the specific psalm type in the Hebrew heading. The headings for examples *a* and *b* are the ones that are often employed to designate the whole Psalter. On a separate paper write the word(s) used to translate these specialized terms in your language. If it is an indigenous expression, provide a brief definition in English.

    (a) _____ — Ps. 145

    (b) _____ — Pss. 17, 86, 90

    (c) _____ — Pss. 32, 42 (This is a song for "teaching" or "making wise" [see Ps. 32:8; 2 Chr. 30:22] or perhaps a song that is "skillfully" composed.)

    (d) _____ — Pss. 16, 56 (The meaning of this Hebrew term is very uncertain; it may be associated with "covering," i.e., expiation/atonement, or it may be a plea for protection since it is often used in psalms of David at times when he was in great danger, as in Pss. 56–60.)

    (e) _____ — Ps. 7; Hab. 3:1 (This uncertain term is perhaps related to "err" or "wander"; it may be a lament.)

    (f) _____ — Pss. 120–134 (This term refers to a type of psalm that was perhaps originally sung by pilgrims on their way "up" to Jerusalem to worship at the temple during one of the annual festivals.)

4. What are some of the different types of song in your own indigenous musical tradition? List a few of the more important ones. Do you think any of these terms could be used to translate one or another of the Hebrew terms for the psalm types? Why or why not?

5. When translating the psalms, different TL compositional styles (*genres*) may be needed for the different psalm types, for example, a prayer of petition as opposed to a song of praise. (This subject will be discussed further in chapter 2.) Can you give any examples of this as far as your language is concerned?

1.7.3 Musical notations

Some psalm titles seem to be or to include musical notations. This category of title includes a variety of terms whose meanings are not at all clear to us now. Most seem to concern the manner in which a particular psalm was to be sung or its specific musical arrangement (melody, sequence of tones). Many scholars think that some of these expressions refer to the names of familiar tunes or types of accompanying music. The title is thought to have identified the music with the words of the opening line or perhaps the most characteristic words, just as the titles of many hymns do today. Often such directions occur in conjunction with the phrase *laməna ṣṣeaḥ* "to ("for"/"of") the choirmaster." This would suggest a separate collection of psalms, perhaps those designated for use on certain special occasions.

Exercise 1.7.3

1. In the spaces below write down the musical notations found in the headings of the psalms listed. Use a literal version such as the NASB or RSV and compare these literal headings with the headings of the CEV, or the TEV footnotes (see also the THP).

    (a) _____ — Pss. 6, 12 (This term means "eighth," perhaps with reference to a deep or bass melody, i.e., an octave lower, or an eight-stringed instrument.)

    (b) _____ — Ps. 46; 1 Chr. 15:21 (This term means "young women," perhaps in reference to a high-pitched, soprano melody.)

    (c) _____ — Pss. 8, 81 (This term is related to the name for the city of Gath which means "wine press," and is probably a tune associated with this city. The term "Gittite" in 2 Sam. 6:11 is similar.)

    (d) _____ — Pss. 4, 6, 54–55 (The meaning of this term, *binginot*, appears to be clear and hence relatively easy to translate.)

    (e) _____ — Ps. 5 (This term, *hannichilot*, should not be difficult to render in your language.)

    (f) _____ — Ps. 9 (This term has nothing to do with the psalm's content. It may refer to a familiar melody.)

    (g) _____ — Ps. 22 (This is probably the name of a certain popular melody.)

    (h) _____ — Pss. 39, 62, 77 (This is perhaps a person's name as in 1 Chr. 16:41–2 and 2 Chr. 35:15.)

    (i) _____ — Ps. 45 (This psalm has two musical notes: _____ the first gives the melody and the second its purpose or occasion, which is quite fitting.)

    (j) _____ — Pss. 53, 88; (This term sounds like the word for "suffering" or "sickness," which fits 88 but not 53. It may indicate a particular melody.)

    (k _____ — Pss. 57–59, 75 (This is the name of a melody that may reflect the psalm's purpose, namely, a plea for help.)

2. Many of the musical terms you have just listed are introduced by the phrase "According to . . ." in English (a rendering of the Hebrew preposition *'al*). How is this normally rendered in your language? Can you suggest a better way of putting it?

3. The musical notation for Psalm 9 illustrates the problem that often confronts Bible translators when attempting to deal with these specific terms. The NIV, NRSV, CEV, and TEV each handle it differently. On a separate sheet of paper list the headings you find in each of these versions and then compare them with the THP. Each approach has its advantages and disadvantages. Which do you prefer best/least with reference to your language and why?

4. Does the fact that the psalms were originally sung during public worship have any relevance to the use of them today in your cultural-religious setting? Explain.

5. Should the original style or manner of composition have any effect on our translation of the Psalter, specifically the version in your language? Is it good to translate the psalms in prose form as ordinary speeches/prayers? Explain your preference.

6. The great diversity that is reflected in these titles would appear to suggest something of the corresponding artistry whereby the psalms were used in Israel's worship and devotional life. What implications does this fact have for their translation and usage by God's people today?

1.7.4 Liturgical directions

Some psalm titles seem to refer to special instructions for using the psalm in worship, although here again there is considerable doubt and disagreement concerning what the original meaning actually was. Some psalms, for example, appear to have been associated with particular days, as for example, Psalm 92, "a song for the Sabbath Day" (NIV). The Septuagint, perhaps reflecting later devotional practice after the exile, adds a designation of selected psalms for each day of the week: Psalm 24 is for the first day of the week, 48 for the second, 94 for the fourth, and 93 for the sixth, for example. Other liturgical directions point to a particular purpose of worship; the heading of Psalm 38, literally, is "to bring to remembrance" (NRSV has "for the memorial offering"). The collection known as the "songs of ascent" would also fit in this category, a fact which shows how these different aspects of the psalm titles overlap in meaning.

Another common liturgical notation is *selah*, which occurs seventy-one times. This term does not occur in a heading, but only in the body of a psalm. No one knows exactly what this word means. It is translated as "musical pause" (or "interlude") by the Septuagint, which is as good a guess as any. Perhaps it was used to designate a place where the chorus was to sing a "refrain" (a key expression summarizing the central purpose or a main theme of a psalm). Or it may have marked a point in the psalm when the singers would stop and only the musical instruments would be played. The latter possibility is suggested by the occurrence in Psalm 9:16 of *selah* with *higgayon*, which seems to mean something like "meditation" (see 19:14). It could apparently also refer to a quiet, or soft, melody (see 92:3b).

Exercise 1.7.4

1. For what liturgical purpose were the following psalms used according to their respective titles: 30, 60, 70, and 100?

2. English versions do not always agree on the precise designation of a particular Hebrew term. For example, in the RSV the heading of Psalm 100 is "a psalm for the thank offering." How is this same expression translated in the following versions: NIV, NRSV, TEV, CEV? Which of the different renderings seems to be the most strongly supported? (The THP is helpful with this.)

3. Are there words to distinguish between "thanksgiving" and "praise" in your language? If so, why would "thanksgiving" be a more precise translation in the title of Psalm 100? (Look at v. 4 and THP.)

4. How has the Bible in your language (or your favorite English or French version) handled the term *selah* (e.g., in Ps. 3:2)? Is there perhaps a better way of handling this term? Explain.

5. Do you support the THP's recommendation to omit *selah* (p. 11, 35)? Give your reasons for or against this position.

6. How is the term *higgayon* in Psalm 9:16 translated in your language or in the version that you are currently using? How is it handled in 19:14a?

7. What does the word "meditation" mean? How can you best express this idea in your language?

1.7.5 Historical references

Thirteen of the psalms include as part of their headings a specific reference to King David's life and experience. These events are recorded in the historical books of 1 and 2 Samuel and sometimes also 1 Chronicles. This is not to suggest that the psalms in question were composed at the same time that the events occurred. Rather, they were no doubt composed as David or some close associate thought back upon these important events. The heading of such a psalm may have been given by the psalm's author, or it could have been added later by an editor of the collection.

There is a great debate among scholars over the accuracy of such historical references. In some cases, these titles seem to reflect a somewhat different oral or written tradition from that contained in the Books of Samuel of the Masoretic text. An example of such a difference is the use of the name "Abimelech" in Psalm 34 instead of "Achish" (cf. 1 Sam. 21:10). Nevertheless, careful study does tend to demonstrate a certain connection between the contents of a psalm (a particular verse at least) and the historical reference that is cited in its title. Thus, the title helps a person understand and apply a given psalm, which is typically written in religious language that is general in nature. The real-life situation of any piece of literature is crucial for providing a context, setting, or background for its content and purpose (i.e., for "contextualizing" the work). Therefore, a decision to automatically omit such headings simply because they may have been added at a later stage in the history of the canon is not a very good idea.

Exercise 1.7.5

1. For the following psalms consult the *NIV Study Bible*'s footnote and the THP in order to determine each heading's most likely historical reference: 3, 7, 18, 34, 51, 52, 54, 56, 57, 59, 60, 63, 142. Write that down along with the actual wording of the heading. Where there is a difference of opinion, write both historical references. Indicate which one seems to you the most fitting.

2. Psalm 30 is sometimes considered to have a historical reference in the heading. What is there in this psalm that seems to fit the setting often specified for it, namely, David's dedication of the property and building materials for the temple (1 Chr. 22:1–6) and the sad incident recorded immediately before this (1 Chr. 21)?

3. Give an example of a psalm for which the historical reference in its heading seems to help a great deal in its interpretation. Tell how it helps.

4. What do you think a translator ought to do with historical titles? Should they be translated exactly as and where they are, omitted entirely, or put in a footnote? Should a chapter and verse cross-reference be given or not? Give reasons for your answers.

1.8 Why "sing a new song to the LORD" in your language

The psalms were composed thousands of years ago in a much different age and social setting. And yet for Jews and Christians of every time, place, and culture these songs are "new" in the sense that they help believers to face the ever-present trials, troubles, and temptations of this life. During crises the appropriate psalm can help give believers a new perspective on their situation, directing them to the almighty and merciful LORD. Thus these songs are vitally renewing and restorative in their effect: they serve to strengthen the people of God in their personal and communal difficulties, no matter how great. The psalms assure them that the King is still on his throne and that he is always managing the affairs of this world to bring them deliverance and new life in the end. Just read Psalm 96 again, to give one example, and you will become convinced of this.

The Psalter is the hymnbook of the saints and has been so throughout the centuries. As it has become available in translation it has provided a model of worship for many of the world's peoples. We will be looking at some of the more specific uses and purposes of various psalms in the next chapter, but for now we might summarize these functions in seven broad categories:

(1) *doxological*—to praise the LORD our God for who he is and what he has done and is doing;
(2) *devotional*—to help us meditate upon the greatness, glory, goodness, and grace of God and to encourage us to make all our needs and problems known to him;
(3) *liturgical*—to provide a pattern for worship and vocabulary for praying, praising, and giving thanks to the LORD as a corporate community of faith;
(4) *theological*—to teach us more about the nature of God and his ways, especially concerning his saving plan and purpose for us;
(5) *confessional*—to give us appropriate words with which we can publicly confess our sins before God as well as profess our faith both to and about him;
(6) *evangelical*—to witness concerning the Lord of Scriptures to those from among all nations whom he has called, together with us, to be members of the holy fellowship of believers;
(7) *relational*—to establish and maintain communication between us and God in all the high and low points of life, the catastrophes and crises, the victories as well as the apparent defeats.

Thus the Psalter provides a psalm for every person and every occasion. God intends that it serve this purpose for those of every language and culture. That is where the essential activity of Bible translation enters the picture and becomes a primary duty and responsibility of the members of his church.

The translation task, of course, must be recognized as a highly specialized and demanding one, one that requires much personal preparation, commitment, training, ability, and experience. Before even beginning to translate the Book of Psalms, one needs to carefully and systematically study the indigenous poetic and musical treasury of the target language, normally one's own mother-tongue. This will provide the necessary resources for rendering the beauty and purpose of Old Testament religious expression for God's people today.

In many cultures of the world people like to express their deepest thoughts and feelings in the form of songs, existing only in oral form or written down in song books. The singing (and dancing) tradition is especially strong in Africa. For example, among the peoples of south-central Africa the following traditional types of song are found: *praise songs* honoring a chief or other important leader; *pounding songs* sung when women grind up grain in a mortar; *hunting songs* sung before, during, or after a hunt; *funeral songs* expressing sorrow at the death of a friend, relative, or chief; *rain-calling songs* invoking the aid of the ancestors during a drought; *initiation songs* of advice to the young as their passage into maturity is celebrated; *planting and harvest songs* sung at the planting and harvest seasons; and *festival songs* for particular times of rejoicing, such as the birth of a child, a wedding, and communal fellowship. Frequently, each type of song is assigned a specific name.

In a society where singing is important, it should also be used for the highest religious purposes—to pray, praise, witness, and give thanks to the LORD God. This is indeed the "new song" of the ancient Psalter and we as translators wish to express it in the fullest, most appropriate language possible through the creative but controlled process of "empathetic translation." To do so, we must ourselves learn to experience the emotive passion and the expressive power of these sacred prayer-songs within the context of our own lives.

Exercise 1.8

1. List five of the most popular types of song in your culture. What are the names for these song types in your language? What is each used for? On what particular occasion is it sung? Are there any traditional instruments used to accompany these songs? Could such instruments be used

along with religious poetry, either during public worship or on some less formal occasion? Explain.

2. Pick two types of songs that you mentioned, ones that are quite different from each other, and describe their main stylistic features, that is, how their structure, content, music, and purpose compare.

3. Would any of these song types be suitable to use as a model in translating at least some of the biblical psalms? Pick the one you think would be the best model and give some more details about its style and use. For example, on what social occasion is it sung? Who sings it? How is it sung? What instruments, if any, are used? Are choruses included? Try to give an actual example of such a song, with a literal translation into English.

4. Have songs such as those you have mentioned been written down or do they exist only in oral form? Could oral genres possibly serve as a pattern for translating and singing or chanting the psalms in your language? Tell why or why not. What are the main problems you would have in trying to adapt the style of an unwritten song you know to fit one of the psalms?

Later in our study of the biblical psalms, you will begin research on the singing tradition of your own culture. Although you may not be able to answer the questions of exercise 1.8 very well right now, you should be able to do so by the time you complete this course. At that point, you will need to decide how the psalms can be most effectively conveyed in your language so that they not only have the right meaning, but also the appropriate impact, appeal, and beauty. Should they be rendered as spoken language, or would a musical rendition be more effective? (Perhaps a separate musical edition of selected psalm-songs can be prepared.) The decision is important because we want to pray and to praise God with the very best our language offers. Remember, the psalms were meant to be sung or recited or orated—perhaps even dramatically "performed"—not read silently to oneself!

2. CATEGORIZING THE PSALMS ACCORDING TO GENRE

We now turn to a consideration of how the different psalms of the Psalter were typically used in the worship life of God's people. We will attempt to determine their principal communicative functions and religious purposes based on a study of their overall content, style, and manner of structural organization.

Although the psalms differ from each other in various ways, they have several major features of structure and style in common, and the various categories are probably not as distinct from each other as the song categories in the oral or literary tradition of your own language. But it is important to recognize that the psalms are not all the same. There are certain variations in the style in which they are written (form), in what they say (content), and also in the purpose or occasion for which they were written (function).

In this chapter some of the principal types and subtypes of psalms will be described. Note, however, that this classification is not based on the Hebrew titles found at the beginning of most psalms. (These categories were presented in chapter 1, at least to the extent possible, for we do not know enough about the Hebrew titles to propose a consistent or comprehensive set of distinctive features.) Nor are they based on the theories of certain scholars who believe that all the psalms were written to be sung either in a specific religious festival, or at a certain season of the year, or to celebrate a particular event in the history of Israel. In most cases information of such a precise nature is highly debatable or completely unknown to us today and cannot be used as a guide for classifying the psalms. Besides, the Psalter is much more diverse and flexible in both its composition and subsequent usage than such theories allow for.

In this chapter, then, we will be classifying the psalms according to their literary genre, for example, songs of praise, songs of petition, songs of thanksgiving, songs of profession, songs of instruction, and so forth. The term *genre* designates a general "class" or "type." It refers to a group of oral or written texts that are similar to one another in some recognizable ways, whether with respect to form, content, function, or usage. This is important because the way we interpret a given literary text is guided to a great extent by our identification of its genre and our knowledge of the formal and semantic features which are commonly associated with that particular type. For example, the way we analyze, understand, and respond to a poem or a hymn is quite different from the way we approach an essay, a sermon, or a newspaper article.

The method of classification described in this chapter is based to some extent upon a given psalm's style and structure, but even more upon its textual content and apparent purpose. The categories are not always clear-cut, however. Frequently, a psalm may be viewed as belonging to more than one category, depending on how we analyze it. For example, within a single composition both petition and praise are often combined, and so we cannot really say that the psalm is one or the other. Furthermore, the psalmist may have written about a number of topics within one psalm.

Nevertheless, the categories proposed here are useful as an introduction to help Bible students recognize some of the important differences between psalms in terms of language and usage. They are not all the same, as many people think, and thus they should not be used—or translated—in exactly the same way. As already mentioned, there are variations in style, in the themes, and in the purposes for which they were written. It is important for Bible translators, especially, to recognize the differences—both large and small—so that they may be reflected as much as possible also in the target language text.

As to the different purposes for which the psalms were written, we can see that there are three main ones for which people speak to God (addressing him in the second person as "you"): to convey (1) petition, (2) thanksgiving, or (3) praise. In *petition*, an individual or the entire community of believers asks God for help in a time of need. In *thanksgiving*, they gratefully and joyfully respond to something specific that the LORD in his mercy has already done. In *praise*, they worship and glorify God for his greatness and goodness as manifested either to humanity as a whole (e.g., the wonders of his creation) or to his chosen people in particular (e.g., his constant protection and provision). Most of the psalms fall into one of these three categories.

But certain other psalms are used to speak, not *to* God, but *about* God, that is, in the third person. These either teach about God and his ways or they serve to instruct people about divine wisdom and a godly way of life. Still other psalms are expressions of trust in which believers profess their faith in God—who he is and what he may be expected to do for them.

All together then there are five *major* functions: petition, thanksgiving, praise, instruction, and profession of trust. But in addition, there are another five *minor* functions which are also important. They are called "minor" because a passage with such a function occurs as part of a psalm that is classified first as having one of the major functions. The five minor functions are repentance, remembrance, retribution, royalty, and liturgy. Usually these particular communicative intentions are expressed only by a few verses within a psalm.

In a passage expressing *repentance*, special emphasis is placed on the psalmist's confession of sin and his heartfelt plea for forgiveness. In a passage of *remembrance*, the history of God's people and the acts of his "steadfast love" (*ḥesed*) are recounted. In a passage calling for *retribution*, believers call upon God, the righteous Judge, to see to it that justice is done in the world for the sake of his name. In a song of *royalty*, praise and prayer are offered for the LORD's appointed king in Zion and his righteous rule on behalf of God's people. Finally, there are *liturgy* psalms, which appear to be specially adapted for use during Israel's public worship services. This is evident, for example, in the amount of exact repetition which they contain and in certain references to specific devotional acts such as a communal procession to the house of worship or the offering of sacrifices.

The diversity of structure and style that is manifested among these ten (and perhaps other) functional categories in the Psalter makes it necessary to begin any analysis with questions such as these: What type of psalm is this overall? Is more than one type combined within it? To be more specific: Does this psalm seem to carry out one of the primary purposes of petition, thanksgiving, praise, teaching, or profession of faith? Does it at the same time emphasize confessing one's sins, remembering the past deeds of the LORD, worshiping him in public, calling out to him for justice on behalf of his people, or appealing to him for the glory of his chosen king? These functions should be noted where they occur in the text before undertaking a more specific study of a psalm's content, structural organization, and stylistic features.

The reason Bible translators, in particular, must learn to see these basic distinctions is in order to find *functionally equivalent discourse forms* in the target language (TL). Petitions, for example, need to be expressed in the way that is most natural for requests and appeals to be made in the TL. The same is true for words of thanksgiving or praise or any other genre. Whether "the natural way" turns out to be poetry or not is beside the point as long as the particular purpose of the TL text-type that has been chosen closely matches the purpose of the original psalm.

The matter of *style*—that is, the characteristic manner of formal composition—is also very important in translation. It must be given the careful attention of skilled mother-tongue speakers. The aim is to approximate the high level of literary excellence and rhetorical power that is displayed by the prayer-songs of Scripture. In other words, the expressions used in a translation should reproduce or at least approximate the emotional impact and aesthetic appeal as well as the intended content that the biblical psalm communicated. This goal requires a thorough study of both the original text and also of comparable TL text-types in their respective linguistic, literary, and sociocultural contexts.

In the different sections of this chapter the major and minor psalmic genres will be described further, with various examples provided as illustrations. These exercises are intended to help students learn to recognize and distinguish the various types of psalms that are found in the Psalter.

2.1 The five major functions

The five principal communicative purposes for which the psalms were used by the people of God are petition, thanksgiving, praise, instruction (teaching), and profession of trust. They correspond most closely to the five basic motivations for prayer, that is, to *ask* God for help, to *thank* him for something that he has done, to *glorify* his great name, to *teach* others about him, and to express one's complete *confidence* in him. As you read and work through the descriptions, examples, and exercises of this section, consider how the psalms can contribute to your own personal worship and the worship of the believing community of which you are a part. Also begin to give some thought to how these ancient prayer-songs might be transmitted more effectively and utilized more fully within the modern-day religious setting.

2.1.1 Petition

The largest number of psalms (or major portions of complete psalms) in the Psalter belong to the category of petition. Sometimes called lament after one of its prominent constituents (as we shall see), petition includes all kinds of prayer to God for help in time of great need, distress, or difficulty. The psalmist may be asking God to protect him from danger, to deliver him from his enemies, or to assist him at a time of serious sickness, physical or spiritual.

There are two main types of petition psalm:

1. *Individual prayers*. These are psalms in which the speaker is appealing for help for himself. They are the most common.
2. *Communal prayers*. These are psalms in which the entire congregation of believers asks God to help the group as a whole.

Intense emotion is often manifested in psalms of petition: despair, anger, sorrow, frustration. However, there are also many expressions of hope and confidence in the LORD's response. In individual petitions the first person singular pronoun "I/me/my" abounds; in the communal type "we/us/our" is prominent. In these psalms "you" refers to God and "they" to the psalmist's enemies. A typical petition contains most of the following seven functional constituents, but not necessarily in the same order (each of these seven "stages" presents a somewhat different communicative purpose):

(a) *Appeal*. A petition normally begins with an initial, general call to God to listen and a plea to help the psalmist in his time of need. Along with this opening appeal to hear the prayer, a vocative is usually present, that is, a divine name in direct address (e.g., "O LORD") as we see in Psalm 17:1.

(b) *Problem*. The opening appeal is often followed by a description of the distress or danger the psalmist or his people are facing. This may be sickness, death, a dangerous enemy, personal weakness, or wickedness (Ps. 6:2), or even some punishment inflicted by Yahweh himself. In this last situation the psalmist may make a bitter complaint or an accusation against God for delaying his help (Ps. 6:3), for "forsaking" the psalmist in the day of trouble, or for allowing the wicked to prosper.

(c) *Request*. Now the psalmist asks more specifically what he wants God to do for him or his people (Ps. 5:8, 11). This element is the "prayer proper." (It is sometimes combined with the "problem," stage b.) In it the psalmist gives one or more of the following reasons why God should hear and help: (1) to show his enemies that the psalmist is righteous because he trusts in Yahweh and lives according to his will; (2) to strengthen the faith and life of others who trust in God; (3) to frustrate the plans and punish the deeds of all the wicked in the world and thereby silence the insults and blasphemy of his enemies; and (4) to manifest the great power, glory, and mercy of Yahweh.

(d) *Defense* or *confession*. In this optional stage the psalmist claims that he or his people are righteous or innocent—that is, not guilty of any specific wrongdoing or overt evil committed against God or man (Ps. 26:5). Alternatively, the personal defense may be replaced by a confession in which the psalmist acknowledges his or his people's wickedness and guilt before the Lord and pleads for divine mercy and forgiveness (Ps. 69:5).

(e) *Profession of faith*. Here the psalmist expresses his complete confidence and trust in God, namely, that he is relying upon the LORD to deliver him (and his people) from all harm and danger. He may include an affirmation that God has helped him or the entire nation in the past (Ps. 54:4). The psalmist may be so certain of God's help that he speaks as if he has already received it (Ps. 6:9).

(f) *Promise*. The psalmist makes a personal vow that he will always thank God for having saved him and/or that he will bring sacrifices of thanksgiving to the temple (Ps. 7:17).

(g) *Praise*. Psalms of petition often close with a final word of praise to the Lord. Sometimes this includes a call to other believers to glorify God too. Specific reasons may be mentioned as to why all people should laud and magnify his name (Ps. 22:25-31).

A characteristic and somewhat surprising feature of the individual petition is the distinct *shift* in attitude and emotion from strong discouragement and complaint to heartfelt trust and hope somewhere after the middle of the psalm (stage e). Thus this type of prayer, even though it may be for the most part an expression of deep sorrow, normally includes a promise of personal commitment (stage f) and a joyful word of praise (stage g) at its close. In other words, the overall tone of the psalm moves from sadness to gladness, from despair to hope. (This dramatic, often sudden, change in perspective and attitude is not quite so evident in the communal, or "national," petitions.) A similar progression is manifested in the Book of Psalms as a whole: petitions are concentrated in the first half, while praises predominate in the second half of the Psalter.

It should be emphasized once more that not all the psalms of petition, especially the communal prayers, include every one of the seven stages. The only element that must be present is the specific request itself (c). Furthermore, some stages may be repeated in other places within the psalm, or the stages may occur in some order other than that given here. Many different combinations are possible. For this reason there is quite a diversity of styles, even though the terminology itself is typically quite general. This makes such psalms appropriate in many kinds of problematic situations in life today even as in Israel of old.

The following is an outline of the individual petition of Psalm 54 (NIV) according to the seven stages:

[1] Save me, O God, by your name; APPEAL (a)
    vindicate me by your might.
[2] Hear my prayer, O God;
    listen to the words of my mouth.

[3] Strangers are attacking me; PROBLEM (b)
    ruthless men seek my life—
    men without regard for God. *Selah*.

[4] Surely God is my help; PROFESSION (e)
    the LORD is the one who sustains me.

[5] Let evil recoil on those who slander me; REQUEST (c)
    in your faithfulness destroy them.

[6] I will sacrifice a freewill offering to you; PROMISE (f)
    I will praise your name, O LORD, for it is good.

[7] For he has delivered me from all my troubles, PRAISE (g)
    and my eyes have looked in triumph on my foes.

In Psalm 54, only element d, "defense," is missing; however, it is implied in the "request," because if someone is slandered, he or she must be innocent of any alleged wrongdoing. There is obviously also some overlapping between the "promise" (f) and the concluding "praise" (g), which actually gives the reason why the psalmist is thanking God. Verse 7 could also be considered a "profession of trust" (e).

The category of petition song-prayers could, of course, be divided into a number of subtypes, depending on the nature of the request or problem the psalmist was facing. One such subtype, for example, is composed of "psalms for protection." In these there is a special emphasis on three elements: (1) a description of the distress (paralleling the "problem"); (2) a declaration of trust (paralleling the "profession of trust"); and (3) a petition for protection (paralleling the "request"). In the third of these stages an appeal is often included that the psalmist's enemies be punished as they deserve. These three stages can be seen clearly in Psalm 3: vv. 1–2, vv. 3–6, and v. 7, with v. 8 acting as a concluding testimony of faith. Other psalms with a similar concern for personal or corporate protection are 27, 35, 55, 56, 64, and 143.

In any classification system like this, there will be differences of opinion as to how to categorize one statement or another. That is to be expected. Our system is not meant to be a "box," but rather a "door" to open onto a broader functional perspective with regard to religious communication. Several possibilities may fit equally well for the same utterance. The point is not to try to determine the single "correct" category. The goal reaches beyond that. Identifying the category has to do with learning (1) how the paired lines of a psalm are arranged with respect to one another to form a complete and unified whole, and (2) how the paired lines often perform different functions in terms of the interaction between man and God. This motivating purpose is what needs to be understood in doing exegesis, and it is what needs to be duplicated as nearly as would be natural in translation.

Exercise 2.1.1a

1. Scan the following psalms of petition and sort them into two groups according to whether they are "individual" or "communal" prayers: 3, 12, 13, 17, 22, 42, 44, 69, 70, 71, 74, 79, 80, 88, 102.

2. What is the main difference you see between the individual and the communal petition?

3. Study Psalms 13, 17, 71, and 79 in detail. For each one list the verses to which each of the seven stages apply. Remember that a given passage may fit more than one stage, and one or another of the stages may not appear. Also indicate the verses that express the strongest emotion in each of these psalms.

4. Select any psalm of petition of your own choosing and analyze it as you did in assignment 3.

5. What is the particular "problem" being faced by the psalmist in 6:2, 12:2–5, 22:16–21, 26:1, 31:18, 62:3–4, 94:20–21, and 102:8–10?

6. The "problem" in the lament psalms mentioned in assignment 5 is often described in terms of drowning, death, and the grave. List the verses in Psalm 88 that contain such references and images. Psalm 88 is a very dark and depressing psalm, and yet it contains at least one statement of confidence and hope. Find this verse and write out these words of trust in full.

7. What is the problem being faced by the psalmist in Psalm 64? What picture does he use to describe his great difficulty? What is the psalmist's request? How does he express his faith in God for help? Again note the picture he uses. According to the final segment of praise in Psalm

64, what will be the result for all people of God's judgment (v. 9)? What will be the result for the righteous (v. 10)?

8. How does the prayer for protection against one's enemies in Psalm 3 illustrate the principle that the punishment should "fit the crime" (see vv. 2 and 7b)? Point out the same principle in operation in Psalm 64.

9. Between which two verses does the major (double) shift from petition to praise occur in Psalm 69? What change do you hear as you move from the first to the second of these passages?

10. Where does a similar break appear in Psalm 71?

11. Where does the change in mood from sorrow to happiness occur in Psalm 22?

12. What can you do to mark such sudden shifts in content, mood (tone), and speech function in your language? Be specific, with an example or two.

13. Songs of lament and petition are found in the prophetic books. See, for example, Habakkuk 1, Jeremiah 11, 14–15, 17–18, and the Book of Lamentations. Pick out one especially powerful example in the prophets. Do you notice any difference between these songs in the prophetic books and what is found in the problem or complaint (stage b) of a typical lament psalm?

14. Examine the communal lament of Hosea 6:1–3. Is this a good prayer or not? Give a reason for your answer.

15. Why is it helpful for translators to be able to identify the various functional stages within a given psalm of petition? Which stage seems to be the most difficult to recognize? Why do you think so?

Some people may see a problem when interpreting psalms of petition, particularly in passages where the psalmist seems to emphasize how good or righteous he is as he presents his case before the LORD (stage d; e.g., Pss. 7, 17, 18, 26, and 44). At other times the psalmist speaks of his enemies as if he hates them and wants them completely destroyed (e.g., 9:3; 79:6, 12). But one must consider the context in which these expressions occur as well as their literary genre. The expressions of hatred may have been influenced by the contextual setting (which we cannot know). Or there may have been some literary reason for the strong words that seem so strange, even inappropriate, to us today.

We must remember that the psalms are Hebrew poetry. They often contain a great deal of non-literal language, figures of speech, verbal irony (saying one thing, but meaning another), and hyperbole (deliberate exaggeration). All such expressions need to be interpreted in a special way. Poetic discourse allows the poet to fully express his feelings to the LORD in the strongest manner possible according to the available forms of literary speech. Strong language is not surprising in a tense religious setting.

In some passages, Psalm 17, for example, it is evident that the psalmist feels the need to defend himself and uphold his innocence of deliberate wrongdoing in order to counteract the false accusations of his enemies. (The Apostle Paul expressed himself similarly in Acts 20:26–27 and 23:1.) In other instances, as in Psalm 26, the psalmist is certainly not claiming the condition of perfect sinlessness for himself. He is merely contrasting his state, that of being in a right (forgiven) relationship with Yahweh, with that of the wicked, who are unrighteous before God, as their deeds clearly demonstrate. The focus may appear at times to be upon the psalmist's outward deeds, but many other prayers stress a concern for the condition of a person's heart (e.g., Ps. 51:10). Indeed, our words and works are a reflection of what is in our hearts (see Ps. 49:3). The main thing is that the LORD's will be done through his chosen people, despite any and all opposition from the unrighteous (Ps. 79:9–10).

Exercise 2.1.1b

1. Note the verses in the following psalms that seem to express a self-righteous opinion: 7, 17, 18, 26, 44. Are there any indications in the text that this was not the psalmist's attitude?

2. Which verse of Psalm 30 expresses a proud and overconfident attitude? What was the result of this overconfidence? What argument does the psalmist use to support his appeal to the LORD?

3. Read Psalm 17 and then tell how you think David views his relationship with God. How does that affect what he says about himself in vv. 1–5?

4. In translating Psalms 7, 17, 18, 26, 30, and 44, you will have to be careful not to give the impression that the psalmist is overly proud or boastful. How can you do this in Psalm 17:3, for example, in your language?

5. Now take Psalm 13, which you already analyzed into its different functional "stages," and prepare an initial translation of it into your language. (If this is English, try not to look at any existing versions as you do your own "first draft.") Make your translation both meaningful and expressive of the psalmist's strong emotions as he pours out his feelings to God. Where does the major shift in feelings occur in this psalm, and what is the specific change that you observe here? How can you highlight this point in your language (or perhaps in a better way in English)?

6. Which is the most difficult verse of Psalm 69 for you to translate? Point out some of its main problems. Why do these cause difficulties in your language? How may these be resolved?

2.1.2 Thanksgiving

Just as a psalm of petition can be either an individual or a communal prayer, so also a psalm of thanksgiving (sometimes termed a "eulogy") may be either personal or corporate. Thus the psalmist may be thanking God either for his gracious help to him as an individual or for what he has done for his chosen people. But there are some key differences between a song of petition and a song of thanksgiving. For one, while a note of praise is usually included in most of the psalms of petition, this function is the primary compositional element of a psalm of thanksgiving (and psalms of praise as well, 2.1.3). In other words, one major difference, or distinguishing marker, between a pure petition and a thanksgiving psalm is the relative amount of praise that is present. Words ascribing glory to God occur both at the beginning and the end of the thanksgiving, whereas they are found only at the end of a typical petition. As a result, thanksgiving psalms tend to be more optimistic in outlook and joyous in their overall emotive tone. This made them particularly suitable for a public service of worship in ancient Israel, and indeed these songs may have been sung during the priests' daily thank offerings.

Another key difference between the petition and the song of thanksgiving involves the time perspective. The thanksgiving commemorates something specific that God has *already done* to help the psalmist himself or the people as a whole. The time orientation is *past,* looking back at the period of distress and deliverance rather than present, as in the petition for salvation right now. In the song of thanksgiving, the crisis is over, the problem has been resolved. It is only fitting, therefore, that the LORD be greatly praised and gratefully thanked. In the prayer of petition, the singer may make a vow to praise God; in the thanksgiving psalm he fulfills that vow. A special group of thanksgiving songs are those which tell how God preserved his people Israel in the past, the so-called *salvation-history* psalms. Examples are Psalms 105, 106, 135, and 136. (This group will be considered in more detail in section 2.2.2.)

The song of thanksgiving has four main parts, or functional stages (although it is sometimes difficult to separate the two middle sections, which are often mixed together and overlapping).

(a) It begins with a *declaration of praise and thanksgiving* to God for his glorious attributes and/or acts of deliverance (Ps. 34:1). Sometimes it leads off with a word of "blessing" with reference to the person who was helped by Yahweh (Ps. 32:1). Often this opening segment includes an invitation to the congregation to join in joyous worship of the LORD (Ps. 30:4).

(b) There follows a *description of the distress* (a "narrative segment"), the dangerous situation that the psalmist or God's people were in. It states why they needed his help (their problem) and how they called upon him (their prayer), as in Psalm 18:5-6.

(c) Often combined with stage b is a *profession of faith,* or a *testimony* that God has indeed helped and delivered. This may include an expression of the psalmist's fervent trust that the LORD will certainly continue to act on his behalf in the future (Ps. 30:11).

(d) This type of psalm ends with a *thanksgiving* and/or a *promise* to give praise to God forever (Ps. 30:12). This may include the mention of an offering of the appropriate sacrifices (Ps. 116:17). There may also be an exhortation for others to join in this song of praise, for example, that even "all the kings" on earth should glorify the LORD (Ps. 138:4).

From the psalms of thanksgiving we can see that Yahweh intends also to deliver the Gentiles, that is, the people of every tribe and nation in the world. He earnestly desires them all to be brought into his kingdom so that they might worship, praise, and give thanks to him for all the wonderful things that he has done for them as Creator, Provider, Savior, and sovereign King of the universe.

Psalm 30 (NIV) is a complex example of a song of thanksgiving:
(The letters in parentheses on the right refer to the four stages listed above.)

[1] I will exalt you, O LORD, 　　for you lifted me out of the depths 　　and did not let my enemies gloat over me.	INITIAL PRAISE	(a)
[2] O LORD my God, I called to you for help 　　and you healed me.	GENERAL DESCRIPTION OF THE DISTRESS	(b)
[3] O LORD, you brought me up from the grave; 　　you spared me from going down into the pit.	TESTIMONY	(c)
[4] Sing to the LORD, you saints of his; 　　praise his holy name.	INVITATION TO PRAISE	(a)
[5] For his anger lasts only a moment, 　　but his favor lasts a lifetime; 　　weeping may remain for a night, 　　but rejoicing comes in the morning.	TESTIMONY	(c)
[6] When I felt secure, I said, 　　"I will never be shaken." [7] O LORD, when you favored me, 　　you made my mountain stand firm; 　　but when you hid your face, 　　I was dismayed.	GENERAL DESCRIPTION OF THE DISTRESS	(b)
[8] To you, O LORD, I called; 　　to the Lord I cried for mercy: [9] "What gain is there in my destruction, 　　in my going down into the pit? 　Will the dust praise you? 　　Will it proclaim your faithfulness?	SPECIFIC DESCRIPTION OF THE DISTRESS (particular appeal)	(b)

> [10] Hear, O LORD, and be merciful to me;
>   O LORD, be my help."
>
> [11] You turned my wailing into dancing;   TESTIMONY OF
>   you removed my sackcloth and   DELIVERANCE   (c)
>   clothed me with joy,
> [12] that my heart may sing to you and not be silent.
>
>   O LORD my God, I will give you thanks forever.   PROMISE OF PRAISE   (d)

Observe the emphatic alternating pattern of functional elements in Psalm 30 (that is, the four stages listed on the preceding page). It is important that when translating, these structural and thematic shifts be represented naturally in terms of distinctiveness, feeling, and effect. Note too that this song of thanksgiving includes the quotation of a specific "petition" as the psalmist vividly recalls his former distress. This example illustrates how the different psalm types may be combined with one another and how one particular stage may recur at different points in the overall progression. Such variety in prayer is the spice of Psalter.

Exercise 2.1.2

1. Tell whether the following psalms are "individual" or "communal" songs of thanksgiving: 34, 41, 66, 67, 75, 92, 107, 116, 118, 124, 129, 136, 138.

2. Which verses of Psalms 34, 41, 66, 92, and 116 correspond to the four parts or stages (a to d) of a song of thanksgiving? Remember that, as we saw in the case of Psalm 30, more than one passage of a given text can be identified as one of these stages, and the same verse may function in more than one way.

3. Psalm 107 is a diverse song of thanksgiving and praise. Four groups of needy people are mentioned who "cried out to the LORD in their trouble." Briefly describe these four groups according to what is said in vv. 4–5, 10–12, 17–18, and 23–27. Write out the refrain that proclaims what the LORD did for all these people. Then write out the refrain that tells how these people should respond to him.

4. Psalm 106 is a lengthy song of thanksgiving of a special type known as a song of *remembrance* (see sec. 2.2.2). Psalms 106 and 107 seem to have been placed together because of a number of similarities between them. Which, to you, are the most important of these correspondences? Where do these two psalms occur in the Psalter, that is, at which major border or division?

5. In Psalm 34, how are those described who call upon the LORD and are delivered? Mention some ways in which the LORD's act of deliverance is spoken of in this psalm.

6. Read through Psalm 18, which is David's personal song of thanksgiving (cf. 2 Sam. 22:1–51). What was David thanking the LORD for (see the psalm's title)? What are the verse numbers of the opening and closing sections of praise (a and d)? In which verses does David speak about his problem and prayer to the LORD?

7. Notice that the dangers of death are frequently described by means of a personification of a place known as "Sheol" (18:5). Where or what is that? (See THP and the NIV-SB at Psalm 6:5.)

8. In Psalm 18, which verses speak of the LORD's response? How this divine reaction described? God is spoken of here as a mighty warrior coming to deliver his people and accompanied by the forces of nature in an awesome display of power and majesty. Such an appearance of God is called a *theophany*. List some of the powerful natural forces mentioned in this passage. Do these suggest anything special in the oral or literary tradition of your culture?

9. The song of thanksgiving in Psalm 18 includes two stages that are generally seen in a petition psalm, namely, the "defense" and the "profession of faith." In which verses do you find these?

10. Make a first-draft translation of Psalm 34. Try your best to render it meaningfully as well as beautifully in your language (even if that is English). Before you start, notice that there are two major shifts in thought and emotion in Psalm 34. These breaks occur after which two verses? What can be done to mark or signal such a break in your language (or in a better way in English)?

11. Which verse of Psalm 34 was the most difficult for you to translate? What do you think is the reason for this? What do you suggest can be done about this problem in your language—or to improve what has been written in the particular English version that you are using?

2.1.3 Praise

Psalms of praise, also called "hymns," are more or less completely devoted to praising the LORD for his greatness and majesty and/or for his constant grace and mercy to his people. All these praiseworthy attributes are manifested in his actions—past, present, and also future. Thus a hymn is usually more general in its content than a song of thanksgiving. It does not refer to some specific situation in the past when God acted on behalf of the psalmist or the people. In most, if not all hymn contexts, God is regarded and praised as the great King who rules over all things, especially as protector of the everlasting kingdom of his holy ones. There is a special focus upon the sovereign LORD, the only true object of worship and personal devotion. Key words in praise psalms are "praise," "give thanks," "glory," "bless," "sing (happily)", and "rejoice." A familiar Hebrew expression that often marks the pure hymn is the joyful command *hallelujah* meaning "praise Yahweh" (see Ps. 149:1 and 150:1).

A hymn of praise usually contains only three parts, and they are closely related:

(a) It always begins with a *summons to praise* the LORD.

(b) The main part of the psalm speaks of the *reasons* why people should praise him. The most frequently mentioned ones are God's acts of creation and the preservation of his people Israel. They are often marked by the transitional conjunction "for" (*kiy*). The reasons are stated either in general terms or with reference to the ancient past, rather than to an act of deliverance in the immediate past as in a psalm of thanksgiving.

(c) It ends with a *concluding call* to thank and praise the LORD, often with increased emphasis, that is, with more enthusiasm and joy than at the beginning.

A good example of a praise hymn is Psalm 100 (NIV):

[1] Shout for joy to the LORD, all the earth.	PRAISE
[2] Worship the LORD with gladness; come before him with joyful songs.	

[3] Know that the LORD is God.
    It is he who made us, and we are his;
    we are his people, the sheep of his pasture.
	REASON

[4] Enter his gates with thanksgiving
    and his courts with praise;
    give thanks to him and praise his name.
	PRAISE

[5] For the LORD is good and his love endures forever; his faithfulness continues through all generations.	REASON

Notice the characteristics of this simple hymn: the overall tone of joy, frequent mention of the name of God, and repeated appeals to praise and give thanks. Also observe its clear two-part structure, in which the second half (4–5) essentially reiterates the first (1–3).

There are many reasons for praising God. One, as already noted, is to acknowledge his wonderful creation and powerful manifestation in nature. Some hymns, the so-called *creation* psalms, may be considered a separate category or sub-genre; for example, Psalms 8, 19:1–6, 104, and 148 focus on this. (These may also be regarded as "wisdom psalms.") In other psalms of praise many more of the "mighty works" of the LORD are mentioned. These may be divided into subcategories as well, for example, those which speak of Yahweh as a great king dwelling in the holy city of Zion (cf. psalms of royalty in sec. 2.2.4), those that teach about the LORD's praiseworthy attributes and the wisdom of those who follow his ways (cf. psalms of instruction in sec. 2.1.4), and those that call attention to God's ever-present protection of and provision for his people (cf. songs of trust in sec. 2.1.5).

Exercise 2.1.3

1. Try to distinguish individual songs of praise from communal songs of praise among the following psalms: 29, 33, 67, 103, 113, 134, 149.

2. Read Psalm 117 (the shortest psalm in the Psalter) and write down the words that correspond to the three basic parts of a typical hymn: (a) the first call to praise God, (b) the reason for praising him, and (c) the closing call to praise him.

3. What is the LORD praised for in psalms 65, 68, 93, 134, 146, 150?

4. Why would Psalm 66 be classified as a song of thanksgiving and Psalm 67 as a song of praise? In other words, which verses of Psalm 66 point to some specific act of deliverance that the psalmist is thanking God for?

5. How is the word *hallelujah* translated in your language? Is it a transliteration of the original Hebrew? If so, what do most people understand by it? Can you suggest a more accurate, idiomatic, or powerful rendering (see THP, p. 889)?

6. Does the literary tradition of your culture, oral or written, include songs of praise to God, the king, or a paramount chief? If so, what are their main stylistic features? Could—or should—any of these features be used when translating the psalms of praise in your language? Explain your answer.

7. What two "creations" is the LORD praised for in Psalm 148 according to vv. 1–6 and 7–14? What repeated line is found at the beginning of v. 5 and v. 13? This repetition divides Psalm 148 into two parts: (a) a summons to praise and (b) reasons for praise. Give the verse numbers of part a (praise) and part b (reasons for praise). Now translate Psalm 148 so that it sounds like a mighty "praise" in your own language. If you are working in English, which of the versions that you have access to seems to do the best job with this hymn? Why do you think so? Could any further improvements be made in the area of naturalness or literary and poetic quality? Try to suggest some improvements.

2.1.4 Instruction

The main purpose of the instructional, didactic, or catechetical songs is to teach the faithful how they might lead a life that is pleasing to Yahweh their King (Ps. 78:1–8). Believers do this by committing their lives to his service—more specifically by obeying the terms of his gracious covenant as set forth in the Torah. (Notice that this Hebrew term, *torah*, so often translated into English by the word "law" literally means "instruction" or "teaching.") In contrast to the strong emotions, positive and negative, that are expressed in the psalms of petition and praise, the psalms of instruction are typically more restrained, meditative, or devotional in style.

God's Torah summarizes everything he wished to make known about how his people are to behave in their daily lives, that is, with reference to both the religious and the secular aspects (which were not separated in the Hebrew way of thinking). This instruction also presents many of his merciful promises of blessing and deliverance for those who remain faithful to him. There are three psalms which focus especially upon the Torah, namely, Psalm 1, 119 (the longest psalm), and 19:7-14 (the "summary" of Psalm 119).

There are other didactic psalms that have more to do with life in general and how the believer ought to follow the holy will of Yahweh and flee what is evil or contrary to his commands. These instructional prayers are frequently called *wisdom* psalms. They teach what "true wisdom" is from God's point of view. They emphasize what constitutes prudent God-pleasing behavior and include strong admonitions to avoid the self-destructive ways of the wicked. The word "blessed" is frequently used to describe the wise person who lives to please God (e.g., Ps. 34:8). "Walking in the fear of the LORD" is another expression commonly used to describe those who honor and obey God (e.g., Ps. 34:9, 11). The blessedness of believers who live to glorify God is frequently taught, contrasting them in strong terms with the many wicked who surround them (e.g., Ps. 34:21). Several of the teaching prayers sound like the debate in Job concerning the question of why evil persons often seem to prosper in this life (e.g., Ps. 37 and 49). The LORD, however, sees what is happening and will one day judge the wicked according to their works (e.g., Ps. 34:15-16, 21; 37:28-38). In addition to strong contrast, other stylistic features characteristic of Hebrew poetic wisdom literature are comparative sayings (e.g., Ps. 37:16), warnings (e.g., Ps. 32:9), general admonitions to listen (e.g., Ps. 49:1-2), picturesque similes (e.g., Ps. 128:3), rhetorical questions (e.g., Ps. 25:12), and representative direct speech of the wicked (e.g., Ps. 73:11).

The following psalms, or significant portions of them, fit into the wisdom category: 14, 25, 32, 34, 36, 37, 49, 73, 78, 92, 94, 111, 112, 127, 128, 133, and 147. Many of these passages sound very much like the sayings of the Book of Proverbs or Ecclesiastes. The pairs of parallel lines in these psalms are often stated in the form of "general truths" and comparisons which apply to the lives of people who seek to follow the teachings of the LORD in contrast to those who live contrary to the divinely established way. A typical contrastive pair can be seen in Psalm 112:1, 10 (note: these are the initial and final verses of this psalm, hence an instance of *inclusion*, 4.1.1):

> Blessed is the man who fears the LORD,
>   who finds great delight in his commands. . . .
>
> The wicked man will see and be vexed,
>   he will gnash his teeth and waste away;
>   the longings of the wicked will come to nothing.

Exercise 2.1.4

1. Read through Psalm 1. What are some of the features that show this to be a good example of a didactic, or wisdom, psalm?

2. Why does the Psalter begin with the particular type of psalm that Psalm 1 is? What does this tell us about how we should view the Book of Psalms as a whole?

3. What is the main theme or "teaching" of Psalm 2? (The fact that this type of psalm immediately follows Psalm 1 suggests that the kingly rule of Yahweh and his Messiah is the central thought that should guide our interpretation of all the rest of the Psalter.)

4. Examine Psalms 37, 49, 73, and 112. Select a verse from each one that calls attention to a special "wisdom" or "teaching," for example, the difference between the righteous and the

wicked. Write these verses out along with their verse numbers. Be able to summarize the specific teaching that is emphasized in each passage.

5. Psalms 111 and 112 are two teaching psalms that have been placed next to one another in the Psalter. Write down the main similarities that link this pair together as "parallel psalms."

6. Using a literal version (NIV, RSV, or NASB), look up Psalm 19:7-9 and 119:9-16. Pick out the words) that refer to the "law" (*torah*). Write down all the different terms along with their verse numbers. If you have a translation in your own language, note how each of these words has been translated. Evaluate these renderings and suggest improvements where necessary. If you do not have a translation, how would you convey these words meaningfully in your language? If you are doing your assignment in English, look up these verses in a meaning-based version such as TEV or CEV to see how the various terms are rendered. Do you see any difference between the literal renderings and the meaning-based ones? Can you suggest any improvements? (Consult the THP and the NIV-SB at these passages.)

7. In your language is *torah* translated literally as "law"? If so, does it give a misleading impression of the wisdom psalms and indeed of the Old Testament as a whole? Can you suggest a more accurate and meaningful term? Explain why you favor it.

8. The longest psalm is 119, which is a teaching psalm. How many paragraphs ("stanzas") does this psalm contain? Notice how each of these breaks is marked in the NIV. The breaks are marked because, in the Hebrew language, each of the lines in one stanza begins with the same letter of the Hebrew alphabet, and each stanza goes in order from **A** (*aleph*) to **T** (*tav*), as it were. The purpose of this poetic device, known as an *acrostic,* was perhaps to suggest the "completeness" of the Torah. Do you think that it is important to draw attention to this poetic feature of Hebrew in the Bible of your language? Tell why or why not. If you think it is important, how would you show the alphabetic order in a meaningful way? (For a helpful article on this particular issue, see Timothy Wilt, "On Translating Acrostics: Perhaps the Form Can Be Represented," *The Bible Translator*, 44:2, 1993, 207-212.)

9. What is the theme of Psalm 119? How do you recognize it as the theme? In your opinion, what is the most important thing that Psalm 119 says about the Torah? (Give the verse number.) Tell why you think this statement is important.

10. Consider the way in which didactic psalms are written, that is, their discourse style or manner of writing, and compare it with literature in your language—either oral or written. Do you have any type of literature that is similar, whether poetic in nature or not? How can you write instructional psalms in your language so that the people would more easily recognize that this is what they are? If you are studying these psalms only in English, compare several versions and select the one that, in your opinion, renders them in a way that sounds most like instruction. Give some reasons for your choice.

11. Sometimes it almost seems as if two complete psalms of different genres are combined into one. Psalms 19 and 34 are good examples of this. Where does the wisdom or instructional portion occur in each of these two psalms? What genre is expressed in the other portion of Psalm 19? Of Psalm 34? Can you suggest any reasons for these functional combinations? How could you indicate in your language where the major break in each of these psalms occurs? In other words, what sort of a literary device would you use as an initial (or final) *discourse marker*?

12. Make a first-draft translation of Psalm 19 in your language. Compare it to the drafts of others in the class who have also done one. Then revise as necessary. Besides the major break at v. 7, there is a minor shift in content and emotional tone at two other points. At which verses are these? Are there stylistic devices in your language that you could use to show these shifts? If you are working in English, examine several versions and pick the one that does the best job of rendering the two different styles that comprise Psalm 19. Explain why you think so.

2.1.5 Profession of trust

In the psalms of trust, the psalmist expresses his complete reliance upon the Lord as the savior and protector of his life. It is not always easy to distinguish these psalms as a separate category. Most of them could easily be classified as either a petition, a song of thanksgiving, or even a teaching psalm. Yet in each of these psalms of profession the main emphasis is on the speaker's unshakable confidence in the Lord. He clearly, concretely, and publicly testifies to his God-centered faith to all who are willing to listen.

These are sometimes called "creedal" psalms because there is a special focus upon one's personal testimony to the faithfulness of the Lord to his covenant with his people (basically the same as stage [e] of an individual petition psalm). In other words, the psalmist does not ask for deliverance from his enemies, nor does he thank God for having already saved him. Rather, he expresses his faith that the Lord continually saves him. As in psalms of instruction, the temporal focus is neither on past time nor the future, but it is timeless. Normally God is referred to in the third person except when he is being quoted, as in Psalm. 46:10–11:

"Be still, and know that I am God;
I will be exalted among the nations . . ."   (*first person* for direct speech)

The Lord Almighty is with us;
the God of Jacob is our fortress.   (*third person* for faith profession)

The reason the psalmist fears nothing and no one is that he firmly believes God is ever present to protect and deliver him. A definite calm, fearlessness, and trust shine through the words to inspire anyone who listens with a sympathetic ear and heart.

Psalm 23 is no doubt the most familiar of the psalms of trust, and it is a good illustration of the difference between this group and those of a didactic nature, such as Psalm 1. The emphasis in Psalm 23 is more upon the confident attitude of the believer's heart than upon his righteous actions in the world, as in Psalm 1. Other psalms of trust are 11, 16, 26, 27, 31, 46, 52, 62, 63, 91, 121, 125, 131, and 139. In some of these only a part of the psalm is a profession of trust, and thus the psalm may be classified as fitting into another category as well.

Exercise 2.1.5

1. Study Psalms 26, 31, 46, 52, and 91. Find a verse in each one that clearly expresses a solid trust in the Lord and write it out. Find a word or phrase in each of these psalms that means "faith/trust/hope." How have these words been translated in your language? Write down the vernacular words and evaluate them for accuracy. Are more powerful expressions available, figures of speech, perhaps? Give some examples, along with a back-translation into English. If you are working in English, compare three different versions with respect to each of the words of trust that you have discovered. After consulting the THP, tell which of the renderings you prefer for each passage and give some reasons why.

2. List the word pictures (similes or metaphors) that speak about the Lord's protection and care for his people in Psalm 11:4, 16:8, 27:5, 62:6, 91:4, 121:3, and 131:2-3. Are these natural ways to refer to God's care in your language—even in English? Point out any difficulties. Do you have any alternatives to suggest?

3. List five figures of speech (word pictures) that help convey the idea of trust and protection in Psalm 23. How have these been expressed in the translation in your language? Are there other figures of speech from your own culture that would convey these concepts more naturally? Would it be appropriate to use them, or would they greatly distort the historical and cultural framework of the Bible? (This matter must be discussed and agreed upon by the members of an established translation committee.) If you do not have a translation in your language, how do

you think you could best express the biblical figures of speech in Psalm 23? List any examples that you can think of, giving a literal back-translation of their meaning into English. If you are using English, compare three English versions with regard to each of the five figures that you have listed and tell which one of the three versions you prefer and why.

4. What kind of a psalm is Psalm 22? What are its distinguishing features? Why does Psalm 23 seem to follow naturally after Psalm 22 in the Psalter?

5. What are some of the main characteristics of a psalm of trust that you see illustrated in Psalm 11? List three of these stylistic features with examples.

6. Psalm 121 is a profession of trust from beginning to end. It consists of four stanzas of two verses each. Looking at the NIV, write down the verse numbers of each stanza. The main theme of this psalm is given in vv. 1-2. What is this theme? The following three stanzas each begin with a line that indicates a different aspect of the main theme. Write down these three distinct facets of trust. What repeated word expresses the psalmist's confidence in God? (It occurs five times.)

7. Psalm 27 is a good example of a psalm of mixed genres; it is a prayer of petition woven together with a profession of trust. Which specific verses belong to each of these two categories?

8. Carefully study Psalm 46 and prepare a first-draft translation of it. What are the features which place this into the category of a song of trust? Observe the symmetrical structure of this psalm: There is a verse that occurs twice as a "refrain." Give the numbers of these two verses. The remainder of the psalm may be divided into three stanzas of three verses apiece. List the verses that belong to each of these stanzas. After completing your first-draft translation, compare it with those done by others in the group. Then try to come up with a single joint version that best conveys the psalm's central message as well as its beauty of expression in your language. (This translation and comparison process should continue for all such exercises in future.)

2.2 The five minor functions

Besides the five major genres, there are several others considered "minor" because they are not as distinct or prominent as the five categories discussed above. These psalms seem to have had a special, more specific purpose in the worship life of the people of Israel, whether for an individual or for the entire congregation. They do not differ very much in terms of form (structure or style) from the psalms assigned to the major types, and usually they may be classified as one or another of them. However, the minor genres do seem to be distinct in purpose, at least in certain portions (especially the liturgical songs), and they are frequently distinct with respect to their content as well.

Some of the better known of these minor types are described and illustrated in this section: songs of repentance, of remembrance, of retribution, of royalty, and of liturgy. Other categories are also possible. Again, it is important to emphasize that many psalms cannot be identified clearly as one type or the other. They are often "mixed." The point of this classification, imprecise though it may be, is to alert us to the importance of communicative purpose in religious discourse and the differences among the psalms based on their various functions. A greater awareness of and appreciation for the diversity manifested within the Psalter will make us better able to convey the meaning of individual psalms in accurate and relevant terms to God's people today.

2.2.1 Repentance

The psalms of repentance (sometimes termed "penitential") may be considered a subtype of the petition psalms, some of which in stage [d] give special emphasis to the confession of sin (see sec. 2.1.1). In expressing repentance the psalmist typically speaks of deep sadness over his own sin, guilt, and unrighteousness and appeals to God to be merciful and to grant him forgiveness. Many different terms to designate human wickedness, both literal and figurative, are found in such prayers, usually concentrated within several closely related verses. These are accompanied by expressions of the deepest feelings of the sinner's heart, in particular, great sorrow for his evil thoughts and actions. Similarly, the terrible results of sin and sinfulness are also expressed in these psalms. Frequently this is described in terms of some sickness or physical affliction, which may be spoken of as a punishment from the LORD. Since sickness and sin are considered to be so closely related in this way, the fervent plea for healing often includes within itself an unexpressed request for forgiveness from God.

There is always some prominent expression of hope in these psalms of repentance. They usually incorporate a number of explicit statements declaring that the individual, or the group, trusts completely in Yahweh, LORD of the covenant, to forgive their sins. The psalmist may also mention the work of God's Spirit in his life, moving him to repent of his wickedness so that God might restore him to a right relationship with himself (e.g., Ps. 51:11). It is the Spirit of Yahweh who creates or inspires a right spirit within the sinner, a heart made right with God which desires to live a holy life in conformity with his will (Ps. 51:12). The psalmist realizes that after God forgives his sin, saves him from his affliction, and heals his body, he is obligated then to live a life pleasing to his Savior. The result of recovery and restoration is often celebrated in words of praise that convey the forgiven sinner's great joy over what God has done for him.

There are seven psalms in the Psalter which have traditionally been designated as "penitential." They clearly express the interrelated ideas of sickness being a result of sin and the confidence that recovery will follow repentance. Such statements are not to be taken too literally, that is, as referring only to physical illness and healing. The "sickness" might also be psychological, social, and/or spiritual in nature. A person may be suffering because of internal conflict or personal guilt, or because of enmity with relatives, friends, or neighbors, or even God himself. Deep down, of course, the cause always has to do with sin and broken fellowship with God, which can be healed only through forgiveness. Having received assurance of forgiveness, the psalmist expresses his faith in the LORD and commits himself to live a consecrated life in service to God and his fellow believers. He is now able to rejoice because he has been "saved" and restored to fellowship as an active member of God's people.

Exercise 2.2.1

1. Pick out the seven penitential psalms from the following group: 2, 6, 32, 33, 35, 38, 40, 45, 51, 100, 102, 125, 130, 143, 144. Draw circles around their numbers.

2. Which of the penitential psalms include strong explicit pleas for the personal or communal forgiveness of sins? Give references for three such passages.

3. Now examine Psalms 32, 51, and 130 in more detail with reference to the seven stages (or parts) that are often present in a psalm of petition: (a) appeal, (b) problem, (c) request, (d) personal defense or confession of sin, (e) profession of trust, (f) promise, (g) praise. On a sheet of paper draw a chart with seven columns, each headed by the name of the respective stages. Try to find a specific verse in each of these three psalms that expresses one or more of the seven stages. Write the verse number in the appropriate column.

4. Notice that the penitential psalms have a prominent element of "instruction" in them (see sec. 2.1.4). List the reference for one instructional passage in each of these three psalms: 32, 51, 130.

5. Now examine Psalms 32, 51, and 130 again. Pick out two vivid word pictures in each one dealing with either sin, repentance, or forgiveness (see also the THP). Write them out along with their verse references. How would you render these expressions meaningfully in your language? If you have an existing Bible in your language, evaluate how well it handles these

terms. (If you are using an English version, use that to make your evaluation.) Can you suggest any ways of bringing out the beauty or forcefulness of these figures of speech?

6. Observe where the major breaks in thought and feeling occur in Psalm 32. Compare the NIV, TEV, CEV, and RSV in this respect. At which verses do all four versions agree that a significant break should be made? Where do they disagree? Tell which version(s) you support at these points of disagreement and give reasons why. Now translate Psalm 32 so that it sounds like a real prayer of sorrow and repentance in your language.

2.2.2 Remembrance

The songs of remembrance, also known as *historical* psalms, are a special type of thanksgiving song (see sec. 2.1.2). They speak about the LORD's faithful provision and protection of his chosen people in the past. They often include a strong expression of faith on the part of the psalmist or the worshiping congregation; thus certain portions may also sound like a profession of trust (see sec. 2.1.5). The two events in the history of Israel that the songs of remembrance mention most often are the Exodus from Egypt (Exod. 14), and the promise of an eternal throne, or kingship, through the descendants of David (2 Sam. 7). In both of these, what is in view is God's redemption of those in need by means of a wonderful deliverance worked by his chosen leader—by Moses on behalf of Israel in the first case and in the second by the Messiah at some future time and on behalf of all people. The LORD's deliverance of his people from slavery on a national scale is seen in these psalms as a model and a guarantee of redemption on a personal level for each and every believer.

The historical psalms also call to bitter remembrance the people's repeated acts of unfaithfulness and disobedience, for which they deserved to be punished by their righteous Lord. Thus these past events of God working out his mercy and justice in the lives of his people are recorded not as a mere history lesson, but rather as (1) examples to warn the present generation not to follow the wicked behavior of those who broke the covenant (Ps. 106:40–43); (2) a strong encouragement to keep walking in steadfast obedience to the LORD (Ps. 105:42–45); and (3) reminders to praise and thank their gracious and glorious King (Ps. 105:1–2). He who once delivered their ancestors would one day do the same for all those who remain in faithful fellowship with him.

Exercise 2.2.2

1. Psalm 78 is a historical psalm, as vv. 3–4 show, and it is also a song of another general type (see vv. 1–2). Name this other major type. Verses 42–43 remind the people of the LORD's salvation. What other sad fact do the following verses also emphasize: 78:8, 10–11, 17–18, 22?

2. According to Psalm 105, what should God's people "remember" (v. 5)? What does the LORD himself "remember" (vv. 8–9)? In what verse is this important fact emphasized again in Psalm 105? How should the people respond to these acts of remembrance (v. 45)?

3. Psalm 106 also speaks about the importance of "remembering." Who is first called upon to "remember"? What is the reason for such remembrance? Who failed to remember in 106:7, 13, and 21? In your language what is the connotation of the word for "remember"? For example, does the word suggest that something important had been forgotten? Is there a better way of conveying the Hebrew meaning in your language, such as "commemorate," "celebrate," or "worship" (cf. THP, p. 892)?

4. What other sins are associated with the sin of not remembering the LORD (see Ps. 106:24–25)? Why are God's people not completely destroyed for such sins (v. 45)?

5. Psalms of remembrance are a specific type of the thanksgiving song. Try to identify the four parts of a typical thanksgiving psalm in Psalms 105 and 106. These are (a) invitation to praise; (b) the problem; (c) testimony to God's deliverance or judgment; and (d) final thanksgiving.

Notice how parts b and c are interconnected with each other. Give the verse numbers of the four parts in each of these psalms.

6. Psalms 135 and 136 are songs of praise. They also call to remembrance the LORD's acts of deliverance on behalf of his people. List the verses of these psalms that belong to each of the three parts of a typical hymn: (a) invitation to praise; (b) reasons for this praise; and (c) concluding praise. Notice that in Psalm 136 the basic reason for praising the LORD is repeated throughout the song in the form of a refrain. Write these reiterated words.

7. At least one important event in the history of God's people is called to remembrance in the following psalms: 66, 83, 107, 124, 136, 137. For each of these psalms write down the event(s) and give at least one verse that mentions these events, plus a cross-reference to a historical book.

8. What genre is Psalm 77? Why do you think so? What are some of the main characteristics of this kind of psalm? In which verses are there strong words of complaint? (They are expressed in the form of questions.) What mighty act of deliverance is called to mind in vv. 16–20? How does this remembrance help the psalmist in his "petition" (see vv. 10–12)?

9. Psalm 95 is a song of praise that includes a lengthy passage of remembrance. What are the people supposed to remember? Why should they remember this? Now prepare a first-draft translation of Psalm 95, keeping in mind that this psalm expresses two important elements: joyful praise in 1–7b and solemn warning in 7c–11. Try to represent these different styles clearly in your translation. Compare your draft with the others in your class and make any revisions necessary. If possible, produce a single joint version that includes the best features of all the drafts.

2.2.3 Retribution

Psalms of retribution come under the general category of petitions, but they are a specific kind of prayer in which the psalmist requests the LORD not only to deliver him (and/or God's people), but also to *punish* the wicked. This small group of psalms plus a number of scattered verses sometimes trouble Bible readers because they appear to be curses in the form of prayers. In them the psalmist calls upon God to bring judgment upon his enemies, especially those who are persecuting him or his people. It sounds as if he is pleading with the LORD to take revenge in behalf of oppressed believers. There are those who say such words and feelings of hatred do not belong in the Holy Scriptures since they are contrary to God's command to love our enemies and pray *for* them, rather than against them (see Matt. 5:43–48).

But again it is important to read these prayers (sometimes misleadingly called *imprecatory*, cursing) in their total context. They need to be understood not from our perspective today, but from the point of view of the cultural and religious setting of their own time. A careful study will show that the psalmist is not really asking God to work vengeance or punish for his own sake. Rather, it is for the sake of the honor and reputation of his holy name. It is the will and righteousness of the LORD God Almighty himself that the ungodly oppressors have violated. God's punishing them will demonstrate his justice for all to see. Thus, what the psalmist is praying for is an act of divine "retribution" (a just judgment) by which God defends his righteous reputation and shows that he is truly God. Such an act of judgment will fulfill God's many promises of deliverance made to the obedient as well as his threats to punish the wicked (e.g., in Deut. 27:24–26 and 28:15–29). By attacking God's covenant people, the enemy were, in effect, insulting God himself, and God will not tolerate such behavior (Ps. 9:11–12).

In these psalms we usually find an urgent call for the LORD to punish the wicked swiftly and severely. Should the enemy continue to afflict God's people, the faithful might begin to doubt or even despair of ever receiving help from the LORD. So they ask God to "vindicate" their faith, that is, to show that they have not trusted in or lived for him in vain (Ps. 37:6, 17, 25). However, the psalmist leaves the entire matter completely in God's hands, knowing that he will act justly (see Ps. 37:8-9; 92:11, 15). It is not right for God's people to take vengeance on their own. Similar prayers for God to exercise his righteous judgment upon evildoers are found elsewhere in the Old Testament, especially in the Book of Jeremiah (e.g., 11:20; 15:15; 18:19-23; 20:11-12; cf. Mt. 23).

In these appeals for justice, the psalmists often use very strong speech, for example, "Do I not hate them that hate thee, O LORD? . . . I count them my enemies" (Ps. 139:21-22). With such words God's faithful people are expressing their great hatred of sin and evil more than hatred of those who were doing wicked things (Ps. 101:8). The language they use emphasizes the outrage they feel over all injustice and oppression. They are especially angry at those who violate the commands of the Torah. These words are not to be taken literally; they should rather be viewed as *hyperbole*, as deliberate exaggeration, the purpose of which is to make the communication more effective (convicting, convincing, compelling). For example, note the strong words of 68:21, 23; 109:12; and 137:8-9. Their aim is to impress the hearers so that they too will want to defend the justice and honor of God. Such words also stand as a *warning* to the wicked to repent, for one day judgment will come (Ps. 92:6-9). Similar expressions are used in the New Testament when sin is being condemned (e.g., Gal. 5:12; 2 Tim. 4:14; Rev. 6:10). Several passages of judgment from the Psalms are applied specifically to evildoers in the New Testament—to Judas, for example (Acts 1:20, quoting Ps. 69:25), and to unbelieving Israelites (Rom. 11:9-10, quoting Ps. 69:22-23).

There are four psalms which, for the most part, can be categorized as petitions for retribution, namely, 35, 69, 83, and 109. In addition, there are psalms that contain some passages of this kind. Examples are seen in Psalms 54, 55, 58, 59, 68, 79, 94, 129, 137, 139, and 140. When dealing with such judgment texts, translators should avoid the temptation to eliminate or reduce the strong language of the original, though in some situations a certain degree of downplay may be required. That may be needed to avoid offense or impropriety of the kind that would make the passage unsuitable for reading aloud in church, for example. Furthermore, it may be necessary in your translation to suggest when certain statements are hyperbolic, or deliberately exaggerated. Then the reader/hearer would know the words are not to be taken in a literal sense. If this is not done, a footnote may have to be used to clarify the meaning; alternatively, the hyperbolic language may have to be toned down somewhat.

Exercise 2.2.3

1. Read through Psalms 35, 69, 83, 109. These are the four primary retribution psalms. Find a verse from each one in which the LORD is forcefully called upon to carry out justice by punishing the unrighteous. Write these verses out in full. Notice that, at times, the punishment the psalmist calls down upon his enemies corresponds to the evil they did against him (see e.g., 35:7-8, 109:17-18). Watch for other instances of this "eye for an eye" principle. Why would such correspondence be of special interest to Bible translators?

2. Point out two examples from the verses that you just selected in (1) that would cause problems if translated literally in your language. Briefly explain the nature of these problems. Suggest a way in which the text may be marked or restated in your language to prevent or at least lessen the likelihood of misunderstanding.

3. Note the implicit information that is present in Psalm 83:9-13. What did God do to the people mentioned in these verses? Does the punishment carried out by the LORD need to be made explicit in some way. If so, how should this be done? Discuss the pros and cons of the various options.

4. After reading Psalm 10, mention three sinful actions for which the wicked deserve to be judged by the LORD according to vv. 3, 5, and 9. How does the wicked person condemn himself by his own words (10:6, 11, 13)?

5. Pick out an obvious passage of judgment in the following psalms and write down their verse references: 54, 55, 58, 59, 68.

6. Identify the hyperbole, or exaggerated expression, in Psalm 137. Write it out. Would this passage be difficult for people in your community to understand? If so, briefly explain why. How would you attempt to resolve the problem in your translation?

7. What is the major genre of Psalm 140? List the verses (if present) that correspond to the seven stages that are typical of such a psalm: (a) appeal, (b) problem, (c) request, (d) defense, (e) profession, (f) promise, and (g) praise. Of the verses that you listed for the "request" stage, which ones are a prayer for judgment upon the wicked?

8. Is there a particular genre of prose or poetry in your language that is used for the purpose of calling upon God (or the ancestors) to punish evildoers and oppression? If so, briefly describe it, especially its specific stylistic features. Could such features be used in your translation to mark the "imprecatory" passages of sharp condemnation in the Psalms? Explain.

9. Translate Psalm 140 in your language, accurately conveying the sense of the original. Use words that sound natural and acceptable to your hearers, despite the strong speech. If you are working in English (or some other major language), tell which of the existing translations you prefer and why.

2.2.4 Royalty

The royalty, or kingship, psalms speak either of Israel's earthly, human ruler—the LORD's "anointed (chosen) one"—or of God as the supreme King. The former are petitions to the LORD for his help in the king's behalf or for his blessing on the king in some special way (e.g., Ps. 20:9). They have to do with situations that were important in the king's life and rule, such as his coronation or enthronement (e.g., Psalm 2), his wedding (e.g., Psalm 45), his wars against the enemies of God (e.g., Psalm 21), his work as a righteous judge and defender of the oppressed (e.g., Psalm 72), his just punishment of the wicked (e.g., Psalm 101), his overall reign (e.g., Psalm 18), and even those times when he had to be punished for unfaithfulness to Yahweh (e.g., Psalm 89).

The songs of royalty—of divine kingship—that extol Yahweh as the glorious King who rules over all nations are, in essence, psalms of praise (see Ps. 47:7-9). Most of the royalty psalms are of this type. Psalms 67, 96, 97, 98, and 99 are examples. There is a natural connection between the two types in that the Davidic king was supposed to be the LORD's representative on earth and act as an intermediary, as a "priest," when the people wanted to make their needs known to God (see Ps. 110:4). Some royalty psalms speak of God as a mighty Warrior who is strong in battle, particularly in defense of Zion (Ps. 98:1), that is, Jerusalem, the holy city where the temple and the Ark of the Covenant were located (e.g., Psalms 46, 48, 76, 84, 87, 132). As King of the universe, however, the LORD has no earthly counterpart; he alone is Creator (Ps. 97:2-6) and he alone is the righteous Lawgiver (Ps. 99:7).

Many of these royal psalms, or at least certain prominent passages within them, are strongly *prophetic* in nature and are to be interpreted as referring either directly or indirectly to the coming Messiah, God's anointed Savior. There was sure hope for the future in the person of an ideal king who would someday rule perfectly and powerfully on behalf of the LORD and his people. Some passages speak of who the Messiah is, his being and attributes, while others tell about what he does. There are additional prophetic passages, not quite so personal in their description, that tell about the circumstances surrounding the promised Messiah's life and the results of his sacrificial death, including salvation also for all nations, including the Gentiles (e.g., Ps. 18:49; see also Rom. 15:9).

It needs to be recognized that most of these psalms which speak of God or his Messiah as King belong to the category of songs of praise (see sec. 2.1.3). They follow the basic threefold structural pattern of a song of praise: (a) opening praise, (b) reasons for praise, and (c) concluding praise. Many of the royal songs also express a strong profession of trust in the LORD. Many societies of the world have a distinct type of "praise poetry" that is chanted, recited, or sung in honor of their king or paramount chief (e.g., the Zulu of South Africa); some form of this may be adaptable for use when translating the royal psalms.

The importance of these psalms is indicated by the fact that they are found in key positions throughout the Psalter, for instance, at the very beginning (Psalm 2) and at the end of Books II (Psalm 72) and III (Psalm 89). The main theme of the entire Psalter could even be summarized in terms of the LORD's kingship: "pray" in the day of trouble to the merciful King who rules all things; "thank" the King for delivering you; "praise" the King for who he is and what he does; "teach" others about the King's great wisdom and mighty works; and, finally, always "profess your trust" in the King through words and deeds that are in keeping with his royal covenant of grace.

Bible translators must pay special attention to the messianic prophecies of the Psalter that are quoted or referred to in the New Testament. This does not mean that such passages should automatically be made the same, with the New Testament verse worded exactly like the one in the Old Testament. The words the New Testament writer used are often somewhat different because these quotations are from the Septuagint (LXX, the Greek translation of the Old Testament). Or he may have been giving only a paraphrase of the original text. But wherever the New Testament quotation does correspond exactly to the passage in the Old Testament, they should be translated the same. This is especially important where messianic references are involved, for example: "Anointed One" (2:2; 84:9), "Holy One of Israel" (89:18), "Savior . . . my firstborn" (89:26–27), "my Lord" (110:1), "a priest forever in the order of Melchizedek" (110:4).

Exercise 2.2.4

1. Look up the following passages and find where they are mentioned in the New Testament: 2:7, 8:4–6, 16:10, 22:1, 22:8, 22:18, 34:20, 40:6–8, 45:6–7, 68:18, 69:9, 69:21, 78:2, 110:4, 118:22. Write out the distinct messianic references. Carefully compare the Old Testament and New Testament passages, using a literal version such as RSV or NIV. Write out any differences in wording between the two. These passages are taken from various psalm types, not just songs of kingship, but circle all those that do come from royal psalms.

2. Do New Testament quotations from the Old Testament need to be *marked* in your language to show that they are quotations? Would readers think that these are the words of the New Testament writer if they are not so marked? Give two examples of such marking. This could be done with transitional words in the text of your translation or just with the printed format. Notice how the printed format of the NIV signals the presence of OT quotations.

3. In the Book of Hebrews we find many Old Testament quotations, especially from the Book of Psalms. Examine Hebrews 1:8–9, 5:5–6, 7:17, 10:7, 10:30, 13:6. Note any major differences between the quotation in Hebrews and the particular psalm from which it was taken. Can you suggest any reason for these variations (see THP)? Again, you will have to use a more literal English version or an interlinear text in order to do this exercise.

4. Psalm 2 is clearly a royal psalm, with many references to kings, the anointed, ruling, and rebelling against rule. However, we may also classify it as one of the five major psalm types (see sec. 2). Which type would this be? Why? Observe that in Psalm 2 there are four parts, or "stanzas." Give the verse numbers for each, with the help of the NIV.

   [A] vv. _____   [B] vv. _____   [B'] vv _____   [A'] vv. _____

Notice that the first and last stanzas as well as the middle two form a chiastic pattern: A B B' A'. What similarities in content and purpose do you see between A and A', and between B and B'? Do you notice any differences here? Explain.

5. Carefully study Psalm 110. Why would you classify this as a song of royalty? What are some of the main characteristics of a royal psalm that are evident? Notice that this praise for the Messiah King is in the form of a prediction. Also observe the two halves of this psalm, each beginning with an oracle of the LORD in quotation marks which is then expanded upon by several verses of warfare imagery. See if you can outline this two-part structure:

   First Divine Oracle: v. _____   Second Divine Oracle: v. _____
   Description: vv. _____   Description: vv. _____

   Make a first-draft translation of Psalm 110 into your language. Then test its impact and appeal by reciting it to your colleagues. Revise as necessary to highlight the "royalty" of this psalm.

2.2.5 Liturgy

Songs of liturgy are the least distinct category of psalms, for they can always be classified as one or another of the nine types already considered. Most are songs of praise or thanksgiving although there are also a number of petition-prayers among them. However, they all have certain formal characteristics suggesting that they were always sung on a particular occasion of public, corporate worship. This may have been at one of the appointed religious feasts or festivals of Israel, such as the Feast of Tabernacles, or during a regular gathering for worship at the temple.

The main characteristic of a liturgical hymn is its arrangement: certain clauses and parallel lines (couplets) are *repeated* (usually exactly) from time to time within the psalm. These reiterated clauses are called "refrains" (or "antiphonal dialogue"). It is thought that these refrains indicate points when either the whole congregation or a selected chorus was to respond in unison to what the worship leader had just spoken. These words—whether solemn and dignified, or joyous and enthusiastic—are words of petition, thanksgiving, praise, instruction, or profession directed to a holy and righteous God who was viewed as being immediately present with the congregation as they were gathered for worship in his name. In addition to helping emphasize the message, the repeated lines also serve an organizational function, indicating the psalm's major divisions (this feature will be discussed more fully in the next chapter).

There are quite a few psalms scattered throughout the Psalter that stand out as having a recognizable liturgical structure especially suitable for public worship. Among this group are Psalms 15, 24, 42–43, 47, 49, 50, 56, 57, 59, 75, 81, 85, 115, 118, 121, 124, and 136. Other psalms or psalm portions may also have been used during special ceremonies. For example, Psalm 67 could celebrate a harvest, and Psalm 68 would make a good processional hymn of victory in battle. Other groups of psalms seem to be dedicated to a particular topic or occasion of religious importance, such as those in praise of Zion (e.g., 46, 48, 76, 84, 87), or the "Pilgrimage Songs" (120–134, also known as "Songs of Ascent"), which worshipers may have sung as they went "up" to Jerusalem to attend one of the annual religious celebrations in the temple. The content of the psalm itself often gives an indication of its particular liturgical function, as do the "Entrance Psalms" (15 and 24) and the "Psalms of Blessing" (91 and 121); it seems likely that Psalm 118:27 would have been particularly appropriate for use during the Feast of Tabernacles (see Lev. 23:40–43).

Exercise 2.2.5

1. Examine Psalms 15, 24, 66, 84, 115, 118, 122. Which one of the five major psalm types do they represent—a song of petition, thanksgiving, praise, instruction, or profession of trust? From each of them choose a verse or two (making note of the references) that shows the song may have also had a special liturgical function. Briefly explain why you think so, based on the general form, content, or apparent purpose of the song (cf. THP and NIV-SB).

2. Carefully study Psalms 42 and 43. Note the verses that are repeated in these two personal petition songs. They are really one song. There are three principal sets of repetition: a *major refrain,* which occurs three times, and two *minor refrains,* each of which occurs twice. Write down the verse numbers of each refrain:

   major refrain: _____   minor refrain A: _____   minor refrain B: _____

3. What is the difference in content and purpose between the major refrain and the two minor refrains of Psalms 42–43? Taking Psalms 42–43 as a unit, let us suppose that each occurrence of the major refrain marks the end of a stanza. Then the whole piece would be divided into three stanzas. List the verses that belong to each:

   I. _____   II. _____   III. _____

   Stanzas I and II present the psalmist's problem while stanza III presents his two petitions to Yahweh. Summarize these two prayers. What structural feature do you see that supports the argument that Psalms 42 and 43 were really a single composition originally?

4. Write the words of the refrains found in Psalms 46, 49, 56, 57, 59A, 59B, and 80.

5. See if you can find another psalm in the Psalter that features a refrain.

6. There is an interesting pattern of refrains in Psalm 107. In vv. 4–32 we find four sets of verses, each of which consists of two parts. The first part of the refrain gives the *reason* why the people "cried out to the LORD" and the second part gives a *command* to the congregation to "give thanks to the LORD." Write out the references for the two verses of the refrain for each of its four occurrences:

   I. _____   II. _____   III. _____   IV. _____

   The second part of each refrain occurs near the end of a stanza. The stanzas tell of God's delivering his afflicted people. Describe each of these four situations of deliverance, noting that vv. 1–3 function as an introduction to the whole psalm. You will find them in vv. 4–9, 10–16, 17–22, and 23–32.

7. Are certain songs or poems in your language characterized by refrains? Write out what you know about them. Is there a need to mark such refrains in your language so that they are recognized as such by readers and hearers alike? Can this be done verbally within the text of the translation? Or would you use a special format in printing, for example, by adding space on both sides of the refrain or by printing the refrain in italics or bold print? Explain your preference.

8. We have already examined Psalm 136. In general, it is a _____ type of psalm, but more specifically we may classify it as a _____ type of psalm. However, its organization as a whole clearly indicates that it is also a liturgical psalm, one that was—and still is—very appropriate for use in a public worship service. What prominent feature makes this psalm so suitable for such a purpose? On what occasion could it serve well today?

9. Prepare a first-draft translation of Psalm 136 in your language. Notice that its special arrangement may cause translators a little difficulty. What is the particular novelty that you see here? Will it cause any problems for you? Explain how you might solve them.

2.3 Conclusion: The importance of genre in the study of the Psalms

Genre analysis has been emphasized throughout this chapter for two reasons. First, understanding the different categories shows Bible students how skillfully the Psalter as a whole has been composed. It demonstrates the great unity in diversity that is characteristic of all excellent literature. Second, we are also able to see that the original authors had particular *intentions* in mind as they composed their poetic works for specifically religious communication. They wanted their prayer-songs to shape the *motives* and stimulate the *emotions* of the people who listened to them so that they would feel the same joy, confidence, wonder, sadness, frustration, or anger which the psalmist himself felt as he wrote. The psalmist's feeling, or set of shifting emotions, corresponds to, or harmonizes with, the specific purpose for which the psalm was written—the five primary functional aims being prayer, thanksgiving, praise, instruction, and profession of trust.

There is, of course, a communicative purpose (at least one) behind every discourse, spoken or written. In other words, the author intends his message to "mean" more than just what the words say. He is also transmitting his feelings, impressions, attitudes, and aims in a manner which corresponds to his audience's knowledge, problems, needs, weaknesses, values, fears, and desires. He does this by formulating his words in a particular way, that is, by using an appropriate speech *style* coupled with a suitable *structural* framework. (The important topic of style will be considered in chapter 5.) He thereby fits the *form* of the message to the total circumstances of the communication event. (An example of fitting the form of a message to the total circumstances can be seen in the difference between a popular chorus sung by a mass choir at a public worship service, and by a mother singing it as a lullaby to a child in her arms.)

The "discourses" of Scripture likewise embody specific functions according to the type of literature they are (e.g., history, laws, proverbs, prophecy) and their different addressees (e.g., Old or New Testament, Jews or Gentiles, Hebrew- or Greek-speakers, righteous or wicked, etc.). This aspect of the communication situation is a vital part of any Scripture text's message. It is part of the total *meaning-package* and needs to be accurately conveyed when translating that passage into another language.

While the intended purpose and the *connotation* (associations, attitudes, values, etc.) of the original message may be specifically stated, such meaning is more often left *implicit* (unexpressed, but "understood") in the discourse itself. That is why it is often ignored or overlooked by translators. This oversight can have serious adverse consequences with regard to the quality of a translation's effectiveness. When something of Scripture has been ignored or omitted, even though unintentional and seemingly minor in nature, the loss must always be a matter of great concern. This applies to the prayer-songs of the Psalter just as much as to any other biblical text.

In Psalm 36, for example, there is a sudden shift in attitude and emotion as one moves from v. 4 to v. 5. The sorrow and disgust that the psalmist feels as he thinks about the pride of the wicked in vv. 1–4 suddenly changes to joyous wonder as he considers the amazing attributes of God in vv. 5–9. Similarly, the declarative and descriptive utterances which predominate in the first two sections of the psalm give way to fervent petitions in the final portion (vv. 10–12). Even within these three stanzas, certain passages stand out from the surrounding text as having a special communicative purpose: Verse 1 announces the topic of the psalm and serves as the introduction to the "oracle"; then the central peak of the psalm is marked by an exclamation of awe in praise of the LORD (v. 7a); finally, the conclusion is marked by another exclamation (v. 12)—this one an expression of confident trust in the LORD's power to fulfill his promises and answer the prayers of his saints (vv. 10–11). It is very important that these different aspects of associated connotative meaning, so closely bound up in the overall structure of the psalm, be manifested in one's translation, for they are a vital component of the psalmist's message as a whole.

Exercise 2.3a

1. Read Psalm 35 from the psalmist's point of view. Then pick out the main *connotations* (or attitudes) and *intentions* (aims) in each of the following verses: 1, 3, 8, 10, 14, 15, 17, 18, 19, 21, 23, 25, 26, 27. Summarize each of these feelings and purposes in a sentence or two (Hint: look for the exclamation marks in a translation such as the GNB, CEV, and NIV).

2. Where do you detect a sudden, sharp shift in tone (emotion) in Ps. 35? What seems to be the reason for this, and how can it be idiomatically indicated in your language (or in a better way perhaps in English)?

3. Examine the translation of Psalm 35 as a whole in your language (or in a literal English version), in the light of your analysis above. Have any of the other main emotions or intentions that you observe been altered or omitted? Note any instances of such lack of communication along with a brief explanation of what seems to have gone wrong. If there is no translation in your language, consider how you could best express these same emotions and intentions so that they will convey the deep feelings and principal purposes of the author.

4. Identify the dominant communicative function of each verse of Psalm 41 and write it down. Note whether or not this function is clearly conveyed in the translation in your language. (Or do this in some English version.) Point out instances where something seems to be missing and suggest ways to correct the rendering so that the *intent* of the original message is transmitted along with its *content*.

4. Now read through all the psalms that you have made a preliminary translation of in this course (13, 34, 148, 19, 46, 32, 95, 140, 110, and 136). Compare your work either with the original Hebrew text and/or with a meaning-oriented version such as the TEV or the CEV. (Also consult the THP and the NIV-SB.) Make the necessary corrections so that your version conveys a closer approximation of the full *feeling* and *effect* of the original. Do the same for the different *purposes,* or *functions*, of the text. Take special note of three of the major errors that you discovered. Tell what the connotation or intention of the original passage was, as you see it now, and what you wrongly communicated—or *failed* to communicate. This exercise will take some time if you do it right, but this will have to be done anyway—sooner or later—in order to produce a meaning-equivalent version in your language.

5. Consider the following diagram (contributed by Murray Salisbury). How does it help to explain some of the key relationships between major psalm genres?

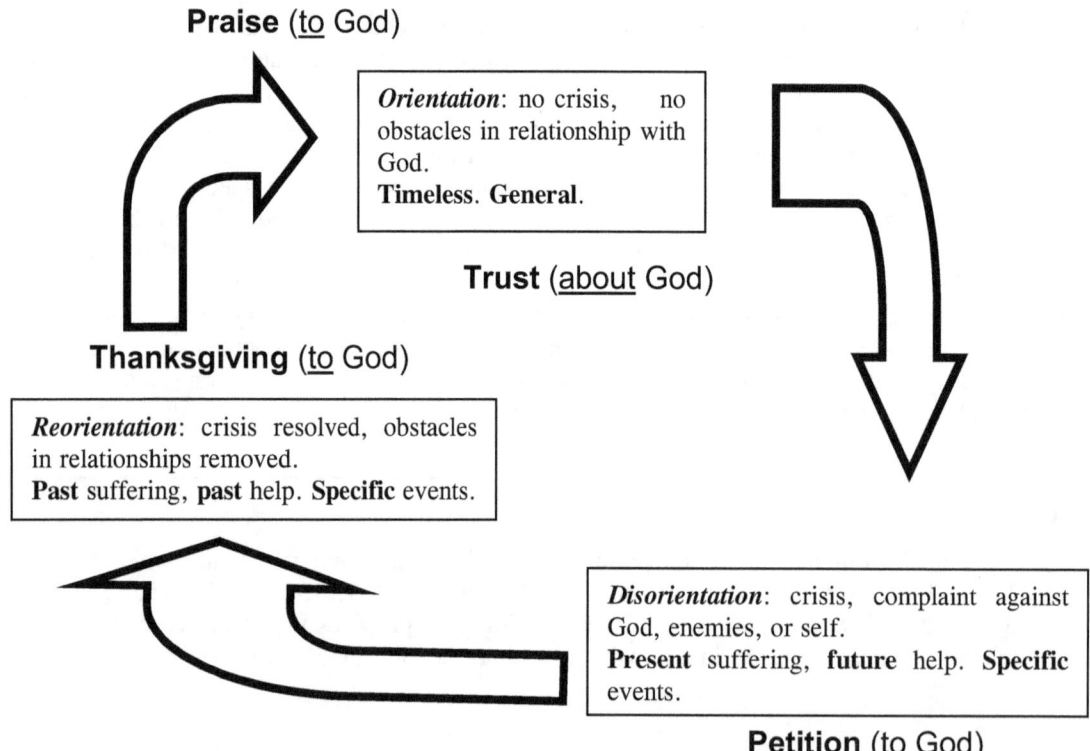

CATEGORIZING THE PSALMS ACCORDING TO GENRE

Exercise 2.3b

In this exercise you will review the different types, or genres, of psalm that we have been studying. Look up each psalm reference, and beside it write the letter of the description that fits it most closely. A psalm's genre cannot be determined on the basis of just a single passage or two, but for the purpose of this exercise, simply assume that the verses cited are representative of the psalm as a whole. Discuss the differences in opinion that are expressed by members of the class/translation team.

1. 48:1 _____
2. 60:1 _____
3. 21:1 _____
4. 119:33 _____
5. 33:3 _____
6. 62:2 _____
7. 112:4–5 _____
8. 99:6 _____
9. 104:5 _____
10. 118:2–4 _____
11. 22:1 _____
12. 106:7 _____
13. 69:24 _____
14. 42:3 _____
15. 149:2 _____
16. 91:9–10 _____
17. 69:21 _____
18. 51:3 _____
19. 79:4 _____
20. 93:1 _____
21. 119:48 _____
22. 34:11 _____
23. 90:15 _____
24. 47:1–2 _____
25. 2:7 _____
26. 20:5 _____
27. 24:3 _____
28. 122:3–4 _____
29. 118:29 _____
30. 116:1 _____
31. 32:5 _____
32. 148:4–6 _____
33. 46:4 _____
34. 109:15 _____
35. 49:20 _____
36. 66:12 _____

Types and Subtypes

(a) song of praise (hymn)
(b) creation psalm of praise
(c) remembrance psalm (salvation-history)
(d) royal psalm (kingship)
(e) royal hymn of Zion (praise)
(f) song of thanksgiving (eulogy)
(g) individual petition (lament)
(h) communal petition (lament)
(i) psalm of profession (creed)
(j) psalm of instruction (Torah)
(k) psalm of instruction (wisdom)
(l) liturgical psalm of worship
(m) the LORD as King passage (messianic)
(n) psalm of retribution (judgment)
(o) psalm of repentance (penitential)

37. 30:1 _____
38. 19:1 _____
39. 19:7 _____
40. 135:8 _____
41. 78:1 _____
42. 19:1 _____
43. 135:5 _____
44. 123:2 _____
45. 130:3 _____
46. 106:48 _____
47. 46:1 _____
48. 90:4 _____
49. 93:3 _____
50. 94:23 _____

Now try to find a passage not in the preceding list, but which illustrates these same psalm types. Write the reference in the blank space provided beside each letter that indicates a different type.

a. _____ f. _____ k. _____
b. _____ g. _____ l. _____
c. _____ h. _____ m. _____
d. _____ i. _____ n. _____
e. _____ j. _____ o. _____

TEN PSALM GENRES[1]

Genre	Components
Petition **(Lament)**	➢ **Appeal** (the psalmist calls to God to listen and pleas for help in a time of trouble, "O Lord...") ➢ **Problem** (more detailed description of trouble, e.g., sickness, threat, weakness, wickedness) ➢ **Request** (what the Psalmist wants God to do); gives reasons why God should help: ♦ to demonstrate God's righteousness ♦ to strengthen faith of all who trust in God ♦ to frustrate plans of wicked and silence their blasphemies ♦ to manifest glory and power of God ➢ **Defense/Confession** ♦ Psalmist's claim of innocence for specific wrongdoing **or** ♦ Confession of individual or corporate sin ➢ **Profession of Faith** ➢ **Promise** (vow to thank God always for saving him or a promise to bring sacrifices) ➢ **Praise** (final word of praise to the LORD)
Thanksgiving **(Eulogy)**	➢ **Praise** (for his glorious attributes and/or acts of deliverance; sometimes leading off with a blessing of the one who has been helped by the Lord) ➢ **Distress** (telling why psalmist or people need help) ➢ **Profession of Trust** (psalmist expresses complete confidence in God to deliver—may include record, or *testimony* of God's past deeds) ➢ **Thanksgiving/Promise to Praise** (vow to praise God, invite others to join, specific sacrifice)
Praise **(Hymn)**	➢ **Summons** (to praise the LORD—*Hallelujah*) ➢ **Reasons** (why people should praise the LORD for deliverance in the ancient past, rather than immediate past as in a Thanksgiving psalm) ➢ **Call** (concluding call to thank and praise the Lord)

---

[1] The following two charts (with several minor adaptations) were contributed by Dr. Lee Fields, who uses the present workbook in teaching a Psalms course at Roanoke Bible College in North Carolina. These may serve as a helpful summary of the material that was presented in this chapter. The results noted on the second chart may be compared with a more general survey to be found in Berry 1995:368–377.

Genre	Components
Teaching (Wisdom)	➤ No set list of components, but **stylistic features** include: ♦ Strong contrasts ♦ Comparative sayings (righteous vs. wicked) ♦ Warnings to the wicked ♦ General admonitions to listen ♦ Picturesque similes ♦ Rhetorical questions ♦ Representative speech of the wicked
Profession of Trust (Confidence)	**Difficult to Identify** because of overlap with Petition, Thanksgiving, and even Teaching. Sometimes called "Creedal Psalms" because of the special focus upon testimony to the faithfulness of the Lord to his covenant ➤ **Thanks/Praise** (same as Petition psalm) ➤ **Profession of Trust** (same as Petition psalm) Distinguishing feature is that the *main emphasis of the psalm as a whole* is the speaker's profession of unshakable faith and confidence in the Lord

Sub-Genre	Emphasized Components
Repentance	*Sub-genre of Petition* with following emphases: ➤ **Confession** (heavy emphasis on confession of sin) ➤ **Profession of Faith** (prominent expression of hope in the LORD to forgive sins)
Retribution	*Sub-genre of Petition* with following emphasis: ➤ **Request** (this request is special in that asks for deliverance of the righteous *and also* for *punishment* of the wicked)
Remembrance	*Sub-genre of Thanksgiving* with following emphasis: ➤ **Profession of Faith** ♦ the LORD's faithful provision and protection in the past despite the people's past failures ♦ also called "Historical Psalms"
Royalty (king only): **Kingship** (Davidic King +/- God's Messiah):	*Sub-genre of Petition* with following emphasis: ➤ **Requests** (what the psalmist wants God to do) ♦ special in that it is made to the LORD on behalf of the king or for the blessing of the king *Sub-genre of Praise* with following emphasis: ➤ **Reasons** (same as praise) ♦ may also contain profession of faith ♦ *Yahweh* is identified as the King and He is praised ♦ often these are prophetic of the promised *Messiah*
Liturgy	➤ **Hybrid** of the other types ♦ can be any of the nine other types, but most are praise or thanksgiving in public worship setting ♦ main characteristic is formal arrangement: certain clauses and parallel lines are repeated exactly ♦ mood is joyous and enthusiastic—celebration!

DISTRIBUTION OF PSALM GENRES

The following chart represents an attempt to classify all 150 psalms by genre. Major genres are in bold type. The sub-genres are arranged under their major genre. An asterisk (*) indicates a dual listed psalm. A plus sign (+) refers to Liturgical Psalms, which are all by definition dual listed. There will of course be differences of opinion with regard to any detailed classification of this nature. However, this attempt provides a good place to begin such a discussion which is aimed at increasing one's awareness of the different genres that are represented in the Psalter—the "pure" forms as well as the "hybrids." Course participants may be assigned as individual small groups to evaluate the listing below and to report their joint findings to the entire class.

Genre	Book 1 (1-41)	Book 2 (42-72)	Book 3 (73-89)	Book 4 (90-106)	Book 5 (107-150)
Petition	3-5, 7, 9, 10, 12-13, 17, 22, 28, 31*, 39, 40*	40, 42+, 43+, 44, 54, 55, 56+, 57+, 59+, 60, 62*, 64, 69, 70, 71	74, 79, 80, 82*, 85+, 86, 88	90, 94	120, 123, 126*, 137, 140, 141, 142
Retribution	35	58, 69	82?*, 83, 89*		109
Repentance	6, 32, 38	51		102	130, 143
Royalty (King)	18*, 20, 21	45*, 61, 72	89*	101	
Thanksgiving	18*, 30, 34, 41?	65, 66+, 67*	75+, 77		116, 118+, 124+, 126*, 129
Remembrance			78*	105-106	107*, 114, 135, 136+*, 138*
Praise	24+, 40*		81+	92, 93, 95, 100, 103, 104	107*, 111, 113, 117, 122, 134, 135, 136*, 138*, 144, 145, 146, 147, 148, 149, 150
Royalty (Messiah)	2, 8, 29, 33	45*, 47+, 48, 50*, 67*-68	76, 84+, 87	96-99	132, 108, 110
Teaching	1, 14, 15+, 19, 36, 37	49+, 50?+, 53	73, 78*,		112, 119, 127-128, 133
Profession of Trust	11, 16, 23, 25, 26, 27, 31*	46, 52, 62*, 63		91	115+, 121+, 125, 131, 139
Liturgical Psalms	15, 24	42, 43, 47, 49, 50, 56, 57, 59 66	75, 81, 84, 85		115, 118, 121, 124, 136

3. CONNECTED PARALLELISM: THE INTERNAL AND EXTERNAL STRUCTURE OF PAIRED LINES IN THE PSALTER

Thus far we have been studying the different types, or genres, of psalms in the Psalter, mostly with respect to their various *functions,* that is, how a given psalm was *used* in the public worship and private devotion of God's people. We now want to take a closer look at the poetic form, style, and manner of composition of the psalms. An understanding of literary form and compositional technique is important because it can often give some crucial insights into the meaning (especially the major and minor themes) and purpose of a psalm. In other words, a careful and complete study of stylistic form is a vital part of the exegetical process without which no analysis can be said to be complete.

3.1 Preparing to study the poetic devices of Hebrew

But how can one investigate the form of a text without knowing the language in which it is written? Indeed, this *is* a rather serious obstacle for those who do not know something about Biblical Hebrew. But it is not an insurmountable barrier. By using a fairly literal version (e.g., NKJV, RSV, NASB, NIV) or an interlinear Old Testament, one can get enough of a picture of the original text to be able to do at least a partial analysis of poetic forms. Commentaries are another source of information. But before turning to the "experts," students should first study a given passage on their own. By following the basic steps for discourse analysis, they can observe how the Hebrew text was composed and begin to understand why it was written in the way it was. It is the methodology, the system of study, that is key to getting the most accurate, consistent, and helpful results. The notes and exercises in this and subsequent chapters will suggest a good procedure to follow when examining the text of a psalm.

The linguistic "form" of a verbal composition, whether oral or written, involves four closely related elements, which together are joint carriers of a given text's total "meaning":

(1) the *sounds*, which make up the spoken words of the text and contribute a great deal to its beauty as it is uttered aloud, particularly in the case of poetry the world over;
(2) the *words*, which in combination both near and far provide most of the semantic content of the discourse;
(3) the *grammar*, which is the rule-governed organization of words into natural and meaningful utterance units (clauses and sentences); and
(4) the *discourse structure*, which is the arrangement of clauses and sentences into larger groupings and patterns of meaning (e.g., paragraphs, episodes, stanzas, sections) that encompass the entire text.

To these four building blocks of form (and content—for the two cannot really be separated) we might add a fifth, the *rhetoric* of discourse. This refers to the selective and skillful use of any of the preceding compositional components in order to construct a more "persuasive" text. Rhetoric adds relevance, impact, beauty, and appeal to the author's message through certain special usages— "literary devices." These are common to all languages, although languages differ in the manner, frequency, distribution, and purposes for which a particular feature is used. (Examples of literary devices are repetition, figurative language, word-order variation, and rhetorical questions.) They operate together to form the "style" of a discourse, meaning the distinctive way it is put together, whether on a large or small scale (e.g., verse, single psalm, psalm type, complete Psalter). Note that every literary genre of both "prose" and "poetry" is characterized by a specific style, and to understand how any particular text conveys its intended meaning, it is essential to examine the different stylistic devices which comprise it.

The use of a given rhetorical device usually results in some "special effect." It may give additional emphasis, it may express or evoke strong emotions, it may focus on some new aspect of truth, or it may make the composition artistically attractive and esthetically pleasing. Whenever heightened feeling, force, or fancy becomes a major motivating factor in the use of the various linguistic features, we are usually dealing with some kind of poetry. Poetry, or poetic discourse, is a distinct type of literature in which the verbal *form* of the message—that is, its style—is accented to a great degree in order to emphasize and embellish the author's intended message as well as make it more memorable. While rhetoric is also found in biblical *prose,* it is of a somewhat different type and is not nearly as obvious or concentrated as in biblical poetry.

The problem for a translator is that the poetic style of Hebrew is different in many important respects from the style of poetry in any target language (TL), whether it be English, French, Spanish, Zulu, Chinese, or Chewa. Each language has its own unique rhetorical resources, its own collection of "poetic devices." The devices of the TL must be carefully studied with respect to both form and function and then compared with those present in the Hebrew text. Some devices may be used in nearly the same way; others will overlap; still others may differ considerably or even completely. Therefore, as we study some of the principal stylistic features of Hebrew poetry, a corresponding investigation of TL poetry must also be carried out. Our aim is to find rhetorical techniques in the TL that are equivalent in effect to those of Hebrew so that the intended meaning of the original text can be preserved in translation to the extent possible. (This important subject will be given special attention in chapter 8.)

Now we turn to consider the most prominent of the poetic devices in Hebrew: parallelism. This chapter will focus on adjacent (connected) parallel lines, and chapter 4 on nonadjacent (distant) parallel lines.

3.2 The nature of connected parallelism: Internal structure

The best-known and most obvious formal attribute of Hebrew poetry is *parallelism,* In essence, a parallelism is simply the product of joining two (sometimes three) relatively short, balanced utterance units together—with a major "pause" somewhere in the middle—to express a complete thought. Such a coupling of poetic lines is effected by formal as well as semantic repetition. The repeated elements may be phonological, morphological, lexical, and/or syntactic, with this repetition bringing about some type of meaningful correspondence that links two lines (usually designated as A and B) closely together, as in Psalm 3:1 (all quotations from the NIV, unless otherwise indicated):

> A: O LORD, how many are my foes!
> B: How many rise up against me!

These poetic lines are more technically known as *cola.* (One line is a *colon.*) Related cola usually occur one right after the other as in Psalm 3:1. This is "near" (connected or adjacent) parallelism. But two or more lines that appear to be parallel may also be found farther away from each other within the text of a psalm. This is "distant" (separated or nonadjacent) parallelism. Psalm 3:2 and 8 are an example:

> A: Many are saying of me, "God will not deliver him." (Ps. 3:2)
> B: From the LORD comes deliverance . . . (Ps. 3:8)

This pair of similar lines that focus on God's saving assistance helps to mark the initial and final boundaries of Psalm 3 (*inclusion,* see ch. 4).

When analyzing near parallelisms, we will look at both their "internal" and "external" organization. The internal structure of two or more parallel lines has to do with the arrangement of the individual word-units within each line or colon. External structure has to do with the various ways in which parallel lines and groups of lines (couplets) are joined together to form larger units of meaning (see sec. 3.3).

In speaking of internal structure, it is the arrangement of "word-units" within a poetic line that is in view. Each of the parallel lines, or cola, that form a poetic couplet generally consists of a simple verb-based grammatical clause. This normally includes the following basic syntactic elements (+ designates an *obligatory* sentence constituent; +/- an *optional* one):

+/- **conjunction** +/- **vocative** + *verb* +/- **subject** +/- **object(s)** +/- **adjunct(s)**

The following is a literally rendered example of this structure:

they-take-a-stand (V) the-kings-of=the-earth (S). (Ps. 2:2a)

It should be noted that in the very literal translation above, the English words are connected by hyphens when they represent a single word in the original. An equals sign (=) then signifies a *maqqeph*, which is the Hebrew equivalent to the hyphen that joins two or more words into a single accent group, forming one lexical item. (The same conventions will be used in all literal renderings in this book.) Thus Ps. 2:2a consists of only two "word-groups" in Hebrew as compared with many more in English.

The term "adjunct" in the formula above refers to all noun-based constructions other than subject or object. This includes, for example, a "prepositional phrase":

and-let-us-throw-off (V) from-us (A) their-fetters (O). (Ps. 2:3b)

Other adjuncts are modifying words, such as adjectives, adverbs, demonstratives, or the "construct" (genitive) construction, normally found following a head noun (e.g., KINGS + "of the earth" in Ps. 2:2).

As the formula above indicates, in Biblical Hebrew, the verb with its inseparable subject marker is the only obligatory constituent in the principal (*verbal*) clause type. A separate subject noun or pronoun is *optional* and, when present, is therefore significant, especially if it is a repeated reference to the same person, place, or thing.

The basic word order in Hebrew prose discourse (e.g., a narrative) is V-S-O, although this arrangement may be varied through "front-shifting" (the placing of some word other than a conjunction ahead of the verb). The purpose of front-shifting is to signal a change in the main topic or to show a contrast or some special emphasis, including the marking of a new larger discourse unit (e.g., a paragraph). The precise reason for such a word order shift can be determined only with reference to the larger context of the line in question (see sec. 5.4.1). A good example of such an arrangement for contrastive, summary purposes is found in Psalm 1:6 (note that [c] = conjunction):

for (c)=he-is-knowing (V) Yahweh (S) the-way-of the-righteous-ones (O),
and (c)-the-way-of the-wicked-ones (S) it-is-perishing (V).

In this passage there is a departure from the normal prose order of syntactic elements, a feature that is frequently found in poetic texts. In the second (B) line, the subject appears before the verb to form a concluding "chiastic" construction (V-S / S'-V'; see further 3.2.2 below).

There is another type of poetic line type (colon) that has no verb. Normally some form of the verb "to-be" is understood (implicit) in these cases. The normal word order in such *nominal* clauses is as follows:

+/- **conjunction** +/- **subject/topic** +/- **vocative** + **complement** +/- **adjunct(s)**

An example of this construction is in Psalm 3:3, the first colon of which can be rendered literally as follows:

and (c)-you (S) Yahweh (Voc) [are] a-shield (C) around-me (A)

The device of front-shifting (or "advancement") can be seen in nominal clauses just as in verb-based clauses. Here, too, it indicates some special discourse function, perhaps to give additional emphasis to a key concept of the text. That is why it is important to note the order of the main syntactic constituents in any A line and to compare it with what is found in its parallel line, as well as in surrounding lines. (You can refer to the original text or an interlinear Old Testament to see what the Hebrew word order is.)

Two cola linked together as parallels are called a "bicolon" (i.e., A + B). It is also possible to find three lines in a parallel arrangement. This is known as a "tricolon" (i.e., A + B + C; e.g., Ps. 1:1). At times, especially in the case of two very long lines, it may be convenient to divide them into a set of four. This is a "tetracolon" (i.e., A + B + C + D; e.g., Ps. 5:11). A single line occurring by itself (with no parallel) is called a "monocolon" (e.g., Ps. 2:12c). The most common pattern, however, is the two-line (A+B) bicolon. The others, the monocolon in particular, are exceptions that may be introduced in order to help mark some important discourse feature, especially a stanza's beginning (e.g., Ps. 11:1a) or ending (e.g., Ps. 11:7c).

One other infrequent feature is what is sometimes termed "internal" or "half-line" parallelism. In this case, the two halves of a relatively long poetic line manifest a parallel relationship with each other. A good example is seen in Psalm 2:2:

```
A1: they-take-their-stand the-kings-of=the-earth   (2)
A2: and-the-ones-ruling they-gather=together       (2)
    B1: against=Yahweh                 (1)
    B2: and-against=his-anointed-one   (1)
```

Here A1 is obviously parallel with A2, and B1 with B2. However, due to the shortness of the B lines, this verse is more accurately analyzed as a 4 + 2 bicolon rather than a tetracolon. In some instances this distinction may not be so easy to make, but the important thing is to observe where the parallelism occurs (whether involving whole or half lines) and what type of semantic connection links the various interrelated meaning segments together.

Another prominent feature of Hebrew poetry is its overall *symmetry* and *balance*. The two (or more) adjacent lines of a parallelism always correspond to, or contrast with, one another in several significant respects—in sound, sense, and/or syntax (e.g., word order). In the case of distant parallelism, complete but textually removed poetic lines may link up with one another to form additional, larger patterns of structure within the psalm. For example, Psalm 73 begins with an affirmation of trust: "God is good to Israel, *to those who are pure in heart*" (73:1). Though the first half of this confessional prayer closes with a lament, "in vain have *I kept my heart pure* . . ." (73:13), the pray-er reaffirms his faith later, just prior to the psalm's conclusion (vv. 27–28), saying "My flesh *and my heart* may fail, but God is *the strength of my heart* . . ." (73:26).

Whether the lines are near each other or relatively far apart, such patterns of textual linkage are much more obvious in Hebrew. This is because the actual sounds of words are used to create additional connections between the lines through alliteration, vowel assonance, grammatical pauses, rhythm, rhyme, or word plays. For example, here is how Psalm 3:1 sounds in Hebrew (approximately!):

| *mah-rabbu ṣaray* | How many are my foes! |
| *rabbim qamim ᶜalay* | How many rise up against me! |

By consulting an interlinear translation we can get some indication of this *interlocking* of form and content between connected cola. The formal harmony of the related A and B lines thus supports and reinforces the parallelism conveyed by the meaning. It is this "paired" organization of the sequence of cola carrying the progression of theological ideas forward in short, measured steps that gives Hebrew religious poetry its special stylistic character.

But in addition to observing the *internal* structure of parallel lines (that of the words in relation to each other), the translator must also analyze the *external* indications of parallelism by identifying the grammatical, semantic, and functional relationships involved between the lines. This is usually done after the psalm's genre has been determined. In section 3.3 we will focus our attention on the various semantic (i.e., meaning) relationships that serve to connect the parallel lines A and B (+/- C). If the Hebrew text or an interlinear version cannot be read, then this consideration of "external parallelism" will have to be done by comparing different English translations, both literal and idiomatic. We will occasionally make use of the formal criteria of internal parallelism such as word class and word order, but only when such evidence is quite obvious and important to the analysis at hand. (More advanced students may continue to investigate such issues in Hebrew, even when they are not explicitly referred to in the following exercises.)

Exercise 3.2

1. You will be studying Psalms 3, 5, 8, 11, and 14 in order to determine which lines are parallel to each other. The first line (colon) of a given parallel set is A, the second B, the third C, and so forth. Thus 1A+B means that the first two poetic lines of v. 1 are parallel; 3C+D means the third and fourth lines of v. 3 are parallel; 6B+C means the second and third lines of v. 6 are parallel. Remember that monocola (e.g., 6A) and tricola (e.g., 2A+B+C) can also occur. Use an interlinear to do this exercise, but remember that if there is a psalm heading/title, it is counted as v. 1 in the Hebrew text. Also refer to the *NIV Study Bible* or the THP for assistance, especially when trying to identify any monocola that are present. Psalm 3 has already been done for you here; check it over before doing the other psalms.

    Psalm 3: 1A+B, 2A+B, 3A+B, 4A+B, 5A+B, 6A+B, 7A+B+C, 8A+B

    [Note that verse 7 could be analyzed in another way, i.e., 7A+B and 7C+D with 2+2+3+3 words. Which interpretation do you prefer and why?]

    Now do Psalm 5, 8, 11, and 14 in the same way. (Other psalms, such as those translated in chapter 2, Exercise 2.3a, may be analyzed in a similar way, if time allows. This same suggestion can be applied to any of the other assignments in this exercise if more practice would prove helpful.)

2. Go over Psalms 5, 8, 11, and 14 again in an interlinear version and list the number of words in each poetic line. Remember that the Hebrew "hyphen" (*maqqeph*) may join two or more words to form a single "word-unit" (i.e., one stress-group). Sometimes initial short words, such as the conjunction *waw* 'and', may be counted together with the following word if this will create a better balance in the numbering pattern. The following shows how this is done for Psalm 3 (v. 1, being the title, is excluded):

    1: 3 + 3, 2: 3 + 4 (excluding *selah*), 3: 4 + 3, 4: 3 + 3 (excluding *selah*), 5: 4 + 3, 6: 3 + 4, 7: 4 + 4 + 3, 8: 2 + 2 (excluding *selah*)

3. Notice the shift in the basic word-count and/or colon pattern that occurs between vv. 7 and 8 of Psalm 3. What do you observe here? Why do you think that this change occurs at this point in the psalm?

4. Notice that Psalm 14 is not easy to analyze into parallel lines due to their great variety:

    1: __+__+__+__ 2: __+__+__ 3: __+__+__+__ 4: __+__+__ 5: __+__
    6: __+__ 7: __+__+__

    Also several verses lend themselves to more than one analysis. Should v. 3, for example, be analyzed as a bicolon, 3A(4) + B(4), or as a tetracolon, 3A(2) + B(2) + C(2) + D(2), or two bicola, 3A1(2) + B1(2) and 3A2(2) + B2(2)? This sort of line analysis may be too complicated to consider now, but it might be interesting for the class to discuss the differences between these three possibilities for v. 3 to see if some agreement can be reached. The important thing is to determine what difference—if any—this would make in the target language. Would one of these interpretations turn out to be easier to translate into your language, or would this matter not have any noticeable effect at all? For example, will one way of segmenting the text produce a more pleasing (rhythmic) sequence of poetic lines in the TL than another way?

5. The final verse of Psalm 14 contains the same problem as Psalm 14:3. Does it have three "long" lines, 5(4)+4+4 = 7A+B+C, or should some attention be given to the correspondence that is found within the final line? In other words, is this a case of "internal parallelism": 7A(5/4) + B(4) + C1(2) + C2(2)? Which pattern of units do you prefer and why? The solution you choose could easily affect your translation; one arrangement would divide the final line into two, the other would not. Notice that there is no word corresponding to "and" in the Hebrew text; it literally reads, "let-him-rejoice Jacob let-him-be-glad Israel." Would a separation of these two short lines be a more effective way of concluding this psalm in your language? Give reasons for your preference. Observe how this problem of line division in 14:7 is handled in the TEV, CEV, NIV, NRSV, and GW (*God's Word*). Which of these versions conveys the internal parallelism most clearly? Which is least successful in this regard? Why do you think so?

We will have a closer look at how the "internal" structure of a pair (or more) of poetic lines affects the nature of their overall parallelism in the following sections.

3.3 The nature of near parallelism: External structure

External structure has to do with semantic relations between lines (i.e., cola). Traditionally scholars have attempted to analyze the meaning (logical + semantic) relationship between parallel poetic lines A and B in terms of three basic categories: (1) similarity, (2) contrast, and (3) addition. In a pairing of *similarity*, the meaning of line B is nearly the same as the meaning of line A (this is called *synonymous* parallelism). In a pairing of *contrast*, line B shows at least one major *contrast* in meaning to line A (this is called *antithetical* parallelism). In a pairing of *addition*, the meaning of line B is necessarily *connected* with the meaning of line A in terms of a time, cause-effect, completion, or statement-reply relationship (this is called *additive* parallelism).

These categories may or may not be helpful, depending on the particular passage that one is examining. But it is important to recognize that they are all variations of a more general relation which we might term *complementation* or *correlation*. In other words, the compositional feature of arranging two or more poetic lines in parallel sets links them in such a way that the B colon "complements" (or "co-relates"—that is, completes, specifies, supports, reflects, reinforces, focuses, or expands upon) the A colon with respect to its content, purpose, impact, and/or appeal.

In general, while there may be a wide range of semantic relations possible between any two poetic lines looked at in isolation, it is usually possible to narrow this range to one or two principal types of logical linkage when dealing with a specific passage in its context. The lack of an explicit marker (e.g., a conjunction) of the connection between A and B is usually the main reason for this ambiguity. When preparing a translation, however, it is often necessary to overtly state what the most likely connection between A and B is. Otherwise, readers/listeners may misinterpret or fail to understand the intended relationship that links the two lines. Consider Psalm 6:3, for example:

A: My soul is in anguish.
B: How long, O LORD, how long?

How is line B related to A? Is the psalmist asking God to tell him how long he *has been* suffering? No, not really. Line B is actually a "complaint" in which the psalmist overtly asks how long he *will have to go on* suffering; but this is in fact an implicit appeal that the LORD would mercifully cut this time short. This may have to be clarified in a translation to prevent confusion, e.g., B: "O LORD, how long will I have to keep suffering like this?"

Whether or not the B colon adds any specifiable content, it often contributes some form of *emphasis* to line A. In many languages, this would even be the effect of pure repetition. Such emphasis may be of several types, each manifesting different levels of intensity depending on the passage concerned and the particular rhetorical device that is used to create it. Exact or partial repetition sometimes occurs in line B, but in addition we often find some specification, an intensifier or exclamation (e.g., a vocative call to God), a figure of speech, or dramatic direct discourse. We will be studying these possibilities in more detail later. Once the variations can be readily recognized, the analyst is usually able to determine the nature and degree of the emphasis between A and B without too much difficulty. Certain commentaries, such as the THP, also draw one's attention to this important literary feature of "seconding" one poetic line by another.

However, in the overall analytical process it is important not to become too concerned about trying to pinpoint either the logical relationship or the difference in meaning between A and B too precisely. That is not the nature of poetry. In contrast to prose, poetry's aim is broader: to encompass a wide area of meaning, describe a novel experience, elicit a particular attitude, evoke powerful feelings, or stimulate the reader's imagination. The meaning of the whole unit (verse, strophe, psalm) is always greater than the sum of its individual parts.

The main principle to keep in mind is this: the two poetic lines must be interpreted together as one, as a *unit* of meaning. There will always be an essential internal *unity* despite any external *diversity*. Even though different formal features with different rhetorical purposes may be used, they all contribute to the harmony of the whole. The A and B lines operate as a closely knit pair—a marriage of poetic utterances, as it were—in order to enhance the main theological or religious message that the psalmist wished to convey. This principle applies to all of the poetic parallels found in a complete psalm. Though each couplet is distinct, they all work together to heighten the total communicative intent and worshipful effect of the complete prayer.

In the rest of this section we will consider in detail the three kinds of poetic complementation mentioned earlier: similarity, contrast, and addition. Remember that the linguistic form of the lines is not our primary focus, though the closer in form that they are, the greater will be the degree of parallelism. Remember also that these categories are not rigid ones. They are simply a convenient means of organizing Hebrew poetry. In fact, there is considerable overlapping among the different categories and a certain ambiguity due to the open and evocative nature of poetry. As a result it is often possible to describe the same couplet in more than one way, depending on its content and context. Even the scholars rarely agree on these issues. Nevertheless, it is helpful to look closely into the different complementary relationships that link two or more poetic lines together as a way to more fully understand the message of a given psalm, to better remember it, and as a means of discovering its great artistic and theological value.

3.3.1 Similarity

The first type of paired relationships is similarity, often termed "synonymous parallelism." In this type of bicolon, line B is relatively similar to A as far as its general semantic content is concerned, but there are usually certain differences of linguistic form: the actual words themselves, their syntactic relationships perhaps, and, of course, their sounds. The semantic similarity serves to reinforce, emphasize, foreground, or specify either the basic thought of the couplet as a whole or a particular element of meaning within it.

This kind of relationship between A and B we will call *base-similarity*. The term *base* refers to the primary poetic line of a pair in terms of form (i.e., the main/independent clause), function (i.e., of major importance), content (i.e., the more general utterance), or simply order (i.e., the first colon to appear, A). Colon B is viewed as being "similar" to A, even though it will frequently (but not always) turn out to be somewhat more specific, concrete, detailed, dramatic, colorful, or intensive. There are certain words and phrases that often occur in B lines because they are characteristic of liturgical language, or they are commonly associated expressions ("poetic word pairs"). Still, the pairs can hardly be thought of as formulaic. The very act of pairing lines in parallel form lends a perceptible progressive movement to the text, which keeps the audience engaged with the flow of ideas, attitudes, and emotions from one couplet to the next.

Consider a literal rendering of Psalm 19:1, for instance:

```
              a                        b                    c
A: the-heavens              / are-ones-telling     / the-glory-of=God;
B: and-the-work-of his-hands / is-one-proclaiming   / the-firmament.
```

In this bicolon, line A consists of three "words" and B of four (note the connective lines of the English interlinear translation). This we write with numerals (3+4) to designate the bicolon's rhythmic, or accentual, structure.

We can observe in the preceding example that the second line reverses the order of syntactic elements, from **S-V-O** in A to **O-V-S** in B. This is called a "chiasmus," a common rhetorical device in poetic literature. A reversal of this sort (i.e., **A-B-C ... C'-B'-A'**) may involve any type of linguistic structure (sound, sense, or syntax), but it is the easiest to detect when the same or similar lexical items are reiterated. Note, however, that English (and other) translations frequently re-order the Hebrew chiasmus so that the text sounds more natural; therefore, to discover them in the original an interlinear version will have to be consulted. A chiasmus is often used to highlight a contrast in meaning. In this case, however, the essential content of the bicolon is not affected. Perhaps a chiasmus is used here simply as an artistic way of introducing the psalm or emphasizing the meaning of the bicolon as a whole, i.e., the unity and completeness of God's creation.

As is often the case in a synonymous parallel, the Hebrew word "firmament" in Psalm 19:1 is not only similar to, but is somewhat more specific than "heavens." Likewise, "proclaims" is a stronger verb than "are telling," and "the work of his hands" states in more concrete terms how "the glory of God" is revealed. But it is important to recognize that line A and line B are not speaking of two separate things. Rather, the idea in line A is the same thing that is described with slightly more detail in line B. The repetition emphasizes the wonderful nature of what God created.

Note that each of the two parallel lines in Psalm 19:1 is made up of three syntactic units: S-V-O in colon A and O-V-S in colon B. This is the normal pattern of couplets in Hebrew poetry, namely, two lines, consisting of two or three primary grammatical elements each. This syntactic feature often turns out to be matched by the number of "words," each of which usually receives a single stress or accent. (In Psalm 19:1 this is 3+4, as we saw.). But the most common word-sequence pattern in Hebrew poetry is 3+3, while 3+2 comes second. Another popular combination is 4+3 (or, like Ps. 19:1, 3+4), but it is not as frequent as the first two.

A variation in these basic lexical and syntactic patterns may occur at any time, especially after a certain pattern has been established. Such a shift often indicates some special rhetorical or compositional purpose in the context of the entire poem. For example, instead of a bicolon, a monocolon or, more frequently, a tricolon can be used for variety. Alternatively, one may find a certain colon that consists of one or four syntactic units (from one to six Hebrew "words"). However, an "exception" can only be determined within the total context of a given psalm; and if a certain line or couplet does prove to be exceptional, it will usually be an indicator of some special meaning, such as to mark a thematic contrast or an important peak. It may highlight the introduction of additional feeling or emphasis to create an emotional climax or extra impact. At other times, the exceptional line serves to signal a discourse boundary; for example, the syntactic reversal noted in Psalm 19:1 probably announces the beginning of the psalm as well as its primary theme.

It is important to stress that the B line does not always represent an addition to A in terms of semantic content. That is to say, the intention may be to emphasize the *unity* of meaning of the pair as a whole, although in many cases there is also a certain progression in thought from A to B. Thus, in Psalm 19:1, "firmament" (i.e., "sky") is a more specific designation of the "heavens." Similarly, "proclaims" is not a different event from "telling"; rather, both verbs are expressing the same figurative idea (personification). Thus, a translator may have to omit "and" in the translation because in many languages "and" often means that something new or different is being added to what has already been said.

There is another important implication for translators here: As we have seen, the B lines often contain close synonyms for words appearing in A lines, with the referent of the synonyms being the same. Therefore, it *is* acceptable for a translator to repeat the word used in line A if the TL does not have a suitable synonym. Consider "firmament/sky," for example. There would be nothing wrong with either repeating, paraphrasing, or using a figure of speech for the word "heavens" in A when translating line B (e.g., "the place up above," "the roof of the world," "the big blue covering"). There may be a certain loss of—or gain in—semantic precision from what is present in the original, but sometimes this cannot be avoided if one is to reflect the original in terms of its literary function. On the other hand, there is obviously a difference in meaning between "the glory of God" and "the work of his hands" (i.e., "everything he has made"), and this distinction should be maintained in the translation—along with the general increase in poetic emphasis that we find in colon B.

In Psalm 19:1 we saw that the number of syntactic elements in line B corresponds to what is found in line A. Such equivalence does not always occur, however. Sometimes one or more of the subunits of A does not have a matching element appearing in B. This is the case in Psalm 38:1:

```
         a              b                 c
A: O-Yahweh  / not=in-your-anger  / you-rebuke-me,     (3)
B:    ***    / and-in-your-wrath  / you-discipline-me. (2)
```

Here, the first element, namely a vocative phrase, as well as the negative found in the second element, is not overtly expressed in line B. Line B consists of only two major units. We say that the first element has been "elided" or "gapped" in colon B (resulting in a 3+2 structure). In some languages, however, it may be necessary to restore the rhythmic balance either by repeating "Yahweh" in B, or by using a synonym such as, "O God," or better still (if possible) through the use of a powerful praise-name, "the Great One of up above," or "Master-Lord," for example. Notice also that while B says essentially the same thing as A in this case (if the negative is included), the effect of the repetition is to add some emotive power to the psalmist's words. It is this rhetorical effect (i.e., for increased impact and appeal) which needs to be reproduced, if at all possible, by a suitable poetic device or literary technique in the language of translation.

Exercise 3.3.1a

1. Read through the psalms translated in the exercises of the last chapter (13, 19, 32, 34, 46, 95, 110, 136, 140, 148). Find five examples of parallel lines (bicola) that are synonymous in nature. Write out these verses with their references. If possible, use an interlinear version and write the two lines in a literal, word-for-word fashion as in the examples of section 3.3.1. Next, circle and draw lines to connect the corresponding syntactic elements in the A and B cola.

2. Look again at the verses you wrote out in assignment 1. Underline any parts of the B lines that seem to be somewhat *different* from the corresponding parts of the A lines, whether they vary in terms of either content, focus, or emphasis. Consult the THP to help you complete this exercise. Be prepared to tell what the difference is in each case and how it might affect the translation into your language. Give a specific example, if possible.

3. In this same set of psalms, see if you can find any instances of a *monocolon* (single line) or a *tricolon* (three lines). Try to find three examples of each. Write down the references to these passages. Indicate which one of these passages has a monocolon or tricolon that seems to mark an opening or closing boundary of a stanza unit.

The various parts of the parallel lines A and B do not always match as they do in Psalm 19:1. In fact, the correspondence between cola may get rather complex and difficult to recognize. This is the case in Psalm 9:9:

```
          a        b         c              d                    e
A: and-he-is  /  Yahweh  / a-refuge / for-the-oppressed, /      ***
B:    ***     /    ***   / a-refuge /        ***         / for-times-of destitution.
```

Here line B contains only one visible element of semantic correspondence with line A, namely, the noun "refuge" in both lines. (It is foregrounded in line B due to the exact reiteration.) Constituents [a], [b], and [d] are left *implicit* in line B; they are not actually expressed in the text but are definitely understood as being part of the author's intended meaning. Element [d] manifests a benefactive and [e] a temporal relationship within the clause. This is an instance of "ellipsis," where words in the immediate context are not directly stated in a subsequent utterance, but their meaning is clearly implied. In some cases, depending on the language and the textual context, it may be necessary to "fill in" the intended content at least a part of such an ellipsis; for example, "God is" may have to be made explicit in line B.

Notice that in line B of Psalm 9:9 a new aspect of meaning is added to the main thought being conveyed. What is added is [e], a time phrase: the LORD helps his people out especially in "times of trouble." However, the final constructions of both lines, which begins with the preposition "for" in the Hebrew, are similar with respect to their form. This is an important feature of Hebrew poetry: there are various degrees of similarity and difference: at the same time *unity in diversity*; in other words, *harmony* despite the *difference*. This applies to both the form and content of the parallel lines A and B (+/- C). The psalmist aims for a special rhythmic effect that will heighten both the linguistic artistry ("style") and at the same time communicate a particular meaning or feeling. The translator's challenge is to try to duplicate this notion of unity along with a similar emotive impact and esthetic appeal, yet also with naturalness in the target language.

The Psalm 9:9 example shows us that we cannot be too rigid when attempting to identify either formal or semantic categories in Hebrew. This is typical of poetry in many other languages: variations and differences, large and small, are frequent, being used to break up or modify an expected pattern. The poet shuns predictability and tries to avoid monotony in order to enhance the religious (theological, moral) message being conveyed. His appeal is to his audience's esthetic sensibility, that is, their feeling for relevance, naturalness, appropriateness, correctness, and beauty. This avoidance of predictable linguistic patterns means that a number of passages may be classified or analyzed in more than one way.

Psalm 145:18 is another example:

```
      a         b                 c                    d
A: near  / (is)-Yahweh / to-all-of=those-calling-him /  ***
B: ***   /     ***     / to-all who they-call-on-him / in truth.
```

Here the first two elements, [a] and [b], are implicit in the B colon, and a new aspect of meaning is added in the prominent concluding position. Formally, this final [d] element serves to create a slight rhythmic imbalance between the lines (a 3+4 syntactic pattern). But more important, it emphasizes the fact that, in the LORD's eyes, one's heart attitude is far more important than outward, routine rites of worship (cf. Ps. 145:19–20).

The next example is Psalm 23:2. Here we see very little formal correspondence at all in most English translations. The similarity appears to exist only on the level of general content, that is, a partial likeness of topic. In other words, lines A and B both speak about the LORD's abundant provision for those who trust in him:

> He makes me lie down in green pastures,
> he leads me beside quiet waters.

However, in the Hebrew these parallel lines are syntactically quite a bit closer in form, as we can see from an interlinear version:

```
         a              b            c
A: In-pastures-of  / greenness  / he-lays-me-down,  (3)
B: beside=waters-of / quietness / he-leads-me.      (3)
```

The two rather different but obviously related pastoral images are poetically linked in order to convey the same basic theological truth. The principle that God generously provides for his people is thus reinforced through repetition.

Earlier we spoke of the *base-similarity* relation, meaning synonymous parallelism. But for the translator it may be helpful to distinguish between two types of synonymous parallelism, based on how closely the A and B lines correspond. We can use the term **base-restatement** for paired cola that are very close in terms of *content* (though not necessarily in terms of *form*, such as the arrangement of a-b-c elements). In the base-restatement category, line B closely repeats the sense of A in different words to stress what was just said. Psalm 19:1 is of this type. But where some aspect of the content of line B is noticeably different, we might use the term **base-amplification**. Here, line B says something quite similar to line A but also *adds* a new and noteworthy element of meaning to the whole. (Both of these relations need to be distinguished from that of *base-addition*, to be discussed later, in which the entire B line is considerably different in content from the A line.)

Two instances of base-amplification have already been given. In both Psalms 9:9 and 145:18, there is an obvious addition in the B lines, but a great deal of implicit information is also present which keeps the lines "synonymous," as it were (*implicit* means not overtly expressed but clearly understood). The category of Psalm 23:2 is debatable: in this verse, cola A and B look quite different on the surface, but underneath (the so-called "deep level" of meaning), we might ask, Are the two lines saying essentially the same thing or not? If the same, the relation is base-restatement (or base-amplification). If not, it is base-addition. The answer to this question may well affect how one decides to translate the bicolon, especially line B.

Another good example of base-restatement is in Psalm 78:4:

A1: We will not hide them from their children;
A2: we will tell the next generation
B1:   the praiseworthy deeds of the Lord,
B2:   his power, and the wonders he has done.

Line A2 of this split bicolon (or tetracolon) restates in a positive way the content of A1, while B2 rephrases the sense of B1. The form of each A and B line is different from its counterpart, but the essential meaning is the same. Thus, we are dealing with two cases of restatement rather than amplification (though the relative correspondence of B1 and B2 could be debated). In any case, B1 + B2 together express the content of what is implied in A1 + A2 (i.e., *base-content*, to be discussed later in this section).

Frequently a synonymous restatement in B will be manifested in more graphic, emphatic, and/or figurative language (see chap. 5). Psalm 69:7 is an example (NRSV):

A: It is for your sake that I have borne reproach,
B: that shame has covered my face.

The personified reiteration of A in line B heightens the sense of shame and isolation that the psalmist expresses here. Notice that line B corresponds only to the second half of line A. It is thus overtly a "partial restatement" of the content of A, with the first part being left implicit in B.

We see then that there are varying types and degrees of correspondence possible with regard to both form and content between the A and B lines of Hebrew poetic parallelism. These range from nearly exact repetition (which is rare, except in nonadjacent parallelism) to complete antithesis, with various degrees of likeness in between. There are also many different types of "additive" linkage that may occur as well as the two semantic opposites of "similarity" and "contrast." These categories offer only a broad framework to start out from, and each couplet or triplet needs to be studied in its own particular compositional context, whether near ("connected") or distant ("separated"). Only a careful, discourse-oriented examination can lead one to the interpretation that seems to best fit the whole psalm. Thus, this is not simply a formal classification of the outward shapes of the paired lines, but rather an explanation of how the lines operate in relation to one another to express the psalmist's overall intended meaning. Nevertheless, the analyst must still learn to recognize the various types of Hebrew rhetorical devices used by the psalmist to embellish and emphasize his message. The crucial issue for Bible translators is this: How can we best duplicate the powerful poetic and persuasive style of psalmic speech in the languages of today?

A particular subtype of either the base–restatement or the base–amplification relation is the ***general-specific*** relation in which colon B presents a more precise, detailed, or concrete instance of what is said in colon A, as in Psalm 51:19 (NRSV):

A: Then you will delight in right sacrifices,
B1: in burnt offerings and whole burnt offerings;
B2: then bulls will be offered on your altar.

The general reference to "sacrifices" in line A is specified in B1 as "burnt offerings." In B2 it is even more specific: "bulls."

In Psalm 47:8, a specific manifestation of kingship is expressed in line B: "holy." Line B is also expressed in more concrete, visual terms than line A:

A: God reigns over the nations;
B: God is seated on his holy throne.

However, line B of Psalm 47:8 could also be viewed more generally as an instance of the figurative restatement of line A.

A special type of the general-specific relation is when B gives an instance of direct speech that exemplifies or typifies a general characteristic or event mentioned in A. Psalm 71:10a–11a is an example:

A: For my enemies speak against me . . .
B: They say, "God has forsaken him . . ."
   (Literally, leʾmowr "saying," which suggests that only the gist or a representative "quote" is being given.)

These instances of the general-specific relation may also be considered a ***base–content*** relation, the *base* (A) being a reference to a speech act and the *content* (B), the direct speech itself. (More will be said about this relation later.)

Now to conclude this section, we will consider Psalm 105:6, a more complex example of similarity. This example illustrates the importance of considering each segment of a given psalm in its wider, compositional context:

```
          a              b             c
A: O-offspring-of / Abraham   / his-servant,      (3)
B: O-sons-of     / Jacob     / his-chosen-ones!   (3)
```

The two lines (3+3) of Psalm 105:6 refer to the same group of people, namely, the nation of Israel. It is they who are the descendants of "Abraham" and also of "Jacob." Although A and B appear to be saying nearly the same thing in different words, we note a distinction in the third element (c) where the relationship between Yahweh and his people is in focus: in A his people serve him (i.e., "his servant"); in B the LORD is said to have chosen them (i.e., "his chosen ones"). The fact that God chose the nation of Israel to be his people and sealed this with a covenant is the basis for all their acts of worship and service. There is thus a heightening of the personal relationship between God and his people that is developed between A and B (i.e., base-amplification). The respective vocative terms of address also shows movement from the more general "offspring" (lit. "his seed") to the more specific "sons" (lit. "children").

When translating this verse, its connection with the preceding verses, especially v. 5, must also be taken into account. Notice that TEV reverses the order of v. 5 and v. 6 so that the vocative in v. 6 precedes the command to "remember" in v. 5. If the Hebrew order of verses is retained, then it may be necessary to make some other kind of change for the sake of naturalness in the TL. For example, v. 5 might be translated as a complete sentence ending with a period, and v. 6 would then start as a new sentence with an emphatic summary of vv. 1–5: "Yes/Indeed, you should do all these things. . . ." Observe that the imperative "do" here applies to everything commanded thus far in the psalm, v. 6 being a climactic utterance that marks the close of the first major discourse segment. The fact that it does mark a boundary is a good reason for giving v. 6 special emphasis and also for leaving it in its original position in the text.

Exercise 3.3.1b

1. Study each of the following synonymous pairs (taken from the NRSV) with the help of the THP and the NIV-SB. Identify the basic syntactic units with the letters a, b, c, (or V, S, O), etc., as was done for the earlier examples of this chapter. Draw circles around the units and join each one with its corresponding unit in the other line(s). If you use colored pens, the corresponding units may be connected simply by using the same color. An interlinear version will enable you to see the parallel segments more clearly. Underline or highlight any elements that are obviously different. Be sure to check carefully for any *implicit* or *added* elements in line B. The following example, Psalm 2:1, has been analyzed for you: Note the chiastic structure (b-c/c-b) and the possible addition of [d] in line B ([d] might also be construed as being part of the verbal idea [b], i.e., "plot vainly"). The question particle of line A, element [a], is viewed as implicitly active also in line B:

   A: why (a) do-they-rage (b)   nations   (c)?   [= 3 words]
   B: and-   as-for-peoples (c) do-they-plot= (b) = <u>vanity</u> (d)? [= 2 words]

   (a) It is you who lights my lamp;
       the LORD, my God, lights up my darkness. (Ps. 18:28)

   (b) They cried for help, but there was no one to save them;
       They cried to the LORD, but he did not answer them. (Ps. 18:41)

   (c) Day to day pours forth speech,
       and night to night declares knowledge. (Ps. 19:2)

   (d) The LORD answer you in the day of trouble!
       The name of the God of Jacob protect you! (Ps. 20:1)

   (e) May he send you help from the sanctuary,
       and give you support from Zion! (Ps. 20:2)

   (f) Let them be put to shame and dishonor
         who seek after my life!
       Let them be turned back and confounded
         who devise evil against me! (Ps. 35:4)

   (g) Let them be like chaff before the wind,
         with the angel of the LORD driving them on.
       Let their way be dark and slippery,
         with the angel of the LORD pursuing them. (Ps. 35:5–6)

   (h) Hear my prayer, O LORD,
         and give ear to my cry;
         do not hold your peace at my tears.
       For I am your passing guest,
         an alien, like all my forebearers. (Ps. 39:12)

(i) Have mercy on me, O God, according to your steadfast love;
according to your abundant mercy blot out my transgressions. (Ps. 51:1)

2. Using an interlinear translation, examine the form of the foregoing passages. Then write the letters of the passages which seem to express the following different aspects of the base-similarity relation:

   base-restatement   *base-amplification*   *general-specific*

3. Find another passage in the Psalms that is an example of a *general-specific* relation. Write it out in its A and B lines, and identify its corresponding syntactic units with a, b, c, (or V, S, O), etc.

4. On a separate piece of paper describe how the two (or more) lines of each of the examples in assignment 1 relate to one another in terms of some "addition" of *content*. In other words, what is it that B seems to say or communicate over and above what is said in A? Focus first of all on the *differences*: Are there any bits of meaning in B that differ in some major respect from what is said in A? Try to explain what this difference in content is. Furthermore, does the B line seem to be more emphatic, colorful, or specific than A in any way? If so, tell how. Also point out any important *implicit* ideas in B, that is, thoughts that are repeated from the A line, but not mentioned explicitly.

5. Be prepared to discuss how you will translate each of these passages in your language, noting especially those places where some restructuring is necessary in order to convey the intended meaning in the best way. For example, you may have to make something explicit in line B that was only implicit (not mentioned) in the original. Give one example showing how you have restated a given passage so that it communicates more clearly and/or poetically in your language.

6. The diverse forms of parallelism are not limited to just two corresponding A and B lines. Cola with similar content may form a pattern that runs over the span of several verses. One pair or one triplet may link up with other sets to form a tightly constructed, often symmetrical whole. Read Psalm 106:1-6 and identify the overall pattern of synonymous or closely related lines. Write out the sequence of cola comprising these six verses on a separate piece of paper. Find one example each of the base-restatement and the base-amplification relationships. Then draw lines or brackets to connect all the individual cola (or complete bicola) which are similar to one another in the sequence. Where does an important break in content and tone occur within these six verses? Describe it. Can you explain the type of shift in the semantic relationship between the A and B lines that occurs beginning in v. 7? Explain the connection between v. 6 and the verses that follow.

3.3.2 Contrast

The type of parallelism that involves a contrast (sometimes termed "contrastive" or "antithetical") is related to that which involves similarity (sec. 3.3.1). But in a contrast relation the emphasis is upon one or more specific *differences* between the content of the two lines, with colon B normally expressing some explicit contrast or opposition with respect to line A. We term this semantic relationship **base-contrast**. The differences are usually quite obvious, and they serve to emphasize one or another of the main thoughts of the psalm, as in Psalm 145:20 (NRSV):

   A: The LORD watches over all who love him;
   B: but all the wicked he will destroy.

If we arrange the word-units of each of these poetic lines in order as they occur in Hebrew, we notice how the form of the original may contribute to the meaning of the whole:

```
              a                    b                   c
A: watching-over        / Yahweh           / all=those-loving-him /
B: and-                 / all=the-wicked-ones / he-will-destroy.
```

The A and B lines appear in the form of a chiasm:

A = verb (a) + subject (b) + object (c); B = object (b) + [subject] + verb (c).

Here the order of the opposing units is reversed: This chiastic reversal highlights the contrasting fates of good people and evildoers in relation to God. "Watching over" is first in line A and "will destroy" is last in line B. This serves to emphasize the main point of the psalmist, which is made clear near the end of the psalm: the positive-negative contrast is used to stress the encouraging message that God always takes care of his people, and they therefore should gratefully praise him (145:21). In this antithetical verse—and others like it—the conjunction *waw*, which is normally rendered "and" in a literal version, may need to be translated as "but" in order to better mark the contrast between A and B.

In a contrastive parallelism the number of syntactic elements may differ from line A to line B, just as in a synonymous parallelism. The reason for this sometimes involves *ellipsis*, that is, the omission in line B of a word corresponding to one found in line A. Whenever there is an ellipsis, a certain prominent concept may then be foregrounded or emphasized by a shift in the normal word order. In Psalm 30:5b the idea being stressed is part of a typical wisdom teaching:

```
         a                  b           c
A: in-the-night       / it-remains / weeping,
B: and-in-the-morning /    ***     / rejoicing.
```

Here, in line B, the psalmist omits line A's verb element (b). He thus leaves the "saints of Yahweh" (v. 4) with the total comfort that not only will good follow evil (as morning follows evening in Hebrew thought), but that blessing ("rejoicing") will be their ultimate state or condition. This idea reinforces the point of the preceding bicolon (Ps. 30:5a), which is also contrastive in nature:

```
         a         b          c
A: for a-moment / [is] / (in)-in-his-anger
B: lifetimes    / [is] / (in)-his-favor.    (Ps. 30:5a)
```

Since in Hebrew the main verb normally occurs first in a clause, we can assume that any word-unit that comes before the verb, is thereby foregrounded. The same is true of whatever word-unit comes first in a verbless (topic-comment) clause. Thus in Psalm 30:5a the psalmist is contrasting—and thereby emphasizing—the fact that although God may punish us for our sins for a time, this period is very short in comparison with our entire life, during which the LORD mercifully protects us.

Psalm 30:5 also illustrates how one bicolon may be combined with another (5a with 5b) to convey a larger unity of meaning. In this case, 5a provides the underlying (divine) reason for the specific (human) experiential result recorded in 5b. Because of God's ever-present favor, a believer can rejoice in all circumstances of life. It is important that this fact about poetic composition not be forgotten during the analysis process. Just as no individual line exists in isolation, no bicolon does either. Rather, except where a text boundary is involved, a parallel pair is always related in a specific way to the bicolon which has gone before and the one which follows. A couplet that is important in terms of the overall structure or thematic content may also be linked by way of some close meaning relationship to one or more other points in the larger composition. Notice again that the elaborate patterning found in Psalm 30:5 helps to establish a discourse boundary; in this instance, it is marking the close of the "strophe" (vv. 4 and 5).

In the examples we have looked at thus far, the contrastive elements between lines A and B are obvious and match rather closely. That is not necessarily true, however, of all the passages that involve the relationship of antithesis. The individual word-units in Psalm 31:8, for example, appear to be quite different from one another:

A: You have not handed me over to the enemy
B: but have set my feet in a spacious place.

Note that the contrastive conjunction "but," which has been supplied by the NIV translators in order to mark the opposition between the two lines, is not actually present either in the Hebrew or in many other versions, such as the RSV and TEV. The contrast here is negative-positive in nature, as the TEV rendering of Psalm 31:8 brings out:

A: You have not let my enemies capture me;
B: you have given me freedom to go where I wish.

But this is more a contrast in general ideas than in specific points, as in the earlier examples. Just as in synonymous parallelism, the syntactic form and word order of the A and B lines may be very similar or very different; the important thing is the meaning of the combination, which always involves at least one major contrast, opposition, or antithesis.

Direct contrastive parallelism is not very common in the Psalms. Where it does occur, therefore, it is usually thematically significant. (Contrastive parallelism *is* found quite frequently in Proverbs, where the difference between the lives of the godly and ungodly is a principal theme of the book.) It is more frequent in the *didactic* (teaching) psalms where it is used to highlight the difference between the blessed way of those who "fear the LORD" (i.e., trust, obey, and worship him) and the evil way of those who refuse to revere and follow him.

Exercise 3.3.2

1. Find the points where specific *contrasts* occur in each of the following passages: Psalm 18:27, 31:23, 34:10, 37:16, 37:21, 37:22, 44:2, 96:5, 126:5, 146:9, 115:17–18. Circle and connect with a line the syntactic elements that contrast with one another. If possible, consult an interlinear translation to do this exercise so that you might observe where any chiasmus or reversal in the word order is found. In Psalm 75:10, for example, we can see how the word order emphasizes the main topic of the verse:

```
             a                   b                    c
A: and-all=the-horns-of/ the-wicked-ones    / I-will-cut-off
B: the-horns-of         / the-righteous-one / they-shall-be-lifted-up
```

It may help to chart the similarities and contrasts that you find between the A and B (+/- C) lines of each of these passages on a separate piece of paper. Then they can be more easily compared and checked. There will usually be at least *two* sets of contrast in each pair of parallel lines, i.e., (x) and (y). They may be noted in the respective boxes under the headings x and y, and z if there is a third pair. The following chart has been filled out for Psalm 75:10 as an illustration of what to do:

Psalm 75:10	**Contrast x**	**Contrast y**	**Contrast z**
Colon **A**	wicked	cut off	(none)
Colon **B**	righteous	lifted up	
Colon **C**	(none)		

2. For Psalm 115:17–18 tell how the two separate sets of parallel lines contrast to dramatically highlight the psalm's conclusion.

3. Find five other examples of contrastive parallelism in the Psalter. Write down their references. Then prepare a chart as above for each passage, filling in each of the primary contrasts you see.

Summarize the main theological point or teaching which these oppositions are intended to convey

4. To translate a contrastive passage, is there any way in your language to bring out the points of contrast between the A and B lines? Is there some word order, a special negative marker, or a medial conjunction such as "but"? Explain and illustrate with reference to Psalm 32:10 and Psalm 34:15–16.

5. Are there proverbs in your language that use opposites to emphasize the ways of the wise as opposed to the foolish? Or does the concluding moral of a folktale ever do this? If so, write down an example or two to explain to the class. Would this apply to translating any of the contrastive passages from the Psalms that you have examined?

3.3.3 Addition

The type of parallelism that involves an "addition" (sometimes called "synthetic" parallelism) is the broadest of the three general categories in that it includes any semantic relation other than close similarity or sharp contrast. Here, the distinct elements of line B correspond much less closely in content to those in line A. Rather, there is a sequential addition, progression, or correlation of meaning. Line B builds upon what was said in line A, completing or reinforcing the thought begun there. Both lines are necessary, as in contrastive parallelism, in order to provide an interpretation for the complete bicolon. Instead of an obvious similarity or difference, however, there is a further logical development of content or a combination of related ideas that links the two lines together.

The three principal types of additive couplet in the Psalms are temporal, causal, and completive. In other words, line B may be linked to A by means of a *time* connection, or by some kind of *cause-effect* progression, or by the addition of certain essential information which *completes* the sense of the unit. It is not always so easy to distinguish the different subtypes, however. There is rarely a clear marker of the relation, such as a transitional conjunction (the common link-word "and" is usually quite ambiguous). In some cases it may be that the psalmist deliberately wanted to allow for more than one possible meaning so as to increase the poetic richness of his message.

Why then should translators even try to specify the sense at all? Why not simply leave the relationship between cola ambiguous? The answer to this question will vary from situation to situation and the type of version that is being prepared. But if a meaning-oriented text is the aim, it would seem that if one possible sense or relationship seems to be particularly called for by the context, or if it appears to fit the TL more naturally with regard to comprehension, or more "poetically" in terms of style—then that option ought to be used. Furthermore, if there is a chance that an ambiguous rendering may allow for the *wrong* meaning to be understood, or cause confusion, then a more explicit translation of the relationship is necessary. This problem is an important issue in translation, one that deserves further discussion. The exercises that follow in this section focus on the way to avoid ambiguity that would result in wrong meaning.

3.3.3.1 Temporal addition

The temporal addition of parallel lines involves a definite progression between events or activities in time. First A occurs, and then B occurs, as in Psalm 25:13:

    A: He will spend his days in prosperity,
    B: and his descendants will inherit the land.

The temporal sequence involved in the preceding passage is not difficult to see. However, many possible instances of this relation are not so clear-cut. A more debatable progression occurs in Psalm 23:6, for example:

>   A: Surely goodness and mercy will follow me all the days of my life,
>   B: *and* [= afterwards] I will dwell in the house of the LORD forever.

In this example, the constituent phrases of the two parallel lines are rather difficult to match up since the only similarity or contrast lies in the presence of two time expressions: "all the days of my life" and "forever" (lit. "for the length of days"). This is characteristic of the category of addition: the less closely the main syntactic elements of lines A and B seem to correspond in content, the more likely it is that we are dealing with an additive bicolon. Yet both lines are equally necessary to convey the intended meaning of the pair. Another problem presented by this example is whether we are dealing with a sequence in time at all: first A, then B. Some scholars consider "house of the LORD" to be a reference to the temple in Jerusalem, the semantic relation between A and B therefore being one of simple "base-addition" (see 3.3.3.3).

In Psalm 25:13 as we saw above, the temporal relation between the A and B cola is a *coordinate* one: one event follows the other and both clauses are more or less independent syntactically. Line B, however, forms a climax, not only in relation to A, but within Psalm 25 as a whole; "descendants" are the greatest covenantal blessing that the psalmist could hope for. Two temporally related cola may be joined in English by the conjunction "and (then)" or "afterwards" or even "next." This is called a ***base-sequential time*** relation. It is very common in the "historical psalms," which recount important events in the history of ancient Israel. Psalm 105:23-27 is an example (modified slightly from the *God's Word* version):

>   A1: Then Israel came to Egypt.
>   B1:   Jacob lived as a foreigner in the land of Ham.
>   A2: The LORD made his people grow rapidly in number
>   B2:   and stronger than their enemies.
>   A3: He changed their minds so that they hated his people,
>   B3:   and they dealt treacherously with his servants.
>   A4: He sent his servant Moses,
>   B4:   and he sent Aaron whom he had chosen.

Notice that each couplet here presents another stage in the temporal sequence. The various A lines state the next event that occurs in the story. That is, they are in a base-sequential time relationship to each other. At the same time, each B line adds more information by means of some synonymous type of relation (e.g., A1 + B1 = *base-amplification*).

There are a number of instances in the Psalms where, rather than a sequence in time, the lines in parallel may speak about two or more different events taking place more or less simultaneously. This is termed a ***base-simultaneous time*** relation. An example is in Psalm 106:24-25 (*God's Word*):

>   A1: They refused [to enter] the pleasant land;
>   B1: They did not believe what he said.
>   A2: They complained in their tents.
>   B2: They did not obey the LORD.

In this passage, a set of actions is presented as if they happened together. (Perhaps they indeed did take place all at once.) This simultaneity stresses the magnitude of Israel's guilt before the LORD and their culpability (vv. 26-27). Since the last line here is the most generic, another way of analyzing this set of lines would be as a *specific-generic* sequence, in which case the first three specific statements would be seen as in a *base-addition* relation to each other.

A subtype of the *base-simultaneous* time relation would be a parallelism in which two or more aspects of the same general event are reported separately. An example of this is in Psalm 105:26 (NRSV):

>   A: He sent his servant Moses,
>   B: and Aaron whom he had chosen.

The LORD did not first send Moses to Pharaoh and then later on send Aaron. Rather, they went together (Exod. 3:13–16). To indicate this simultaneity, the B line may need some appropriate marking in many languages. In English, for example, "also" could be used instead of "and" in B.

In other instances of temporal coupling, one of the lines (either A or B) may, in the Hebrew, be explicitly marked by a conjunction, prepositional phrase, adverb, and/or a nonfinite form of the verb as being *subordinate* to its parallel. In other words, one line (or often, only a half-line) will be grammatically independent, and the other dependent. The dependent clause normally adds some information about the main event that the other line is reporting. We call this relation ***base–circumstance***. An example is Psalm 31:22b (NRSV):

    A: But you heard my supplications
    B: when I cried out to you for help.

Here line B is dependent upon A. It is an adverbial clause of time, marked by the temporal conjunction "when" (actually the preposition *b-* "in" in Hebrew). The principal event in A speaks of the LORD's hearing; the secondary one gives the circumstances, namely, the psalmist's crying out. This crying out is a more specific expression of "supplications" in line A (hence A+B also manifests a *general-specific* relation). When translating this into some languages, the order of the A and B cola may have to be reversed to reflect the natural temporal sequence of events: first I "cry" and then God "hears."

    But when I called to him for help,
        the LORD heard my prayer.

The difference between "sequence," "simultaneous occurrence," "circumstance," and "addition" is not always clear in the original text. Such distinctions may not be very important in poetry anyway, at least not in every TL. But then again, there may be some languages in which the relation may need to be made explicit. Thus, for the sake of classification, we might reserve the designation "circumstantial time" for those cases where there is an obvious subordination in importance or an actual dependent construction in Hebrew, e.g., where the verbal appears in the form of an infinitive. An interlinear version will usually show this. Often an English version will help because of the use of a conjunction such as "when," "after," "while," "until," or "before," even though in most cases these words are simply renderings of the single Hebrew conjunction *waw*, "and" or the preposition *b-*, "in." Translators have used the different English conjunctions in order to try to indicate the temporal relation more explicitly or naturally within a particular context.

Sometimes two or more of the various temporal relations are combined. Psalm 28:2 is an example (NRSV):

    A: Hear the voice of my supplication,
    B1:   as I cry to you for help,
    B2:   as I lift up my hands toward your most holy sanctuary.

Lines B1 and B2 are clearly parallel. (To be precise, they are half-lines.) They are in a simultaneous-time relationship to one another, but with B2 being emphasized due to its length and occurring second. This pair, in turn, describes the particular circumstances that pertain as the psalmist is making his "supplication" (line A). In other words, B1 and B2 tell of two secondary actions (or aspects of one complex event) that occur while the primary activity of A is taking place. Thus the relation of base–circumstance is combined with base–simultaneous time.

Exercise 3.3.3.1

1. Identify each of the following verses as to its **temporal** relation. Before each verse write the letter that fits it best: (a) *base–sequential* time, (b) *base–simultaneous* time, (c) *base–circumstance*.

___ They track me down; now they surround me;
   they set their eyes to cast me to the ground. (Ps. 17:11, NRSV)

___ When the Almighty scattered kings there,
   snow fell on Zalmon. (Ps. 68:14, NRSV)

___ . . . the earth quaked,
   the heavens poured down rain . . . (Ps. 68:8a, NRSV)

Now check these verses in the NIV, TEV, and CEV. Do their renderings appear to agree with what you have marked? Do you notice any possible differences of opinion? If so, what are they?

2. Is the relation between the A and B lines of Psalm 68:7 one of base-sequential time, base-simultaneous time, or base-amplification?

   O God, when you went out before your people,
      when you marched through the wilderness . . . (NRSV)

   Explain your answer. What kind of semantic relation links Psalm 68:7 and 8a?

3. A literal rendering of Psalm 68:18a reads as follows:

   you-went-up to-the-height; you-led a-captive; you-received gifts from-the-man.

   In the following quotations, note how the different English versions indicate the *temporal* relations between the clauses. Mark the relation between lines A and B, and between B and C, as either a, b, or c as in assignment 1. If you feel that a relation of *similarity* fits better (see sec. 3.3.1), then indicate that instead.

   (NIV)   When you ascended on high,
              you led captives in your train;   _____
              you received gifts from men . . .   _____

   (TEV)   He goes up to the heights,
              taking many captives with him;   _____
              he receives gifts from rebellious men.   _____

   (NRSV) You ascended the high mount,
              leading captives in your train   _____
              and receiving gifts from people . . .   _____

   (GW)   You went to the highest place.
              You took prisoners captive.   _____
              You received gifts from people.   _____

   Which set of temporal relations would sound most natural or appropriate in your language? (Note: You should *not* have indicated that any of these involves a similarity relation.)

4. Find five more examples in Psalms of the relation we call "temporal addition." They may be (a) base-sequential time, (b) base-simultaneous time, or (c) base-circumstance. Write the five passages out on a separate sheet of paper. Try to find instances where different transitional conjunctions are used in English between the A and B cola and circle them. Then check a Hebrew interlinear, if possible, and note what conjunction or preposition, if any, was used in the original. Write that above the English conjunction on your paper. Finally, indicate which type of temporal relation appears to be linking the cola—a, b, or c—as you did in the earlier assignments.

3.3.3.2 Causal addition

The A and B lines of an additive pair are sometimes linked in a *cause–effect* relation. In this relation, the action of B is an effect of the action reported in A, or, we could say, in some way A causes B to take place. We call this semantic relationship a *causal* addition.

Causal addition is a very common way of joining two cola together. There are a number of important subtypes in this broad category: **reason–result, means–purpose, means–result, condition–consequence, concession–contraexpectation,** and **grounds–implication**. While it is not always possible to clearly distinguish one from the other, especially in Hebrew poetic texts, this classification helps us to be more conscious of the various ways in which poetic lines (cola) may be related. The relatedness may occur at the lower level or the higher levels of discourse structure with respect to both "near" (connected) and "distant" (separated) parallelism.

The following is Psalm 116:2 in the NRSV:

> A: Because he inclined his ear to me,
> B: therefore I will call on him as long as I live.

Here the NRSV has marked the causal relation very clearly, in fact, almost too explicitly for a poetic text. "Because" shows the **reason**, and "therefore" shows the **result**. Note that, in the Hebrew, the second conjunction is simply *waw* "and." In many languages it is not necessary to signal both components of this logical relationship as overly as the NRSV does, especially in poetry, where a more condensed, or abbreviated, manner of expression is in order. Condensation is often needed because of a particular rhythmic pattern or because the text is more suggestive and evocative in nature.

Notice how difficult it would be to segment the two lines of Psalm 116:2 into corresponding lexical parts, whether similar or contrastive. Nevertheless, the A and B lines are closely linked to one another, related by means of a grammatical chiasmus: in A the order is "he" + "me," in B the order is "I" + "him." Another good example of this reason–result relation is found at the beginning of Psalm 46, vv. 1–2a. In the NRSV rendering, as well as in the Hebrew (ʿal-ken), the internal connection is marked by an appropriate conjunction:

> A1:   God is our refuge and strength,
> A2:   a very present help in trouble.
> B: Therefore we will not fear . . .

Other ways of expressing "therefore" (showing result) in English are "that is why," "consequently," "for this reason." Notice that in Psalm 46:1–2 one could also decide to mark the reason lines, A1 and A2, by turning them into dependent utterances: "Because God is our refuge . . . we will not fear. . . ." But this would be too long and complex, especially for poetry. Besides, it seems more appropriate, at least in English, to give the statement about "God" more emphasis by making it an independent clause/sentence. Of course, these are matters that have to be determined in accord with what sounds natural and "poetic" in a given TL.

A special type of *reason–result* relation is **ground–conclusion**. (Some would consider this a relation on its own.) Here, the ground (comparable to reason) provides some pertinent evidence or proof on the basis of which an important conclusion (comparable to result) is drawn. An example of this relation is seen in the central climax of Psalm 48 (v. 8), which concludes the first half of the psalm:

> A: The things we had only heard about, we have now seen
> B1:   in the city of the LORD of Armies,
> B2:   in the city of our God.
> C: God makes Zion stand firm forever. (*God's Word*)

Here line C is the climactic conclusion of the testimony, or ground, presented in summary form in A, B1, and B2. B1 + B2 are synonymous expressions of location in relation to the A base. Line C is marked by means of the juxtaposed mention of "God," with no intervening conjunction (i.e., a feature termed *asyndeton*), and due to its summary, assertive nature as an independent utterance. A corresponding emphatic conclusion marks the end of the second half of this psalm in v. 14 (forming a boundary-marking relation of *closure*, cf. 4.1.4). Notice how the NRSV (and others, e.g., NJB) subordinates this important C statement in a relative construction, thus hiding it, through an erroneous interpretation of the relations involved in this passage:

> . . . in the city of our God
> which God establishes forever.

In the proverbial close of Psalm 49:20, a final bicolon gives the summary-conclusion for a ground that is expressed by the psalm as a whole (my own translation):

> A person who has wealth without understanding
> is no better off than a dumb animal.

Reason–request is another type of *cause–effect* connection related to reason–result; it is common in all sorts of psalmic exhortation and appeal. A typical example appears in Psalm 82:8, which is the concluding climax of the psalm (NRSV):

> A: Rise up, O God, judge the earth;
> B: for all the nations belong to you.

This semantic relation of *request–reason* (or *reason–request* depending on the order in which it appears) in Psalm 82:8 takes the form of an appeal, a strong petition, or even a command in line A, which is the "request." The "reason" (basis or grounds) for this request is then given in line B. The reason is emphasized by virtue of its discourse-final position and the clause-initial independent pronoun: "for as for you (*kiy-ʾattah*), you inherit. . . ." Again, it is important to note that in idiomatic speech the order of the two lines, A-B or B-A, may differ from one language to another. Also the specific markers or conjunctions used to signal the relationship between them will probably differ.

It must be kept in mind that a cause-effect relation may link not only cola, but bicola as well. One such example is Psalm 117:1–2:

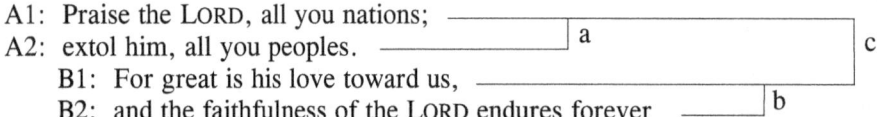

> A1: Praise the LORD, all you nations;
> A2: extol him, all you peoples.
>   B1: For great is his love toward us,
>   B2: and the faithfulness of the LORD endures forever

[Note: The small letters indicate the semantic relation between two cola, e.g., a = A1 + A2.]

The first two lines, A1 + A2, are obviously alike in meaning and also in form. They are in a *base-restatement* relation of similarity (see **a** in the diagram above). Lines A1 and A2 express a request, a hortatory command, or a prayerful appeal. The last two lines, B1 + B2, are also synonymous with respect to one another. They are in a *base-amplification* relation (see **b** in the diagram), and they give the reason that motivates the imperative in A. But note that a single relationship, *request-reason* (**c** in the diagram) links up the two bicola. In translating this, it might sound more natural, depending on the particular TL, to combine A1 with B1 and A2 with B2. Perhaps an even greater shift in arrangement may be necessary, such as placing B1 + B2 first and then A1 + A2:

> God's love toward us is very great;
>   and the faithfulness of the LORD endures forever.
> Therefore praise Him, all you nations;
>   extol him, all you peoples.

However, this last alternative may not be acceptable in many situations since it inverts the original order of the two verses.

Other variations of cause–effect can be seen linking more than two poetic lines. Psalm 107:1 is one such example:

> A: Give thanks to the LORD,
> B1: for he is good;
> B2: his love endures forever.

Here the two B lines are in a *general–specific* relationship of similarity to one another. The general statement that "God is good" is followed by a specific aspect of his goodness: "his love endures forever." These two lines together express the *reason*, or underlying basis, for the *request* in line A. A second request is not present in this case, as it was in 117:1 above.

These examples illustrate how important it is to analyze a psalm's sequence of poetic lines, especially how they are joined together, in order to get an idea of how the author organized his thoughts and emphasized his main ideas within the original composition as a whole. The point is first to better understand a biblical poetic text and then to find a natural and equally effective way of expressing these same relationships in a contemporary language.

Exercise 3.3.3.2a

1. Pick out three examples of a reason–result or reason–request relation in the set of psalms that you worked on in chapter two: 13, 19, 32, 34, 46, 95, 110, 136, 140, and 148. Use two different English versions (e.g., RSV, TEV, NIV, CEV, GW). Try to find translations that are different in each case. Write these passages out. Then label the relations you see. Be sure to indicate which version you are using. If you can use an interlinear version, compare the different English translations with the original Hebrew. Also refer to the comments in the THP and the NIV-SB. Which version do you think is more accurate? Why? Which version would be easier or more natural to translate in your language? Tell why this is the case.

2. The following is Psalm 56:4 in the NIV:

> A: In God, whose word I praise,
> B: in God I trust; I will not be afraid.
> C: What can mortal man do to me?

Compare this rendering with the TEV, GW, and CEV renderings. Then try to identify the relations that tie the cola together. It may be helpful to divide line B into two cola. Where do you find the relation of grounds–conclusion? What has TEV done with the order of the lines? Can you see any reason for this?

3. Find another example of the relationship of grounds–conclusion anywhere in the Psalms. Write it out, along with its reference, using the English version that seems to express the grounds–conclusion link most clearly.

Psalm 79:11b illustrates a *cause–effect* relation that is somewhat different from the ones presented so far:

> A: By the strength of your arm
> B: preserve those condemned to die.

In this case the psalmist is asking the LORD to deliver those who are in danger of death. He confidently expects that God will be able to fulfill his petition by means of his great power. Thus the relationship between A and B here may be called ***means–request***.

This relationship is similar to the ***means–result*** relationship, which Psalm 17:4 exemplifies (NRSV):

A: As for what others do, by the word of your lips
B: I have avoided the ways of the violent.

The English preposition "by" (i.e., Hebrew *k-* or *b-*) helps to mark the *means* relationship here. Note that in GW the relation is interpreted as *reason*: "I have avoided cruelty *because of* your word."

The *means-result* linkage in Psalm 34:4 is even more debatable:

A: I sought the LORD, and he answered me;
B: he delivered me from all my fears.

Two things should be noted in this example. First of all, it would be possible to interpret the relation between A and B in some other way, such as *base–sequential* time (or perhaps even *general-specific*), but this would seem to be less precise. Second, there is a semantic relation between the two parts of the A line itself: "I sought the LORD" being *means* and "he answered me" being *result*. In this line two separate "events" are linked, each of which serves as the nucleus or central core of a "proposition" (in grammatical terms, a simple clause). Now when two events happen to occur within one poetic line, as in Psalm 34:4a, an "internal" division of that line is possible. However, in this study, we will not always go into such detail. We will usually deal only with complete poetic lines (or half-lines if they consist of two to three word-units in parallel). The purpose at this stage is simply to sharpen our awareness of the nature and development of meaning in Hebrew poetry.

The NRSV, NIV, and NASB are helpful to us because they show the line segments. The translator who does not know Hebrew should consult one of these versions or an interlinear text. They normally indicate the SL poetic lines (or half-lines) by means of punctuation and/or by their rules of indentation, in which the beginning of a new line is indicated by being farthest to the left, and the beginning of each line parallel to A is indented slightly. The remainder ("overlap") of any line (A, B, or C) is indented still farther. The following example shows how the NIV segments Psalm 78:17–18:

[17] But they continued to sin against him,   (A=3)
        rebelling in the desert against the
            Most High.   (B=3)
[18] They willfully put God to the test   (A=2)
        by demanding the food they craved.   (B=2)

Each verse here consists of two poetic lines. The two lines of v. 17 consist of three word-units each (in Hebrew), and the two lines of v. 18 of two word-units each. The bicolon of v. 17 is divided at the comma, but in v. 18 the division is shown, not by punctuation, but only by the indentation. Notice that the words "Most High" at the end of v. 17 are a part of the B line. This fact is shown by its being indented so far to the right. The words were placed on a third line due to a lack of space within the two-column format of the printed page.

The narrow print columns in most English Bibles unfortunately obscure the parallelisms found in the Hebrew text. The GW version (and special editions of some of the others) overcomes this problem with its single column of print on the page. Another possible solution (suggested by Alan S. Duthie) would be to use the two column print format more creatively by reserving the left side for the A lines (or any C line of a tricolon) and the right column for the B lines. Thus the preceding example would be reformatted as follows:

A	B
[17] But they continued to sin against him,	rebelling in the desert against the Most High.
[18] They willfully put God to the test	by demanding the food they craved.

Observe that a bit of extra space between the horizontal lines may be necessary in order to make the text more legible and therefore also readable aloud.

Now we turn to the logical relations between these four cola. Notice that v. 17 could be classified either as *base-amplification* or as *general-specific*. Verse 18 is a good example of *result-means*: The people demanded food from God (B), and "by" their action (note the preposition, in this case Hebrew *l-*) the result was that they tested God's power and willingness to provide (A). Verse 18 as a whole provides a specific instance of the general sin that was reported in v. 17. This account of Israel's unfaithfulness becomes most specific in vv. 19–20: there direct speech is used to illustrate the people's "sin," "rebellion" (v. 17), and "willful demands" (v. 18) against God.

Closely related to means-result or means-request is the ***means-purpose*** relation, which always conveys the notion of deliberate *intention*. Psalm 78:71 is an example of means-purpose:

> A: . . . from tending sheep he [God] brought him [David]
> B1: to be the shepherd of his people Jacob,
> B2: of Israel his inheritance.

The purpose for which the LORD chose David and took him away from his flock was to place him as a royal shepherd over his people Israel (B1 + B2 = *base-amplification*). TEV seems to interpret the relation here as one of subsequent action (i.e., *base-sequential time*):

> . . . where he looked after his flocks,
> and he made him king of Israel,
> the shepherd of the people of God.

However, the Hebrew infinitive construction (with *l-*) is more precisely understood as *purpose* in this particular context.

Differences of interpretation of this relation are possible, of course, in some contexts, especially when there are no explicit markers in the Hebrew. Psalm 66:6 (NRSV) is an example:

> A: He [God] turned the sea into dry land;
> B: they [Israel] passed through the river on foot.

Here one could interpret the connection between A and B as being *base-sequential time*. But in this case, the two lines serve as the basis for a call to praise God in line C: "come, let us rejoice in him." In other words, the relation of lines A–B to C is *reason-request*. Therefore, it is more likely that the relation of A to B is either means-result or means-purpose. This could be expressed more clearly in the following manner:

> God turned the sea into dry land
>   [in order] (or [so]) that Israel might cross over it on foot.

Therefore, one cannot be dogmatic. The point of this method of analysis is simply to provide a clearer idea of the options available, both with regard to exegesis (SL) and also to re-expression (TL). Translators need to explore the different possibilities that appear to be relevant and select the one that would seem to fit the context and sound the best—the most "poetic" and stylistically most natural in the TL.

Sometimes a petition or a command is given in order to carry out a certain specified objective. We call this relation ***request-purpose***. Psalm 24:7 is an example:

> A1: Lift up your heads, O you gates;
> A2: be lifted up, you ancient doors,
> B: that the King of glory may come in.

Here the two A cola are synonymous (i.e., *base-restatement*). These two, in turn, act together to indicate the means whereby the purpose specified in B may be carried out. The conjunction "that" represents an interpretation of the Hebrew *waw*. In English, the purpose relation might be indicated even more specifically by the phrase "in order that," but that does not sound very poetic.

Unfortunately, one cannot always depend upon the conjunction used in an English translation to determine the meaning relation between two cola. The Hebrew, in many instances, has no explicit conjunction or uses a general transitional word, typically "and" (*waw*). (Note that a common conjunction like *kiy* is significant with respect to semantics, e.g., to indicate a reason ["for"], and/or pragmatics, e.g., to indicate a different participant perspective or opinion.) To discover the precise relation, translators must carefully study the surrounding context (with the help of reliable translations and exegetical commentaries), and come to their own conclusion. An examination of the actual Hebrew text or an interlinear version may clarify things as well. Consider Psalm 67:1-2 as rendered by the New Jerusalem Bible:

> [1] May God show kindness and bless us,
> and make his face shine on us.   *Pause*
> [2] Then the earth will acknowledge your ways,
> and all nations your power to save.

The conjunction "then" (also in CEV) seems to suggest sequential time, but the original Hebrew infinitive here would more strongly support *purpose*, as in the TEV, for example (see also NIV, NRSV, REB): "God, be merciful . . . so that the whole world may know your will." The two bicola (vv. 1 and 2) are thus linked by the relation of request–purpose.

Upon closer analysis, some passages turn out to be rather more complex than they may first appear. For example, what is the relation that links the two parallel lines of Psalm 51:7 (NRSV)?

> A: Purge me with hyssop, and I shall be clean;
> B: wash me, and I shall be whiter than snow.

Lines A and B are clearly synonymous. Their relation is *base–restatement*. But within each line are two half-lines with a *means–purpose* relation, which tends to be hidden by the conjunction "and." In order to see this better, the passage may be reworded as follows:

> Purge me with hyssop *so that* I may be clean;
> wash me *so that* I might be whiter than snow.

Psalm 59:12 is an even more complex example. Its literal translation is as follows:

> A: the-sin-of=their-mouth the-word-of=their-lips
> B: and-they-will-be-caught in-their-pride

This is how the TEV renders these words:

> Sin is on their lips; all their words are sinful;
> may they be caught in their pride!

NIV tries to make the relation between the cola more explicit:

> A1: For the sins of their mouths,
> A2:   for the words of their lips,
> B: let them be caught in their pride.

A1 and A2 are obviously synonymous as well as alike in form. Their relation is base–similarity (*restatement*). But what is the relation between them and the B line? The repeated conjunction "for," which is not present in the Hebrew, is supplied to indicate the *reason* for the *request* in line B. One could also use the conjunction "because" (GW) or "so" (CEV)—or begin the B line with "therefore" (which would fit in with the TEV rendering). It is up to the translator to determine as accurately as possible the semantic relationship between lines and then decide how to express this most naturally and forcefully in the TL.

Exercise 3.3.3.2b

1. Search the Psalter and see if you can find one clear example of each of these four relations: (a) *means-result*, (b) *means-request*, (c) *means-purpose*, and (d) *request-purpose*. (The order of the two parts of the relation may be reversed in the text.)

   Write your selections out along with their references, indicating which version you used. <u>Underline</u> the markers such as prepositions or conjunctions that helped you recognize a certain relation.

2. Now look up these same four passages in a Hebrew interlinear translation and one more English version. If you don't have access to an interlinear, use two different English versions. Make a note of any problems or differences that you discover in the interpretation of the relations. After studying the context of each passage and the THP's comments, tell which translation you prefer and why. Do you prefer it because of the relative ease of rendering the passages in your language? Explain any interesting translational issues that you encounter.

3. Analyze the three semantic relations that exists between the poetic lines of Psalm 37:14:

   > A1: The wicked draw the sword
   > A2: and bend the bow
   >   B1: to bring down the poor and needy,
   >   B2: to slay those whose ways are upright.

   a (A1–A2), b (B1–B2), c (A–B)

   a = _____ b = _____ c = _____

   The CEV rendition of Psalm 37:14 is as follows:

   > The wicked kill with swords
   > and shoot arrows to murder
   >   the poor and the needy
   >   and all who do right.

   Which of the three relations is not expressed very clearly in the CEV?
   Would the CEV be a good model to follow in this regard in your language? Why, or why not?
   If not, how could you improve the translation, either in English or your language?

Another type of *cause-effect* relation is the **real condition-result**. An example is in Psalm 7:12 (TEV):

> A: *If* (ʾim) they do not change their ways,
> B: God will sharpen his sword.

In this verse, the condition in line A is real and the result stated in B will most certainly take place if the condition is met (or, in the case of a negative condition like this, if it is not met). Sometimes such a relation extends over several verses, as in Psalm 89:30–34:

> A1: If his sons forsake my law
> A2:   and do not follow my statutes,
> A3: if they violate my decrees
> A4:   and fail to keep my commands,
> B1:   I will punish their sin with the rod,
> B2:   their iniquity with flogging;
> C1: but I will not take my love from him,
> C2   nor will I ever betray my faithfulness.
> C3: I will not violate my covenant
> C4:   or alter what my lips have uttered.

Notice that the letters given to poetic lines above are not in keeping with our usual usage (i.e., the B and C lines are not parallel to A, but build sequentially upon it in stages). The usage here is intended to highlight the similarities and differences that are found in this passage, which begins with four *real conditions* (A1–4) similar in meaning to one another (i.e., *base-restatement*) followed by the certain *result* (B1–2), namely punishment, if the sinful actions of A occur. Notice that B1 and B2 are similar in meaning to each other (i.e., *base-restatement*). Then the unit concludes with the four synonymous lines of C1–4 balancing those of A, i.e., *base-amplification*, a strong contrast with the A + B warning in a relation of *base-contrast*. (Note the two sets of contrasts: human evil action vs. God's gracious action.) In other words, the LORD will surely punish (B) his people for their sins and wickedness (A), but he will never forsake them or break his covenant with them (C). (It may be that there is a *general-specific* relation linking C1–2 and C3–4.)

A less common kind of *conditional* relation may be called **unreal condition–result**, which is a contrary-to-fact condition plus a potential consequence. It is illustrated in Psalm 66:18:

> A: If I had cherished sin in my heart,
> B: the LORD would not have listened.

In this example, the condition part of the relation is again explicitly marked by the Hebrew conjunction ʾ*im*, "if." In English, the conjunction "then" is sometimes used to signal the result part, but it is not really necessary since "if" is usually sufficient on its own. The problem with this type of condition is that it did not really happen. Line A is actually saying, "I did *not* set my heart upon evil." Thus the underlying meaning of line B is the opposite of what seems to be stated; the result, in fact, was that "the LORD *did* listen to me." Therefore, this relation has to be clearly marked in the TL so that the passage is not misinterpreted (e.g., by the auxiliary verbs in English above: "If...had / would not have").

A third type of conditional relation that sometimes occurs in the Psalms (and elsewhere in the Bible) is called **condition–unexpected result**. This one is more difficult to recognize because it is usually not very clearly marked either in Hebrew or in English. Psalm 118:18 is an example:

> The LORD has chastened me severely,
>   but he has not given me over to death.

On first reading, especially in view of the conjunction "but" (*waw*), one might think that this couplet expresses a simple contrast and that its line A is linked to line B in a *base-contrast* relation. A closer look, however, reveals that this is not quite accurate (i.e., there are not two sets of contrasts here). Rather, the relationship involves a more complex type of cause-effect sequence, namely *condition–unexpected* result (or *condition–contraexpectation*). Here in the A line is a condition that would lead one to expect a certain result, but it does not, in fact, happen. Instead, in B there is a surprise: an unexpected outcome is reported. Thus the condition in line A carries with it a certain amount of implicit information. This is shown for Psalm 118:18 in brackets and italics below (notice the conjunctions that are commonly used as markers of this relationship in English):

> A: [*Even if/although*] the LORD has chastened me severely,
>   X: [*people would surely have expected me to die*]
> B: [*nevertheless/however*] he has not given me over to death.

Line A expresses the "condition," that is, the hypothetical circumstances. Line X is the implicit thought in the middle. It is not stated, nor did it really occur. But it indicates the result people normally would have expected to follow after A. Line B then gives the *surprise*—what truly did happen, or the situation that actually exists, contrary to everyone's expectation in X. The only major English version that expresses this implicit relation in Psalm 118:18 is the Jerusalem Bible (and New Jerusalem Bible). It does so by means of a conjunction:

> *Though* Yahweh punished me sternly,
>   he has not abandoned me to death.

The implicit content may not always be so easy to determine. Commentators themselves may not be agreed about what is going on beneath the surface of the text. This is the case for Psalm 39:8:

> A: Save me from all my transgressions;
> B: do not make me the scorn of fools.

This bicolon might be analyzed as a simple *contrast*: "save me but do not make me (look foolish)." Alternatively, one might see a certain *similarity* between the two lines, "save me from both my transgressions and also the scorn of fools" (cf. GNB, which links the couplet with "and"). However, a closer look at this passage in the light of its context seems to indicate a more complex set of relations. The sequence may be stated as follows, with brackets again enclosing the implicit elements:

> 1: Save me
>   2: [I am in trouble]
>   3: [because of] my sins.
> 4: [If you do not save me],
>   5: fools will mock me.

Thus line 3 gives the *reason* for the *result* expressed implicitly in 2, and both lines together act as the *reason* (grounds) for the *request* (appeal) of line 1. Line 5 then gives the *result* of the implied *real condition* in line 4. Taking the analysis a step further, we observe that (4 + 5) together act as another *reason* for the request of line 1.

This is not to suggest that this passage ought to be translated according to this outline. But readers (or hearers) of the translation should be able to follow the basic argument without too much difficulty and without missing the point of the appeal. If, in checking the translation or teaching about a passage of this nature, it is found that readers cannot follow the meaning, some of the implicit information may have to be expressed.

Problems in interpretation often arise because certain aspects of the meaning are not stated explicitly in the text. Nevertheless, they are part of the total content that the original author intended to communicate to his audience.

But why *is* meaning left implicit? First of all, something very *familiar* to the original audience did not need to be expressed for them to get the whole picture. Second, material may have been omitted so the audience would work harder at understanding the message; this often helps people to *remember* it better. This kind of ellipsis is appropriate in translating as well. Third, *brevity* is a feature of poetry in Hebrew, and this may well be the case in the TL as well. Poetic language is often concise in order to fit the expected *rhythm* patterns or to evoke certain associations of meaning in the listener's mind.

The problem is that today's readers of the Bible do not have the same background information or speak the same language as the original audience. This makes it harder for them to interpret many texts. Passages that may have been perfectly clear to the original Hebrew-speaking hearers are not always so easy for us to understand now. Sometimes it seems that two or more interpretations of a certain verse are possible, perhaps even intentional, especially in poetry. But such "ambiguity" can often (but not always) be resolved when we study the passage in detail and investigate the wider context (including closely related psalms and similar passages). It is also helpful to examine the overall semantic content of problematic cola, the word order, the presence of emphatic words, and the markers of compositional boundaries. But such clues to meaning, even when they are explicit, do not always resolve every problem. The analyst must be careful, therefore, not to jump to hasty conclusions or be too rigid in the matter of interpretation, for this can easily lead in turn to an error in translation. That includes trying to be too specific or precise when the original text allows for several possible construals.

Exercise 3.3.3.2c

1. Study the following passages. Tell which semantic relation you think is present between A and B in each one: (a) *real condition-result*, (b) *unreal condition-result*, or (c) *condition-unexpected result*.

    ____ If we had forgotten the name of our God . . .
    would God not have discovered it . . . (Ps. 44:20a, 21a)

    ____ If an enemy were insulting me,
        I could endure it;
    if a foe were raising himself against me,
        I could hide from him. (Ps. 55:12)

    ____ If I go up to the heavens,
        you are there;
    if I make my bed in the depths,
        you are there. (Ps. 139:8)

    ____ . . . if your sons keep my covenant and the statutes I teach them,
    then their sons will sit on your throne for ever. (Ps. 132:12)

    ____ Unless [= if . . . not] the LORD builds the house,
        its builders labor in vain. (Ps. 127:1a)

    ____ If the LORD had not been on our side . . .
        they [= enemies] would have swallowed us alive . . . (Ps. 124:1a, 3b)

    ____ . . . if I have done evil to him who is at peace with me . . .
    then let my enemy pursue and overtake me . . . (Ps. 7:4a, 5a)

2. Now check each of the preceding passages in the TEV (or CEV) to see how they have been handled there. Note where any apparent differences occur. Be prepared to discuss and evaluate these in class.

3. Find two more examples of the *condition-result* relation in the psalms you studied in chapter 2. Write them out on a separate sheet, giving the reference. Tell what type of relationship is involved, a, b, or c (as in assignment 1).

4. More than one type of conditional relation is exemplified in Psalm 37:23–24. What are these types?

    ____ If the LORD delights in a man's way,
        he makes his steps firm;

    ____ though he stumble,
        he will not fall,
        for the LORD upholds him with his hand.

    How is the final line of v. 24 linked to what is stated before it?
    This relationship is one of _____ + _____ .

5. Both the RSV and the TEV renderings of 37:23 sound quite different from that of NIV:

    The steps of a man are from the LORD,
        and he establishes him in whose way he delights. (RSV)

    The LORD guides a man in the way he should go
        and protects those who please him. (TEV)

Each of these translations may cause a certain misunderstanding. Can you explain what some of the problems are? Consult the THP or some other exegetical commentary. How does the CEV change the focus of the first line of v. 23?

6. The English word "(al)though" (e.g., in 37:24) is not easy to translate. How can you best express this relationship in your language?

7. Examine the semantic relations linking the internal cola that comprise verses 10-12 of Psalm 118. Do you think that the relationship here is one of *base-contrast* or *condition-unexpected result* or does it vary from one verse to the next? Give a reason for your answer.

3.3.3.3 Completive addition

As we have seen, the semantic relation between parallel lines of Hebrew poetry may be similar (synonymous), contrastive (antithetical), or additive, and the subtypes of the additive category include the temporal, causal, and completive. The first two of these sub-types were discussed in sections 3.3.3.1 and 3.3.3.2. Now we will look at the semantic relation that we term ***completive addition***. It includes whatever does not fit in any of the other additive categories, temporal or causal. In this subtype, line B is very closely related to line A in meaning, but not in terms of similarity, contrast, time, or cause-and-effect. Rather, it adds some important information to "complete," complement, or fill out, the content of line A.

The completive addition category of parallelism itself has several subtypes. We will consider them here in the order of their relative frequency. First is the relationship of qualification or, as we will call it, ***base-attribution***. This is seen particularly in descriptive passages where the B line either defines, modifies, characterizes, or gives more detailed information about some important noun or pronoun found in line A. In English it is usually expressed by a relative clause introduced by a conjunction such as "which," "who," or "that." Psalm 31:19 contains four such relative clauses:

> A: How great is your goodness,
> B1: which you have stored up for those
> C1: who fear you,
> B2: which you bestow in the sight of men on those
> C2: who take refuge in you.

The attributive lines C1 and C2 each state a characteristic of the demonstrative "those" in B1 and B2. The two B lines each express qualities of the head noun "goodness" in line A. This *base-attribution* relation is marked by a relative pronoun in most modern translations. But sometimes it is omitted for poetic purposes, to make the text sound more condensed or rhythmic, as in the NIV's rendering of Psalm 54:3:

> A: Strangers are attacking me;
> B: ruthless men seek my life—
> C: men [who are] without regard for God.

Here lines A and B, which are synonymous in meaning and also have the same syntactic form, are in a *base-similarity* (restatement) relation. Line C, which characterizes "men" in line B, is in a relation of *base-attribution* with line B. We can see a progressive intensification in this description of the wicked. They are not only strangers, they are also *ruthless*; they not only attack, but they even want to *kill* me; they not only disregard *me* (implied in the preceding), but also they have no regard for *God*. One way to highlight this progression would be to translate line C as an independent unit, as in the NRSV:

> B: . . . the ruthless seek my life;
> C: they do not set God before them. (CEV: Not one of them cares about you.)

The relation of C to A + B in Psalm 54:3 could also be regarded as one of base–addition (see below), which is more strongly supported by the Hebrew text. If this is taken to be the relation here, C would be more independent and/or distinctive in nature.

Another important type of attributive relationship involves illustration with some sort of simile or metaphor, as in Psalm 1:

Blessed is the man
    who does not walk in the counsel of the wicked . . . (v. 1)
He is like a tree
    planted by streams of water . . . (v. 3)

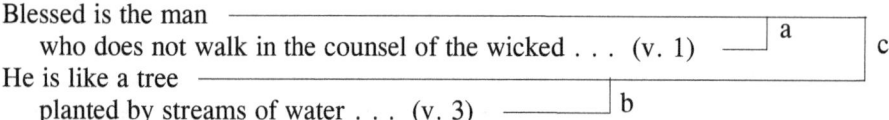

In this case, the relations **a** and **b** each appear to exhibit a *base-attribution* relationship, qualifying the nouns "man" and "tree" respectively. Set **c**, however, is an instance of the *base-comparison* relation (see below).

As we have seen, the dependent "attribution" colon is always attached to some noun or pronoun found in the "base." Other, less prominent relations may be in view when the focus of the base in A is a verb or verbal form, for instance, the relation of **base-location**, an example of which is found in Psalm 116:18–19 (NRSV):

A: I will pay my vows to the LORD
B1:   in the presence of all his people,
B2:   in the courts of the house of the LORD,
B3:   in the midst of you, Jerusalem.

The place where the psalmist will fulfill his promise to God is specified in the three B lines. The threefold synonymous restatement strongly emphasizes it. He worships the divine source of help in the location where God's presence was concretely symbolized, namely, the Temple in Jerusalem. The city of Jerusalem is here addressed with a vocative in the final line of the set, B3, as though it were a person. This is a figure of speech known as *apostrophe*. These words form an appropriate climax to this psalm of thanksgiving.

Another, more complicated example of the *base-location* relation occurs in Psalm 84:3:

A1: Even the sparrow has found a home,
A2: and the swallow a nest for herself,
B1:   where she may have her young—
B2:   a place near your altar . . .

The two A lines, here synonymous (*restatement*), together form the base for the two B cola, which both specify the place where the birds have found a home. B2 also refers to the sacred quality of this setting. In addition, B1 conveys an implicit notion of purpose, *why* the birds wanted to make a nest there. But since the main emphasis of Psalm 84 appears to focus upon the holy setting, the *base-location* relation would seem to be the one in view. Remember that more than one semantic relation may apply to a given bicolon, one acting as a complement to the other to enrich and extend the overall meaning being communicated.

A relatively minor completive relation is that of **base-manner**. A complex example is found in Psalm 55:20–21 (NRSV):

A1: My companion laid hands on a friend
A2: and violated a covenant with me
B1:   with speech smoother than butter,
C1:   but with a heart set on war;
B2:   with words that were softer than oil,
C2:   but in fact were drawn swords.

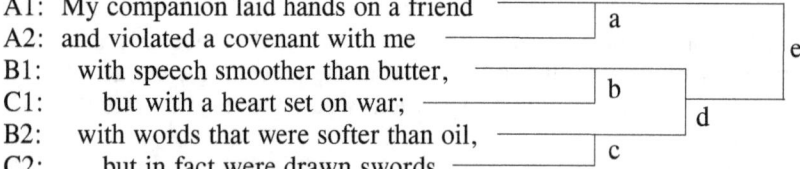

Here A1 and A2 exemplify the *means–result* relation (a); B1 with C1 (b) and B2 with C2 (c) are both in a *base-contrast* relation with one another. Thus A1 + A2 together act as the *base* for the twofold *manner* (e) relation of B1–C1 + B2–C2 (d). Manner tells the *how* of a particular event—the way in which the action was carried out. It is often marked in English by the ambiguous preposition "with." In Psalm 55:20-21, the repeated "with" (*asyndeton* in Hebrew) serves to emphasize the act of treachery (covenant violation) that is being lamented in A1–A2. That is, it was characterized by verbal hypocrisy that undoubtedly led to actual physical violence (cf. 55:3-5).

There is another type of completive relation that may be termed **base-response**. A couplet with this relation is seen at times in the liturgical psalms, where one utterance is spoken by the worship leader—the cantor—immediately followed by a reply from the chorus or entire congregation. The clearest example of this is in Psalm 136, where the group response embodies the psalm's theme, forming a sustained rhythmic string of utterances in an iterative binary sequence. The following is vv. 1–3:

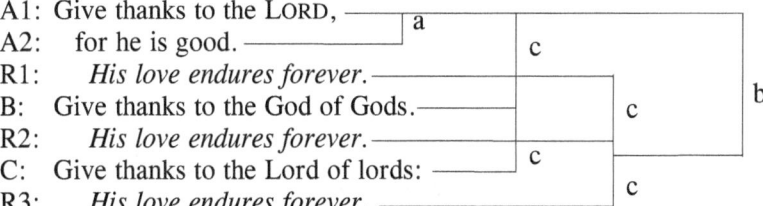

A1: Give thanks to the LORD,
A2: for he is good.
R1:   *His love endures forever.*
B: Give thanks to the God of Gods.
R2:   *His love endures forever.*
C: Give thanks to the Lord of lords:
R3:   *His love endures forever.*

Here **a** = *request-reason*, **b** = *base-response*, **c** = *base-similarity* (restatement). The psalm's opening (A1 + A2) is distinctive in that it includes a binary clausal connection. So does the song's final line in v. 26, which is in a synonymous relation with the song's first three verses, thus artfully forming an *inclusio* around the whole liturgical piece.

In contexts where direct speech is used to dramatize the text, the relation of **base-content** frequently appears. The content is what is said, thought, or perceived, and it is usually in focus, as in Psalm 30:6:

A: When I felt secure, I said,
B: "I will never be shaken."

Line B here gives the actual words (the content) which the person in line A said or thought to himself. (Note that line A includes the relation *circumstance-base*.) Such use of direct speech gives emphasis to the content—as well as the personal attitude that it reflects. This is another example of two different semantic relations possibly applying to the same bicolon. Thus the relation could also be interpreted as *reason-result*; taken like this, line A would begin "Because" and line B (now including "I said") would be the resultant speech act.

A clearer instance of the *base-content* relation is Psalm 53:1:

A: The fool says in his heart,
B: "There is no God."

This type of connection between two parallel lines may also occur in indirect speech, with a dependent clause being the object of a verb of saying or thinking, as in Psalm 44:

. . . our fathers have told us
what you did in their days . . .

Another possible type of secondary completive linkage is that of **base-comparison**. We have a clear instance of this in Psalm 103:11 (actually, *comparison-base*):

A: For as high as the heavens are above the earth,
B: so great is his love for those who fear him...

This comparative relationship is continued in the next two verses, which constitute the theological core of Psalm 103, situated at its midpoint.

The *base-comparison* relation may also designate a simple likeness or analogy, as in Psalm 35:14:

> A1: I went about mourning
> B1: as though for my friend or brother.
>
> A2: I bowed my head in grief
> B2: as though weeping for my mother.

Here a pair of *base-comparison* couplets occur next to each other. The two bicola, which emphasize the psalmist's great grief (i.e., the point of the comparison), are in turn linked to each other by the relation of *base-restatement*. The underlying comparative relation may be easily confused with that of manner (as above) or attribution, the latter especially where a simile is involved, as in Psalm 78:57:

> A: Like their fathers they were disloyal and faithless,
> B: as unreliable as a faulty bow.

In this instance, the B colon adds another negative attribute, unreliability, with reference to "they" (as well as to "their fathers") in line A, and is not related to any "event." The comparison actually occurs *within* each line; therefore, the linkage between the two is more accurately classified as *base-attribution* or *amplification*, rather than *base-comparison*. However, in some languages it may not be natural, desirable, or even possible, to maintain these semantic distinctions.

A rather general and important completive relationship is that of ***base-addition***. In this couplet line B amplifies or elaborates upon something stated in line A; B is clearly a new idea, but it is also closely related in meaning to what is said in A. We observe such an addition in Psalm 50:18:

> A: When you see a thief, you join with him;
> B: you throw in your lot with adulterers.

The dependent "when" clause in line A *could* be taken as a separate thought expressing sequential time (more precisely, reiterated time, i.e., "whenever") in relation to its base in the second half of the line. These are two distinct events, it is true, but in terms of the original Hebrew this first clause is all part of line A since it consists of just four word-units. Therefore, it may be better for the sake of simplicity to consider which relation seems to be in focus for the line as a whole: the complete line A acts as a base to which line B is an addition. In other words, the sin of adultery is cited along with that of stealing as a separate *additional* accusation by the LORD against the wicked. Notice that we are not dealing with a case of synonymy here, e.g., *base-amplification*. Nor is there a progression in time between A and B, so it is not *base-sequential* time. Rather, one distinct and equally important thought is "added on" to complete or complement another. This type of relation is especially common at the higher levels of poetic discourse structure when one larger unit ("strophe" or "stanza") is linked to the next to further develop the message of the entire psalm.

Another clear example of the *base-addition* relation occurs in Psalm 10:3 (TEV):

> A: The wicked man is proud of his evil desires;
> B: the greedy man curses and rejects the LORD.

The psalmist is not talking about two different people here, as the TEV rendering might imply, but only one. It is another aspect of the ungodly man's wickedness that is in view in line B: his greed and rejection of the LORD. This particular psalm is full of additive relations as the pray-er builds his case against the wicked. A little later we hear the impious person condemn himself (additively) in his own words, in v. 6:

> A: ... "Nothing will shake me;
> B: I'll always be happy and never have trouble."

A line of addition may be stated in positive or negative terms, as in the preceding passage. A potentially confusing example of the use of a negative is found in Psalm 1:5:

> A: Therefore the wicked will not stand in the judgment,
> B: nor sinners in the assembly of the righteous.

Here we are not really dealing with an *alternative*, as the conjunctions "nor" or "or" may suggest. Rather, the B line presents an additional aspect of the same impossibility. Reference is to a single, complex event. The semantic relationship between these two lines may be viewed as *base-similarity*, *-restatement*, *-amplification*, or *-addition*, depending on how closely one views the two lines as matching in terms of form and content. In this case, probably *base-amplification* is the most likely.

Psalm 1:1 may give us an instance of the relatively rare **base-alternative** relation:

> A: Blessed is the man
> B1: who does not walk in the counsel of the wicked,
> B2: or stand in the way of sinners,
> B3: or sit in the seat of mockers.

These three B lines are viewed as related by means of "or" alternation. That is, the negative exclusion applies to each activity, in turn, and neither one nor the other can be said to characterize the "blessed person" in line A. All three B lines stand in a *base-attribution* relationship to A.

Another example of the *alternative* relation is Psalm 118:8 (NRSV):

> A: It is better to take refuge in the LORD
> B: than to put confidence in mortals.

For the psalmist there is no doubt as to whom one should trust; the alternative is unthinkable. The preceding example also involves a strong personal evaluation or judgment. Such convictions or attitudes of course need to be clearly conveyed in any translation.

In several of the preceding examples, we have encountered the problem of when and where to divide the parallel lines A and B. This is especially difficult to do on the basis of the English versions alone. Consider Psalm 35:14, for instance, which reads as follows in the NIV:

> A1: I went about mourning
> B1: as though for my friend or brother.
> A2: I bowed my head in grief
> B2: as though weeping for my mother.
>
> Literally: as-a-friend=as-a-brother for-me I-walked-about
> like-the-weeping-of=a-mother a-grieving-one I-bowed-over

An examination of the Hebrew original reveals that, taken as a whole, each English synonymously paired couplet, both A1–B1 and A2–B2, together consists of three words each (or four if one disregards the hyphen). Thus structurally, according to the actual line construction, these lines would probably be regarded as constituting only one colon each, that is, A1–B1 = A and A2–B2 = B. Semantically, however, each consists of two distinctly related segments (half-lines) of meaning in a *base-manner* relation. A1–B1 and A2–B2 in turn are linked to each other by a *base-restatement* relation.

This issue of determining the poetic lines ("colometry") brings up a technical aspect of analysis which we cannot deal with further in this introductory study. Instead, we will adopt the procedure of following the arrangement of lines/cola set out in the NIV. Exceptions may be made, however, when two distinct and semantically significant clauses are included within a single line, as in Psalm 10:13, where the parallel line (in Hebrew) includes a segment of direct speech. Such instances of "internal" (half-line) parallelism are also common in lines that are exceptionally long in the Masoretic text, especially if they contain several verbs. Psalm 35:17 is an example:

A:	O Lord, how long will you look on?	(3 words)
B1:	Rescue my life from their ravages,	(3 words)
B2:	my precious life from these lions.	(2 words)

The chiasmus in the Hebrew B lines (object + prepositional phrase / prepositional phrase + object) suggests internal parallelism and therefore distinct semantic relations (i.e., *base–amplification*). B1 and B2 in turn are related to A by way of contrast (i.e., *base–contrast*). Such a construction must be distinguished from a tricolon, like the tricolon in Psalm 35:15:

A:	But when I stumbled, they gathered in glee;
B:	attackers gathered against me when I was unaware.
C:	They slandered me without ceasing.

The analysis of Psalm 35:15 is complicated by the presence of many "event" words, each of which suggests a separate clause (or semantic proposition). In this passage, considering the lines as complete wholes, line A is linked to line B by the relation of *base–amplification*, and A + B to line C by the relation of *base–addition* (or possibly, *general–specific*). Thus the degree of exegetical precision will have to be decided pragmatically. In short, any study can be carried out in greater or less analytical detail depending on the nature of the text at hand and the translator-exegete's particular abilities, needs, and goals.

On the whole, the NIV, in its translation of the Psalms, pays careful attention to both the micro- and the macrostructure of the original Hebrew. Microstructure refers to the individual lines and their constituents; macrostructure to the composition of paragraphs or strophes. The notes found in the *NIV Study Bible* often make reference to these aspects of meaning. Hence the NIV is more helpful for analytical work than many other modern versions. For one thing, it does not collapse (or combine) two or more poetic lines. However, translators are encouraged to consult other versions (e.g., GNB, CEV, NRSV) for the sake of comparison. The comments in the THP are also very useful with regard to poetic structure.

We will conclude this section with an extended example from Psalm 80 to illustrate our recommended procedure with regard to line division. As just mentioned, every distinct "event"—whether an action (e.g., I sinned), or a feeling (e.g., I am sorry), or a state (e.g., I have peace)—can function as the core of one side of any semantic relation. Usually there is just one event per line, but this is not always the case. Sometimes, in order to better reflect the different aspects of internal meaning, a single long Hebrew colon must be divided in two, as we saw in Psalm 78:4 i.e., (A1–A2 and B1–B2).

Occasionally, even a short colon will contain two very distinct and independent events, making it advantageous for the sake of a more complete analysis to view it as two different propositions. Psalm 80:18b is an example. Its literal rendering is "revive-us and-on-your-name we-will-call." We need now to ask what the two events in this colon are and what the relation between them is. While it might be taken as a real condition–result relation ("if you revive us, we will call upon your name"), or even as sequential time–base ("after you revive us, we will call . . ."), it is probably best to call it *request–purpose* (= intended result). In other words, as the basis for (and climax of) their appeal to Yahweh, the people make a promise that once he has "revived" (i.e., delivered) them, they will be in a position to praise and thank him in return: "revive us and we will call on your name" or, better yet, "Revive us *so that* we might call on your name."

In Psalm 80:19, the very next verse, is the psalm's final summary refrain (cf. vv. 3, 7). This is an even more interesting example. Literally it reads:

A:	Yahweh God-of armies, restore-us!
B:	cause-to-shine your-face and-let-us-be-saved!

How many events are in these two lines? What is the relation between them? (The NIV, TEV, and THP may help answer these questions.) Perhaps the best way of analyzing this bicolon is to divide the B line in two in order to highlight the ultimate intended result, which is a divinely worked act of salvation. Such an analysis would give the following:

> A: Restore us, O LORD God Almighty.
> B1: Yes, be merciful to us,
> B2: so that we may be saved.

In this case, line B2 indicates the hoped-for *result* (or *purpose*) of the event stated in B1. The latter refers to the *means* whereby salvation is to be carried out, namely, by the exercise of God's great mercy. (TEV has "Show us your mercy, and we will be saved.") Colon A is linked to B1 + B2 by the relation of *base-amplification*, as suggested by the connective "yes." Another possible connective is "indeed," or even "please." In a reiteration of this kind, an initial emphatic word or intensifier like this may be a more effective rendering than a conjunction, especially if the conjunction would suggest a different relation between the lines.

Thus, there is no single "right" way of analyzing such poetically paired lines. There is normally not just one "correct" answer. This needs to be emphasized. The procedures offered here provide a way of examining and evaluating difficulties so that exegetes and translation teams are better prepared to handle the diversity of potential meaning they will confront in Hebrew poetry and the different ways of representing this in another language. For this reason, a comparison of a number of translations with regard to a specific passage is always helpful. There is a lot more to be learned, but this is best done through experience with actual texts in specific situations.

Remember too, no passage of Scripture exists in isolation. The lines and strophes of a psalm must always be considered in relation to one another and in the light of the complete psalm and its primary functional characteristics (i.e., the *textual* context). This is an essential procedure all translators, preachers, teachers, and other Bible interpreters would do well to follow.

Exercise 3.3.3.3

1. Using either the NIV or the NRSV, try to find one good example of each of the seven additive correlative relations: *base-attribution*, *base-location*, *base-manner*, *base-content*, *base-comparison*, *base-addition*, and *base-alternative*. Choose examples not already mentioned in the text. Refer first to the psalms that you worked with in chapter 2. Perhaps, as a result of doing this assignment, you may wish to revise your rendering of some of those passages.

2. Now compare your selections and translations with those in the GNB and CEV. Note any apparent disagreement between the GNB and CEV as to one colon's relation to another. Be prepared to give the class a detailed evaluation of one example in which the GNB and CEV interpret a relation differently. Which of the versions do you prefer? Why? (The THP and an interlinear version translation will help you do this assignment.)

3. There are three relations that are not always so easy to distinguish from one another: (a) base-restatement, (b) base-amplification, and (c) base-addition. See if you can differentiate them in the four passages below, all from Psalm 81. Write the letter of the relation (a, b, or c) in front of the bicolon that it seems to fit best. Be prepared to explain and defend your choices.

> ____ A: He says, "I removed the burden from their shoulders;
> B: their hands were set free from the basket." (v. 6)

> ____ B: I answered you out of a thundercloud;
> C: I tested you at the waters of Meribah. (v. 7b–c)

> ____ A: You shall have no foreign god among you;
> B: you shall not bow down to an alien god. (v. 9)

> ____ A: But you would be fed with the finest wheat;
> B: with honey from the rock I would satisfy you. (v. 16)

3.4 A summary of the semantic relations between parallel lines

The following is a list of the interlineal connections presented in this chapter. It is important to recognize the relations that may exist between two poetic lines, or the two principal events of a single line—or, indeed, between two clusters of several lines or entire stanzas. For each relation below a summary and sample passage (based on the NIV) is given to help in remembering it. In most cases the "base" proposition generally occurs first in Hebrew, but in some couplets the *base* may appear either first *or* second (A-B or B-A). This is not necessarily the characteristic order of every TL. Some languages may prefer one way or the other.

Keep in mind that more than one relation is possible between the lines of a given pair; thus, the various examples below may be debated and substituted for by better illustrations of a particular relation. In cases of ambiguity, one must try to find the relation that fits most naturally and meaningfully in the light of the immediate context as well as within the framework of the entire composition. This is especially important when translating the Psalms and other Hebrew poetry. The list that follows is not exhaustive, but these twenty-five semantic relations are the main ones found in the Psalter.

Relations involving *similarity, or synonymous* parallelism (see sec. 3.3.1)

1. **base–restatement**: Line B is very similar in meaning to line A. (61:1)
2. **base–amplification**: Line B adds some significant aspect of meaning to line A. (61:3)
3. **general–specific**: Line B is a more specific instance or example of what is said in line A. (60:12)

Relation involving *contrast* (see sec. 3.3.2)

4. **base–contrast**: Usually two elements in line B contrast with the corresponding segments of line A. (145:20)

Relations involving *temporal* addition (see sec. 3.3.3.1)

5. **base–sequential time**: In line A the first event occurred, after that in line B a second event occurred. (105:23)
6. **base–simultaneous time**: The events of lines A and B occurred at relatively the same time. (105:26)
7. **base–circumstance**: The event in A is primary, and in B another, subordinated, circumstantially related event is reported. (31:22b)

Relations involving *causal* addition (see sec. 3.3.3.2)

8. **reason–result**: Because one event happens, therefore another occurs. (116:2)
9. **ground–conclusion**: Line A provides the basis/evidence for the conclusion in line B. (48:8)
10. **reason–request**: Because of the event in line A, there is a request/command in line B. (82:8)
11. **means–request**: By means of an event in line A, a request is made in line B. (79:11b)
12. **means–result**: By means of the event in line A, the event in line B occurs. (17:4)
13. **means–purpose**: A is done in order that B may occur/happen. (78:71)
14. **request–purpose**: The request of line A is made in order to achieve the event in line B. (24:7)
15. **real condition–result**: If the event in line A happens (or is true), then the one in line B results (or is also true). (7:12)
16. **unreal condition–result**: If one event (A) had happened (it didn't), then the other (B) would have occurred (but it didn't). (66:18)
17. **condition–unexpected result**: Even if/although one event (A) happens (or is true), the other (B) occurs (is true), contrary to expectation. (118:18)

Relations involving *completive* addition (see sec. 3.3.3.3)

18. **base–attribution**: The quality in line B applies attributively to a noun or pronoun in line A. (53:4)
19. **base–location**: The event of line B occurred where the main event line of A took place. (116:18-19)
20. **base–manner**: Line B tells how the event of line A was carried out. (55:20-21)
21. **base–response**: Line B provides a formal reply to what is said in line A. (118:2-4)
22. **base–content**: Line B gives the content/object of the verb in line A, often a verb of speech. (30:6)
23. **base–comparison**: Line B is compared to line A in terms of likeness/degree. (118:9)
24. **base–addition**: The distinct content of line B is added to that of line A. (68:31)
25. **base–alternative**: Line B provides an alternative to what is stated in line A. (1:1)

More detailed information and exercises on the semantic relations that can link poetic lines, whether adjacent or separated in the text, are given in the books *Exploring Semantic Structures* by E. A. Nida (Munich: Wilhelm Fink, chap. 5), *Translating the Word of God* by J. Beekman and J. Callow (Grand Rapids: Zondervan, chaps. 17–19), *Meaning-based Translation* by M. Larson (Lanham, Md.: University Press, chaps. 25–28), *A Manual for Problem Solving in Bible Translation* by M. Larson (Grand Rapids: Zondervan, chaps. 17–20), and *Introduction to Semantics and Translation*, 2nd ed., by K. Barnwell (Dallas: SIL, chaps. 17–20). It would be helpful to study these books before attempting to analyze and translate the Psalter.

Exercise 3.4a

As you do this exercise, consult the THP and the *NIV Study Bible* and look the passages up in your own Bible (or a draft translation) so that you can study their context. The verses you will analyze are quoted in full from the RSV on the next page.

(1) First, for each verse, identify all of the distinct propositions, that is, the units that appear to express an independent idea, whether they correspond with a poetic line/syntactic clause or not. Usually each proposition will be organized around a key event or state. Label these as A (A1, A2 . . .), B (B1, B2 . . .), C (C1, C2 . . .), etc., to show the ones which seem to parallel or correspond with each other most closely.

(2) Describe the paired semantic relationship that exists between any two lines (bicola) or groups of lines (cola clusters) that you have designated in A. (Refer to the listing of interpropositional relations given in section 3.4.) Begin with the most closely related cola and work up to the larger clusters that are present. Draw lines to show the connections, that is, from the smaller to the larger organizational units within a given passage. Psalm 44:20-22 has been done for you as an example.

(2) If you detect any emphasis, specification, focus, or some other aspect of "heightening" in the B line, then underline the word or phrase where this is located. Describe the precise nature of the intensification and its effect in the text. This part of the exercise should be written out on a separate sheet of paper.

Before you begin working on this exercise, see how such an analysis is done for Psalm 44:20-22:

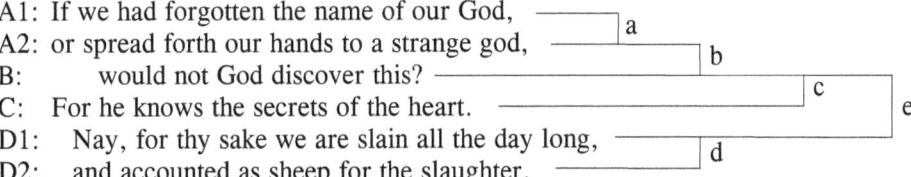

A1: If we had forgotten the name of our God,
A2: or spread forth our hands to a strange god,
B: would not God discover this?
C: For he knows the secrets of the heart.
D1: Nay, for thy sake we are slain all the day long,
D2: and accounted as sheep for the slaughter.

a = *base–addition*: A2 gives another, more emphatic, instance of sin in addition to A1.

- **b** = *unreal condition-result*: A1-A2 state a condition that was not true, and this emphasizes the people's claim of faithfulness to God and their innocence before him (B).
- **c** = *conclusion-grounds*: Since God knows everything (C), it would not have been possible for the people to deceive him (A-B).
- **d** = *base-comparison*: The hyperbole of D1 is expressed as a simile in D2; a base-amplification relation is also involved.
- **e** = *condition-unexpected result*: Even though the people were (or claimed to be) innocent of idolatry (A-C), nevertheless their enemies were destroying them—hence their bitter lament to God.

Would you like to revise any aspect of the preceding analysis? If so, please do this, with reasons.

Note that vv. 20–22 repeat the same basic argument of vv. 17–19: the people complain that they are being punished unjustly. This repetition heightens their plea and builds up to the emotional appeals found at the psalm's conclusion in vv. 23-26.

Now analyze the following passages according to steps 1—3 given above. For the longer examples, it is helpful to begin the analysis with the lines that are most *closely* related and built up from there:

(27:3) Though a host encamp against me,
  my heart shall not fear;
 though war arise against me,
  yet I will be confident.

(26:3) For your steadfast love is before my eyes,
  and I walk in thy faithfulness. [alternate reading]

(31:5) Into thy hand I commit my spirit;
  thou hast redeemed me, O LORD, faithful God.

(37:16) Better is a little that the righteous has
  than the abundance of many wicked.

(37:17) For the arm of the wicked shall be broken;
  but the LORD upholds the righteous.

(35:4) Let them be put to shame and dishonor
  who seek after my life!
 Let them be turned back and confounded
  who devise evil against me!

(32:5) I acknowledged my sin to thee,
  and I did not hide my iniquity;
 I said, "I will confess my transgressions to the LORD";
  then thou didst forgive the iniquity of my sin.

(50:3) Our God comes and will not be silent;
  a fire devours before him,
  and around him a tempest rages.

(77:2) In the day of my trouble I seek the Lord;
  in the night my hand is stretched out without wearying;
  my soul refuses to be comforted.

(31:23) Love the LORD, all you his saints!
  The LORD preserves the faithful,
  but abundantly requites him who acts haughtily.

(4:7-8) Thou has put more joy in my heart
  than they have when their grain and wine abound.

> In peace I will both lie down and sleep;
>> for thou alone, O LORD, makest me dwell in safety.

(69:4) More in number than the hairs of my head
>> are those who hate me without cause;
> mighty are those who would destroy me,
>> those who attack me with lies.
> What I did not steal
>> must I now restore?

(17:3) If thou triest my heart,
> if thou visitest me by night,
> if thou testest me,
>> thou wilt find no wickedness in me;
>> my mouth does not transgress.

(139:11–12) If I say, "Let only darkness cover me,
>> and the light about me be night,"
> even the darkness is not dark to thee,
> the night is as bright as the day;
>> for darkness is as light with thee.

(78:21–22) Therefore, when the LORD heard,
> he was full of wrath;
>> a fire was kindled against Jacob,
>> his anger mounted against Israel;
> because they had no faith in God,
> and did not trust his saving power.

(109:28) Let them curse, but do thou bless!
> Let my assailants be put to shame;
> may thy servant be glad!

Which passage was the *most* difficult for you to analyze? Why? What was the special problem involved?

Now consult an interlinear Old Testament and/or several other English versions to see if they give you help with any problem you had in determining the semantic relations between the lines of the passage you found most difficult. Does this additional study lead you revise or clarify your previous interpretation in any way? Explain. Does any English version appear to differ from the interpretation you have arrived at? Which version? In what way(s) does it differ?

Exercise 3.4b

In this exercise, which is intended for more advanced students, we will examine a complete prayer, Psalm 11, to determine the semantic relations between parallel lines. On a separate sheet of paper, write each line as set out in the NASB, RSV, NRSV, or the NIV. If possible, consult an interlinear to check on the division of lines. Then study each set of two or more lines in their context and identify the semantic relation between them. (Refer to the listing in sec. 3.4.) Draw connecting lines to link up the particular cola that you are dealing with. Finally, see whether you are able to join some of the pairs to form larger groupings of the text, again drawing lines to connect the more closely related segments. For example, how is v. 6 (A + B) related to v. 7 (A + B+ C)? Or how is v. 4 (A' + B') related to v. 5 (A)?

Now observe the overall thematic "movement" of this psalm of trust:

- —In which verse does the psalmist confess his faith?
- —Where does he express the reason or basis for this faith?
- —Where is the midpoint of the psalm?
- —Where is the main "problem" stated?
- —Where is the "solution" to this problem given?
- —Which verse expresses the deep frustration of the psalmist?
- —Where do we find a warning for the wicked?
- —How does the final verse of this psalm link up with the first verse?
- —What is the theme of Psalm 11?

Now do you see a larger thematic pattern or structure of organization here? In other words, how are the larger clusters of cola (i.e., several verses) related to one another? Is it simply *base-restatement*, *base-amplification*, or *base-addition*? Or can you detect a more specific relationship between these bigger chunks of petition and/or praise?

The following is a diagram of one way (not necessarily the only way) of linking the groups of cola (i.e., bicola/tricola) in Psalm 11. Fill in the term for each relation indicated by the lowercase letters in boldface type below. To simplify this exercise, consider each bicolon or tricolon as a complete unit. To the right of the diagram, list these relations in the space provided by the respective letters. Select the term that you think best fits each set from the twenty-five given in section 3.4.

If time allows, you may now either translate this psalm into your mother tongue—or make a corrective adaptation of an existing translation that you have available, based on your preceding discourse analysis.

PSALM 11

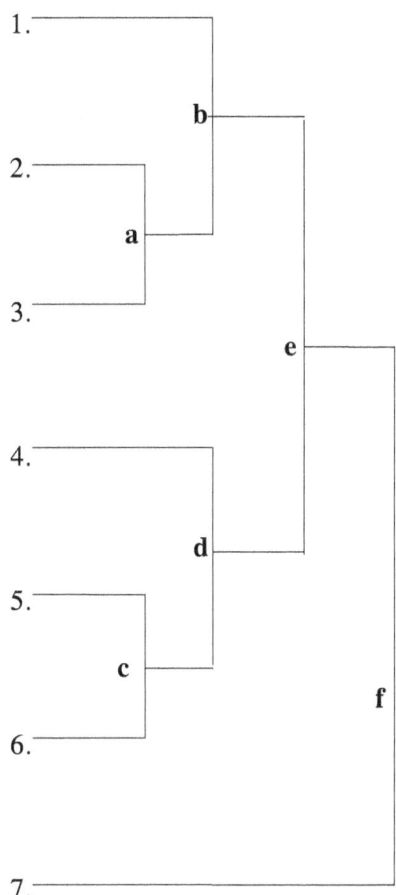

a = _____ – _____

b = _____ – _____

c = _____ – _____

d = _____ – _____

e = _____ – _____

f = _____ – _____

Exercise 3.4c

In this exercise, which again is for more advanced students, you will do a similar type of step-by-step analysis (as in exercise 3.4b) of the sequence of cola in Psalm 14.

1. On a sheet of paper, write out the couplets and then build them up in paired sets, from the most closely related ones to the larger clusters of cola. Draw lines to connect the cola that you see as being joined by parallelism. You will see that two of the verses of this psalm are best analyzed as containing four poetic lines (*tetracola*), and two others as containing three lines (*tricola*).

2. Write out your answers to the following questions in preparation for the propositional analysis:

   What is this psalm's genre? Why do you think so?
   In which verse(s) does the psalmist express his faith in God?
   In which verse(s) does he express a petition to the LORD?
   If you divide Psalm 14 into two main parts, what are they?
   What is the function of v. 4 within the structure of the whole psalm?
   Where does the climax, or peak, of this psalm occur? What makes you think so?

Now, just as you did for Psalm 11, give the term for each semantic relation that links couplets and also the larger clusters. Write it in the spaces provided to the right of the following diagram:

ANALYZING THE PSALMS

PSALM 14

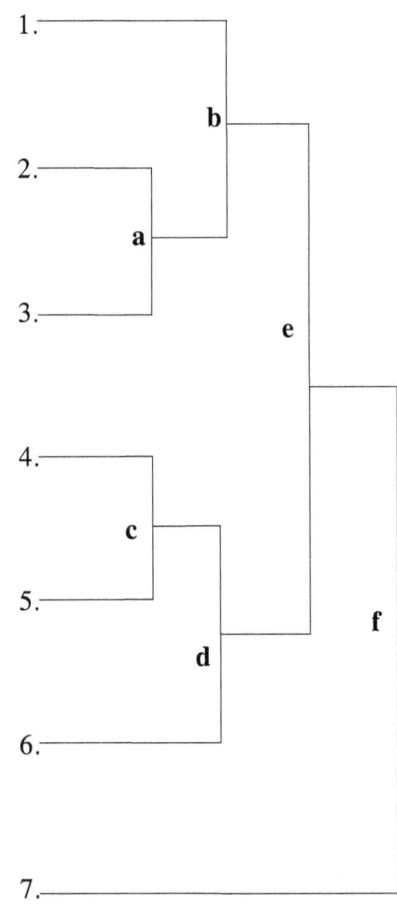

a = _____ – _____

b = _____ – _____

c = _____ – _____

d = _____ – _____

e = _____ – _____

f = _____ – _____

It may be more accurate to analyze Psalm 14 as being composed of *three* major sections, each one of which is marked by a dramatic opening utterance. Study the text again along with your diagram above and determine what these three main divisions are. (Also read the comments in the THP and the NIV-SB.) Then give a short title or section heading for each of the three parts, summarizing its content and/or purpose.

	verses	*summary*
I.	_____ :	_____
II.	_____ :	_____
III.	_____ :	_____

Where does the *emotive climax* of Psalm 14 occur? What are the textual markers of this crucial point? Does this seem to be the same as the *thematic peak* of this psalm? Explain.

Again, if time allows, translate this psalm idiomatically in your language—or make a corrective adaptation of some existing version.

Exercise 3.4d

With the help of a Hebrew interlinear, write out the lines of Psalm 23 in order. After each line, write the number of word-units that it contains. Now look at the next page which shows one possible way of diagramming the structure of Psalm 23. Try to identify the relations that link all of the paired cola and cola clusters. Write the label of each relation in the space next to the boldface letters below (the letters correspond to those on the diagram). The first one has been filled in for you as an example. You may want to discuss the different possibilities with another member of the class.

a = ____base____ + ____addition____

b = _____ + _____

c = _____ + _____

d = _____ + _____

e = _____ + _____

f = _____ + _____

g = _____ + _____

h = _____ + _____

i = _____ + _____

j = _____ + _____

k = _____ + _____

l = _____ + _____

m = _____ + _____

n = _____ + _____

o = _____ + _____

p = _____ + _____

q = _____ + _____

r = _____ + _____

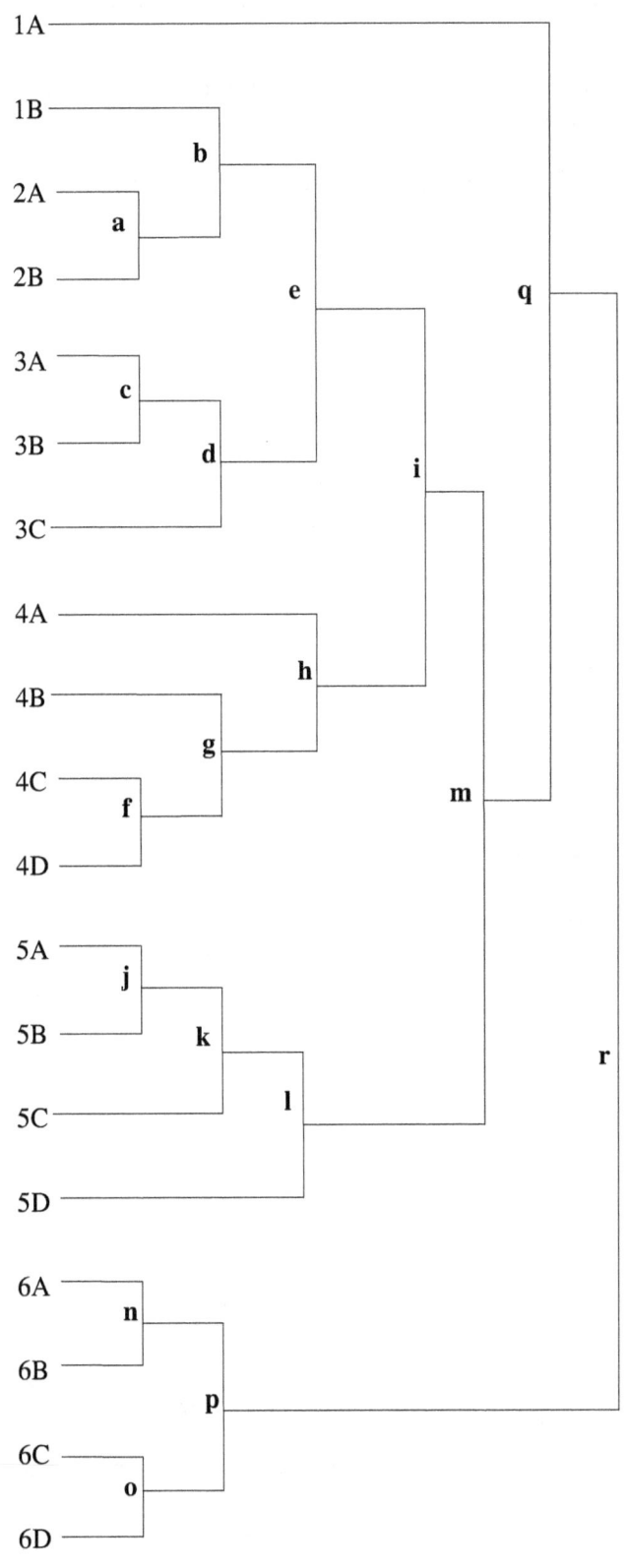

Exercise 3.4e

Each class member (or translation team member) should select a *short* psalm and prepare a written analysis of it as in the previous exercise. First, divide the psalm into poetic lines. Next, determine the semantic relation between the separate lines of every bicolon or tricolon, and then between the larger units—the cola clusters. Finally, try to diagram the discourse structure, drawing lines as shown in the previous exercise. Compare your diagram, especially the chief divisions, with the segmentation that you see in the TEV, NIV, and CEV. Also look at the recommendations given in the THP. Make any revisions that you now feel are necessary. Be prepared to present your "discourse analysis" of this psalm to the entire group. Include any potential problem areas in your language or special implications for translation that you noted during your study of this psalm.

4. DISTANT PARALLELISM:
THE MARKING OF TEXT BOUNDARIES IN THE PSALTER

Most Bible students consider the literary device of parallelism only when they see it within a verse. This is what, in chapter 3, we called connected or "near" (adjacent) parallelism. But parallel bicola and tricola may be joined together to form clusters, and these, in turn, may be combined in ever larger units to form an entire psalm. It is important to recognize that the same sort of correspondence seen in paired lines is manifested also between higher-level units of Hebrew poetic discourse. Such correspondence, or parallelism, serves to demarcate boundaries, as well as thematic peaks, within the text as a whole. This sort of parallelism is what we call "distant" parallelism. It functions to reinforce and to foreground crucial aspects of the semantic organization of the entire composition. In other words, the related parallel lines may be separated from one another by a number of verses and placed in positions that are essential to the development of the complete message that is being poetically conveyed.

This type of parallelism is based on the principle of selective and positioned repetition, termed *recursion*. It is a feature that enabled people to follow along when psalms (or other poetic texts) were being sung, chanted, or recited in a public worship service. Verbal structuring of this kind also helps us today to see the larger organization of a psalm (as well as other passages of Scripture), whether a prayer of petition, thanksgiving, praise, instruction, or profession of faith. We can see the main ideas the psalmist wished to convey both to and from the Lord on behalf of the religious community.

In this chapter, we will survey the higher-level discourse features involving various kinds of recursion, which the psalmists used to construct a prayer-song. The aim is to enable translators to recognize these devices and their significance in a particular psalm. Such knowledge will be immensely helpful in both interpretation and translation. Opportunity to practice the basic analytical procedures will also be given as each feature is presented.

4.1 How separated parallelism reveals text boundaries

There are four major devices the Hebrew poets used in order to highlight the boundaries and other important points in a poem. These features are as follows:

Inclusion, which marks the beginning and ending of the same discourse unit.
Junction, which marks the ending and the beginning of adjacent discourse units.
Aperture, which marks the respective beginnings of different discourse units.
Closure, which marks the respective endings of different discourse units.

4.1.1 Inclusion

Inclusion is the first type of distant parallelism that we will consider. It is one of the most common literary techniques in Hebrew (and in most other world literatures as well, including the Greek New Testament). It is important because it serves to demarcate a complete textual unit, whether small (strophe) or large (an entire psalm). For example, the words of Psalm 8:1 and 8:9 are exactly the same. The distant B line (v. 9) repeats the A line (v. 1), emphasizing the psalm's main theme, the surpassing majesty of the Lord. In this type of text *bounding* device, one element occurs at the beginning and its parallel at the end of a given compositional unit. The second element is similar in several key respects to the first—in terms of form and/or content. This is also known as an *inclusio*. It signals that the unit "includes" everything between the A and B lines. It is a device frequently used in the hallelujah psalms: the repetition stresses the purpose of these hymns as proclaiming universal praise to the LORD (e.g., 103:1a, 22b).

Sometimes the parallel A and B cola occur, not at the beginning and end of a psalm, but elsewhere at key points *within* the text. Or it is possible for either A or B to occur at the beginning or end of a given psalm, and the other to be found within the text. An example is Psalm 22:1 and 22:11, as we will see in the exercise below.

The balanced, often symmetrical pattern formed by the reiteration of ideas is a common feature of Hebrew poetry. Parallelism functions to artistically *embellish* the discourse at the same time that it *demarcates* its structure and *emphasizes* its main ideas.

As the examples of the following exercise will illustrate, the distant parallel cola are not usually an *exact* repetition of each other. However, it is generally true that an *inclusio* is most obvious and hence effective as a signaling device when the corresponding words and ideas between the separated parallel lines, A and B, do match very closely. Remember that just as in connected parallelism, the semantic linkage between the related lines may be similar, contrasting, consequential, or in some other way complementary or completing in nature.

Exercise 4.1.1

1. Look at vv. 1 and 11 of Psalm 22 and write down the words that correspond to each other in some way, whether by similarity or contrast or some other relation that was presented in chapter 3:

   22:1: _____
   22:11: _____

   What point is being emphasized by the speaker of these words? What is his purpose in saying them? That is, what is the function of these words?

2. There are other examples of *inclusion* found in Psalm 22. Compare vv. 12-13 with v. 21. Write out the words that correspond:

   22:12-13: _____
   22:21: _____

   The next pair of verses is vv. 22 and 31:

   22:22: _____
   22:31: _____

   What do you notice about the way in which the three *inclusions* segment Psalm 22? Between which two verses does the major break of the psalm occur? What is the prominent shift found at this juncture? Is an explicit signal of such breaks necessary in your language? Do you think an overt marker would be helpful in English? If so, what would you suggest to clarify the text's larger organization?

3. Write down the words that are similar in v. 4 and v. 5 of Psalm 20:

   20:4 (A): _____
   20:5 (B): _____

   In Psalm 20:4-5, the *inclusion* serves to mark off a much smaller unit within the psalm, one that corresponds to a paragraph in prose discourse. In poetry such a unit is called either a *strophe* or a *stanza*. It is a strophe if several such units are uneven in length; it is a stanza if the units are relatively equal in length. If we consider Psalm 20 as a whole, we reasonably conclude that the corresponding words of v. 4 and v. 5 represent its central theme or main point. This suggestion is reinforced by another similar *inclusion* that bounds the psalm as a whole. Write the words that make up this inclusion.

   20:1: _____
   20:9: _____

In this case, the *inclusion* reveals to whom the pronoun "you" refers. What does that tell us about the special function of this psalm?

4. What is the special semantic relation that links the first and last verses of Psalm 16?

    16:1: _____
    16:11: _____

4.1.2 Junction

In contrast to *inclusion*, which functions to delineate the outer boundaries of the *same* unit of discourse, *junction* highlights the boundary between two *different* discourse units. This text-initial repetition of a certain concept found at the end of the previous unit is often called a "tail-head" construction. (The technical term is *anadiplosis*.) A good example is found in Psalm 7, where vv. 10–11 repeat v. 9, the last line of the previous unit.

Exercise 4.1.2

1. Write out the semantic elements that correspond in Psalm 7:9 and 10–11. What linguistic feature indicates that these verses belong to *different* strophes and not the same one?

    7:9: _____
    7:10–11: _____

There is another indication that 7:9 and 7:10–11 each belong to different strophes, namely the double *inclusion* on each side of the common "boundary." Write the corresponding semantic features in the spaces below:

    7:1: _____
    7:9: _____

    7:10–11: _____
    7:17: _____

In this case, the *junction* in the middle of Psalm 7 provides a summary of its main theme and purpose. What is it? How does this fact relate to the genre of Psalm 7? (Note that in quite a few psalms we find such a major division at or near the structural midpoint of the discourse as a whole.)

2. What corresponding expression helps to mark the *junction* between v. 7 and v. 8 of Psalm 6?

    6:7: _____
    6:8: _____

Again there is a significant shift from v. 7 to v. 8. What is that? What else helps to distinguish v. 8 as the beginning of the final strophe of Psalm 6?

Although tail-head repetition (*anadiplosis*) is not by itself a very clear indicator of a border, it works together with other *disjunctive* poetic devices to support the presence of a border. A *junction* in the text is most noticeable when it is characterized by a great deal of synonymous or even exact lexical correspondence. In other words, the strength of *anadiplosis* as a boundary-marking device varies according to the amount of recursion that supports it.

3. There is a major *junction* in Psalm 2, marked by repetition. Write it out.

    2:6: _____
    2:7: _____

What else do you see that would indicate a border here? In other words, what *change* in the discourse is present in v. 7? The presence of a repeated "key word" marks a minor (i.e., not fully developed) *inclusion* between v. 7 and v. 12. What is this word?

4. What is the parallelism that forms a strong *junction* between v. 3 and v. 4? Which other linguistic markers are present, confirming this linkage? What marks the break or border, on the one hand, and what marks the bridge on the other side?

4.1.3 Aperture

Parallelism of the respective *apertures* (openings) of consecutive or separated (non-contiguous) strophes is yet another important boundary marker. This rhetorical device, which is used to mark the start of a new unit, is also called *anaphora*. An example is vv. 22 and 25 of Psalm 22:

22:22 (A): I will declare your name to my brothers; in the congregation I will praise you.
22:25 (B): From you comes the theme of my praise in the great assembly; before those who fear you will I fulfill my vows.

These partly synonymous verses mark the respective beginnings of the two adjacent strophes, vv. 22–24 and 25–28.

Parallel *apertures* may also occur in strophes that are nonadjacent, that is, they are separated from each other in the text, as in Psalm 35.

Exercise 4.1.3a

1. Read Psalm 35. Write out the similar words that appear in v. 19 and v. 26:

    35:19: _____
    35:26: _____

    Give the final verse numbers of the strophes that v. 19 and v. 26 mark the *apertures* of: 35:___ and 35:___ (This second one should be easy!) Does the discourse unit that begins at v. 19 extend all the way to v. 26? What rhetorical markers would suggest that a new strophe begins in v. 22?

    What then are the verse numbers that belong to this strophe? ___ Notice how we are using the text boundaries of these different poetic units to get an idea of the structure of the psalm as a whole.

2. What verse in Psalm 66 is similar to v. 16? ___ Give the verse numbers of each of the strophes that begin at these two points: from 16 to ___; from 5 to ___. Note the discourse markers that help you to determine the end point of each of these strophes (we will be studying these in more detail later).

3. Verses 1–2 of Psalm 66 correspond in many respects to which other verse(s)? Give the verse numbers of each of the strophes that begin at these two points: from 1-2 to ___ ; from 8 to ___. What markers indicate that a new strophe begins also at v. 13?

    On the basis of your answers to questions 2 and 3, you should be able to divide Ps. 66 into five strophes. Give the verses that belong to each one: a) ____ b) ____ c) ____ d) ____ e) ____ .

4. Of what value are such markers of a psalm's internal structure? How can this information be used in the process of interpretation and translation?

5. Find another good example of *aperture* in a different psalm and write out the matching lines below:

   ___ : ___ : _____

   ___ : ___ : _____

   Does the meaning of these lines relate in any way to the major theme of the psalm as a whole? Explain:

Parallel *apertures* are sometimes seen in more than two stanzas of a psalm, as in Psalm 81. Here the element of "listening" found in v. 8 is repeated in v. 11 and v. 13. These correspondences serve to distinguish the beginnings of three strophes: 8–10, 11–12, and 13–16. Other evidence to support such a division can be seen as well. Observe (hear!) how the notion of listening or not listening to God is revealed as an important aspect of the message of Psalm 81.

Aperture usually involves some sort of synonymous repetition. But other types of parallel relationship may also be used to bring out the correspondence of the strophe beginnings. In Psalm 73, for example, the pray-er makes use of a dramatic *contrast* in the apertures of the initial and final strophes in the first half of the psalm; that is, v. 1 and v. 13 are in sharp contrast with each other.

In translating, it is important to indicate the divisions of the units whose boundaries are marked by parallelism so that the sequence and arrangement of thought reflects that of the original text as closely as possible. Markers such as opening conjunctions, closing formulas, particles of emphasis, or vocatives may be needed in the target language to reinforce the demarcation and bring out the movement of the main thoughts of the psalm from one to another in the overall flow of the text.

As already mentioned, an *anaphoric* series can occur a number of times within a given psalm, as for example, Psalm 78, where the idea of vv. 10–11 is repeated in vv. 17, 32, 40, and 56. These unit-initial verses all contribute to the development of the theme stated at the end of the psalm's introduction in v. 8, and they contrast with the theological principle stated in v. 7. There is a sudden (and shocking!) shift in this repeated pattern of ideas at the onset of the psalm's final poetic unit. Notice where this change occurs and how the theme alters at this point.

Such a shift is a common technique of Hebrew poetic composition. A clear pattern of form and/or content is established, then somewhere along the line there is a significant change. At this juncture, some new (often contrasting) idea is introduced—one which is thereby emphasized because of its variation from the preceding sequence of thought. Normally some prominent structural markers also appear at this point of change. Recognizing such a consequential difference within a progression based on similarity is a crucial factor in the analysis of biblical poetry.

Sometimes not just single lines, but entire bicola match each other in certain important respects. In other words, there is a parallel between A + B of the first occurrence and A + B of the second occurrence (and third, etc.). This technique can be seen in the short strophes of Psalm 34.

Exercise 4.1.3b

1. Write out the matching bicola of Psalm 34 in the spaces provided:

   34:15 A1: _____
         B1: _____

   34:17 A2: _____
         B2: _____

34:19 A3: _____
       B3: _____

What is Psalm 34's central theme? Notice how this theme is emphasized by the pattern of recursion. What important variation then occurs at the beginning of the final strophe of this psalm? What other key term do you see repeated? (This is another instance of *anaphora*.)

2. At which verse in Psalm 78 is there a sudden shift in content to mark an *aperture*? How does this strongly contrast with what has been said in this psalm? Why do you think that this dramatic shift is placed at this point in the psalm?

3. Observe where the key verses of *aperture* are located in Psalm 132. Notice that there are several different sets of these corresponding ideas. See if you can use these to propose a discourse structure for the psalm as a whole (there are five major poetic units/*strophes*).

4.1.4 Closure

A parallel pair of lines sometimes marks the respective *endings* of larger poetic units, instead of the beginnings. As in the case of aperture, so also in *closure* the strophic units themselves may be adjacent to each other or separated. The technical term for such "closure" is *epiphora*. An example of epiphora can be seen in Psalm 71, in v. 13 and v. 24, though the correspondence of these two lines is not exact. (See the following exercise.) An example of figurative epiphora marks the closure of two strophes in Psalm 81 (vv. 8–10 and 13–16).

As can be seen in Psalm 71, the *center* of larger poetic units is often prominent—important with respect to content/theme and intent/purpose, as well as in relation to the larger structure of the whole piece. In other words, central points may serve as formal and functional "peaks" of the discourse segments demarcated by aperture and/or closure. Such central verses are also frequently marked stylistically by other poetic devices.

Another good example of *closure* is found in vv. 29 and 36–37 of Psalm 89. Here the principal correspondences have to do with the establishment of David's line and throne and their eternal continuance. An *inclusion* is also evident as we compare vv. 34 with 36–37. Notice the abrupt thematic reversal unexpectedly introduced after the positive peak found in vv. 35–37. The psalm's negative peak occurs in vv. 50–51 with the "taunts" and "mockery" of the LORD's "anointed servant" on the part of his "enemies." This is the climax of another *epiphoric* refrain seen at the conclusion of strophes in vv. 41 and 45. An important idea is then recalled in v. 49. (In what other verse does this notion occur?) These patterns of repetition help to reveal the larger structural, and in this case also the thematic, organization of this psalm. The praise, divine promises, and professions of faith which characterize the first and larger portion of Psalm 89 (vv. 1–37) act as the foundation upon which the heartbroken and bitter appeals of part two (vv. 38–51) are based. In other words, the semantic relation of the psalm's two parts is *grounds-request*. The structure of the whole helps us to decide how v. 52 fits into the thematic organization of Psalm 89. What is the larger compositional pattern being developed here?

The close of each of the five "books" of the Psalms is marked by the device of *epiphora*, and *closure* for the Psalter as a whole is marked by an entire psalm, namely the joyous hymn of celebration, Psalm 150. Read these passages and note the repeated elements which serve to mark the concluding boundaries of each of these major structural units.

Exercise 4.1.4

1. Look at Psalm 71:13 and 24. Write out the words of lines A and B that correspond:

   71:13 (A): _____
   71:24 (B): _____

   In what way is line B different from line A? How is this difference significant as far as the psalm's overall meaning is concerned?

   Verses 13 and 24 come at the ends of parts one and two of this psalm respectively. The two halves are each marked by an *inclusion* as well. Write down the important conceptual correspondences of these units in the spaces below:

   71:1-2: _____
   71:12: _____

   71:15: _____
   71:24: _____

   The midpoint of Psalm 71 occurs in v. 14. Why is this verse especially significant? What is the genre of this psalm? How does the genre affect the analysis of its discourse structure? Now look at the second line of v. 14: this promise forms the theme of the final strophe of Psalm 71. What are the verse numbers of the final strophe?

2. The structural devices of *anaphora* and *epiphora* are often complementary; in other words, they work together to demarcate the significant units of a given psalm, namely, its *apertures* and *closures*. Psalm 35 illustrates the harmonious operation of such recursion within a poetic text. We have already seen how anaphora in vv. 19 and 26 signals the onset of new segments. Following the short introduction in vv. 1-3, three occurrences of epiphora, each covering two verses, then divide the remainder of the psalm into three stanzas. Record the major similarities of these instances of closure in the spaces below:

   35:9-10: _____
   _____

   35:17-18: _____
   _____

   35:27-28: _____
   _____

   Give the verse numbers of the three stanzas that follow the psalm's introduction: (a) vv. _____ (b) vv. _____ (c) vv. _____ .

   Direct quotation also acts as an *epiphoric* device in this psalm. List the five verses that incorporate a segment of direct discourse. Notice that the last three of these function to divide the third stanza into three strophes. Give their verse numbers: (a) vv. _____ (b) vv. _____ (c) vv. _____ .

   How do the speakers of the third quotation differ from those of the previous two? The end of the second stanza in v. 18 is distinguished, not by a portion of direct speech, but by a switch to direct address to the LORD. How does this compare with v. 28? Notice that the verses on either side of v. 18 are similar to a pair of verses that each begin a series of requests for punishment upon the psalmist's enemies. Which verses belong to these two *imprecatory* sequences?

How do these segments of direct speech serve to highlight the theme of Psalm 35?

_____

3. An elaborate pattern of repetition operates to demarcate the text of Psalm 67 in a very symmetrical manner. Which repeated words (a *refrain*) appear in Psalm 67 and where are they found?

   v. ____ : _____
and v. ____ : _____

On the basis of these repetitions, it is possible to divide this psalm into three stanzas. Give the verse numbers of each stanza and tell how each one is related in meaning to the other:

A. vv. _____ = _____
B. vv. _____ = _____
C. vv. _____ = _____

There are several other instances of structural parallelism in this psalm. Can you point them out and suggest how they help to distinguish the text's overall organization?

_____
_____
_____
_____
_____

We can diagram this psalm in terms of its semantic relations between adjacent cola, as we did earlier. Such a diagram shows how the patterns of separated (distant) parallelism tend to be complemented by patterns of connected (near) parallelism (or vice versa). We will do this in assignment 4, which follows.

4. The following diagram is a structural-semantic (or poetic-propositional) outline of Psalm 67. You must fill in the terms for the various relations according to the sequence of lowercase boldface letters. (You may need to refer back to section 3.4 for help with this exercise.)

PSALM 67

```
1A ─┐
    ├ a ─┐
1B ─┘    │
         ├ c ─┐
2A ─┐    │    │
    ├ b ─┘    │
2B ─┘         │
              │
3A ─┐         │
    ├ d ─┐    │
3B ─┘    │    │
         ├ h ─┐
4A ─┐    │    │
    ├ f ─┘    ├ m ─┐
4B ─┘         │    │
         ┌ e ─┘    ├ n
4C ─┘              │
                   │
5A ─┐              │
    ├ g ──────── i ┘
5B ─┘

6A ─┐
    ├ j ─┐
6B ─┘    │
         ├ l
7A ─┐    │
    ├ k ─┘
7B ─┘
```

a = <u>base-restatement</u>

b = _____

c = _____

d = _____

e = _____

f = _____

g = _____

h = _____

i = _____

j = _____

k = _____

l = _____

m = _____

n = _____

The preceding diagram is just one of several possible ways of organizing this psalm. It is somewhat different from the ones we did earlier. What is different about it? (Carefully examine its middle section.) This difference suggests the presence of a common poetic structure called an A-B-A' "ring" construction, in which A and A' are more closely related to each other than both are to B. How would you describe the relation between **m** and **n**, that is, between A + A' and B? Which verses fit into each section? A: vv. _____ B: vv. _____ A': vv. _____

Now consider vv. 2, 4, and 7: which words or thoughts are repeated in these verses? Notice that the repetition occurs at the end of each unit. What is this compositional marking device called?

DISTANT PARALLELISM

5. As we saw in assignment 2, a repeated "refrain" (i.e., a line or two repeated almost exactly) helps us divide a psalm into its major parts. Let us consider a few other psalms that contain such a refrain. In Psalm 46, for example, in what two verses does a repeated refrain occur? Write this bicolon in the space below:

   A: _____
   B: _____

   How does such repetition help to mark the major divisions of this psalm?

   There are two instances of epiphora in Psalm 46. They signal the closing boundary of a unit. In which verses do these occur? v. _____ and v. _____ .

   What is the *similarity* between these verses?

   What is the *contrast*?

   These correspondences serve to divide Psalm 46 into two parts, the first longer than the second. Give the verse numbers of the two parts.

   Where do you think another division could be made in this psalm? Explain why you think this break in the text is needed (or not needed).

   It is important to observe that wherever there is a sudden shift in *form* (e.g., a rhetorical question), *content* (e.g., a new subject), *tone* (e.g., from negative to positive), and/or communicative *purpose* (e.g., from warning to promise of blessing), there will often be a new structural beginning (aperture). The sharper the shift, the more likely it is that a discourse break is present. We may conclude, then, that Psalm 46 is divided into __ strophes, each of which consists of __ verses. What is the principal theme of each strophe and the psalm as a whole? Try to formulate suitable section headings for this psalm.

   I. _____
   II. _____
   III. _____
   Whole: _____

6. Psalm 56 also contains a refrain that divides the discourse in a symmetrical way. In which verses does it occur? What are the two principal ideas that constitute this refrain?

   56:3–4:   A = _____
             B = _____

   56:10–11: A = _____
             B = _____

   Psalm 56 is a psalm of "thanksgiving" (*eulogy*). Review the functional segments of such a psalm in chapter 2 (2.1.2). Then tell what the psalmist is doing in each of the three sections marked by the two occurrences of the refrain that you noted above:

   56:1–2:   _____
   56:5–9:   _____
   56:12–13: _____

   Remember that discourse analysts must always keep the larger compositional picture in mind. This helps them to discover the meaning of the individual parts, as well as the whole piece, especially those verses that seem obscure or ambiguous when considered on their own.

4.2 How convergence and harmony reveal text boundaries

A pertinent question could be raised at this point: How can we recognize the boundaries of a psalm's poetic units simply by noting the parallel cola, especially when they are so separated in the text? And what if there are no instances of distant parallelism or other patterns of repetition to guide us in seeing a particular psalm's overall organization?

Uncertainties like these can be resolved because parallelism is not the only feature marking text boundaries in biblical poetry. There are two other features of discourse organization (in prose as well as poetic passages) that help the analyst to segment a particular text. First is the *convergence* (coming together) of additional poetic and rhetorical devices at points of special compositional importance. These will tend either to support or to disallow the analyst's early guesses based on patterns of parallelism.

Second, one structural feature and pattern tends to support another to produce a *harmony* of the formal, semantic, and functional elements within the complete discourse. Apparent anomalies or exceptions usually turn out, upon further study, to fit somewhere and somehow within the total plan of established arrangement. The well-formed literary discourse is built up into a *hierarchy* of larger and smaller units. These are normally marked by a diverse assortment of components and interrelationships on a number of different levels of textual organization. The analyst must look to see how they all operate together to communicate the original author's message.

4.2.1 Markers of a beginning

A psalm's structure as a whole will determine how the analyst divides it into smaller units of composition. But where does one begin? Perhaps the first thing to look for in a given psalm is its *obvious* internal beginnings. By "obvious" is meant those apertures that are clearly marked in the text. The *most* obvious signal would be any prominent shift, or change, in form or content. Such a change, or a combination of them, often indicates the start of a new segment of the discourse. The following is a list of features that commonly "shift," signaling a new unit. Thus they are onset markers of the compositional border between two poetic units, whether units on the same or different levels of the structure as a whole.

(1) *topic*: a change in the subject being spoken about

(2) *speaker*: a change in the speaker of the words of the text

(3) *addressee(s)*: a change in the person or group being spoken to

(4) *discourse genre*: a change in communicative function

(5) *setting time*: a change in temporal orientation: past, present, or future

(6) *situation*: a change from positive to negative circumstances from the psalmist's viewpoint

(7) *mode of speaking*: a change from indirect to direct speech, or vice versa, usually accompanied by some pronominal shift

(8) *word order*: especially if a chiasmus or another such pattern is involved

(9) *tone*: a change in attitude or emotion

(10) *formal mood*: a change from statement to question or command/request or vice versa

The first five markers tend to be more important in the exercise of structural analysis. Furthermore, one must be especially careful in the case of features (5) and (10) because the Hebrew verb always requires a certain amount of contextual interpretation, especially in poetry, depending upon the situational setting, the semantic cotext, the psalm's genre, and the particular element being dealt with. For this reason, translations sometimes differ in the tense or mood they use for a given verb. Thus, the features of mood and tense can be used only as secondary or supporting indicators of a break in the text, and they must always be confirmed by some primary compositional marker.

It is important to recognize the need for more than one indicator of a new compositional unit: the greater the number of shifts that "converge," or appear together, in a particular passage, the more certain one can be that a break in the text actually occurs there. The combination of markers, including the different types of separated (non-adjacent) parallelism noted in 4.1, is what indicates that a new segment is being initiated.

Exercise 4.2.1a

1. Study the following passages in their immediate context. Tell what kind of a shift you see in relation to what has gone before. In other words, identify the text markers ("cues") that indicate a new starting point in the psalm. On a separate piece of paper, and consulting the THP, mention all of the markers you can find for each passage: 36:5, 27:7, 27:13, 28:6, 29:3, 31:6, 31:9, 31:14, 31:19, 31:21, 32:3, 32:6, 32:11. The first one, 36:5, is done as an example:

   36:5 — Here we see a shift in *topic* (from the wicked person to the LORD), in *genre* (from description to praise), in *addressee* (from general to specific, God now being the one spoken to), in *tone* (from dejection to joyful hope), and in *word order* (a syntactic chiasmus is present). This convergence of markers makes the break between v. 4 and v. 5 quite apparent. Note also the subtle *epiphora*: in v. 4, the wicked man lies on his bed plotting evil; in v. 12, the evildoers lie fallen in defeat on the ground. This shows that v. 4 is well marked as the close of a unit, while v. 5 begins a new poetic paragraph.

2. Read through several other psalms and choose four *internal* unit-opening verses that illustrate at least three of the ten possible markers of a break. For each verse that you choose, be sure to mention *all* of the markers of aperture that you can find, including inclusio, anaphora, epiphora, and anadiplosis (see p. 105).

3. Now check the GNB, CEV, and NIV and see which version agrees most fully with all four of the internal breaks that you have noted.

In addition to the ten kinds of shift already listed, there are other linguistic and literary features which often (but not always) occur at the beginning of a new unit. In the prophetic literature, for instance, there are certain *formulaic* openers: "Hear the word of the LORD" or "Thus says the LORD" or "And it will be (or, come to pass)" or "Therefore" plus a word of judgment. In the Psalms, such formulas are not as common (but note an initial "Blessed..."; e.g., 1:1, 32:1-2, 41:1, 112:1, 119:1-2). Since the Psalter's poetry is "lyric" (personally expressive) and "liturgical" (religious or worship-oriented), it has specific forms, such as *eulogy* (praise + thanksgiving), *lament* (complaint + petition), *homily* (teaching + admonition/ exhortation), and so forth, each with its own kind of markers, including some of the various shifts we have mentioned. The following are four other features which frequently appear at a point of *aperture* in the psalms (the first three frequently occur together):

(1) an *imperative* (e.g., "Sing joyfully to the Lord" in Ps. 33:1)

(2) a *vocative* (e.g., "you righteous!" in Ps. 33:1)

(3) explicit mention of the *divine name*, often in vocative form (e.g., "Your love, O Lord, reaches to the heavens" in Ps. 36:5)

(4) a *rhetorical question* (e.g., "How long will you assault a man?" in Ps. 62:3)

Remember, these markers of a new unit do not operate in isolation. Rather, they tend to coincide with the other signals already mentioned—the repetition patterns and prominent shifts in form, content, and/or intent. Together then they function to distinguish a particular boundary that is manifested in a poetic text.

Exercise 4.2.1b

1. Find four examples of the use of the four markers just listed to show the internal *aperture* of a new poetic unit within a given psalm (not its very beginning).

2. For the verses you selected, mention any other signs of an *aperture* that you see.

3. Which of these verbal signals of a new unit would be the clearest indicators in your language? Which would be the least likely to imply a new unit? Is there any other type of marker in your language that typically occurs in poetic discourse to indicate the onset of a new strophe, e.g., an exclamation such as "ah!" or a specific genre-marker (e.g., of lament poetry)?

4.2.2 Markers of an ending

Just as *aperture* is signaled by certain stylistic devices, so the *closure*, or ending, of a particular unit of poetic discourse may be marked by such features. Recognizing them is more difficult, however, because the formal and semantic cues are not as clear. In fact, they are ambiguous because the same devices may appear in a closure as in an aperture. They may even occur at a point of special thematic emphasis ("peak")—frequently in the center and/or at the close of a strophe or stanza. For this reason, it is even more important not to rely on a single stylistic device on its own as the indicator of an ending. These markers must always be considered in conjunction with one another as well as with the overall patterns of discourse arrangement, based upon repetition.

Once again, the greater the "convergence" of indicators and the more functional "harmony" among the various features present, the more credible is the presence of a concluding discourse boundary. After careful study, one usually finds that every psalm gives evidence of a general agreement, even a symmetry, of textual organization. That is, its various units and levels of structure fit together in a mutually complementary manner, and the whole is structurally well formed. Any major exception is frequently significant with regard to the principal thematic point and communicative purpose of a given psalm.

As noted earlier, the various points of *aperture* within a text are perhaps the easiest of all the boundary markers to recognize. It is reasonable to assume that if there is a new beginning somewhere, it must be preceded by an ending, one that will be marked for *closure*. Hence, we can now look for such a marker; as we do so, we will see that concluding cola tend to be *emphatic* utterances. This is because, in addition to concluding a unit, they often also serve to stress its main idea. To create emphasis, they incorporate dramatic linguistic and literary features such as the following (a partial listing):

(1) *direct speech* (e.g., "Do not let them think, 'Aha, just what we wanted!'" in Ps. 35:25)

(2) *vivid imagery* (e.g., "they will vanish, vanish like smoke" in Ps. 37:20)

(3) *condensation*, a short, strongly worded utterance (e.g., "Nothing can shake me at all!" in Ps. 62:2 [lit. not=I-will-be-shaken greatly])

(4) *asyndeton*, the absence of an initial or medial conjunction (e.g., "Therefore everything shouts and sings for joy!" in Ps. 65:13 [lit. they-shout indeed=they-sing])

(5) *intensification* or *exclamation* (e.g., "Indeed, each man is but a breath—*Selah*" in Ps. 39:11)

(6) *change in usual word order* (e.g., "Your deeds bring shouts of joy from one end of the earth to the other" in Ps. 65:8, TEV [lit. outgoings-of-the=morning and-the-evening (= frontshift) you-cause-songs-of-joy])

(7) *repetition* (e.g., "Everyone has turned away, they have together become corrupt; there is no one who does good, not even one!" in Ps. 53:3)

(8) *verbless clause* (e.g., "You, O God, are my fortress; you are the God who loves me!" in Ps. 59:17 [lit. for=God my-fortress God-of my-love.])

(9) *strong contrast* (e.g., "For evil men will be cut off, but those who hope in the LORD will inherit the land" in Ps. 37:9)

(10) *vocative* (e.g., "Strike them with terror, O LORD!" in Ps. 9:20)

The convergence of a number of these dramatic features would mark a *closure* very forcefully. A good example of such a combination of many markers is in Psalm 62:8. Literally it reads "God a-refuge=to-us *selah*," meaning "Surely God is our refuge!" Here, four of the preceding indicators apply, namely: 3, 4, 7, and 8. *Epiphoric* parallelism is also present (i.e., a conceptual correspondence of v. 8 with v. 2).

It is important to keep in mind that many of these poetic devices may also be found in cola of aperture. Therefore one must thoroughly consider the structural design of a given psalm as a whole and the "correspondence" of its various interrelated elements and levels before deciding upon the boundaries and stressed points of any of its parts.

Determining the overall organization of a psalm is something like assembling a jigsaw puzzle, fitting together larger and smaller segments of text instead of a picture: The analyst carefully studies all of the possible borders, both large and small (especially the larger ones), in order to see how they relate to one another. As more and more of the pieces are joined together and a larger pattern develops, the easier it is to fit the rest into the total picture. Finally, the structural organization of the whole will enable one to make a reasonable guess as to how to incorporate the most problematic or ambiguous passages.

Exercise 4.2.2

1. Examine the following verses in the Psalter (in an interlinear version if possible): 3:8, 4:3, 5:12, 6:3, 10:11, 11:3, 12:4, 13:2, 14:7, 17:12, 18:29, 19:6, 20:5, 27:6, 29:9, 30:10, 31:22, 32:5. These verses all come at the end of a strophe or stanza. Now, from among the devices described in section 4.2.2, list the ones you see in each of these verses. Also mention any other distinguishing feature you happen to notice. To help you analyze these verses, Psalm 51:17 is presented here as an example:

   A: the-sacrifices-of God [are] a-spirit broken,
   B: a-heart=being-broken and-contrite O-God not will-you-despise.

   Here we observe the convergence of all but one of the features on our list: (1) direct address to God, (2) the related imagery of "spirit" and "heart," (4) asyndeton before both cola, (5) a negative intensifier, (6) a chiastic construction, (7) the repetition of "sacrifice" from v. 16, (8) a verbless A colon, (9) a strong contrast between what is said in v. 16 and v. 17, and (10) a vocative (in line B: "O God"). The device not included is "condensation" (3). It seems to have been replaced by its opposite, expansion (there are five words in the B line), which may also be significant. The word "God" near the beginning of the bicolon is repeated near its end. In addition, there is a significant sound parallel in the bicolon's initial and final words: *zibḥey*, 'sacrifices-of,' and *tibzeh*, 'you-will-despise'. Finally, the terms "spirit" and "heart" reiterate the key words of the psalm's central strophe (vv. 10–12).

   You might also note the features that serve to mark v. 18 as a unit *aperture*. What are these?

   ---

2. List the devices of closure which seem to be important in the poetry of your language.

   ---

3. Look at each of the verses of assignment 1 in the TEV and CEV. Write down the places where these versions do not agree on the point of *closure*. Be prepared to discuss the pros and cons of the different structural formats of these two versions.

4. Examine Psalm 118:7, 14, 21, and 28. Write down the corresponding words and ideas of these verses on a separate sheet of paper. All four verses must be considered together, along with their preceding context, because the similarities are not the same in each case. Then explain why it is likely that these verses occur at the ends of their respective units (i.e., as points of *closure*), and not at their beginnings (i.e., *aperture*). Also note the *inclusion* that demarcates Psalm 118 as a whole.

5. Now carefully study Psalm 98 in the NIV and, if possible, also in an interlinear version. Make an analysis of its strophic structure. What are the main divisions of this joyful hymn? What markers do you see that lead you to your conclusions? Do these same markers indicate *closure* in your language? If not, why not? What indicator(s) might you use in your language to mark the final border more clearly? (Write out assignments 5 and 6 on a separate sheet of paper so that it can be handed in for an individual evaluation. Later we will use these papers in class to discuss the importance of discourse markers in the religious poetry of the Bible as compared with your own oral or written tradition.)

6. Tell how an accurate determination of the structural organization of Psalm 98 helps one to better understand the development of its theme and its overall rhetorical purpose. Note any specific elements that distinguish this universal song of praise and what these would signify to the psalmist's religious constituency. Would the same effect be evoked in the intended audience of your translation? Explain.

4.3 Summary of the marking functions of separated parallels

An analysis of the patterns of *recursion*, both near and distant, corresponding as well as contrastive, is an important part of the study of Hebrew poetic discourse. Reiteration is frequently used to signal the boundaries of units: separate bicola, tricola, strophes, stanzas, cantos, and even complete poems. A structure-marking recursion of form and content may occur at the beginning and end of the same unit: this is an *inclusio*. It may occur at the end of one unit and the beginning of the next: this is an instance of *anadiplosis* (e.g., *inter*-strophic: "all the earth" in Ps. 98:3/4; *intra*-strophic: "music" in Ps. 98:4b/5a). It may occur at the respective beginnings of different units: this is *anaphora*. And it may occur at the corresponding endings of different units: this is *epiphora*. But such instances of separated/nonadjacent/distant parallelism (as opposed to connected parallelism) always need to be examined together with other literary features (as listed above) according to the principles of convergence and harmony in order to determine the precise points of *aperture* and *closure* within a given psalm. The purpose of this type of analysis is threefold:

(1) To better understand how the original author formulated his text, consisting of various interrelated parts and wholes, lines and levels, in order to effectively convey important theological and religious truths and to carry out certain spiritual and ethical purposes.

(2) To gain knowledge by which we can improve our methods of communicating the same message in a meaningful way to diverse worldwide audiences today. In many cases, this will require an accurate translation of the original text in a completely different language and culture, utilizing natural linguistic and literary equivalents, including the appropriate markers of style and structure, both oral and written, that are appropriate to each indigenous discourse genre and also to the setting of religious communication in which the translation will be used.

(3) To guide us in the layout of a translation on the printed page so *readers* can more readily see and follow the larger discourse structure of the original through the text format. This, along

4.4 Some extended patterns of parallelism

To conclude our discussion of parallelism in Hebrew poetry, we need to consider several patterns of recursion in the Psalter that are more extensive and elaborate than those presented so far. In certain instances, they are so large that they encompass an entire psalm. In such cases, the arrangement that results will overlap with the linear organization discovered by the methods discussed earlier. Such patterns serve to highlight both form and meaning and to draw them together into a unity and harmony of purpose within the poetic work as a whole.

An example of a psalm with an extended symmetrical pattern is Psalm 132. It contains two general petitions that divide the complete text in half, into two major portions. The second of these is related to the first by *anaphora* (see sec. 4.1.3) In other words, the verses that mark this division (v. 2 and v. 11) are similar, though not the same in content.

```
v. ___   A: _____
         B: _____

v. ___   A: _____
         B: _____
```

If we look for all the internal markers of *aperture* and *closure* in Psalm 132, each of the following verses appears to be the beginning of a new segment (strophe): 2, 6, 10, 11, 13, and 17. This may or may not be the case, however. The symmetry of the whole, that is, the overall balance in the number of lines for the corresponding sections must be considered, too.

Exercise 4.4

1. What is similar about the four strophes of Psalm 132 that begin in vv. 2, 6, 11, and 13? Notice the larger parallel pattern that they form. Summarize the content of each of the two halves of this psalm: vv. 1–9 and 10–18. How does the little strophe at the end, vv. 17–18, fit into the total picture in terms of form and function. What purpose does it serve within the psalm as a whole? What markers come together in v. 18 to highlight this as the conclusion of the entire psalm?

2. Examine the translation of Psalm 132 in several English versions (and in your own language, if such a translation exists). Observe how it has been arranged. Are there any noteworthy differences from the analysis that you have made? Evaluate the differences for accuracy and naturalness with regard to the discourse features of a contemporary target language, either English (French) or your language.

4.4.1 The unfolding, step-by-step pattern

An unfolding, step-by-step ("terrace") pattern is seen in some psalms. It may be an extension of the overlapping or "staircase" type of parallelism that is sometimes found in adjacent lines, e.g.,

Ps. 77:16 (NIV):   *The waters saw you*, O God,
              The waters saw you and writhed;
                 The very depths were convulsed.

(In the Hebrew, the third line is marked as a climax by an exclamation and a chiastic syntactic arrangement.)

This complex pattern of parallelism transforms Psalm 132, for example, into an artistic unity of form, content, and purpose. In such a poem, there is a *sequence* of important religious concepts and key terms that reiterates something said earlier in the text, point by point or topic by topic. This can be seen in the second half of Psalm 132, as shown in Exercise 4.4.1.

Exercise 4.4.1

Summarize the prominent similarities and the overall meaning progression of the whole of Psalm 132 by writing the major correspondences (similarities or contrasts) in the spaces provided below:

A1 (v. 1): _____

  B1 (v. 2): _____

    C1 (vv. 3–5): _____

      D1 (vv. 6–7): _____

        E1 (v. 8): _____

          F1 (v. 9): _____

A2 (v. 10): _____

  B2 (v. 11a): _____

    C2 (vv. 11b–12): _____

      D2 (v. 13): _____

        E2 (v. 14): _____

          F2 (v. 15–16): _____

A3 (vv. 17–18): _____

The following is one possible way of indicating these correspondences (the words and concepts of special note are indicated in italics):

A1: petition—O LORD, *remember David* and all his hardships (1)

  B1: report—*he* (David) *swore an oath to the LORD*, the Mighty One of Jacob (2)

    C1: quote—a promise: "*I will find a place for the LORD*
                      a dwelling for the Mighty One of Jacob." (3–5)

      D1: a call to go to the *dwelling place* of the LORD (6–7)

        E1: invitation to the LORD to come to his *resting place*
           along with the *ark* of the covenant (8)

          F1: wish—"May *your priests be clothed with righteousness*;
             may *your saints sing for joy*." (9)

A2: petition—(O LORD) *do not reject your anointed one* (the king), for the sake of *David* (10)

   B2: report—*the LORD swore an oath to David* (11a)

      C2: quote—a promise: "*I will place one of your own descendants on your throne* for ever and ever." (11b-12)

         D2: *the Lord* has chosen Zion *for his dwelling place* (13)

            E2: the LORD declares Zion to be his eternal *resting place* where he will sit enthroned [upon the *ark*] (14)

               F2: grant—"*I will clothe her priests with salvation,* and *her saints will* ever *sing for joy*." (15-16)

A3: promise—the LORD declares that he will bless *the anointed one* and establish his kingship for *David's* sake (17-18)

How does this extended step-by-step unfolding structure function to emphasize the principal theme of Psalm 132? Does it help for the printed format of the text to be arranged accordingly to highlight the main aspects of this important message? Could such formatting be used in the translation of Psalm 132 in your language? Explain what could or could not be done and why.

4.4.2 The inverted pattern

Another common type of extended parallelism is the "inverted" sequential pattern. It sometimes appears in the larger organization of poetic discourse for the purpose of compositional artistry and thematic highlighting. It involves a *chiasmus* (X) within a high-level discourse unit, that is, a reversal in the order of corresponding elements from the first part of the overall structure to the second:

A - B - (C - N . . . N' - C') - B' - A'

This type of pattern consists of at least four elements (i.e., A + B + B' + A'), and it may extend to any number (N + N'). However, the number of elements does not usually go beyond seven or it becomes too difficult to recall. We have already observed the presence of "minor" structural inversions in some psalm texts. The following is a longer example from Psalm 12:3-4 (the parallel terms are underlined):

    A May the LORD cut off

      B all flattering lips

        C and every boastful tongue

          D that says,

        C' We will triumph with our tongues;

      B' we own our lips—

    A' who is our master?"

Here, the inverted structure mirrors the content of the petition which it expresses. The psalmist prays that Yahweh would reverse the impious boasts of the wicked and teach them through a just punishment who their true master is, namely, the LORD alone.

Exercise 4.4.2a

1. Study Psalm 30 in the NIV, especially with regard to its larger discourse structure. How many poetic segments, or strophes, does this psalm have? Which verses are included in each unit?

2. Identify the various markers that give evidence that these strophes do indeed begin and end where you have indicated. On a separate sheet of paper, write out the signals of *aperture* (and *closure* too, if relevant) for each of the poetic "paragraphs" of this psalm. The first segment has been done as an example:

   v. _1_: *The type or genre of this psalm is indicated by the psalmist's praise to God for some past deliverance (= "thanksgiving psalm"). The first line includes a vocative opener with the name of God ("LORD"). There is also a contrast in the final line which states what did* not *happen to the psalmist.*

   v. ___ : _____

   v. ___ : _____

   v. ___ : _____

   v. ___ : _____

3. What similarity to the opening line is found at the very end to indicate an *inclusio* for the psalm as a whole?

4. Now we will look at the verbal parallelism that runs throughout Psalm 30. It takes the form of a chiastic *inversion*. See if you can outline this structure by identifying the various words and concepts that seem to correspond (i.e., by means of similarity, contrast, statement-response, cause-effect, etc.) in the parallel pairs shown below. These pairs are indicated by means of the capital letters, verse numbers, vertical lines, and the different degrees of indentation at the left-hand margin.

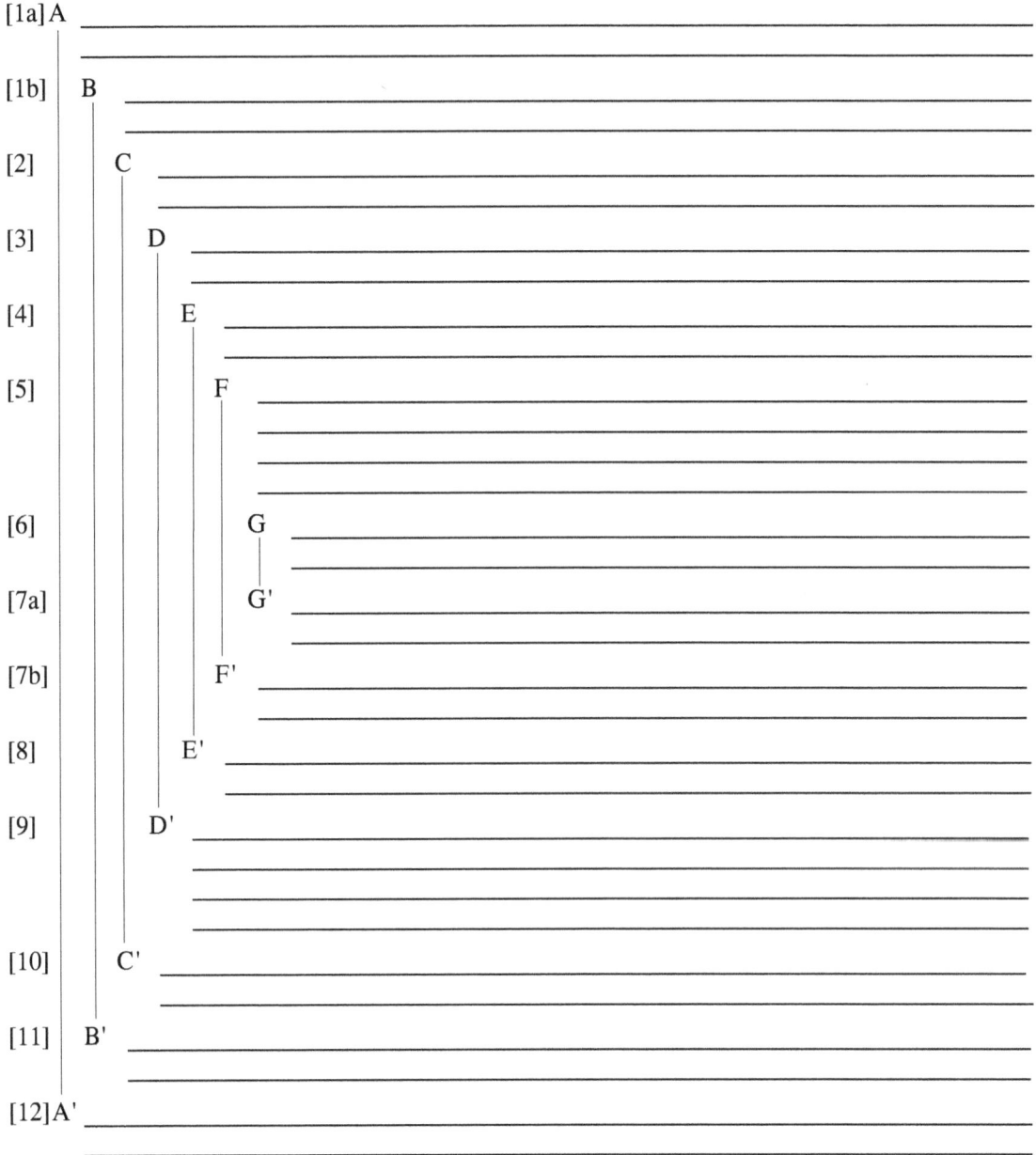

5. Where is the central core of this psalm and what is thematically significant about this particular pair of passages?

6. The outer borders, A-B and B'-A' indicate the major communicative purpose of Psalm 30, which involves a grounds–implication (reason-response) type of relation. Tell what this communicative purpose is. The following diagram gives an idea of how this psalm is symmetrically structured in the form of an inversion. (Its main correspondences are written in italics.) This is not the only way of organizing the principal ideas of this text, but it does seem to be valid in view of the repetition involved. See if you agree:

[1a] A *I will exalt you, O Lord,*

[1b]   B for you *lifted* me out of the depths,
and *did not let my enemies gloat over me.*

[2]   C *O Lord my God, I called to you for help*
           and *you healed me.*

[3]   D O L<small>ORD</small>, *you brought me up from the grave;*
               you spared me from going down into the pit.

[4]   E *Sing to the Lord,* you *saints of his;*
                   praise his holy name.

[5]   F For *his anger* lasts only a moment,
                       but his favor lasts a lifetime.
                       Weeping may remain for a night,
                       but rejoicing comes in the morning.

[6]   G *When I felt secure,* I said,
                           "*I will never be shaken.*"

[7a]   G' O L<small>ORD</small>, *when you favored me,*
                            you made my mountain stand firm;

[7b]   F' but when you *hid your face,*
                       I was *dismayed*.

[8]   E' *To you, O Lord, I called;*
                   to *the Lord I cried for mercy*:

[9]   D' "What gain is there in my destruction,
               in my going down into the pit?
               Will the dust praise you?
               Will it proclaim your faithfulness?

[10]   C' *Hear, O Lord, and be merciful to me;*
           O L<small>ORD</small>, *be my help.*"

[11] B' You *turned* my wailing into dancing;
         you *removed* my sackcloth and *clothed me with joy,*

[12] A' that my heart *may sing to you* and not be silent.
        O Lord my God, I will give you thanks forever.

Notice that the relation between the two parallels may be one of *contrast* rather than similarity (e.g., D and D'). It may also be observed that when there is an *even* number of units in such structural inversions, as is the case here, the main thematic point of the psalm tends to occur on the *final* outer boundary, that is, in the A'–B' elements. However, in Psalm 30 the central core (i.e., G–G') is also significant in terms of the message. Here it marks the psychological and spiritual turning point of the psalmist's prayer as he goes on to recall his earlier change from self-sufficiency to desperate faith. This even incorporates a segment of his former prayer to God in direct speech (D'-C'). The center of such chiastic constructions becomes especially important when there turns out to be an *odd* number of units because a principal peak in the content of the message is usually highlighted there. This will be evident when we analyze Psalm 54 in the next exercise.

Exercise 4.4.2b

1. To the extent that you are able, prepare a propositional, semantic-structure analysis of Psalm 30 according to the method described in chapter 3. Identify the binary relations at the verse level and, if possible, at the colon level; that is, specify the relations between the individual cola. You may check your analysis by referring to pp. 51–52 of the 1995 UBS monograph entitled

Discourse Perspectives on the Hebrew Poetry of the Scriptures, by E. Wendland (ed.). A diagram of the semantic propositional relations appears there.

2. Compare these two methods of analysis—the sequential (propositional) and the inverted (topical)—to chart the discourse organization of Psalm 30 as a whole. Do the two compositional patterns complement each other or conflict with one another? Explain your answer with two examples from Psalm 30.

3. How does the chiastic organization of Psalm 30 help you to understand and interpret the overall message? How does the study of a psalm's discourse structure enable you to format it typographically (visually) on the printed page? Briefly, what suggestions can you make about how to display the text of Psalm 30 in a meaningful and readable way?

Exercise 4.4.2c

Psalm 54, though short, has a very interesting compositional structure—or, rather, several complementary and overlapping patterns. As we try to identify these, we will see what they can tell us about the psalmist's message. First of all, examine Psalm 54 in the NIV. Note where the breaks occur and indicate the reasons for them. In the blank spaces below, fill in the terms for the type of markers that you see at each boundary. The first aperture has already been analyzed as an example.

v. 1: *imperative + vocative + divine name + strict parallelism* _____
v. : _____
v. : _____
v. : _____
v. : _____

Now consider what the psalmist is doing as he speaks each of the verses of his prayer: What *verbal action* (speech function) is he performing? What is the point or purpose of his words? Or we could say, what communicative effect (*illocutionary force*) does he want his words to have upon the persons to whom he is speaking (cf. the *NIV Study Bible* notes)? Describe these successive utterance functions in the spaces below (some may be synonymous):

v. 1: *an APPEAL to God for help (i.e., vindication, deliverance)* _____
v. 2: _____
v. 3: _____
v. 4: _____
v. 5: _____
v. 6: _____
v. 7: _____

Summarize in one line what you consider to be the central theme of Psalm 54. How does this theme relate to the genre of this psalm?

It is possible to view the different functions you just noted as matching one another in paired, but separated, fashion to form an inverted arrangement. Examine the following diagram of the prayer's inverted structure to see whether or not you agree with the general functional pattern shown:

[1] A   Save me, O God, by your name;   BASIS for the petition
          vindicate me by your might.

[2]   B   Hear my prayer, O God;   PETITION (general) to God
              listen to the words of my mouth.

[3]	C	Strangers are attacking me; ruthless men seek my life— men without regard for God. *Selah*	REASON for the petition
[4]	D	Surely, God is my help; the Lord is the one who sustains me.	EXPRESSION of trust in God
[5]	C'	Let evil recoil on those who slander me; in your faithfulness destroy them.	RESULT (intended) of the petition (specific)
[6]	B'	I will sacrifice a freewill offering to you; I will praise your name, O LORD, for it is good.	PROMISE to God
[7]	A'	For he has delivered me from all my troubles, and my eyes have looked in triumph on my foes.	BASIS for the promise

Here the parallel segments correspond not so much in their exactness of wording or content but in their petitionary purpose. It may be debated, therefore, whether this is in fact a genuine inversion, or simply a convenient matching of ideas. What do you think? The important thing for translators is to make sure that the overall pattern of principal themes and topical emphases as well as the sequence of major communicative motivations or intentions is clearly understood. These may then be reproduced in the target text, using the natural linguistic and rhetorical features of the target language.

What does the inverted structure suggest about the main idea(s) of Psalm 54? How does the central element, D, provide the foundation for everything that is said in this prayer? Can the printed format be arranged in a way that will highlight this main thought? What about indenting the other parallel ideas? Would that help the reader's understanding? Present your personal opinion with several reasons either way.

In our earlier examination of the genre we called *lament* (a petition to the LORD 2.1.1), we noted that this type of psalm often consists of seven basic functional elements. See whether you can match the verses of Psalm 54 with each of these parts:

(1) *appeal*   v. _____   (4) *request*   v. _____   (7) *promise* v. _____
(2) *problem*   v. _____   (5) *defense*   v. _____
(3) *complaint* v. _____   (6) *profession* v. _____

Now examine Psalm 54 more closely, observing the skillful manner in which the psalmist has organized these typical lament elements in a balanced way, at the same time also highlighting the principal thought of the composition as a whole. His poetic technique includes the use of so-called word pairs—closely associated lexical items (see chap. 6), such as "name–might" and "save–vindicate" in v. 1, and in v. 2 "hear–give ear" and "prayer–words of my mouth."

Indeed, the lexical parallelism is very tight between the respective lines of the individual bi- and tri-cola. But the semantic relations between adjacent bicola, or verses, are not always very obvious. In fact, it seems almost as if the corresponding verses of the inverted pattern are more closely linked together. Thus the development of meaning in this psalm is as follows:

The psalmist begins by stating the basis, A, for his initial appeal in B. This was the foundation upon which his faith rested, namely the might and reputation ("name") of God. (Note that the divine name *Yahweh* is not explicitly mentioned until the end of the psalm, in v. 6b.) Similarly, the pray-er concludes A' by affirming the basis, or reason, for the promise which he has just made in B'. This vow to thank and praise God in B' corresponds to the earlier prayer that he made to God in B, a petition which the psalmist, in fervent trust (perhaps based on past experience), considers to have been already answered. In both C and C' he speaks about the specific source of his troubles, namely his enemies. Notice that the seemingly harsh call for vengeance (the imprecation in C') is not made for the psalmist's own sake, as personal revenge, but rather because his adversaries justly deserve such punishment: they are "men without regard for God" (C). Thus, he calls upon God to defend his holy honor and at the same time to vindicate his (the psalmist's) confidence in God's power to deliver his people (cf. v. 1). The central core of the lament presents the theme: a firm confession of faith in the Lord (D), specifically in his ability to help and sustain all those who put their trust in him.

In sum then, we can see the close connection between the middle of the psalm and its beginning and ending; that is, the initial appeal (A) is answered in deliverance and victory (A'). This fact, in turn, is a justification of the psalmist's strong trust in God (D).

The start, finish, and center are crucial points of emphasis in Hebrew prayer-poems. Time and again, we see that the poetic couplets placed in these positions express the key aspects of the theological and/or ethical message. These same thematic emphases, as well as the various logical relationships which join them into a unified composition, also need to be conveyed in a translation, along with as much as possible of the emotive power and literary beauty of the original text.

Exercise 4.4.2d

Now we will take a closer look at the logical relationships that tie Psalm 54 together. Study the diagram below and compare it with the sequence of paired parallel cola of the complete text. Then try to identify the semantic relations that join the poetic lines together to form ever larger groups. Write these in the blank spaces to the right of the diagram. Then compare your results with those of another student to check for any differences. Discuss these points of disagreement and try to resolve them. Any outstanding differences can be brought to the class for further discussion as time allows.

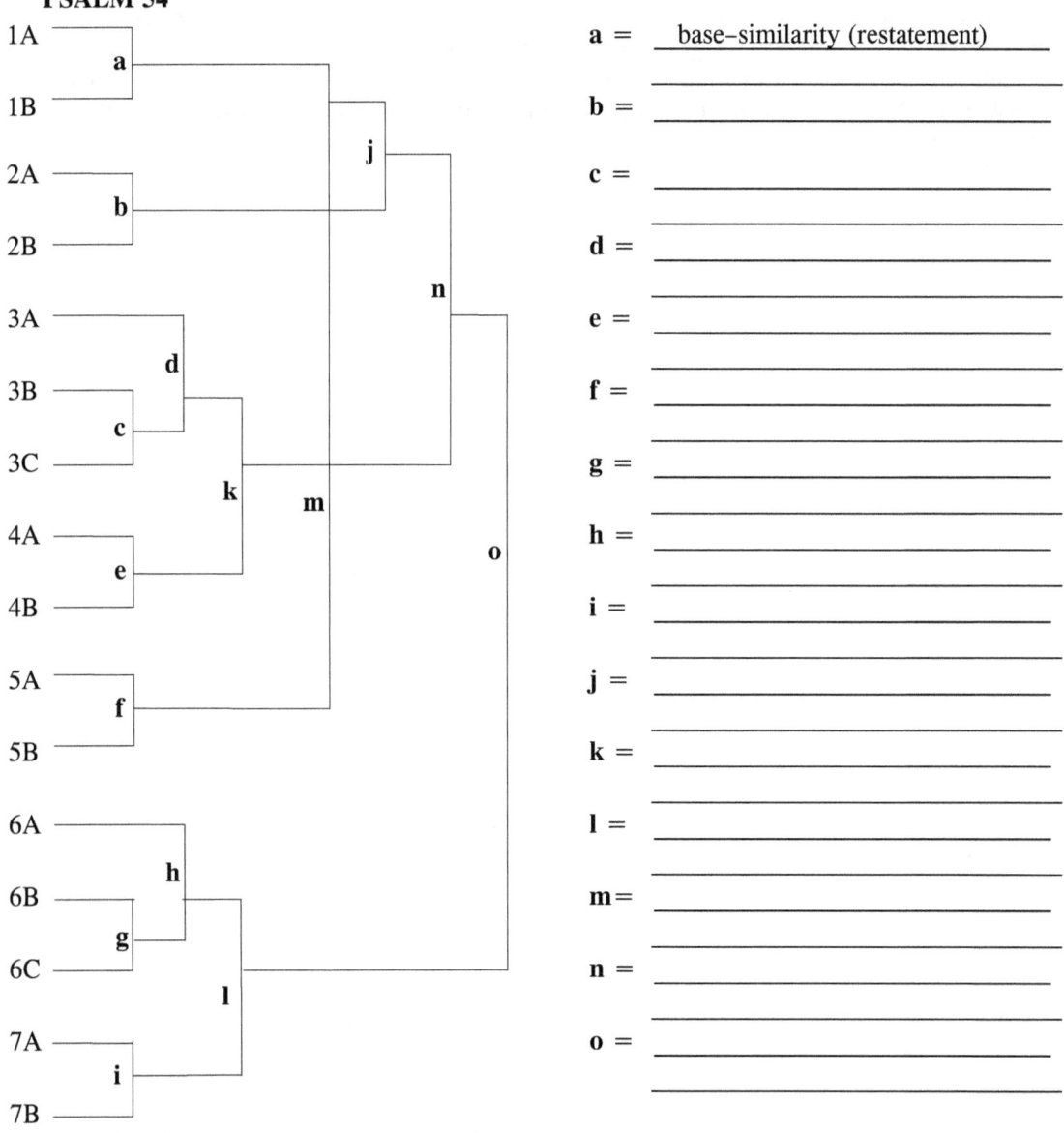

PSALM 54

a = base-similarity (restatement)
b =
c =
d =
e =
f =
g =
h =
i =
j =
k =
l =
m =
n =
o =

Considering this psalm as a whole, where does the most significant break occur? What is the evidence that leads you to this conclusion? Can you suggest a reason for this? What is happening as far as the internal development of the discourse goes? What is the psalmist's point here?

According to the propositional analysis above, v. 5 appears to be out of position; that is, it relates to v. 1 in particular. Can you suggest any reason for this in view of where the major break in the psalm occurs? Is this psalm a natural way of praying to God in your own language and culture? Point out any features in the development or arrangement of this Hebrew prayer that sound strange or unnatural in comparison with typical prayers that you hear in your language. Are these likely to cause any misunderstanding? Explain.

Exercise 4.4.2e

Make a complete structural analysis of Psalm 64 by answering the following questions:

1. List the five constituent strophes. Give reasons for the way you have segmented the text, mentioning the key signals that serve to mark the boundaries (*aperture* and *closure*) of the individual strophes. Write these down on a separate piece of paper.

2. Prepare an analysis of the whole psalm, identifying the various semantic relations between bicola or colon clusters and writing them out in the spaces below:

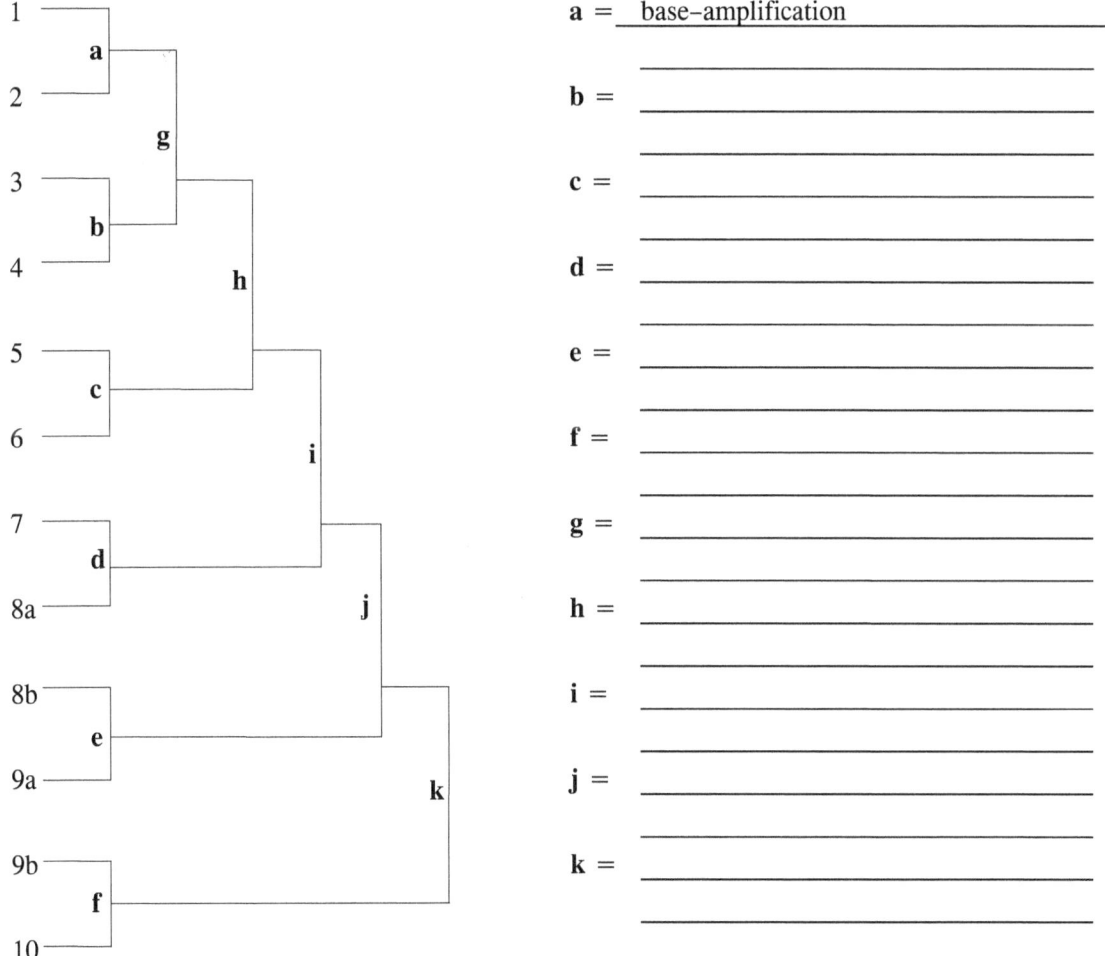

a = base-amplification

b =

c =

d =

e =

f =

g =

h =

i =

j =

k =

Observe the impressive manner in which this psalm is progressively built up. Where would you expect the thematic peak to be? Why? There is a little *asymmetry* in the sequence of cola in vv. 8-9. What is this in terms of the text, and how does it affect the meaning of this section?

3. In view of the corresponding key terms in each of the parallel segments, it may be that Psalm 64 was also intended to operate as a *chiasmus*. See if you can construct this inversion by filling in the blank spaces beside each capital letter with the verses that belong to each segment. Then give

a summary of the content that corresponds between each linked pair of similar letters. Also underline the key terms from each parallel set.

verses   *topical/lexical correspondences*

A ___ : _____

    B ___ _: _____

       C ___ _: _____

          D ___ _: _____

          D' ___ _: _____

       C' ___ _: _____

    B' ___ _: _____

A' ___ _: _____

What is emphasized in the central core of this inverted structure (D-D')? What is the psalmist's main message in the final conclusion? (In this, an "even"-membered chiasmus, it is the ending that is especially highlighted.) What special encouragement is given in this psalm for the people of God? Is this message relevant today to the people of your culture? Explain. How does the structure of Psalm 64 as a whole help to communicate its highly emotive message?

5. LOWER-LEVEL STYLISTIC FEATURES OF HEBREW POETRY

Parallelism, both near and far, with major and minor correspondence, is probably the most important aspect of style in Hebrew poetry to consider when doing a discourse analysis. Parallelism provides *continuity* in a text, which has to do with the smooth forward progression of both form (structure) and content (theme) from one point to another. In the process, as we have seen, it helps to *demarcate* the discourse into distinct compositional segments on several levels of structural organization. This is done through the reiteration of key words and corresponding concepts at the initial and concluding boundaries of the larger poetic units.

But in addition to parallelism, there are a number of other literary devices that can help mark discourse boundaries within the text. These include figures of speech, rhetorical questions, shifts in word order, emphatic utterance, and direct speech. These usually involve, to a greater or lesser extent, some sort of *discontinuity*—an interruption that makes the audience pause and take notice. This sort of "heightened" language creates a measure of surprise or interest in the discourse at the point where it appears. Listeners/readers then give extra attention to how the words are being used and why. Thus the use of these rhetorical devices always adds a degree of emphasis, especially when a number of them occur together in combination. Oftentimes, such a convergence of forms also helps to indicate the beginning or ending of a particular segment of the text, or it may serve to highlight some aspect of special significance to the poet's central theme or sub-theme (the emotive "climax" or topical "peak").

These stylistic features used in conjunction with parallelism build the unique discourse structure of a given literary composition. Together they create the larger form and framework of message organization used by the poet to convey his intended meaning. (By *meaning* is meant semantic content plus rhetorical purpose, including impact, appeal, and relevance.)

In this chapter we will survey a number of the more important of these special poetic techniques: that is *repetitive, figurative, condensed, varied,* and *resonant* language. At the end of the chapter (sec. 5.7) we will note once again some of the primary communicative functions of such stylistic devices.

5.1 Repetitive language

In chapters 3 and 4 we saw how parallelism operates to give unity to a psalm at the same time that it helps divide the text into discrete units. A crucial aspect of the analysis of the different types of parallelism to be found in a psalm, then, is to examine the various kinds of repetition that it manifests. Especially important—due to its visibility (or hearability)—is the recursion of lexical items, whether key terms, phrases, or entire clauses. Such iteration, which includes the introduction of opposing or contrasting ideas, is the foundation for the distinctive Hebrew poetic technique of balanced parallel expression. As we have seen, it is also often employed at the higher levels of a discourse, both to shape its overall organization and to stress items of particular importance.

But repetition involves much more than lineal parallelism, which is generally manifested in two-part structures such as a bicolon. It also includes the reiteration of individual sounds, words, ideas, and grammatical categories. Although it is difficult to recognize this feature in all of its variety, without a knowledge of Hebrew, it *is* relatively easy to detect the repetition of *words*, and even of *concepts* expressed by synonyms and antonyms, with the help of a literal translation. In this section we will concentrate on the easily discerned feature of lexical repetition. Where phonological, morphological, or syntactic repetition is involved, it will be pointed out and discussed if it is important in a given passage.

5.1.1 Individual words

Earlier, we focused our attention on patterned lineal repetition in Hebrew poetic discourse. This we might call *recursion* to distinguish it from non-structured, primarily (individual) lexical *repetition*, to which we now turn our attention.

Repetition refers to the kind of limited restatement which does not, on the surface of the text, seem to be part of a larger structural arrangement. It may occur within a single bicolon to highlight that unit's function in the text (i.e., as an aperture or closure), or it may be dispersed more or less throughout a text, positioned irregularly within a pericope, where it serves to develop the main theme or to stress some significant supporting idea. Another very important structural function of repetition is that it supplies *cohesion*, or topical connectivity, to the particular discourse segment in which it is found. This is an important aspect of all well-formed texts, whether literary or otherwise. For not only do distinct boundaries mark a compositional unit, but such a unit by its very nature is also connected *internally*. That is, it hangs together from beginning to end, as well as being linked by its external boundaries with other segments within the larger whole, whether adjacent or distant. In the exercise that follows, we will look at the feature of lexical iteration in relation to certain key terms that are repeated more or less exactly within a given span of discourse.

Exercise 5.1.1

1. Count the number of times the following lexical items (or words formed from the same stem) appear in the psalms referred to. A very literal translation (e.g., NASB) or interlinear version will be needed for this exercise. Next, do another count, this time including any synonyms of the key words listed below. Then tell how the ideas that these repeated words express or relate to the main message of the psalm, or how the repetition functions to foreground a point of special compositional importance in the discourse.

psalm	word	times	*thematic and/or structural significance*
3	deliver(ance)		
6	LORD		
7	righteous(ness)		
13	how long?		
24	glory		
29	voice of the LORD		
48	city		
66	praise		
77	remember		
84	LORD Almighty		
89	faithful(ness)		
112	righteous(ness)		
121	watch over		
122	peace		
126	joy		

2. Are any of the repeated terms or concepts referred to above difficult to express in your language? Do any of these words have to be rendered differently due to the context? Describe any problems that you encounter in this regard. How can such difficulties best be handled in order to convey the intended meaning?

3. List four of the repeated expressions that are found in Psalm 118. Then tell how these are related in meaning, both to one another and to the main message of the whole psalm. Do any of the repeated sets have some structural significance? If so, explain what this is.

4. Find another psalm in which a key term is repeated three or more times. Tell how this word or phrase relates to the main theme or a sub-theme of this psalm. Can it be rendered by the same expression on every occasion in your language? Explain.

5.1.2 Word pairs and related sets of terms

One of the prominent stylistic features of Hebrew poetry is the periodic occurrence of word pairs, often called *doublets*. The words of a doublet are paired words in the same grammatical class (e.g., both are nouns or both are verbs) and closely related in meaning or reference. The first word of the pair tends to be better known and more frequent. It generally appears in line A of a bicolon, and the second word of the pair in line B. The following are examples: "head"—"skull" (Ps. 7:16, JB); "mounted up"—"went down" (Ps. 107:26, NRSV); "desert"—"desert of Kadesh" (29:8, JB); "wine"—"oil" (Ps. 104:15, NRSV); "hear"—"listen to" (Ps. 61:1); "my teaching"—"words of my mouth" (Ps. 78:1, NRSV); "king"—"royal son" (Ps. 72:1). In most cases, the terms occur in the same order, and hence a reversal may be of some rhetorical or structural importance in the text. (For a listing of a number of well-known parallel pairs, see Index 5 of W. Watson's *Classical Hebrew Poetry*.)

In some psalms, terms that are synonymous or contrastive in meaning, or belong to the same general semantic field, or have the same referent, are used in sets larger than just a pair. Such larger groups of synonyms are used to convey the principal theme or to highlight some particular aspect of the message being communicated, as will be seen in exercise 5.1.2a.

Exercise 5.1.2a

1. A relatively large number of word pairs occur in Psalm 54. (This may be an indication that this text is of *oral* origin.) Identify each pair, filling in the blanks. Then look up the verse given in parentheses to see if this same pair (or a synonymous pair) is used elsewhere.

v. 1 (cf. 106:8)	= _____	+ _____
v. 1 (cf. 76:9)	= _____	+ _____
v. 2 (cf. 39:12, 49:1)	= _____	+ _____
v. 2 (cf. 88:2)	= _____	+ _____
v. 3 (cf. 86:14)	= _____	+ _____
v. 4 (cf. 68:17)	= _____	+ _____
v. 5 (cf. 94:23)	= _____	+ _____
v. 6 (cf. 116:17)	= _____	+ _____
v. 7 (cf. 138:7)	= _____	+ _____

2. Does the secular or religious poetry of your language, oral or written, use synonyms in this way, either in pairs or in larger sets? Describe any noteworthy similarities to, or differences from, Hebrew poetic style, along with some examples, if possible.

3. In the psalm indicated, write out all the words and phrases (including figures of speech and obvious contrastive terms) that are related to the topic indicated. Following each word or phrase, write in parentheses the verse number in which it is found.

psalm	topic	*synonymous (or contrasting) expressions*
19	law	_____
27	temple	_____
34	righteous	_____
	deliver	_____
51	sin	_____
71	proclaim	_____

77	miracles	_____
	water/storm	_____
81	Israel	_____
90	days/years	_____
92	enemies	_____
104	mountains	_____

3. Write down all the words in Psalm 145 that are related in meaning to "say/speak." In what way does this repetition emphasize the psalm's main theme? Do the same thing for all the words expressing "time" in Psalm 90 and relate this to its theme.

4. Psalm 119 is known for containing many words that refer to the same topic. What is this topic? Give an example of a passage where many such words occur and list them.

   _____

   Are you able to reproduce this diversity in your language, either literally or in a figurative way? Explain. Cite several examples.

5. Examine the lexical pattern of repetition in Psalm 148. How does it serve to structure the entire psalm? What is the point of all this repetition?

6. Many scholars think that Psalms 111 and 112 are "twins," that they were composed together by the same poet and intended to be sung together. Carefully compare these two psalms. Write out any terms or expressions that you find in *both* psalms, noting also the respective verse numbers. What is the common theme of these two psalms?

7. In Psalm 106 the principal repeated ideas may be grouped into two general categories. What are these?
   A. _____   B. _____

   How do these two sets of concepts relate to the main purpose of this psalm?

8. Try to find another psalm, but not 136, that contains a great deal of repetition. Explain how this repetition functions to tell us something about the psalm's structural organization or its thematic meaning. Now check the TEV or CEV and note the places where the repetition has *not* been retained. Evaluate what was done, giving reasons for your opinion.

Hendiadys is another type of iterative technique. It is a figure of speech in which a single complex concept, normally an entity modified by some quality, is expressed by two distinct, but related nouns, often joined by "and" (*waw*). The following is an example:

   Fear and trembling have beset me . . . (Ps. 55:5)

Remember, the conjoined components of a hendiadys are not to be considered separately, but as a single unit. In line A of Psalm 55:5, the psalmist is not talking about being troubled by two different things, but rather by one, a great fear that may indeed have had the physical consequences of a trembling body (i.e., cause => effect). This same experience is more intensively described in line B: "horror has overwhelmed me."

   A hendiadys can also be formed by verbs rather than nouns, as illustrated in the next passage:

   When may I *come and see* the face of God? (Ps. 42:2)

The focal verb in this case is not "come." (It is sometimes omitted in translation as, e.g., in CEV.) Rather the important action is "see"; that is, the psalmist eagerly desires close fellowship with his God in a worship experience. The "see" concept is intensified by "come" in this hendiadys; alternatively, "come" may be interpreted as expressing the ingressive *mood*, i.e., "*begin* to see."

The next example, Psalm 69:17, also illustrates a verbal hendiadys construction, but there is no linking conjunction. The manner in which the principal event is to be carried out is indicated by the minor event. In the NIV this hendiadys is rendered "answer me quickly, for I am in trouble," but literally it is:

    and-not=you-hide your-face from-your-servant,
    for=trouble [is] to-me; make-haste [a] answer-me [b].

Exercise 5.1.2b

1. Underline the hendiadys in each of the following texts (all very literal renderings). Tell what special sense or significance it has in its verbal context. Note any specific problems that you encounter in translating these related expressions in your own language. Consult several modern English translations and cite those that do a good job of handling these instances of hendiadys.

   — I would lead them to the house of God with the sound of joy and thanksgiving . . . (Ps. 42:4)

   — Vindicate me, O God, and plead my case . . .
   from a deceitful and evil person deliver me! (Ps. 43:1)

   — You sit against your brother you speak,
   against the son of your mother you give slander. (Ps. 50:20)

   — May they be shamed and may they be confused together,
   the ones seeking my life to take it. (Ps. 40:14)
   (*Note:* The adverb *yaḥad,* "together," often marks a hendiadys in the Hebrew text.)

   — Send forth your light and your truth;
   as for them, let them guide me,
   let them bring me to the mountain of your holiness and to your dwellings. (Ps. 43:3)

   — He scatters, he gives to the poor his righteousness enduring forever . . . (Ps. 112:9)

   — Oh, they are for destruction in suddenness,
   they are swept away, they are completed in terrors. (Ps. 73:19)

   — May they be ashamed and may they be dismayed forever,
   and may they be disgraced and may they perish. (Ps. 83:17)

   — God spoke from his sanctuary,
   I will triumph, I will parcel out Shechem . . . (Ps. 68:6)

   — He alone is my rock and my salvation . . . (Ps. 62:2)

   — . . . you have established strength because of your enemies,
   to silence the foe and the avenger. (Ps. 8:2)

2. Find and analyze one example of hendiadys from Psalm 42 and one from Psalm 71. Can you suggest a more idiomatic way of translating these?

5.2 Figurative language

As we saw, the feature of repetition, whether exact or synonymous in nature, contributes a great deal to the "continuity" of discourse. We now turn to consider a compound feature that may contribute to a certain *discontinuity* within a text, namely, figurative language. This literary device, if not too common or overused, creates a little break or shift in the flow of discourse that causes the reader or hearer to pause and take notice. Lexical iteration can also serve this purpose if the repetition happens to be concentrated within a relatively short span of the text. For example, the psalmist's mockery of pagan idols in Psalm 135:15–18 is suddenly cut short by a repeated call to "praise the LORD" as his prayer reaches its climax in vv. 19–21.(Notice the inclusio that is formed with the beginning of this psalm in vv. 1–3.)

By "figurative language" is meant the poet's use of certain words, phrases, and even entire clauses or sentences in a way that is noticeably different from normal usage. The words mean something other than what one would initially expect upon reading or hearing them. They are not used "literally," that is, in their most common, or general, sense, but convey some additional meaning, one that often appeals to the listener's imagination and sensory perception.

The use of figurative language—if it is fresh and creative—normally requires the persons addressed to exert greater mental effort to determine the intended sense. But they are compensated by the novelty, beauty, or forcefulness of the expression and given a modified or even a completely new perspective on familiar persons, objects, and events. Frequency of use is an important factor here, for when a figurative expression is employed often, it becomes familiar, even expected, and its vividness and impact are correspondingly decreased. However, due to the *ritual* (evocative) function of language, reiteration may serve to enhance the effect of certain important religious symbols and images of great sociocultural significance, for example, the "wine," "oil," and "bread" referred to in Ps. 104:15.

Many figurative devices (e.g., metaphors and similes) involve the mental picturing of something, which we call the *topic* (T), by an *image* (I), on the basis of a recognized point of similarity between the two (or a set of closely related features). This point of similarity is often called the *ground* of comparison (G).

The topic is that entity or event which the poet wishes to describe or explain in a vivid, forceful, unusual, or simply non-repetitious way. Alternatively, he is dealing with a concept or experience that is difficult to describe using ordinary language. Hence he uses a concrete (sense-related) image, an illustration from the everyday world of human life and reality. By using the image in a new or unexpected verbal context he draws attention to the topic. In Scripture, the topic often has something to do with God—his will, works, and ways—in an effort to express something about the *inexpressible*, namely, the One who stands above all human knowledge and the semantic potential of language. The imagery may also serve to express the strong feelings and attitudes of the poet in an effort to arouse the same in his listeners/readers. The aim is to evoke a more forceful response to, or a closer identification with, the message. Indeed, it is such "word pictures" that give poetry its special rhetorical power to affect our understanding, memory, emotion, and volition so deeply.

Imagery always involves some form of *comparison* or a close semantic *connection* between the topic and image. The more novel, unusual, or unexpected the imagery is, the greater its impact upon the reader or listener. As noted above, commonly used pictures do not usually make a great sense impression, but they may still be highly valued due to their familiar or referentially significant associations, especially in religious literature with a long liturgical and teaching tradition.

5.2.1 Simile

When a comparison between a topic (T) and its image (I) is explicit, then we are dealing with a figure of speech known as *simile*. In a simile, the ground or basis of comparison (G) may be stated or left unexpressed, but there is always an overt *marker* (M), such as "like" or "as," to indicate the non-literal nature of the expression:

> They are *like* a lion eager to tear. (Ps. 17:12)

In the preceding example, the topic, image, and ground of comparison, respectively, are "they" (the people under discussion), "lion," and the rapaciousness common to both. Notice that the ground of comparison is suggested here by the words "eager to tear." The primary, nonfigurative sense of these words is violent behavior, a desire to destroy. This is how the topic being referred to, "they," is described as behaving.

It is important to study the context of any simile carefully in order to determine the main point of similarity, that is, the "ground of comparison." A simple example is found in Ps. 38:13: "But I (T) am like (M) a deaf man (I), I do not hear (G)." The topic and the image may be similar in more than one respect; still, the context often will make it possible for the analyst to identify the component of correspondence that is primarily intended.

The following example is a case in point: "He lurks in secret like a lion in his covert" (Ps. 10:9). In this passage the image of the lion again appears, but the context shows that a somewhat different point of similarity is in view: stealth and cunning, used for a harmful purpose. This is suggested by the words, "lurk in secret" and "in his covert."

In most passages, however, the simile's ground of comparison is not explicitly stated; it is left *implicit*. The psalmist expected that the original reader or hearers either knew it or could readily figure it out from the context. For today's receptors, however, this cannot be taken for granted, especially since they may not be familiar with the sociocultural or ecological context of many of these images. For example, in "He made my feet like hind's feet" (Ps. 18:33), it is not so easy for us today to immediately identify the ground of the comparison. However, in this case, the ground is suggested in the B line of the bicolon. Here, examining the context proves helpful: "He enables me to stand on the heights" (NIV), that is, firmly—without falling.

To analyze a given biblical simile then, we normally follow these three steps: First we must discover or discern the *image* in the passage at hand. Next, we locate the *topic* that the image is descriptively referring to. Finally, we examine the surrounding context as well as any other passages in which the same image appears in order to specify the most relevant *ground* of comparison. This would be the particular way (or ways) in which the image and topic appear to be related, that is, the specific associations that their combination would most likely evoke in the minds of the intended audience within its Ancient Near Eastern religious and cultural setting.

Exercise 5.2.1

1. Analyze the following two similes:

    Let them vanish like water that flows away. (Ps. 58:7)

    T = _____   I = _____
    G = _____

    My bones burn like glowing embers. (Ps. 102:3)

    T = _____   I = _____
    G = _____

    The "ground" for each of these similes is found in the immediate context. It is always necessary to fully examine every instance of imagery within its own compositional setting, including the other words with which the figure is used as well as the surrounding verses, in order to gain a correct or more precise interpretation. Most exegetical commentaries along with the THP or the NIV-SB will help you to do this. It is always good to consult such books to see if there is something that you may have missed, especially with regard to the original biblical setting of such imagery.

2. Find and analyze the simile in Psalm 2:9:

    T = _____   I = _____
    G = _____

    Now analyze the similes in the following passages; notice that the ground of comparison is not explicitly stated:

Psalm 14:4 T = _____ I = _____
          G = _____

Psalm 36:6a T = _____ I = _____
           G = _____

Psalm 36:6b T = _____ I = _____
           G = _____

Psalm 78:52 T = _____ I = _____
           G = _____

Would any of these similes be difficult to translate meaningfully in your language? If so, mention some of the problems that you would anticipate. Usually such difficulties have to do with the basis of comparison, when the image does not call to mind the same common ground that the original readers or hearers would have thought of.

3. Find five additional examples of a simile in the psalms. Analyze them in the spaces below:

Psalm ____ T = _____ I = _____
           G = _____

Psalm ____ T = _____ I = _____
           G = _____

Psalm ____ T = _____ I = _____
           G = _____

Psalm ____ T = _____ I = _____
           G = _____

Psalm ____ T = _____ I = _____
           G = _____

Point out any special problems you would face when trying to render these similes literally in your language and cultural environment. Can you suggest any possible solutions?

5.2.2 Metaphor

A metaphor functions in much the same way as a simile, except more directly and thus often more forcefully. It is a figure of speech in which a *topic* is immediately associated with an *image*. A metaphor differs from a simile in that it is not openly stated that a comparison is being made. That is, there is *no* overt marker such as "like" or "as." This makes the mental connection between the "image" (I) and its "topic" (T) more immediate; thus the comparison usually conveys greater impact as in "I *am* a worm" (Ps. 22:6a). Here the topic is "I," the image is "worm," and the *ground* of comparison, which is explicitly given in the nearby context, refers to something that is scorned and despised (v. 6b).

As we see in the preceding example, the colon (whether A or B) that is parallel to the one containing the image is often very helpful in providing guidance for interpretation. In most metaphors in the Psalms the ground of comparison is not explicitly stated in the text, but the context (coupled with one's knowledge of the biblical world and related biblical literature) is usually enough to indicate the desired connection. This is true for Psalm 18:2, "The LORD is my rock," and Psalm 22:16, "Dogs are round about me." But in other passages, one must carefully study the relevant historical, cultural, biological, and geographical setting as well as the religious practices of ancient Israel. An example of this is Psalm 60:8, "Moab is my washbasin" (or "waterpot," i.e., a common household utensil normally used by servants).

Sometimes even the topic of a metaphor may be left partially or wholly implicit and only the image is present. We see an instance of this in Psalm 43:3; "Oh (God), send out thy light and thy truth; let them lead me." In this case, the images of light and truth are related and are most likely a reference to God's Word (the *torah*) (cp. Ps. 40:10).

Some images, such as "snow" (Ps. 51:7), cause difficulty simply because they do not have a close equivalent in the target culture. Another example of this is in Psalm 9:9, "The LORD is a stronghold for the oppressed." Here, the "stronghold" is a high rocky place or a thick wall surrounding a city or some strongly fortified structure within city walls. Such hills and strongholds were places to which people could flee for refuge or protection when enemies attacked (cf. Ps. 11:1). But this image is not familiar to most people today (for whom mountains are simply barriers to cross or places for recreational activities). However, there might be a similar hiding place in some cultural settings, some specific location to which people can flee for safety. But suppose there is not; then the translator must find some other meaningful way to render this verse. If it can be done so as to preserve the original poetic impact, that would be the best option (e.g., through the use of related imagery or an ideophone) .

Exercise 5.2.2a

1. In Psalm 52:8 we find an important Old Testament figure (a simile). Check a commentary, the THP, a Bible handbook, study Bible, dictionary, or encyclopedia in order to determine the significance of the *olive tree* in the life-setting of the people of Palestine. What is the ground of comparison for this simile (cp. Ps. 93:14)?

    Do the same for the following simile:

    When the Almighty scattered the kings in the land,
    it was like snow fallen on Zalmon. (Ps. 68:14)

    T = _____   I = _____
    G = _____

2. Identify the topic, image, and ground of comparison in the following metaphor:

    You anoint my head with oil. (Ps. 23:5)

    What Hebrew custom is being referred to here and what is its significance? What would a literal translation of this picture mean in your cultural setting? Do you have any custom that is similar either in *form* (i.e., outward features) or *function* (i.e., social purpose)? Explain.

3. Use the THP to help you to interpret this complex verbal metaphor: "I will bridle my mouth" (Ps. 39:1).

4. What does the psalmist mean when he describes God metaphorically as being "a father to the fatherless" (Ps. 68:5)?

5. Find five additional metaphors in the psalms and analyze them below. You may need to refer to the *NIV Study Bible,* a commentary, or the THP for assistance.

    Psalm ____   T = _____   I = _____
                  G = _____

    Psalm ____   T = _____   I = _____
                  G = _____

    Psalm ____   T = _____   I = _____
                  G = _____

    Psalm ____   T = _____   I = _____
                  G = _____

Psalm _____   T = _____   I = _____
          G = _____

6. Of the metaphors referred to in assignment 5, which one would make the greatest impression in your language and culture? Explain. Which one would be the most difficult to translate? Why? How can you best render this figure in a meaningful, powerful way?

Both metaphors and similes may be "extended"; that is, one image may lead to another one closely associated with it, and perhaps to yet another one, to form a cluster of related pictures, which may be continued either implicitly or explicitly throughout an entire psalm. Consider Psalm 64:3-4, for example (cf. 64:5-8):

> [Evil men] whet their tongues like swords,
> [they] aim bitter words like arrows,
>   shooting from ambush at the blameless,
>   shooting at him suddenly and without fear.

This imagery is drawn from warfare, likening the psalmist's enemies and God's enemies to swordsmen and archers. Such imagery is very appropriate in this particular context that entreats God for protection from dangerous conspirators (cf. Ps. 37:14-15). The figurative topic of warfare is a common one in the Psalter; however, the details of the individual images that are used to depict the plight of God's people and his coming to their defense tend to vary considerably so these passages do not become monotonous and lose their impact (e.g., Pss. 2, 18, 60, 110, 149).

More frequently used than an extended image are combinations of *different* pictures that form a long, diverse chain of images. The primary ideas in such a chain may be either similar or different in nature, but the overall topic or point is the same. In the two passages that follow, several distinct images are found in each one:

> As smoke is driven away,
>   so drive them away;
> as wax melts before the fire
>   let the wicked perish before God! (Ps. 68:2)

Notice that the respective grounds of comparison in the two images here are somewhat different. However, they *are* related in that smoke and melting wax both vanish relatively quickly. In the next passage the first double simile's ground of comparison is explicit (durability), while that of the second simile is implicit (refreshing, life-giving):

> He will endure as long as the sun,
>   as long as the moon, through all generations.
> He will be like rain falling on a mown field,
>   like showers watering the earth. (Ps. 72:5-6)

Notice that the CEV has made the ground of comparison of the second simile explicit in its translation: "helpful as rain that refreshes the meadows." This may be required in some other languages as well. Furthermore, it may be necessary to specify the nature of the "field" as being "plowed" or "planted" (instead of "mown") in order to fit the local cultural setting.

Exercise 5.2.2b

1. A great deal of imagery, both extended and combined, is used to heighten the impact of the message in *Psalm 80*. Give the topics and grounds for each of the similes or metaphors listed below. Be sure to study the context of each figure as well as the psalm as a whole to help with your interpretation; consult the CEV and THP as well.

v. 1 "Shepherd": T = _____
        G = _____

    "flock": T = _____
        G = _____

    "shine forth": I = _____   T = _____
        G = _____

v. 5 "fed (them)": T = _____
        G = _____

As in v. 1, when the image is an action, or is connected with an action, the interpretation is more difficult than when the image is a thing (noun). In such cases, one must try to reconstruct the entire scene or situation that is being alluded to by the figure in order to determine which aspects of it apply to the topic. This is especially true for an extended figure, as we have in v. 5 (see the THP for some guidance).

v. 8 "grapevine": T = _____
        G = _____

    "you planted it": T = _____
        G = _____

v. 9 "clear the ground for it": T = _____
        G = _____

    "it took deep root": T = _____
        G = _____

v. 10 "its shade": T = _____
        G = _____

v. 11 "its branches": T = _____
        G = _____

v. 12 "broken down its walls": T = _____
        G = _____

    "pick its fruit": T = _____
        G = _____

v. 13 "the boar from the forest": T = _____
        G = _____

v. 15 "the root": T = _____
        G = _____

v. 16 "burned it with fire": T = _____
        G = _____

2. The abundance of images—similar and contrasting, pleasing and shocking, yet all skillfully woven together—is what makes Psalm 80 so beautiful, a powerful expression of the poet's lament to the LORD. Is it possible to convey this same emotional impact in your language? Point out where any special problems occur in this text with respect either to interpretation or translation.

3. Notice how the text of Psalm 80 is structured. A repeated refrain occurs three times at the end of each of its three major segments. (This is the repetitive compositional device termed closure, or *epiphora*.) Which verses make up these three poetic sections, or strophes?

   I. vv. _____   II. vv. _____   III. vv. _____

The third and longest of these strophes may be considered to be divided into two parts by a two-verse figurative appeal similar to the refrain already noted. In which verses does this appeal occur? Thus there are four strophes in the psalm as a whole. The final two strophes (making up section III) present the extended figure of the vine, a very important image in OT literature. Consult a reference work to learn why this is so significant.

4. What kind of an impression would the extended imagery of Psalm 80 make in your language? What problems may you encounter if people do not fully or correctly understand these pictures? If you were to remove the imagery, how would you translate the passage meaningfully, based on the THP suggestions (pp. 715–17)? Is there some other way you could handle this problem?

5. Summarize the poet's message in each of the three sections of Psalm 80:

   I. _____
   II. _____
   III. _____

How to deal with figurative language in teaching and translation

The figurative language of the Bible frequently poses problems for exegetes and translators. There are several general guidelines that may be helpful in this regard:

First, try to *retain* the biblical image, if possible; but do so only if it does not convey a wrong, misleading, or nonsense in the TL. The reader/hearer should recognize that figurative language is being used and be able to determine its intended sense and significance from its context. This includes the particular *connotations*, or emotive associations that are evoked by the imagery in its context of usage.

Second, if the image is unknown or doesn't convey the same "meaning" (content + feeling + forcefulness + beauty) in the cultural setting of the receptors, then try to find the *closest, natural equivalent* figure in the TL. If one is available, use that instead. A somewhat different image may be substituted *if* it communicates with a similar purpose, impact, appeal, and relevance. But this solution is acceptable only if the original figure has no special or symbolical significance in the biblical setting, for example, "wild dogs" for "dog" in Psalm 22:20, or "water buffalo" for "wild oxen" in Psalm 22:21. However, the figure of a grapevine should not be replaced because it frequently represents the people of Israel in the Scriptures (e.g., Hos. 10:1).

Third, if the image is difficult to understand and the context sheds no light on it, or if it has no meaning at all in the TL, then try to explicitly state *both* the image and the point of similarity, if this can be done concisely and naturally as is appropriate for a poetic text. Translating like this, to convey both form and meaning, often involves making explicit what was left implicit in the source text. But you will need to test such a rendering for intelligibility, literariness, and clarity of focus.

Fourth, if the meaning cannot be communicated economically by explicitly stating it along with the image, then again try using a TL *substitute*, where available, this time *modifying* the substitute (e.g., by an adjective or prepositional phrase) to conform it more closely with the original form and/or function. Remember that all such modification in the interest of meaningfulness should also sound "poetic" in the TL, if at all possible.

Fifth, if none of the preceding solutions seem to work, then simply state the *meaning* of the figure in a nonfigurative way—in plain, literal language. Obviously, the forcefulness and attractiveness of the original message will be lost, but perhaps this may be compensated for through the use of some other rhetorical device(s) in the same passage, for example, an ideophone, intensified descriptive phrase, alliteration, or a wordplay in the TL.

A sixth means of transmitting the intended sense of an important biblical figure is to use a carefully worded footnote to describe or explain it. It is helpful to use such a note to explain a complex, difficult, and/or theologically significant figure even where one of the preceding solutions is used. Of course, a footnote, even if it is actually referred to, generally helps only a reader, not those who are listening as someone else reads the text of Scripture aloud.

More discussioin of figurative language can be found in chapter 5 of *The Cultural Factor in Bible Translation* (UBS, 1987).

Exercise 5.2.2c

1. Prepare a detailed study of the imagery that is found in the well-known *Psalm 23* (as was done in Ex. 5.2.2b). But do not assume that you already know what all of the figures mean; rather, carefully study their background as outlined in the THP or some other good exegetical commentary. Observe where a sudden shift in the prevailing imagery occurs and the significance of this within the psalm as a whole. Finally, discuss how you would meaningfully render the various figures with equal vigor in your language.

2. Of all the figures that you noted in Psalm 23 which two would be the hardest to translate in your language? Why is this?

3. Are there some similar or functionally equivalent figures in your language that you could use to translate these two figures of Psalm 23? Explain, along with an example or two.

4. Which of the six possible solutions mentioned above would work best in handling the two special problems that you have pointed out?

5. Try to find an example from any other psalm, either in your language or from the CEV or TEV, that would illustrate an application of three of the six possible solutions. Be sure to specify which solution you are illustrating in the case of each example given.

5.2.3 Metonymy

Metonymy is the application of a figure of speech (a *metonym*) that involves the *substitution* of the name or designation of one thing for that of another closely associated with it. For example, a king is often referred to as "the Crown," or the name of a capital city for the government of the land, e.g., "London" (= U.K.). Thus the literal idea (we might also call this the *topic*) is replaced by a figurative term (the *metonym* or *image*), usually a noun, having to do with such notions as time, place, attribution, or cause-effect, to mention some of the most important. The poet has the literal meaning of the concept in mind as he writes, but he employs some other conceptually (often conventionally) related word, used nonliterally, to refer to it. Note that there is no comparison involved in metonymy as was the case with simile and metaphor; it is simply a lexical replacement or substitution. Psalm 5:9 is an example: "with their *tongue* they speak deceit". In this case, the tongue as a physical instrument is used to refer to what the wicked say, that is, their words.

As will be seen in some of the examples of the following exercise, one figure of speech (e.g., a metonym) often occurs in the same passage with another (e.g., a metaphor) to express some important thought in a powerful way. But such a figurative combination may be difficult to communicate in translation. This is especially true if the translator fails to understand the meaning underlying the original images in the Hebrew. However, the THP is usually an excellent source of help in determining the intended sense.

Exercise 5.2.3

Study the following passages in their context, and carry out the following four steps of analysis, referring to the TEV, CEV, the *NIV Study Bible*, the THP for assistance, and any other commentaries you have at your disposal:

(a) *Pick out* the metonym, and underline it. (More than one may be present.) If some figure other than metonymy is present (e.g., a metaphor), try to distinguish which is which.

(b) Try to determine the specific *type* of metonymy. That is, does it have to do with an association based upon *time* (T), *place* (P), *attribution* (A), *cause-effect* (CE), or something else (SE)?

(c) Write down the nonfigurative *meaning* (i.e., the "topic") of the metonym.

(d) Decide whether the metonym would convey its intended meaning in *your language*. If not, is there some other figure that could be used instead? Describe the different translation possibilities. Which of them do you prefer?

metonym	*type of metonymy*	*nonfigurative meaning*
if there is wrong in my hands (Ps. 7:3)		
purge me with hyssop (Ps. 51:7)		
pour out thy anger on the nations (Ps. 79:6)		
you shall eat the fruit of the labor of your hands (Ps. 128:2)		
I love thee, O Lord, my strength (Ps. 18:1)		
the Lord is my light and my salvation (Ps. 27:1)		
pour out your hearts before him (Ps. 62:8)		
you prepare a table before me (Ps. 23:5)		
no scourge will come near your tent (Ps. 91:10)		
the snares of death encompassed me (Ps. 116:3)		
then I called on the name of the Lord (Ps. 116:4)		
all the earth bows down to you (Ps. 66:4)		
they set their mouths against the heavens (Ps. 73:9)		
he who has clean hands and a pure heart (Ps. 24:4)		
the Lord is my strength and my song (Ps. 118:14)		
thou hast defiled his crown in the dust (Ps. 89:39)		
he who avenges blood is mindful of them (Ps. 9:12)		
sing praises to the Lord, who dwells in Zion (Ps. 9:11)		
kiss the Son, lest he be angry (Ps. 2:12)		
They say, "A deadly thing has fastened upon him." (Ps. 41:8)		
do not lift up your horn on high, or speak with insolent neck (Ps. 75:5)		

5.2.4 Synecdoche

Synecdoche is a specific type of metonymy, or figurative substitution, in which a *part* of something is used to refer to the *whole* (or vice versa), or a *particular* is used to refer to the *general* (or vice versa). There are two instances of synecdoche in the following passage:

> For not in my *bow* do I trust,
> nor can my *sword* save me. (Ps. 44:6)

These each refer to *any* and *all* man-made weapons or human means of defense. Together they heighten the contrastive notion that underlies the psalmist's complete trust in God.

The following verse presents a synecdoche in which the *whole* refers to a certain *part* of the whole:

> *All nations* surrounded me. (Ps. 118:10)

Here a great many people—but certainly not everyone in the world—surrounded the psalmist. Notice that the whole-part type of synecdoche normally produces a degree of exaggeration or overstatement and thus is akin to *hyperbole* (see sec. 5.2.8).

A special form of synecdoche called *merismus* makes use of a pair of terms, words which represent two very different, extreme, or opposite aspects of something, in order to highlight the whole idea. In Psalm 92:2, for example, the meaning of the poetic word pair "morning and night" is "at all times" (see sec. 5.1.2 for more on word pairs):

> ... to proclaim your love in the *morning*
> and your faithfulness at *night* . . .

The following are three more examples of merismus. The "sea" and "dry land" refer to the entire universe; "flesh" and "blood" refer to all portions of sacrificed animals; "lends his money" and "does not accept a bribe" refers to all types of financial transaction.

> The *sea* is his, for he made it,
> and his hands formed the *dry land*. (Ps. 95:5)

> Do I eat the *flesh* of bulls
> or drink the *blood* of goats? (Ps. 50:13)

> ... who *lends his money* without usury
> and *does not accept a bribe* against the innocent. (Ps. 15:5)

Would these paired figures have the same sense in your language?

Exercise 5.2.4

1. Note all those figures referred to in section 5.2.4 that would cause difficulty if rendered literally in your language. Is it possible to clarify their intended meaning? Explain, with examples (and a back-translation into English).

2. Underline and give the nonfigurative meaning of the synecdoches in the following passages. Then suggest how they can be best translated in your language. If you notice any of the other figures that we have already studied (simile, metaphor, metonymy), analyze them in the same way and suggest how the combination serves to emphasize the psalmist's utterance.

   — For all day long I have been stricken,
   and chastened every morning. (Ps. 73:14)

   — As for man, his days are like grass,
   he flourishes like a flower in the field. (Ps. 103:15)

   — All who see me mock at me. (Ps. 22:7)

   — They came upon me in the day of my calamity. (Ps. 18:18)

   — The Lord loves the gates of Zion. (Ps. 87:2)

   — For thy servants hold her stones dear,
   and have pity on her dust. (Ps. 102:14)

   — And let all flesh bless his holy name. (Ps. 145:21)

   — In thee our fathers trusted. (Ps. 22:4)

   — May gold from Sheba be given him...
   Let grain abound throughout the land. (Ps. 72:15-16)

   — Great peace have those who love thy law. (Ps. 119:165)

   — The works of his hands are faithful and just. (Ps. 111:7)

— You know when I sit and when I rise;
   you perceive my thoughts from afar. (Ps. 139:2)

— Therefore my heart is glad, and my soul rejoices
   my body also dwells secure. (Ps. 16:9)

— Bless the LORD, O my soul;
   all my inmost being, praise his holy name. (Ps. 103:1)

— When the cares of my heart are many,
   thy consolations cheer my soul. (Ps. 94:19)

— His mischief returns upon his own head. (Ps. 7:16)

— Shout for joy to the God of Jacob. (Ps. 81:1)

— My lips will pour forth praise . . .
   My tongue will sing of thy word . . .
   Let thy hand be ready to help me. (Ps. 119:171-73)

Note that in Psalm 119:171-73 there is more than one synecdoche, while in Psalm 60:3-5 (next example) synecdoche and metonymy occur together, as they so often do in Hebrew poetic language. After studying Psalm 60:3-5, underline the figures and give their nonfigurative meaning. Then suggest a meaningful translation in your language. Notice that an internal discourse break seems to be needed (cf. TEV, CEV, NIV, and THP). Where would you make this break? Why?

— Thou hast given us wine to drink
     that made us reel.
   Thou hast set up a banner
     for those who fear thee,
     to rally to it from the bow.
       That thy beloved may be delivered,
   Give victory by thy right hand
   and answer us! (Ps. 60:3-5)

3. Find two other instances of metonymy and synecdoche in the psalms. List their references and give their respective interpretations. Then suggest how you would render them with the same import and impact in your language.

The types of figurative language that will be described in sections 5.2.5–5.2.8 do not occur as frequently in the Psalter as simile, metaphor, metonymy, or synecdoche. Nor are they as difficult to interpret unless they happen to occur in combination with other figures. Even so, translators need to be aware of them so that they can correctly identify them and determine their rhetorical purpose and aesthetic effect in the biblical text.

5.2.5 Personification

Personification is a figure of speech in which an inanimate or lifeless thing or abstraction is represented as if it were a human being, a living person. Parts of the body, for example, may be personified:

Their *tongue* struts through the earth. (Ps. 73:9)
The *eyes* of all look to thee. (Ps. 145:15)

The translator needs to consider what the intended meaning of such a passage is, and whether the personification would sound natural in the target language. Notice that a personification may be interpreted both as personification and synecdoche. In Psalm 145:15, for example, "eyes" signifies the people, "all" of them. Sometimes it may simultaneously be personification and metonymy, as in Psalm 73:9, where "tongue" signifies what the wicked say. The closeness of personification and synecdoche is especially notable when the figure occurs in parallel with the word "soul," as in Psalm 119:81-82:

> My *soul* [= I myself] languishes for thy salvation . . .
> My *eyes* [= I] fail with watching for thy promise . . .

The same is true when names of places are used to refer to the people who live there, as in Ps. 97:8:

> *Zion* [= people of Jerusalem/God's city] hears and is glad,
> and the *daughters* [= inhabitants of the villages] of Judah rejoice.

Of course, our purpose as translators is not simply to attach labels to figures of speech. Rather, we want to understand their intended meaning (including any connotation) in order to more accurately and idiomatically communicate them in translation.

The following examples show how vivid personification can be:

> Let the *sea* roar and all that fills it . . .
> Let the *floods* clap their hands;
> let the *hills* sing for joy together. (Ps. 98:7-8)

> His *lightnings* lighten the world;
> the *earth* sees and trembles. (Ps. 97:4)

Such vividness is particularly appropriate when speaking about the works of God. He is so great and glorious that the poet needed a special way of talking about him. Heightened language was also good for expressing strong feelings, motives, and attitudes. It helped listeners experience the same sort of emotions.

Some personifications involve abstractions. Psalm 85:10-11 is an extended example:

> *Steadfast love* and *faithfulness* will meet;
> *righteousness* and *peace* will kiss each other.
> *Faithfulness* will spring up from the ground,
> and *righteousness* will look down from the sky.

This passage, so full of personification, leads off the final, climactic stanza of the psalm. Such figures signal this climax well. In some languages, however, it is not possible to personify an abstract noun. In this case, the translator would have to make the human participants explicit (at least for the first set), whether "God" or "people," to make sense: "God demonstrates great steadfast love; surely he loves his people without fail." Perhaps the heightened nature of the original language can then be communicated in some other way, such as through the use of emphatic particles, a fitting figure of a speech, a shift in the normal word order, an exclamation, or a rhythmic utterance pattern.

Exercise 5.2.5

1. Find three instances of personification in the Psalter besides those given in section 5.2.5, at least one of which involves an abstraction. Write them out on a separate piece of paper. Then tell how you would translate them in your language with the same functional effect. Be sure to consider the context of each passage.

2. What do you think is the purpose of personifications such as these in the Bible? Are similar modes of expression used in the poetry of your language? If so, what is their nature and purpose? If possible, give some examples from your own tradition, written or oral.

3. Psalm 85:10-11 is a particularly difficult passage to translate. Mention some of the problems that you see. Tell how you would handle them creatively in your language (see THP, pp. 748-49).

5.2.6 Anthropomorphism

Anthropomorphism is a figure in which God, or some other spirit being who is not a human, is spoken of as though he had a human body. This sort of language occurs quite often in the Bible, including both poetic and non-poetic passages. How else can humans conceive of, talk about, or understand the unseen and almighty LORD of the universe, except in terms of their own lives and experiences? We have to depend on human language, inadequate though it is, to derive and develop our understanding of God's nature, and this is why we liken the Indescribable One to a mere mortal. Psalm 89:13 is an example:

> Thou hast a *mighty arm*;
> strong is thy *hand*, high thy right *hand*.

The same anthropomorphic *image* may have different senses in varied contexts:

> In his *hand* are the depths of the earth . . .
> for his *hands* formed the dry land. (Ps. 95:4–5)

> Thou openest thy *hand*;
> thou satisfiest the desire of every living thing. (Ps. 145:16)

> For thy arrows have sunk into me,
> and thy *hand* has come down on me. (Ps. 38:2)

Notice that there is a difference of meaning associated with God's "hand" in each of the preceding passages, that is, with reference to his activities of creation, provision, and chastisement. The translator needs to consider whether any of these anthropomorphisms can be used in the target language and still convey the intended meaning. If they cannot, he needs to find another effective way of translating them.

Some other poetic anthropomorphisms are: "to see his [God's] face" (Ps. 11:7), meaning to live in his presence, as TEV has it; "lift up your hand, O God" (Ps. 10:12), meaning to help the needy or punish their oppressors (TEV); "the little man/daughter of [God's] eye" (Ps. 17:8), equivalent to the English "apple of one's eye" (NIV). Many others could be listed as well.

Exercise 5.2.6

1. Identify all of the anthropomorphisms and personifications in the following literal translations of the Hebrew. What is the significance of each one in its context? Choose three of the most difficult ones and explain how they may be rendered meaningfully in your language. Again, check out other English (French, Spanish, Russian, etc.) translations for possible models to follow.

    —You will hide them in the secret of your face. (Ps. 31:20)

    —Send out your light and your truth; let them lead me. (Ps. 43:3)

    —Bow down your ear to me. (Ps. 31:2)

    —All my bones shall say, "LORD, who is like you?" (Ps. 35:10)

    —His eyes see; his eyelids will examine the sons of men. (Ps. 11:4)

    — . . . O Yahweh, at the blast of the breath of your nostrils. (Ps. 18:15)

    —For he remembered that they were but flesh . . . (Ps. 78:39)

    —O LORD, heal me, for my bones are troubled. (Ps. 6:2)

    —Let Ethiopia hasten to stretch out her hands to God. (Ps. 68:31)

—Bless the LORD, O my soul;
and all that is within me, bless his holy name. (Ps. 103:1)

—Yahweh looked down from heaven on the sons of man . . . (Ps. 14:2)

—He who sits in the heavens shall laugh;
Yahweh shall mock at them.
Then he will speak to them in his anger,
and he will trouble them in his wrath. (Ps. 2:4–5)

—If I forget you, O Jerusalem, let my right hand forget. (Ps. 107:5)

—The sun knows his time for setting. (Ps. 104:19)

—And its place knows it no more. (Ps. 103:16)

—Evils have encompassed me without number. (Ps. 40:12)

—Why do you stand far away, O Yahweh?
Will you hide in times of distress? (Ps. 10:1)

—Surely goodness and mercy shall follow me. (Ps. 23:6)

—How often did they provoke him in the wilderness
and grieve him in the desert! (Ps. 78:40)

—For he knows our frame,
he remembers that we are dust. (Ps. 103:14)

2. Sometimes the psalmist describes a powerful manifestation of the LORD in nature using anthropomorphic terms (called a *theophany* in commentaries). Usually this has to do with God's coming to earth either for judgment or deliverance. Psalm 18:7–15 is an example. Select five of the outstanding instances of anthropomorphism in these verses, then summarize the purpose of this passage in the context of the psalm as a whole. What is the point of speaking about God in this manner? Select three of these figures that are difficult to translate in your language. Why are they so difficult? How would you render them in a meaningful, yet poetic, way?

5.2.7 Apostrophe

Apostrophe is a figure of speech in which the poet interrupts his discourse to speak directly to some absent person(s) or thing(s) as though actually present and capable of listening. Apostrophe therefore always involves some form of *direct address*, which is often marked as such by a *vocative*. It is usually used in dramatic contexts where the psalmist wishes to express some very strong emotions, such as joy or anger. It may also be employed to announce the beginning of a new section in the psalm (i.e., an aperture). Psalm 2:10 is an example:

Now therefore, *O kings*, be wise;
be warned, *you rulers* of the earth.

In many languages there is a special way to mark a vocative. In Chewa, for example, a separable personal pronoun is used together with the proper name or noun of reference. Languages also differ as to the normal position of the vocative expression in its clause, whether at the beginning, middle, or end. In Chewa it is at the beginning, thus signaling the connotation of the utterance immediately, whether positive (pronoun first) or negative (pronoun second). In some other languages, placement of the vocative varies according to the type of text and the situational context. It is important for every translator to be aware of the vocative structures in the target language in order to see how best to express figurative apostrophe.

Exercise 5.2.7

1. On a separate piece of paper, write out the instances of apostrophe (A) that you find in the following passages and indicate the ones which also involve a personification (P): Psalm 6:8, 24:7, 31:23, 87:3, 103:1, 114:5, and 148:3, 7.

2. Psalm 148 is virtually one big apostrophe! Explain the significance of this feature with reference to the purpose of the psalm as a whole. Which persons or things addressed in this psalm are the most important from your perspective? How is the overall structure of the psalm affected by who is being addressed? Where does the climax of Psalm 148 occur? Why do you think so?

3. Find two other verses in the Psalter where things or non-humans are addressed. Does such poetic usage sound natural in your language? If not, is there a way of rendering these passages so that they are more meaningful? Give an example.

5.2.8 Hyperbole

Hyperbole is a figure of speech in which there is an intentional exaggeration or overstatement. What is actually said is obviously more than is meant to be literally understood. Hyperbole is a means of emphasizing the ordinary, intended meaning and, in the process, the poet's strong feelings as well. Frequently it is based upon, or associated with, another type of figure, such as a whole-for-the-part synecdoche, a simile, or a metaphor:

>   simile: They have poured out their blood *like water*. (Ps. 79:3)

>   metaphor: My tears have been *my food* day and night. (Ps. 42:3)

In addition to emphasizing some important idea, personal opinion, or deep feeling in the biblical text, a hyperbole may function in place of a superlative or intensifying adjective, as in Psalm 69:4:

> More in number *than the hairs of my head*
> are those who hate me without cause.

In this passage, the psalmist uses a simile to exaggerate his complaint to the LORD, which in effect is that his enemies are "very many."

Exercise 5.2.8a

1. There are three figures in Psalm 42:3. Identify and interpret them and then point out the exaggeration in the statement as a whole. What is the psalmist trying to emphasize here?

>   figure 1: _____
>   figure 2: _____
>   figure 3: _____
>   What is the psalmist's point? _____

2. Identify the hyperboles in the following lines. Tell how they foreground the psalmist's intended meaning. In addition, what strong emotion (if any) does the utterance also seem to convey in the light of its context? In the case of some of these passages, you may disagree that any hyperbole is present. If so, analyze the imagery and tell what you think it means in the context specified.

>   — . . . all night long I flood my bed with weeping
>   and drench my couch with tears. (Ps. 6:6)

>   — On the wicked he will rain fiery coals and burning sulfur. (Ps. 11:6)

>   — he rained flesh upon them like dust,
>   winged birds like the sand of the sea. (Ps. 78:27)

— Will evildoers never learn—
those who devour my people as men eat bread. (Ps. 14:4)

— . . . you have uprooted their cities;
even the memory of them has perished. (Ps. 9:6)

— . . . Though you test me, you will find nothing;
I have resolved that my mouth will not sin. (Ps. 17:3)

— Though an army encamp against me,
my heart shall not fear. (Ps. 27:3)

— The cords of death entangled me;
the torrents of destruction overwhelmed me. (Ps. 18:4)

— He asked you for life; you gave it to him—
length of days forever and ever. (Ps. 21:4)

— The valleys of the seas were exposed
and the foundations of the earth laid bare
at your rebuke, O LORD. (Ps. 18:15)

— I have been blameless before him
and have kept myself from sin. (Ps. 18:23)

— They set their mouths against the heavens,
and their tongue struts through the earth. (Ps. 73:9)

— With your help I can advance against a troop;
with my God I can scale a wall. (Ps. 18:29)

— . . . foreigners cringe before me.
They all lose heart,
they come trembling from their strongholds. (Ps. 18:45)

— They mounted up to the heavens
and went down to the depths. (Ps. 107:26)

— . . . they seize the poor and drag them off in their net. (Ps. 10:9)

3. Point out three instances of hyperbole in Psalm 38.

4. In some languages, hyperbole is not very commonly used. Or its usage may be restricted to certain sociocultural situations, such as a public debate, a love song, or a folktale dialogue. Where this is the case, its use in other situations (e.g., in a sermon or liturgical prayer) may sound strange and out of place. The translator needs to stay alert to the likelihood that a literal translation of a hyperbole will be misunderstood and the wrong meaning conveyed to reader and hearers alike. Which of the passages listed in assignments 2 and 3 might be difficult to understand if rendered literally in your language? Why is this the case? How might you reword them in order to communicate the intended sense and emphasis? Check other translations for possible ideas here.

5. Find three other passages involving difficult hyperbolic language in the Psalms. Specify what the problem would be in translating them in your language. How might you deal with it so as to preserve the intended sense and significance of the figure?

Hyperbole is often called upon to highlight the righteousness of the faithful (Ps. 18:23) and the sinfulness of the wicked (Ps. 14:4). It is also used to foreground the terrible retribution that is going to befall evildoers in the coming judgment (Ps. 9:6). Hyperbole is especially evident in the so-called *imprecatory* psalms (see sec. 2.2.3). One cannot interpret these psalms that call for utter condemnation and gruesome punishment in strictly literal terms. It must be kept in mind that this type of psalm (cf. 2.2.3) involves exaggerated language being employed poetically for a particular rhetorical purpose. The words are highly emotive, urgent, and intended to warn all deliberate and degenerate sinners of the judgment that most certainly awaits them if they do not repent of their evil ways.

Recognizing the presence of hyperbole can sometimes throw light upon what at first appears to be some puzzling theology. It can also help resolve an apparent contradiction or conflict in meaning in a particular passage, as for example, in Psalm 83, which will be studied in assignment 3 below.

Exercise 5.2.8b

1. Take note of all the hyperbolic language in the following examples. What is the point being emphasized?

    — May the LORD cut off all flattering lips
    and every boastful tongue. (Ps. 12:3)

    — . . . may their path be dark and slippery,
    with the angel of the LORD pursuing them. (Ps. 35:6)

    — May their eyes be darkened so they cannot see,
    and their backs be bent forever. (Ps. 69:23)

    — Charge them with crime upon crime;
    do not let them share in your salvation. (Ps. 69:27; cf. v. 29)

    — May they be blotted out of the book of life
    and not be listed with the righteous. (Ps. 69:28)

    — May his children be fatherless and his wife a widow. (Ps. 109:9)

    — May . . . the sin of his mother never be blotted out. (Ps. 109:14b)

2. Would any of the preceding passages be difficult to understand if translated literally into your language? Give two examples where you think that problems might occur. In each case, indicate the specific difficulty and suggest what you might do to solve it without losing the forcefulness of the passage entirely. Consult the TEV, CEV, or some other dynamic English translation to see if the strong language has been modified in any way. Point out two good examples of this.

3. Observe the poetic structure at the thematic peak and emotive climax of Psalm 83 (vv. 16–18):

    A1 Cover their faces with shame
        B   *so that men will seek your name, O LORD.*
    A2 May they ever be ashamed and dismayed;
    A3 <u>may they perish</u> in disgrace.
        B1 Let them know that you, whose name is the LORD—
        B2 that you alone are the Most High over all the earth."

    Identify the apparent contradiction in the passage above (cf. also TEV, CEV). How does interpreting the underlined portion as a hyperbole help you resolve the contradiction here? How does the literary structure of this section support such an interpretation? Noting the climactic progression of cola in both A (= appeal) and B (= purpose) will help you answer this. How could you translate the apparent contradiction so that an audience will understand it correctly?

5.3 Rhetorical questions

The literary device known as *rhetorical question* is not based on imagery; but, like the other figures, it is a form whose meaning is not what it appears to be on the surface of the text. Rather, there is some deeper significance, especially with respect to connotation and intention.

A rhetorical question causes a pause in the flow of discourse. It is an open invitation to the listener to participate in the discourse by responding to the question form. To this extent, it can be said to interrupt the progression or development of the argument, exposition, complaint, or conversation wherever it occurs. Often a number of rhetorical questions appear in a series. Then, of course, the whole set contributes to the unit's *continuity* even though normally, in isolation, it contributes to textual discontinuity.

A rhetorical question is different from a "real" question in that it is not intended as a request for information. That is to say, it does not seek a direct "answer." Rather, the hearers are to observe the particular feeling, attitude, or point of emphasis to which the question draws their attention.

The following is an example of a rhetorical question at the beginning of a psalm:

"My God, my God, why have you forsaken me?" (Ps. 22:1)

Was the psalmist here asking the LORD to explain why he seemed so far away and deaf to his prayers? No, he knew that he had no right to demand an explanation of God. But he was troubled. He could not understand why it appeared God had abandoned him, allowing his enemies to triumph over him, for he was a true believer and faithful worshiper of Yahweh. Clearly, this is not a request for information, but a complaint about the speaker's current situation in life and the at times inexplicable justice of God. Such bold rhetorical questions are typical of the lament genre of Hebrew poetry. In this case, the RQ serves to highlight the theme of the first half of the psalm (22:1–21): "LORD, you surely ought to help me in my time of need because I trust in you and depend on you for help." It also conveys the psalmist's deep frustration and grief. He felt deserted and left alone, even by the One who he assumed to be the closest to him—his God!

Many rhetorical questions appear, on the surface, to call for a yes or no answer, but they are more than just a means of emphasizing the positive, yes, or negative, no. In fact, such an RQ highlights the content of the entire utterance. This function becomes clear if we turn the question into a statement form. For example, consider Psalm 56:13 rendered literally (the words in brackets are implicit in the Hebrew text).

[Do you] not [keep] my feet from falling
[so that I am able] to walk before God in the light of the living?

In the NIV and RSV (and most other translations), this passage is rendered in the form of a statement in order to make the text sound more natural in English, although in Hebrew it is an RQ. Notice that this is the last verse in the psalm. The highlighting function of an RQ is quite appropriate here in such a climactic location. The same may not be true for this dramatic question form in another language.

Psalm 56:7a is yet another RQ, rendered literally here:

Upon [= by means of] iniquity shall they escape?

This must be interpreted as a rhetorical question (in contrast to the TEV, RSV; cf. the discussion in THP); otherwise it would cause semantic problems in its context. Examining the context of such questions is vital for ascertaining the idea, mood, opinion, or attitude the poet is intending to emphasize. In the case of Psalm 56:7, line B sheds light on line A. The implicit answer to line A is a resounding "Of course not," strengthened by the compelling plea in line B: "In your anger, O God, bring down the nations" (NIV). But if line A were taken literally to be a negative declaration instead of an RQ, it would lead the translator to misinterpret the passage and perhaps even the entire psalm, e.g., "On account of their iniquity, let them escape!"

In addition to stressing the content of the expected reply and the emotion of the speaker, a rhetorical question may also function to express the speaker's *attitude* (e.g., certainty or uncertainty, sympathy or hostility, surprise or steadfastness) or *intention* (e.g., a desire to warn, rebuke, encourage, express irony, and/or exhort the addressee). We see this in line A of Psalm 56:7 where the RQ conveys the psalmist's anguished doubts over the unwarranted attacks of his enemies. This is evident also at the end of the next verse where the RQ contrastively expresses the poet's certainty that God will one day execute justice: "Are they [my tears = sufferings, an instance of metonymy] not [written] in thy book?" (RSV).

Another common function of the RQ is to introduce a new topic or even the principal theme of a particular psalm, as we see in Psalm 15:1:

> O LORD, who shall sojourn in thy tent?
> Who shall dwell on thy holy hill?

Here the parallel questions emphasize the expected answer, which is explicitly given in verse 2 as the principal theme of the Psalm. Due to the element of discontinuity that an RQ introduces into the discourse, it often functions to announce the beginning of a new strophe, that is, an *aperture* (e.g., Ps. 24:3, which is similar to the RQ of 15:1). This may be the case also in the next example, though this is debatable. But it is clear that this RQ serves the somewhat different function of calling to mind an important theological truth:

> Who, then, is the man who fears the LORD?
> *He* [= the LORD] will instruct *him* in the way chosen for *him*. (Ps. 25:12)

Line B highlights an aspect of the godly character of the person referred to in line A. (Note: the pronouns need to be clarified.) This verse thus highlights a key religious principle. Such an RQ is sometimes termed a "wisdom question," appearing as it does in texts that are didactic in nature. But the basic purpose of the RQ remains the same, namely, to emphasize some feature of its answer.

Exercise 5.3

1. Study the following rhetorical questions in context and determine the sense, feeling, attitude, and function conveyed by each one. What is the main idea that each intends to emphasize? Note any special function each may have in its specific context, (e.g., beginning a new section, stating an aspect of the central theme, foregrounding the respective opinions or emotions of the righteous and unrighteous, or dramatizing the interpersonal relationship between the psalmist and his God.)

   — Who is like you, O LORD? (Ps. 35:10)

   — Who will rise up for me against the wicked? (Ps. 94:16)

   — Who can proclaim the mighty acts of the LORD . . . ? (Ps. 106:2)

   — Who knows the power of your anger? (Ps. 90:11)

   — Who, then, is the man who fears the LORD? (Ps. 25:12)

   — Who is the man who desires life . . . ? (Ps. 34:12)

   — What is man that you are mindful of him? (Ps. 8:4)

   — How then can you say to me:
   Flee like a bird to your mountain. (Ps. 11:1)

   — What right have you to recite my laws
   or take my covenant on your lips? (Ps. 50:16)

   — They say, "How can God know?" (Ps. 73:11)

> — Why should the nations say,
> "Where is their God?" (Ps. 79:10)

Notice that Psalm 79:10 is a rhetorical question in which another RQ is included. Determine the meaning of each one separately.

2. Sometimes rhetorical questions occur in pairs, or even in a series as in Psalm 77:7–9, a dramatic and highly emotive passage that is a complete strophe:

> Will the LORD reject forever?
> Will he never show his favor again?
>   Has his unfailing love vanished forever?
>   Has his promise failed for all time?
>   Has God forgotten to be merciful?
>   Has he in anger withheld his compassion?

What is the obvious "answer" which each of these questions emphasizes? How did the psalmist himself determine the expected answer (Ps. 77:10–12)? What do you think he was *feeling* as he prayed these words?

3. In Psalm 77:13 the psalmist states his conclusion in the form of a rhetorical question: "What god is so great as our God?" What emotion is he experiencing here? How does the greatness of God, emphasized in this way, bring out the primary theme of the entire psalm? Make an observation concerning where this RQ occurs within the discourse structure of the psalm as a whole.

4. Do a similar analysis of the series of RQs in Psalm 88.

5. Give some examples of different types of RQs that you have heard or used in your language. Try to specify their function or at least the particular sociocultural or literary context in which they are used. Tell how RQs are formally marked in your language as being distinct from "real" questions that request information.

6. Now go over the list of examples in assignment 1. Which RQs could be rendered by a question form in your language and still have the same sense and impact? Which would need to be adjusted to an emphatic statement or some other type of rhetorical device? Give two examples of such an adjustment. How do you preserve the special emphasis or emotion of the original text? Check several other translations as you do this exercise.

7. Try to find two examples of RQs in the psalms (besides those already mentioned) that perform the structural function of marking an aperture or beginning of a section or strophe. Give evidence for your conclusions. Can RQs be used to perform this same function in your language? Explain.

5.4 Condensed language

Condensation is found in most types of poetry the world over. It may operate with respect to either form or content. In Hebrew poetry it is normally the product of parallelism, which often calls for the poet to express his point concisely so that it will fit within the span of a single colon (poetic line), which in Hebrew rarely extends beyond five words.

Formal condensation is called *contraction*; it contributes a great deal to the rhythm and beauty of the language as it is being spoken (or sung) and heard. Semantic condensation is called *compaction*; it adds much to the depth of meaning and richness of connotation of a particular poem. Both types are frequent in the Psalter.

5.4.1 Contraction (condensing the form)

Contraction is the deliberate omission of certain words or parts of words that can be clearly understood from the context. Several so-called "prosaic" particles (i.e., the sign of the direct object, the definite article, the relative pronoun, and prepositional forms) are omitted so regularly in verse that their absence constitutes one of the characteristic features of Hebrew poetry.

The poet may employ contraction because of the restriction on line length, as already mentioned, and also simply to make what he says more unusual, emphatic, or memorable. Attentive receptors perceive that something is missing, or not completely apparent, as they hear or read the text—they notice any unexpected order in the arrangement of words. This forces their minds to work a little harder at that point, and the intended meaning is therefore drawn to their attention. At other times, the poet employs contraction in order to make the sound of the text more attractive or beautiful, especially when the shortening creates a pleasing rhythm.

If Hebrew poetry is translated literally, the contractions often cause problems for the readers or hearers. They may not even realize that something has been left out. They have no way of determining what has been left implicit. The omissions may result in their misunderstanding the meaning of the passage. Here, for example, is a literal translation of Psalm 34:17:

> They cry, and Jehovah hears,
> and saves them out of all their distresses. (NKJV)

To determine who "they" refers to, you may decide to look at the immediate context, verse 16. This might lead you to think that "they" refers to the wicked. In the NIV verse 17 is rendered "the righteous" in the place of "they." This is justified in view of the larger context (see v. 15) and the meaning of the psalm as a whole.

The preceding example is actually an instance of *ambiguity* rather than of formal contraction since the subject is not elided, grammatically speaking. It is just that the referent of "they" is unclear due to the subject's being a pronoun. But for practical purposes, we will treat such cases of ambiguous pronoun reference due to the lack of a full noun subject as a type of formal contraction. This is because an explicit subject *could* have been included for the sake of clarity, but was not in order to preserve the poetry of the passage.

In the next example, Psalm 105:40, we see that the pronoun referents are left ambiguous in the NIV (cf. also NRSV):

> They asked, and he brought them quail.

In the wider context (v. 37), the referents of the respective subjects can be discovered, however, because they are stated explicitly. But it may be necessary for meaningfulness in some languages to bring the intended referents even closer, e.g., "his people" in verse 39 of TEV.

In Psalm 111:1 there *is* a genuine contraction. Literally, it reads as follows:

> I-will-extol YHWH with-all # heart.

Here it is the personal pronoun "my" (simply a noun suffix in Hebrew) that has been elided (as shown by the space mark [#]). Most modern translations "fill in" such gaps with the intended sense; that is, they state explicitly what was left implicit in the original. When this is not done, difficulties may arise for some readers, especially those who do not know how to use the preceding context to guide them in the interpretation of a passage.

In Psalm 103:9, the grammatical *objects* are elided. The intentional omission of part of a grammatical construction is termed an *ellipsis*. Modern translations usually fill in such blanks that exist in the original Hebrew. The literal reading of Psalm 103:9 is this: He will not always chasten _____, nor will he keep _____ forever. The NKJV renders this passage as follows:

> He will not always strive *with us*,
> nor will He keep *His anger* forever.

But sometimes these formal gaps are not filled in by the more literal English versions. For example, Psalm 26:9 in the NIV reads:

> Do not take away my soul along with sinners,
> my life with bloodthirsty men.

Here the verb phrase of the B line, which is elided in Hebrew, is likewise unexpressed in the English. It is "understood" from the A line and hence left implicit. To translate line B meaningfully in some other language the verb phrase may have to be expressed, however (e.g., CEV: "Don't punish me with death . . . ."—or, more poetically: "...extinguishing my life along with those killers").

The deliberate omission of a corresponding verb in the B line is a prominent stylistic feature of Hebrew poetry. It is even given a special name, *verb gapping*. (The linking verb "to be" is often left out in prose texts as well as in poetry.) Most English translations automatically include this word when necessary, to clarify the sense. Consider this literal rendering of Psalm 4:2:

> A: sons-of man until=when my-glory to-shame
> B1:   you-will-love delusion
> B2:   you-will-seek a-lie

Here the A line is unintelligible. But if the linking verb *h-y-h* is supplied, it forms a construction along with the preposition *l-* "to" to mean "it becomes, it changes into": "How long, O men, *will you turn* my glory into shame" (NIV; cf. TEV). The opening interrogative particle "how long" that appears in the A line is elided in both B1 and B2, but virtually all English versions supply it (e.g., TEV: "How long will you love what is worthless . . . ?"). (Note that the CEV turns this second RQ into a direct statement.)

Of course, Bible scholars and commentators will sometimes disagree as to exactly which words should fill in a particular contraction in the original text. For example, a literal rendering of Psalm 57:2 reads as follows:

> I will cry to God most High,
> to God who performs _____ for me.

Some versions insert "all things" as the object of "works" (GW, JB). Commentators make various suggestions: "his mercy," "his promises," "my desires," and so forth. Luther adds "my sorrow." NIV has "fulfills *his purpose*"; TEV, "supplies my *every need*."

What should translators do when it is not obvious just what words to supply when filling in such a gap, especially if the versions they are consulting do not agree? Sometimes a good commentary, like the THP, will help. The *NIV Study Bible* may prove helpful on occasion. But most often one will simply have to examine the context of the passage on one's own and come to a decision based on that, combined with what sounds most meaningful and moving in the target language.

Exercise 5.4.1

1. After studying the context of each of the following passages in a more literal translation (e.g., NASB or an interlinear version) as well as a number of other versions and commentaries, identify all the possible contractions or omissions. Supply whatever you think has been left out:

   — If I forget you, O Jerusalem, let my right hand forget. (Ps. 137:5)

   — Enter his gates with thanksgiving, his courts with praise. (Ps. 100:4)

   — You shall fix on your string against their faces. (Ps. 21:12)

   — This I had for I kept your commands. (Ps. 119:56)

- He who chastens the nations, shall he not punish?
  He who teaches man knowledge? (Ps. 94:10)

- God is a righteous judge, and God is angry every day. (Ps. 7:11)

- For a day in your courts better than a thousand. (Ps. 84:10)

- You have destroyed all who go lusting away from you. (Ps. 73:27)

- Therefore the wicked shall not stand in the judgment,
  nor sinners in the company of the righteous. (Ps. 1:5)

- Turn again, O Yahweh, her captivity, like the south streams. (Ps. 126:4)

- Gird your sword on the thigh, O Mighty One,
  your glory and your majesty. (Ps. 45:3)

- O Yahweh do not rebuke me in your wrath,
  and in your fury chasten me. (Ps. 38:1)

- By day the LORD directs his love,
  at night his song is with me—
  a prayer to the God of my life. (Ps. 42:8, NIV—NB. the textual note, cf. 42:3)

How would these passages have to be rendered in your language? To what extent do the contractions have to be "filled in" for the sake of the meaning? Choose any three of these that pose special problems and explain the nature of the difficulty.

2. Is such *formal* contraction a feature of the oral or written poetry in your language? Give an example or two, if possible.

3. Select a passage from the Psalms other than those already mentioned in which you detect an instance of formal contraction. What seems to be missing? Does this need to be replaced in a translation in your language? Remember, such a procedure does not really add any meaning. It simply states explicitly words that are implicit in the original text.

5.4.2 Compaction (condensing the content)

Compaction is a condensation or shortening of the poetic line with reference to its content. (Of course, this cannot be completely separated from its form.) Compaction is a common literary technique often seen combined with the use of imagery and other types of figurative language wherein the poetic "picture" replaces prosaic explanation. For example, feel for yourself the intense pain the psalmist was experiencing when he wrote, "My bones burn like glowing embers; my heart is blighted and withered like grass" (Ps. 102:3b–4a).

Many African Bantu languages have a good possible equivalent for such vivid sensory images: the *ideophone*. An ideophone, which functions as a dramatic predication, can similarly convey a complete scenario in a word. In Chewa, the word *waliwali* is an example: it refers to the "glowing embers" of Psalm 102:3; and the word *kwinya* refers to the "withered grass" in Psalm 102:4.

Allusion is a special type of content-cutting technique in which passing mention is made of some well-known fact in a people's history, literature, social institutions, customs, way of life, traditional beliefs, geography, and so forth. It is abbreviated because the addressees need no explanation; they are assumed to know all about it. In the Bible, the Psalter in particular, there are many allusions to the religion of Israel, its precepts and practices, as well as to the history of their covenant relationship with Yahweh. The psalmist often makes only an indirect reference to such matters as he develops the main theme or some subtopic of the message. It was not necessary to give much detail; the intended audience was already well acquainted with the subject and the situation. The allusion, whether a general suggestion or a specific reference, thus enriches the content of the message without wordiness. It is a good way of illustrating some important point of background or of involving the audience by evoking a particular feeling or attitude.

In Psalm 4:2, for example, we see not only ellipsis, but also a twofold contrastive allusion: to "glory" (= the glorious [God] of Exod. 16:7 and 1 Sam. 4:21) and to "shame" or "lie" (= the shameful lying/false gods/idols of Hos. 9:10 and Amos 2:4). The use of these devices in Psalm 4:2 makes the passage a difficult one to translate because today's readers, who come from a different time, place, and cultural-religious setting, are frequently quite ignorant about the things alluded to. Most of the time they will not recognize that there *is* an allusion in the text, or they may not recall the details supposedly evoked by the passing reference. Therefore, they will certainly miss the point that the poet is trying to make and thus this particular aspect of the intended message will be lost to them.

How to translate allusions is an important consideration in any meaning-oriented Bible translation strategy. The degree of potential "loss" has to be determined and evaluated with reference to the particular passage, the nature and purpose of the translation being carried out, and the cognitive principle of "relevance" (the ease and economy of text processing, on the one hand, and the conceptual benefits to be derived from the information in question, on the other).

Take, for example, the well-known passage "Cleanse me with *hyssop*, and I will be clean" (Ps. 51:7). The general thought of this request is quite clear in its context. The words "cleansing" and "clean" in a context that speaks of sin (vv. 5, 9) obviously refer to the act of forgiveness, especially since the implied agent is God. Most readers will leave it at that; they will be satisfied that they have a general understanding of the verse, even though they don't know what hyssop is. But surely the psalmist had some reason for using this noun. What is hyssop anyway? Most people do not know and do not take the time to find out. A Bible dictionary reveals that hyssop is a small type of aromatic plant having a straight stalk and many branches. Its leaves and bark had little hairs on them, enabling the branches to hold quite a lot of liquid. For this reason a branch of hyssop was very useful as a sprinkling device for water or blood in the religious rituals of ancient Israel. At the time of the Passover, for example, Moses commanded the elders of the people to take hyssop, dip it into the blood of a slain lamb, and sprinkle it on the doorframe of their houses (Exod. 12:22). The hyssop was also specified in the Mosaic Law as the means of sprinkling blood in the ritual to purify someone who had been healed of an infectious skin disease, "leprosy" (Lev. 14:4). It was also used to sprinkle water on persons who had defiled themselves through contact with a dead body (Num. 19:19–22).

So how does the allusion to hyssop enrich the significance of Psalm 51:7? Notice what is involved here: a defiled, religiously "unclean" person is unable to get rid of or atone for his guilt through any human means. God alone can cleanse him. A spiritual purification is needed. This is achieved through a sacred sprinkling as prescribed in the *torah*. The allusion to hyssop in Psalm 51:7 also calls to readers' minds the notion of blood—the blood of a substitutionary sacrifice, which was necessary to cleanse people of sin and guilt before God. This important theological element of the original meaning is missed when readers do not recognize the allusion to Israel's covenantal system of sacrifice evoked by the word "hyssop."

In the TEV, mention of "hyssop" has been replaced with a statement of the simple meaning. In other words, the allusion itself does not appear. The rendering is "Remove my sin, and I will be clean." Any translator must ask, What would a literal translation of the words "cleanse me with hyssop" mean in the target language? Would there be any problem of understanding? Is it possible to adjust the literal form so that the intended meaning of the passage is more clearly stated? Can one combine a reference to the form with some indication of the meaning?

GW renders Psalm 51:7, "Purify me from sin with hyssop." But if the allusion is retained like this, there is still the problem of how to replace the emotive impact of the original figure and its associations. It may be that an explanatory footnote would be an answer, or at least a partial solution.

In exercise 5.4.2 there are several examples from Psalm 60. These passages illustrate both the expressive power as well as the interpretive problems associated with the use of allusion. On the one hand, these brief, compacted references greatly expand the meaning potential of the psalm. They invite the listener into the rich thought-world of the text. On the other hand, if the allusions are not recognized, they make even the shortest of cola almost impossible to interpret correctly. Then the audience is effectively excluded from the author's intended meaning. Another danger is that they can easily be misinterpreted and give rise to all sorts of far-fetched and erroneous ideas.

Exercise 5.4.2 also demonstrates the need for the translator or exegete, using such aids as dictionaries and commentaries, to thoroughly investigate all strange and unfamiliar terms in a given poetic verse. To ignore them is to throw away the key by which the readers of the translation can unlock a greater portion of the intended meaning of an allusive passage. It may not be possible to fully identify an allusion right in the text itself. But, in the case of important ones, a footnote along with relevant cross-references should be supplied, drawing attention to both the allusion's significance and its relation to the psalmist's message. Such descriptive or explanatory footnotes cannot simply be borrowed from some other Bible version. They must be carefully thought out and worded in a way that fits the sociocultural and religious setting of the target language. However, such footnotes should "explain" no more than what is absolutely necessary to the intended meaning of the biblical text.

Exercise 5.4.2

1. Consult a Bible dictionary, the THP, and the notes and cross-references of the *NIV Study Bible* to learn more about the allusions in the passages below. What is being alluded to? What is the particular significance of the allusion in relation to its context? Is there any way that you might express these allusions in your language so that the readers will realize there is a deeper level of meaning present, which they need to investigate? How far can you go to make *explicit* what is *implicit* in the original text? Discuss in class the possible ways these allusions could be rendered in a meaning-oriented version.

   — I have installed my King on Zion, my holy hill. (Ps. 2:6; see the footnote in TEV)

   — . . . the birds of the air, and the fish of the sea,
   all that swim the paths of the seas. (Ps. 8:8)

   — For he who avenges blood remembers;
   he does not ignore the cry of the afflicted. (Ps. 9:12)

   — On the wicked he will rain fiery coals and burning sulfur. (Ps. 11:6)

   — . . . strong bulls of Bashan encircle me. (Ps. 22:12)

   — You prepare a table before me . . .
   You anoint my head with oil. (Ps. 23:5)

   — I will exalt you, O LORD,
   for you lifted me out of the depths. (Ps. 30:1)

   — . . . you removed my sackcloth and clothed me with joy. (Ps. 30:11)

   — They feast on the abundance of your house;
   you give them to drink from your river of delights. (Ps. 36:8)

   — Here I am, I have come—
   it is written about me in the scroll. (Ps. 40:7)

   — "I have made a covenant with my chosen one,
   I have sworn to David my servant." (Ps. 89:3)

— But for those who fear you, you have raised a banner
to be unfurled against the bow. (Ps. 60:4)

— In triumph I will parcel out Shechem
and measure off the Valley of Succoth. (Ps. 60:6)

— Ephraim is my helmet, Judah my scepter. (Ps. 60:7)

— Moab is my washbasin,
upon Edom I toss my sandal;
over Philistia I shout in triumph. (Ps. 60:8)

— . . . (he) touches the mountains and they smoke. (Ps. 104:32)

— He determines the number of the stars and calls them each by name. (Ps. 147:4)

2. Which of the allusions in assignment 1 would cause the most difficulty in your language? Explain the problems involved and some possible solutions. Consult some of the standard translations that you have available to see how they have handled these semantic issues.

5.5 Varied language

Language that is deliberately varied from the usual or ordinary way of saying things tends to sound "poetic," especially in combination with other stylistic features. To a certain extent, varied wording would be a natural outgrowth of the general technique of parallelism, for the second, or "B," line is almost always made to differ from the "A" line in some respect, while maintaining the essential semantic similarity (or some other unity of relationship) between the two. Thus in line B there will normally be at least one word or phrase that noticeably varies from its correspondent in A. Remember, though, that the meaning of the bicolon (or tricolon) is a product of, and is often meant to be greater than, the sum of the two or more parallel expressions. This poetic principle has already been abundantly illustrated.

In this section, we will consider several other grammatical features in Hebrew poetry that manifest some variation from what is the norm in prose discourse with respect to word order, tense/aspect and voice, and pronominal reference. In discussing these, it will often be necessary to refer to the original text or an interlinear version; hence the discussion will be kept brief. Nevertheless, these devices need to be mentioned, if only briefly, so that they can be understood when pointed out in exegetical commentaries.

5.5.1 Variation in word order

In chapter 3 it was noted that the regular order of main words in the prose clause is V-S-O. In poetic discourse, however, this order is not always followed, but rather an order based on importance, prominence, relevance, or simply sound (rhythm). In other words, some syntactic unit (excluding a conjunction or other transitional expression) may appear *before* the verb. This position indicates a foregrounding of the first element, whether for a semantic reason (e.g., to highlight a contrast), a structural reason (e.g., to announce a strophic aperture), a pragmatic reason (e.g., to mark a change in attitude or tone), or a thematic reason (e.g., to indicate a new topic). Of course, such possible discourse functions must always be determined on the basis of a thorough text study that includes all of the structural features noted in chapter 4. It could also be that the varied word order is introduced simply for the sake of *rhythm* (though we have little knowledge of this aspect of biblical poetry), or for *euphony* (i.e., to create pleasant sounds). In any case, our conclusions with regard to the poetic function of the variation are always to be proposed as tentative. Moreover, they must be supported by other stylistic criteria.

Most variations of the normal Hebrew word order are erased in translation, even in relatively literal versions, simply because the target language (e.g., English) does not allow for this particular order. Therefore, only those who have access to the original language can appreciate it. But to show its importance, the rhetorical feature of varied word order in the Psalter will be illustrated here with a partial analysis of Psalm 82. In the literal rendering of Psalm 82 that follows, the syntactic elements that in Hebrew occur *before* the verb are written in italics, and other salient terms are underlined or boldfaced. The symbol X marks a chiastically ordered bicolon. Note that the macrostructure of Psalm 82 is itself organized as a larger topical chiasmus, as can be seen by the reversed parallel arrangement of the internal poetic segments.

      A1 ***God*** he-is-presiding in-the-council-of=**god** (i.e., divine council);
X   A2 *in-the-midst-of* **gods** he-is-judging.

      A3 until=when (= how long) will-you-judge=unjustly?
      A4 *and-the-faces-of* wicked-ones you-are-showing-partiality-towards=selah.

          B1 judge=(the)-weak-one and-(the)-fatherless;
X   B2 (the)-poor-one and-the-one-being-oppressed maintain-rights!

          B3 rescue (the)-weak and-(the)-needy-one;
X   B4 *from-(the)-hand-of* wicked-ones deliver!

              C1 not(hing) do-they-know and-not(hing) do-they-discern;
              C2 *in-darkness* they-walk-about;

                  D they-are-shaken all=the-foundations-of (the)-earth!

              C1' *as-for-me*=I-said **gods** (are) you,
              C2' and-sons-of the-**Most High** (are) all-of-you

          B1' surely *like-a-man* you-will-die,
          B2' and-*like*-other-of the-*princes* you-will-fall.

      A1' rise-up O-**God** judge the-earth!
      A2' for=*as-for-you* you-will-inherit from-all-of=the-nations.

The emotive low point of this psalm appears in the structural center (D). The bitter conclusion of D can be seen to contrast in theme and tone with the outer borders, A1–A2 and A1'–A2', which picture God in complete judicial control of all of earth's events. Most of the text is devoted to a lament over the injustice and oppression of the wicked, beginning in A3–A4 and building up to a contrastive peak in C1'–C2' (where the wicked are ironically praised) and B1'–B2' (where they are roundly condemned). C1'–C2' contrasts with C1–C2, which describes the spiritual poverty of all self-proclaimed worldly "gods." All of the B lines deal in some way with God's judgment—of the weak (B1–B4) and of the powerful (B1'–B2'). Chiastically arranged bicola in A1–A2 and B1–B4 perhaps suggest the bitter inversion of justice that the psalmist is experiencing.

Front-shifted elements in the first half of the psalm also emphasize the prominent topics of "the wicked" (A4) and the "darkness" (C2) they practice. On the other hand, fronted full pronouns ("me" in C' and "you" in A2') draw attention to the contrasting perceptions of this situation on the part of man as opposed to God. And, significantly, the ultimate fate of all the wicked is highlighted by the word order in B1'–B2': One day they will fall and die like anyone else, only to face the righteous judgment of the God who owns all nations (A1'–A2'). Thus virtually every word of this dynamic little psalm is carefully chosen and positioned to highlight a message of comfort to the suffering people of God. On the surface of the text, things may sound disorganized and pessimistic, but the carefully positioned organization on the micro- and macrostructure brings out the positive nature of the psalmist's passionate and trusting appeal.

Exercise 5.5.1 (especially for students who can refer to the Hebrew text or an interlinear)

1. Examine Psalm 12, making a note of all front-shifted elements and any that appear to be placed in line-final position for a special reason. After studying the structure and style of the psalm as a whole, make some suggestions as to the possible function of the variations in word order that you have observed.

2. Compare TEV and RSV's renderings of Psalm 12. Note any places where an original front-shift in the Hebrew has been preserved in the English translation. What is the effect of this (in English)? Are there any places where you think that the focus or emphasis manifested by the Hebrew word order might have been meaningfully preserved in English? If so, give an example or two of how you would word these lines, in English or any other language.

3. What are the functions of word order in your language, in particular, any variations from what is regarded as the norm? Can you utilize this feature in translating the psalms more precisely? Give two examples from Psalm 12.

4. Consider once again the *irony* of the segment C1-C2 of Psalm 82 above (v. 6). Irony is another important poetic-rhetorical technique that is especially common in the prophetic literature. When using verbal irony, a speaker intends to say something that is quite different, or even the opposite, of what his words literally seem to mean. Often some strong emotion and a certain amount of criticism are also involved—that is, directed at the apparent addressees. With this in mind, explain the irony that is present in Ps. 82:6 (cf. THP) and how you would mark it in YL. Try to find another good instance of irony in the psalms: What does it mean and how would you translate it?

5.5.2 Variation in verb usage (tense/aspect and voice)

Strictly speaking, Hebrew finite verbs do not express "tense," past, present, or future. They do not distinguish the precise time when an activity or event takes place. Rather, the verb appears to be marked with respect to what is known as "aspect." Two principal aspects are distinguished: completed action (the so-called "perfect" or "suffix" form) and uncompleted action (often termed the "imperfect" or the "prefix" form). The terms *perfect* (P) and *imperfect* (I), used in older Hebrew grammars, will be retained here for ease of reference.

In narrative, the Hebrew perfect verb usually denotes what in English, for example, would be a past-tense verb (including present perfect, pluperfect, and the immediate past). The Hebrew imperfect denotes everything else, most notably present and future time. A special distinction in the usage of the verb in Hebrew narrative concerns sequences of verbs that refer to the same type of time-action. These are linked into cohesive sets by the conjunction *waw*, "and," which is attached directly to the verb in clause-initial position. However, the second and all subsequent verbs in a string will manifest the alternative tense-aspect from that which is indicated on the first, or head, verb: P + *w*I + *w*I + *w*I (i.e., *waw* consecutive imperfect, the *wayyiqtol* form) or I + *w*P + *w*P + *w*P (i.e., *waw* consecutive perfect, the *weqetal* form). The former type of sequence is characteristic of narrative discourse, while the latter construction also appears frequently in non-narrative prose texts (e.g., in prophetic or legislative discourse). Any deviation from these two basic patterns indicates some type of information that is taken off the main line of discourse development for some special purpose, e.g., to mark a structural boundary, a new participant or topic, or content that is highlighted.

However, the prose verbal patterns just described are not always, or even usually, seen in Hebrew poetry. Rather, the verb forms of poetic discourse often seem to follow a somewhat different logic, governed more by the desire to maintain a rhythmic balance between parallel lines or by some other sound-related constraint. As a result, it is not always so easy to determine the particular time setting of a given event or series of events. The regular prose rules, for example, that a *w*I form designates a past action of some sort, do not necessarily apply. Instead, one must carefully consider the context to see whether a certain temporal situation is indicated or at least suggested by other forms, such as a temporal adverb or adverbial time phrase, reference to a past situation, or a vow to perform some religious action in the future. For example, in the following complaint (Ps. 38:11), the psalmist uses the same verb in both lines of the bicolon, obviously in a present sense, but the verb in the first line is the imperfect form as expected, while the verb in the second line is the perfect form. Literally, it reads:

> my-beloved-(friends) and-my-companions from-before my-wound they-*stand* (I);
> and-my-neighbors from-afar-off they-*stood* (P).

Some commentators (e.g., Watson, pp. 279–80) view this as an attempt to avoid exact parallelism in a case where the same lexical stem was employed. At any rate, the passage does illustrate the *flexibility* of usage allowed in poetic discourse. Thus, it sometimes happens that the temporal reference of a certain verb may be debated by commentators and be rendered differently by different versions, as is the case for Psalm 31:17, which reads literally:

> Yahweh not=let-me-be-ashamed for I-*cried* (P)-out-to-you;
> let-them-be-shamed wicked-ones let-them-be-quiet in-Sheol.

With respect to the perfect verb of line A, the NIV, GW, and NAB construe the tense as a past in English, whereas the CEV, TEV, NRSV, and JB see it as a present. Either rendering fits the context in this instance. But that is not always the case. At times a completely different perspective results from the choice of tense, as we can see by comparing a literal rendering of Psalm 40:6 with its translation in the NIV and TEV:

> a-sacrifice and-an-offering not=you-*desired* (P);
> ears you-pierced for-me;
> a-burnt-offering and-a-sin-offering not=you-*required* (P).

> Sacrifice and offering you *did not desire*,
>   but my ears you have pierced,
> burnt offerings and sin offerings
>   *you did not require*. (NIV)

> You *do not want* sacrifices and offerings;
>   you *do not ask for* animals burned whole on the altar
>   or sacrifices to take away sins.
> Instead, you have given me ears to hear you. (TEV)

Remember, it is not possible to deal with tense-aspects issues when a poetic passage is considered in isolation. Rather, it must always be studied in the light of the structure and function of the complete strophe in which it is contained, and ultimately from the perspective of the entire discourse.

Exercise 5.5.2

1. Compare the difference between the NIV, CEV, and TEV renderings of Psalm 40:6 with regard to tense usage. Which seems to fit the immediate context of the passage better? Which tense seems more appropriate to use in your language? Why do you think so? Mention two other ways in which the NIV, CEV, and TEV translations differ, either from each other, and/or from the literal version.

2. How do the NIV, CEV, and TEV differ with regard to tense in Psalm 11:6? Which tense sounds more natural in the context? Why?

3. Compare the NIV, CEV, and TEV renderings of Psalm 39:9 and Psalm 40:9, answering the same questions as in 2 above.

4. Find one more example in the Psalter where two or more major versions differ with respect to tense usage. Which version seems more correct and why (cf. also the THP)? Which tense would you use in your language.

5. Chart the sequences of and shifts in tense usage in English in Psalm 22 and Psalm 132. How does this feature relate to the discourse structure of these psalms in their entirety? In other words, does the shift in tense seem to be related in any way to the organization of the psalm as a whole?

5.5.3 Pronoun shifting

In Hebrew poetry we sometimes see an unexpected altering of pronouns as to person and number within connected segments of text. (The technical term for this is *enallage*.) This can be very confusing. In some cases the pronoun change may have a special function: Just as in the case of a change in tense-aspect (e.g., from past-completed to present-uncompleted action), so also a pronominal shift from the third to the more dramatic first or second person forms, for example, may serve to announce the aperture of a new discourse unit. Where this *is* the case, however, other clearer markers of a compositional boundary (e.g., structural *anaphora*, a vocative plus an imperative, direct speech, etc.) will always be present to confirm the boundary.

In this section, however, we will focus on apparently random changes *within* a given poetic segment, even within the same verse or colon set. In most instances this involves a shift between the second and third person singular with reference to God. A good illustration of such pronoun shifting is seen in Psalm 40:16–17 (RSV):

> But may all who seek thee
> rejoice and be glad in thee;
> may those who love thy salvation
> say continually, "Great is *the LORD*!"
> As for me, I am poor and needy;
> but *the Lord* takes thought for me.
> Thou art my help and my deliverer;
> do not tarry, O my God!

In this passage, which powerfully concludes the psalm as a whole, the psalmist alters the prevailing second person address in the prayer mode to refer in v. 17 to God in the third person as "the Lord." (That there *is* a change here is somewhat obscured by the bit of direct discourse in 16b: "Great is the LORD.") Most idiomatic English versions modify the anomalous line to conform with the rest. CEV, for example, has: ". . . but, LORD God, *you* care about me. . . ." (Note that it would have been more correct to have used "Lord" here instead of LORD because the Hebrew word is ʾ*adonay* in the original.)

Psalm 41 is distinguished by a somewhat different pattern of variation in personal reference. Verse 1 is ambiguous in this regard:

> Blessed is he who has regard for the weak;
> *the LORD* delivers him in times of trouble.

The difficulty here lies in the first line: to whom does "he" refer? As the THP notes: "This is somewhat strange, since nothing else is said about this in the rest of the psalm" (391). Normally, one would expect a prayer of petition as this is (read the entire psalm) to lead off with an utterance of direct address to God, that is, with a vocative that includes a second person pronoun, e.g., "Blessed are you, O LORD, who have regard for the weak." But that is not what we find here or elsewhere in the Psalms with the word "blessed, happy" (*ashre*), which always has a human complement. God *is* referred to in line B, but with the third person as "the LORD." There is also an ambiguity in the pronoun "him": Does it refer to the "he" or "the weak" (singular in Hebrew) of line A? CEV attempts to remedy this problem as follows: "You, LORD God, bless everyone who cares for the poor, and you rescue those people in times of trouble." But this solution does not completely resolve the ambiguity of reference. GNB attempts to clarify things with a different interpretation: "Happy are those who are concerned for the poor."

We might ask if there is any reason for the somewhat strange use of the third person pronoun in v. 1, other than to announce the beginning of Psalm 41. A wider discourse perspective might help answer this; in verse 4 there is an unexpected change from third person references to the first person as speaker. Thus it is likely that the psalmist pray-er was referring to himself with the indefinite third person pronoun in verses 1–3, including the anomalous initial line where "he" functions as the primary agent (elsewhere it is the *object* of divine action). The sudden shift that we have in v. 4 may function then as an important structural and functional signal in the psalm's development as the psalmist begins his urgent petition to the LORD in the *first* person.

A similar sort of referential change occurs at the end of Psalm 41 to mark this prayer that concludes Book I of the Psalter. Notice the shift from verse 12 to verse 13, in which the psalmist changes from addressing God directly ("you") to the use of a third person form:

> In my integrity *you* uphold me
> and set me in your presence forever.
>
> Praise be to *the LORD*, the God of Israel,
> from everlasting to everlasting! (NIV)

In the CEV rendering, again a pronominal adjustment is made, so it is clear that God is being addressed throughout:

> You have helped me because I am innocent,
> and you will always be close to my side.
>
> You, the LORD God of Israel,
> will be praised forever! Amen and amen.

However, this harmonization tends to smooth over the definite break between the end of the psalm proper (v. 12) and the doxology that concludes Book I as a whole (v. 13).

As the preceding example shows, pronominal usage in the psalms is not always straightforward. Every translator must therefore consider how such shifts in Hebrew would sound in the target language. Would it be desirable to maintain consistency in this regard as in the CEV? Is there something special in the discourse that a given shift is marking? Then one must also ask: Are changes in the pattern of personal reference, such as we find in the Hebrew, sometimes found in the poetry of the target language? Even if they are, their purpose must be understood before the Hebrew forms can be translated literally. And, as has been stressed throughout this study, any consideration of function must include the larger discourse structure, for example, the use of a shift in pronouns to indicate the start of a new poetic unit.

Exercise 5.5.3

Using a literal translation such as the RSV or NASB, find three passages besides the ones already considered above in which there is a sudden shift in the pronominal reference. Write these lines out on a separate sheet of paper. Underline the forms that cause special difficulty.

Can you suggest *why* these shifts occur in the Hebrew? Does there appear to be a special discourse function in any of the examples you noted? Give reasons for your conclusion. Propose how you would reword these lines in your language to make them sound more natural. If this would not be necessary, explain why not.

5.5.4 Other less frequent kinds of variation

Besides the features considered so far in section 5.5, there are others that are used less frequently, for example, variations in verbal conjugation, gender-matched parallelism, the deliberate break-up of stereotyped phrases, the use of archaic or rare words, the inclusion of additional terms in a B line (i.e., a "ballast variant"), the introduction of an extra word at the onset of a line ("anacrusis"), and construction of a "run-over" line (i.e., "enjambment"). There is also a special type of psalm construction known as an *acrostic*. In an acrostic psalm, each successive line begins with a new letter in the order of the twenty-two letters of the Hebrew alphabet. Psalms 9–10, 25, 34, 37, 111, 112, 119 ("the great acrostic"), and 145 are all arranged as alphabetic acrostics. But we have not discussed these devices because their meaningful significance in the original text is less apparent than the others, hence also their implications for translation—that is, how they may be matched *functionally* in the target language.

Most of the other stylistic features discussed in this section are visible in a literal translation such as the RSV or NASB, so it is usually not too hard to discover them. But it is not enough simply to recognize their presence in the text, one must also look to see how these devices interact with one another to perform a given communicative *purpose* or set of purposes in the discourse (see 5.7). This too is an important aspect of biblical meaning, but it is often overlooked in exegetical studies, thus in translation work as well.

5.6 Phonological resonance

Since the psalms were for *oral* presentation, they were composed to appeal to the ear. One way of doing this was to cause the sounds of Hebrew to resonate, to vibrate with one another during utterance. Such resonance contributed beauty, feeling, contrast, and emphasis especially in the performance of the liturgical psalms. Examples of special phonological marking are found in Psalm 27:6; 19:14; 40:6–10; 51:15–17; 107:21–22; 116:17. Of course, some knowledge of Hebrew is necessary for a full appreciation of this important dimension. It is only by reading the original Hebrew aloud that such features as *assonance* (clusters of repeated vowels) and *consonance* (clusters of repeated consonants) can be recognized.

Assonance and consonance (also called *alliteration*) are two phonological devices the psalmists often used to stress a particular idea, evoke a mood, or foreground a major contrast in the text. In Psalm 98:7, for example, the parallel of the word "sea" (with its *m* sound being echoed in line A) is the word "earth" (with a repeated *b* sound in line B). Together these words (a word-pair) present a picture of completeness:

yirʿam hayyam umloʾo	let-it-resound the-sea and-its-fullness;
tebel wəyoshbe ba	the-earth and-those-living in-it.

(In the literal English rendering, note that the words connected by a hyphen constitute one word in Hebrew.)

Psalm 137:3 provides an example of a combination of sibilant sounds /s-sh-ts/ that serve to accent the scornful "song" (*šir*) the Babylonian captors are using to torment the exiles, who are foregrounded by the repeated /u/ vowel in "us/our":

ki šam šəʾelunu šobenu	for there they-asked-us our-captors
dibre-šir wətolalenu śimḥa	[for] the-words-of=a-song,
	and-our-tormentors [for a song of] joy;
širu lanu miššir ṣiyyon	sing for-us from-the-song[s]-of Zion.

Sibilants combined with fricatives and nasals are prominent in Psalm 140:3. This bicolon also provides an example of *onomatopoeia*, sounds intended as an imitation of something that can be heard in the natural world. Here one can almost hear the hissing of the dangerous serpents as they are being described:

> *šanənu ləšonam kəmo-naḥaš*　　they-make-sharp their-tongue as=a-serpent;
> *ḥamat ʿakšub taḥat śəpatemo*　　the-poison-of a-viper [is] under their-lips.

Occasional rhymes are used in Hebrew poetry in combination with selective word placement such as word order shifts. Rhyme audibly highlights some aspect of meaning in the text. An instance of initial rhyme occurs in Psalm 102:6:

> **damiti** *liqʾat midbar*　　I-am-like unto-a-great-owl-of the-wilderness;
> **hayiti** *kəkos ḥarabot*　　I-am an-owl-of the-abandoned-ruins.

Here the sound correspondence between the initial verbs in each line draws attention to the comparison of the owl, a bird that inhabits deserted places, and typifies the psalmist's own loneliness.

More commonly rhyme occurs at the end of the lines, as in Psalm 3:2:

> *yhwh ma-rabbu ṣaray*　　O-Yahweh, how=they-are-many my-foes;
> *rabbim qamim ʿalay*　　many [are] those-rising-up upon-me.

Here the phonological similarity at the end of the two lines foregrounds the antagonists mentioned at the lines' end. Repetition also highlights the psalmist's major concern in this lament, namely, the multitude of his enemies.

In Psalm 76 there is a less regular rhyming pattern. Praise names that sound alike are carefully positioned throughout the text to keep the spotlight upon the awesome LORD God whose "name is great" (v. 1): *nodaʾ*, 'the-one-who-is-known' (v. 2); *naʾor*, 'the-one-lighted-up' (v. 4); *noraʾ*, 'the-one-being-dreaded' (vv. 7, 12); *moraʾ*, 'the-one-being-feared' (v. 11).

Sound patterns connect with meaning in the device known as *punning*, in which one word is played off another which sounds similar, if not identical. Lexical "puns" occur quite often in Hebrew poetry, as, for example, in Psalm 129:5–6:

> may-they-be-shamed (*yebošu*) and-may-they-be-turned back
> 　　all-of the-ones-hating Zion.
> may-they-be like-grass-of the-housetops
> 　　which-before it-grows it-withers (*yabeš*).

In this figure, the verbal image, "withers" (*yabeš*), is linked by its sound to the topic, "may they be shamed" (*yebošu*). Notice that the topic is the first word in verse 5 and the image the last word in verse 6 (Hebrew).

Another kind of punning that occurs frequently is the use of the same lexical root in two different senses (e.g., in Ps. 27:3: *taḥaneh*, 'she encamps' and *maḥaneh*, 'army') or in association with diverse agents or entities. Psalm 35:1 is an example of the latter, where the psalmist's petition is phonologically linked with its object:

> contend (*riba*) O-Yahweh with those-contending-with-me (*yəribay*);
> combat (*ləḥam*) with those-combating-me (*loḥamay*).

A pun can be quite subtle, as we observe in the judgment announced in Psalm 6:10:

> they-will-be-shamed (*yebošu*) and-they-will-be-dismayed greatly all=my-enemies;
> they-will-turn (*yašubu*) and-they-will-be-shamed (*yebošu*) suddenly.

The inversion of consonants in the medial verb here audibly reinforces the reversal in the fortunes predicted for the psalmist's enemies. (For more on the possibilities and importance of punning in the Bible, see Nick Lunn, "Paronomastic Constructions in Biblical Hebrew," *Notes on Translation* 10:4, 1996.)

Much more could be said about "sound effects" in Hebrew poetry, for this is a very prominent aspect of the psalmists' oral-aural rhetoric. But since most students will not be able to investigate this device in the original language, we will not go into further detail. But translators and exegetes must be aware of it and take note where such features are discussed in commentaries. The significance of sound patterning should be seriously considered wherever it occurs. Natural poetic patterns of phonological resonance also need to be built into the text of any translation of the Psalter, employing features that are functionally equivalent within target language and its oral and/or written tradition.

Exercise 5.6a (to be assigned to students who are familiar with Hebrew)

1. As you read through the following passages in the Hebrew Bible or an interlinear version, make a note of any significant sound feature such as assonance, consonance, rhyme, or punning, and then suggest any special effect on the overall meaning that these devices might possibly have: Psalm 5:9; 15:3; 18:10, 12; 28:5; 46:9; 83:2; 85:1; 93:3–4; 109:13; 127:1; 148:3–5. Consult the THP for help with this exercise.

2. Are phonological features like these commonly found in your language, either in poetry or prose? If so, give some examples. In translating any of the passages you just read, would it be possible to use some appropriate sound device in your language to convey the emphasis or feeling that you see in the Hebrew? Or could you compensate for the loss through some other poetic technique? Give an example or two.

In Hebrew as in all poetry there are regular rhythmic patterns of alternating sound and silence (i.e., "beats" and "pauses"). *Rhythm* is not so obvious as rhyme perhaps, but it is very important nonetheless. A consistent rhythm gives to a psalm a sense of unity, progression, harmony, balance, and beauty. The recurring stresses upon key words in a relatively short poetic line creates a forward movement in the sound structure. On the other hand, a sudden break or more prolonged modification in the prevailing rhythm can signal the onset of a new unit or a discourse peak.

Rhythm that takes place in a regular, predictable way is called *meter*. Although meter is not, strictly speaking, a feature of Hebrew verse, there is definitely rhythm. The student can get some idea of the varying *balance* of word-beats by examining an interlinear version or a very literal English translation.

Major nouns and verbs each receive one accent, as in the following example from Psalm 26:2 (RSV):

Prove['] me, O LORD['], and try['] me;
test['] my heart['] and my mind['].

Here, in the actual Hebrew text, there are three primary accents per line, that is, one for each word or word group. This rhythmic unit would be designated as a 3+3 (or 3:3) pairing.

The 3+3 pairing and the 3+2 pairing are the most common doublet patterns in Hebrew poetry, certainly in the Psalms. But many variations are possible, with single lines ranging in length between one and five Hebrew "words" (accent groups).

For centuries biblical scholars have debated whether Hebrew poetry has meter or not. Most likely it did not, not in the strict sense of a predictable pattern of stresses. But regular rhythmic sequences and fixed patterns of more limited scope frequently do appear to embellish and demarcate the discourse. Thus, as with every other poetic feature, it is important to observe where a significant *alteration* occurs with regard to the number of beats in a line, for this may mark a compositional boundary in the text, either initial (aperture) or final (closure). For example, there may be a change from mainly three-beat lines to two-beat lines. Or suddenly an extra long line (e.g., five beats) or short line (one beat) may appear. We may also find a single, non-paralleled line (a monocolon) or an additional third line in parallel (forming a tricolon). Such rhythmic shifts and unusual lines may serve as clues to some special rhetorical or structural function in the text, for example, to help distinguish a thematic peak point within the psalm.

As will be seen in exercise 5.6b, rhythm patterns may serve to mark the peaks and boundaries of compositional units in poetic discourse. But such sound structures should not be used as unit markers without the occurrence of some of the other important signals of breaks and borders discussed in previous chapters. It is only when taken together (i.e., "convergence" and "harmony," see 4.2) that they enable us to see how the Hebrew poet arranged his thoughts and feelings.

Exercise 5.6b

1. The following is a word-for-word English rendering of Psalm 3. Observe the hyphens in order to determine what constituted a "word" (i.e., accent-group) in the Hebrew. The equals sign (=) signifies *maqqeph*, the Hebrew equivalent of a hyphen, which joins two or more closely related words into a single stress group, that is, one compound lexical unit. Count the number of words in each line and indicate the total for each parallel pair of lines (couplet/bicolon) as follows: $n + n$. Draw a vertical line to divide each verse into its constituent lines (2 or 3). Do this for each verse of Psalm 3 and write the numbers in the spaces provided. Verse 1 has been done for you.

   Consult the NIV for help in seeing the line breaks. The NIV normally puts some punctuation mark (a comma, semicolon, full stop, or question mark) at the end of every English equivalent to a poetic line in the Hebrew. Although there are exceptions to the rule (a closing comma may occur simply to signal apposition), the NIV is a fairly reliable guide to the Hebrew line breaks. Note: Do not include the liturgical interjection *selah* in your count.

verse	interlinear text	$n + n$
verse	*interlinear text*	
[1]	Yahweh how=they-are-many my-foes | many those-rising-up against-me	3 + 3
[2]	many those-saying to-my-soul there-is-no salvation for-him by-God *selah*	__ + __
[3]	and-you Yahweh a-shield around-me my-glory and-one-who-lifts-up my head	__ + __
[4]	my-voice unto=Yahweh I-cry and-he-answers-me from-the-hill-of his-holiness *selah*	__ + __
[5]	As-for-me I-lie-down and-I-sleep I-awaken because Yahweh he-sustains-me	__ + __
[6]	not=I-will-fear ten-thousands-of people who every-side they-are-drawn-up against-me	__ + __
[7]	arise Yahweh deliver-me my-God for=you-struck all-of=my-enemies jaw the-teeth-of the-wicked-ones you-broke	__ + __ + __
[8]	to-Yahweh the-deliverance on-your-people your-blessing *selah*	__ + __

   What is the average poetic-line (colon) length in this psalm? Two of the verses in Psalm 3 do not fit the established pattern. Is there an explanation for this? (The exceptions may help to signal a special point of emphasis or a discourse boundary.)

   What is the psalm's genre? (Knowing the genre may also help in discovering points of emphasis.)

   Which verse marks the climax of the prayer? (It represents the central petition of this psalm.)

   Which verse marks the concluding doxology of benediction?

2. Following the same instructions as above, analyze the rhythm pattern of Psalm 149:

   [1] praise Yahweh sing to-Yahweh song new praise-him in-the-congregation-of holy-ones   __ + __ + __

[2] let-him-rejoice Israel in-the-one(s)-making-him the-sons-of=Zion
let-them-be-glad in-their-king   __ + __

[3] let-them-praise his-name with-dancing with-a-tambourine
and-a-harp let-them-make-music=to-him   __ + __

[4] for=delighting Yahweh in-his-people he-crowns humble-ones with-salvation __ + __

[5] let-them-rejoice holy-ones in-honor let-them-sing-joyously upon=their-beds __ + __

[6] praises-of God in-their-mouth and-a-sword-of two-edges in-their-hand   __ + __

[7] to-make vengeance on-the-nations punishments upon=the-peoples   __ + __

[8] to-bind their-king with-fetters and-their-nobles with-shackles-of iron   __ + __

[9] to-do against-them judgment being-written glory this
for-all-of=his-holy-ones praise=Yahweh   __ + __ + __

What genre is this psalm and what does this lead you to expect concerning its overall structure?

What is the average line length in Psalm 149 in terms of beats? In which two verses does a variation occur in the usual number of lines and in the number of beats? From the point of view of its structure, these two verses help to mark the _____ and the _____ of Psalm 149.

3. Are certain poem or song genres marked by a particular rhythm or accent sequence in your language? If so, describe them. Could any of these genres along with their rhythmic patterns be used as a model when translating the Psalms—whether exactly or in some modified form? Explain.

5.7 Multifunctional language

Discourse function (i.e., the intended communicative purpose of a discourse) was considered in chapter 2, where we focused on the ten psalm genres: petition, thanksgiving, praise, instruction, profession of trust, repentance, remembrance, retribution, royal celebration, and liturgical expression. We also had occasion to consider the communicative purpose in chapter 3 when analyzing the semantic relationships between parallel poetic lines. There it was pointed out that no two (or three) cola are ever completely synonymous, even if their vocabulary is very much the same. Rather, something is always *added* in the semantic movement from line A to line B; that is to say, "A, and what's more, B!" or "not only A, but also B" or "A, and indeed B as well." Even exact repetition, which rarely occurs in any case, will contribute a certain emphasis to the progression of thought or reinforce a particular focus of thematic attention. Occasionally this addition in sense or significance (e.g., emotion, specification, intensification, figuration, or personalization) can be noticed in a good translation. Comparing several versions also helps us see it. For example:

> Then he will *speak to* them in his <u>wrath</u>,
> and *terrify* them in his <u>fury</u>. (Ps. 2:5, RSV)

Clearly "terrify" is stronger than "speak to," and "fury" is more intense than "wrath," though this latter point could be debated. The following is the TEV rendering of Psalm 2:5:

> Then he *warns* them in <u>anger</u>
> and *terrifies* them with his <u>fury</u>.

Of these two versions of Psalm 2:5 we should ask ourselves which is better as a guide or model for translation (in English) and why. One must remember, however, that the progressive development, variations, and distinctions of the Hebrew are not very apparent just from reading some translation. A reliable commentary (e.g., THP), if not the original text, needs to be consulted.

It will also be helpful to look at function, with regard to the individual line, from a *speech act* perspective. A speech act has to do with the more specific purpose that an utterance has in the process of oral or written communication between two or more individuals or groups. Since the psalms are personal or corporate prayers to God (who is believed to be present and listening), certain communicative "acts" are carried out as they are being uttered. The psalms may be analyzed in terms of speech acts even though no response of God is recorded (unless supplied by the psalmist as direct speech). In the sequence of poetic lines we see six general functions commonly being carried out, often one in conjunction with another, hence the term *multifunctional*. These major functions, briefly defined and illustrated, are as follows:

1. *Declarative*: an utterance that asserts or teaches some fact about the nature and works of God or man, something concerning his/their attributes and actions.

    Blessed is he who has regard for the weak [assertion about man];
    the LORD delivers him in times of trouble [assertion about God]. (Ps. 41:1)

    For the LORD watches over the way of the righteous,
    but the way of the wicked will perish. (Ps. 1:6)

2. *Expressive*: an utterance that manifests the deep personal emotions, attitudes, values, and expectations of the psalmist, whether positive or negative in nature.

    But I am a worm and not a man,
    scorned by men and despised by the people. [neg] (Ps. 22:6)

    Surely goodness and love will follow me all the days of my life,
    and I will dwell in the house of the LORD forever. [pos] (Ps. 23:6)

3. *Affective*: an utterance that aims to influence the thinking, feelings, and/or actions of the addressee or audience, using a command or an appeal either to effect a change in their behavior or reinforce the status quo and what is taken for granted.

    But you, O LORD, be not far off;
    O my Strength, come quickly to help me. (Ps. 22:19)

    Refrain from anger and turn from wrath;
    do not fret—it leads only to evil. (Ps. 37:8)

4. *Relational*: an utterance that seeks to open, maintain, enhance, or close communication (prayer) with someone, especially God. This relational purpose is often associated with a certain *ritual* function that aims to promote unity and solidarity within the community of faith (typical of *liturgical* discourse). This type is often combined with one of the three preceding functions.

    How long, O LORD? Will you forget me forever?
    How long will you hide your face from me? (Ps. 13:1; + *expressive*)

    I will sing to the LORD,
    for he has been good to me. (Ps. 13:6; + *declarative*)

    Praise the LORD.
    Praise the LORD from the heavens,
    Praise him in the heights above... (Ps. 148:1; + *affective*)

5. *Performative*: an utterance that in and of itself changes the status of the addressee or which alters the relationship between speaker and hearer (e.g., included direct discourse). Any utterance of God presented as direct speech needs to be carefully examined with regard to this particular function.

> I will proclaim the decree of the LORD:
> He said to me, "You are my Son;
> today I have become your Father. (Ps. 2:7)

> But I trust in you, O LORD;
> I say, "You are my God." (Ps. 31:14)

6. *Artistic*: an utterance that is poetically embellished (e.g., by figurative language, wordplay, rhythm) so as to enhance the effectiveness of any of the other functions just listed, especially the three primary ones—declarative, expressive, and affective.

> Cleanse me with hyssop, and I will be clean;
> wash me, and I will be whiter than snow. (Ps. 51:7; + *affective*)

> They spread a net for my feet—
> . . . They dug a pit in my path— (Ps. 57:6; + *expressive*)

> Praise him, sun and moon,
> Praise him all you shining stars. (Ps. 148:3; + *relational*)

When attempting to determine the function of a poetic form, it often seems that several possibilities fit equally well, which may indeed be the case. Our objective here is not to try to discern right from wrong or the one and only possible answer, but simply to discover the great variety and potential of meaning that is inherent in the poetry of Scripture. It is this manifold complex of content and intent (including impact and appeal) that must be communicated in translation, to the extent that this is possible, given the poetic resources of the target language.

Translators may find that for their purposes the six general functions listed here need to be broken down into subtypes of communicative purpose (sometimes termed *speech illocutions*), e.g., warning, encouragement, rebuke, promise, and so forth. It is important, too, for them to keep in mind that the basic functional elements are usually accompanied by different attitudes and emotions on the part of the speaker—love, hate, anger, joy, grief, frustration, determination, commitment, and so forth. Such diverse psychological states must be investigated and conveyed, as accurately and naturally as possible, in the process of translating the text into an appropriate TL poetic equivalent. The translator needs to consider, for example, what the intense feeling is that accompanies the words in the following three passages:

> I am worn out from groaning;
> all night long I flood my bed with weeping . . . (Ps. 6:6)

> Away from me, all you who do evil,
> for the LORD has heard my weeping. (Ps. 6:8)

> O LORD, our Lord, how majestic is your name in all the earth! (Ps. 8:1, 9)

This may seem obvious enough, but the point is this: Have the author-intended rhetorical speech aims and accompanying emotive aspects of the passage in question been conveyed clearly, correctly, and with corresponding power and beauty in its textual context and in the intended TL setting of use (including the sociocultural and religious situation)? Remember, a psalm should not sound like a sermon! Propositional content, while extremely important, is not the only aspect of "meaning" that needs to be considered during the analysis, interpretation, and communication of biblical discourse, psalmic lyric poetry in particular.

Exercise 5.7

1. Study each of the following passages in its context to determine what appears to be its primary communicative function (and any apparent sub-function/illocutionary force too, if possible). Also, what prominent emotions or attitudes seem to be conveyed as well? Write your comments alongside each text.

> O LORD my God, if I have done this
>   and there is guilt on my hands—
> then let my enemy pursue and overtake me;
>   let him trample my life to the ground . . . (Ps. 7:3, 5)

> He who digs a hole and scoops it out
>   falls into the pit he has made. (Ps. 7:15)

> He says to himself, "Nothing will shake me;
>   I'll always be happy and never have trouble." (Ps. 10:6)

> Hear, O LORD, my righteous plea;
>   listen to my cry.
> Give ear to my prayer— (Ps. 17:1)

> I love you, O LORD, my strength. (Ps. 18:1)

> The law of the LORD is perfect,
>   reviving the soul.
> The statutes of the LORD are trustworthy,
>   making wise the simple. (Ps. 19:7)

> May the words of my mouth and the meditation of my heart
>   be pleasing in your sight,
> O LORD, my Rock and my Redeemer. (Ps. 19:14)

> My feet stand on level ground;
>   in the great assembly I will praise the LORD. (Ps. 26:12)

> Rejoice in the LORD and be glad, you righteous;
>   sing all you who are upright in heart! (Ps. 32:11)

> See how the evildoers lie fallen—
>   thrown down, not able to rise! (Ps. 36:12)

> I confess my iniquity;
>   I am troubled by my sin. (Ps. 38:18)

> My heart grew hot within me,
>   and as I meditated the fire burned;
>   then I spoke with my tongue. (Ps. 39:3)

> Praise be to the LORD, the God of Israel,
> from everlasting to everlasting.
>   Amen and Amen. (Ps. 41:13)

> Let death take my enemies by surprise;
>   let them go down alive to the grave . . . (Ps. 55:15)

> I am in the midst of lions;
>   I lie among ravenous beasts—
> men whose teeth are spears and arrows,
>   whose tongues are sharp swords. (Ps. 57:4)

> I will sacrifice fat animals to you
>> and an offering of rams;
>> I will offer bulls and goats. (Ps. 66:15)
>
> Praise be to God,
>> who has not rejected my prayer
>> or withheld his love from me! (Ps. 66:20)

2. Would it be difficult for you to convey certain aspects of the intended communicative purpose, the obvious *emotion* (feeling), the rhetorical *power* (forcefulness), or the literary *beauty* (artistry) of any of these passages in your language? Explain why. What might you do to solve the problem? Give a concrete example.

3. Choose two of the passages in assignment 1 and compare their rendering in the NIV with their translation in the TEV, CEV, or LB (Living Bible). What differences do you detect with regard to function, feeling, or artfulness? What does a reliable commentary (e.g., THP) have to say about this? Now come to your own conclusion. Present your findings to the class for discussion.

4. Examine the following psalms for *direct speech* attributed to God: 2, 12, 35, 46, 50, 68, 75, 81, 82, 89, 90, 91, 95, 105, 110, 132. List three different purposes for such divine speech, and give examples of each. Note one instance in which God's words seem to be directly related to the theme of the psalm as a whole, and another in which it occurs at an important juncture within the psalm's structure, that is, either at an aperture or closure, or at a high point in terms of content ("peak") or emotion ("climax").

5. Examine the following psalms for direct speech attributed to the wicked: 10, 11, 12, 13, 14, 40, 41, 42, 49, 70, 71, 74, 79, 137. List two different reasons for their evil talk. Give one example where such self-incriminating direct speech appears to perform an important structural function in the psalm.

6. Determine the primary *speech purpose* of each verse in Psalm 32 according to the six basic functions listed in section 5.7. (You may break these down into more specific "illocutions" if desired.) Observe the various groupings of "speech acts" that emerge from your study. Note their progression and tell how they relate to the theme and purpose of the psalm as a whole.

6. CONTENT: WHAT THE PSALMISTS PRAY AND PRAISE ABOUT

In working through the material of the preceding chapters, we have had occasion to consider the religious subject matter of the psalms only in a cursory way. We now take a closer look at its rich theological content. We will examine the principal topics and themes, explore how these are related to one another, and then survey certain key terms. It is important to look at the topics and themes before the specific terminology because individual words have meaning only in relation to their larger textual context as well as the external situational setting.

While various aspects of the text have already been carefully studied, the nonverbal situational setting cannot be specified with any measure of certainty and we have not focused on this. Nevertheless, the very nature of the psalms as prayers and hymns—along with their diverse generic subdivisions—suggests a number of possible occasions of use, involving personal meditation, public worship, and external proclamation, both polemical and confessional. We cannot be too specific in this regard, however, because of the relative *generality* of the Psalter's vocabulary. That is, the same basic vocabulary appears in individual lament, corporate lament, thanksgiving, confession of sin, profession of faith, and other genres as well. Very few particular personal names, dates, events, and historical situations are mentioned, except in the so-called historical psalms and the titles. Although the imagery may be detailed, the figures tend to be conventional, even stereotyped, and may frequently be applied to any number of situations. This lexical flexibility serves to extend the range of referentiality of any given psalm, making it relevant and applicable to many different occasions.

It is also important to consider the psalmic "cast of characters" and their interaction, and this will be done first (sec. 6.1). Next, we will consider some of the major theological topics and themes about which the psalmists and their characters were concerned, life and death issues which still have great relevance to the people of God today (sec. 6.2). Finally, we will consider a number of the key terms and phrases of the psalms (sec. 6.3). They are the vehicles for the religious thematic content. We will give special attention to certain idiomatic expressions and those terms which, from the linguistic or translational perspective, may seem strange and unfamiliar to today's receptors.

6.1 The cast of psalmic participants

When the psalmist conveyed his deeply felt convictions, concerns, feelings, and desires, he often expressed himself in a way that revealed a state of intense emotion in his interaction with God. Whether psychologically and spiritually positive or negative, this involved either strong feelings of attraction and communion, or feelings of serious separation and estrangement. In addition to these two primary participants, the psalmist and YHWH, his LORD, there very often is a third set of persons mentioned (only as a general group), namely, opponents, enemies, persecutors, or troublemakers of some sort. These three form a "triangle" of agency and influence, whether for good or bad. This might be diagrammed as follows:

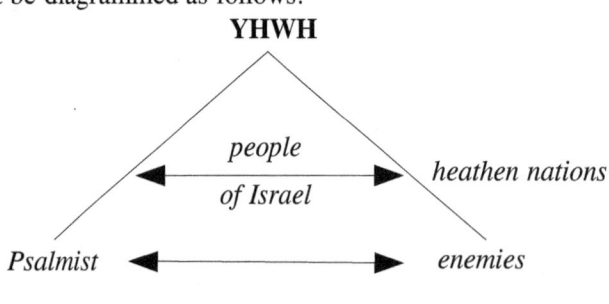

Besides the three major characters, we see in the diagram two other participant groups that may stand in relation to one another within the thematic framework of a given psalm. The psalmist himself often stands as a representative of the *people of Israel* as a whole (or more specifically, the worshipping community). Much more distant in communicative terms (actually, closer in many respects to the "enemies") are all the *heathen*, or non-Israelite, nations of earth. These two groups are secondary participants in that they are normally set in the background of the compositional development; however, they may emerge in a psalm at any time, usually only by way of reference. We find all five participants included in Psalm 2: the psalmist as the commentator, the One enthroned in heaven (v. 4), the heathen nations/kings (who also represent the enemies) (v. 1), and God's people (v. 12b). But in this psalm, instead of the major conflict being between the psalmist and his own adversaries, as is usually the case, here the psalmist stands outside the action and reports the LORD's final victory over all those who oppose his people and his purpose in the world.

A more typical example is in Psalm 3:1, which speaks of the wicked hating the righteous (cf. v. 7). The enemy is even given a voice in the disparaging remark cited in verse 2. But the confident faith of the psalmist breaks through his initial despair at the end (v. 8a) as he proclaims, "From the LORD comes deliverance!"

A similar scene is set in Psalm 4 (Psalms 3 and 4 being an example of topically "adjacent psalms"). Here the psalmist addresses his unrighteous and idolatrous opponents directly (vv. 2–3), confidently responding to their taunts in 6a. The LORD's "blessing" referred to at the end of Psalms 1, 2, and 3 is spoken of in 4:7–8 in less general terms: God has filled the psalmist's heart "with joy" and now he can "sleep in peace" and "safety."

At the end of the Psalter, we find the same basic cast of characters, but their relative importance has changed somewhat in keeping with the overall movement from lament to eulogy, from prayer to praise. Thus greater prominence is given to the secondary participants, particularly the psalmist's fellow-worshipers (see Ps. 149:1–6) and all the lowly and oppressed in the land (e.g., Ps. 146:7–9). But the wicked are ever present in the world, and God's faithful people must still rely completely upon him for ultimate justice (Ps. 149:7–9). In the very last psalm, it is instructive to note the almost total foregrounding of the gracious One who has been the "producer" and "director," as well as the "leading player," throughout the progressive drama of life and death in the history of God's saints.

At times the dramatic interaction of participants plays a prominent *structural* role in a psalm's composition. Take Psalm 86, for example, noting the sequence of personal pronouns in particular. This lament may be divided into four main sections on the basis of the persons being referred to, whether they are involved actively (i.e., in dialogue) or passively (i.e., merely mentioned). In the first section, verses 1–7, the psalmist ("I") makes his initial appeal to the LORD ("you") for help in a time of great trouble, with the reasons for doing so based on Yahweh's proven attributes (vv. 5–7). The second section, vv. 8–10, is a profession of faith in which the supreme greatness of God ("you") is foregrounded in contrast to all other gods as a witness to the pagan nations ("they"). In the third section, vv. 11–13, the psalmist ("I") comes more to the fore again as he prays for a life of piety befitting the glory of God ("you"). Everything come to a climax in the lament's concluding strophe (vv. 14–17) where the petition is expressed in more specific terms. The three primary psalmic participants are all seen in Psalm 86: the psalmist ("I") pleads to his merciful LORD ("you") for salvation from ruthless enemies ("they"). The final outcome is never in doubt, for the psalmist, in verse 17, takes his loving covenantal relationship with Yahweh as a "sign" of present protection and future deliverance (cf. vv. 7, 13). In fact, a periodic recurrence of the emphatic independent personal pronoun "you" (*ʾatta*), occurring in verses 2, 5, 10, 15, 17, may be intended as a verbal "sign" of the LORD's never-failing presence on behalf of his oppressed people.

There is considerable value in viewing the psalms, both individually and as an interlocking set, from the perspective of *who* the participants are and *how* they happen to be interacting with one another. Indeed, there is this benefit, even for the personal worship experience of the analyst. For one thing, it encourages any reader or listener to "participate" in the spiritual drama, one which may be taking place even on the stage of her/his own life. In short, it is an aid to identification and empathy with the psalmist.

But besides the personal benefit, such a participant-oriented point of view is a great help for functional analysis, and this kind of investigation is particularly necessary in psalmic studies. These prayers, professions, and hymns have not been recorded in Scripture for purely esthetic, informational, or inspirational ends. They have a much wider communicative purpose. Written in readily applicable terms, they are intended to express the highs and lows—and the plateaus—of the believer's life, both individually and in relation to the believing community. Thus they can enrich and edify the contemporary church when contextualized linguistically and socioculturally. The Psalter is not to be regarded as a quaint, alien, archaic hymnbook but rather as a diverse inventory of intensely personal case studies. Each psalm presents a poetic record of religious "action" ready to be appropriated at any time for a corresponding purpose by members of today's assembly of the saints.

In his excellent study of the Psalms entitled *Sing Unto God a New Song* (Indiana University Press, 1995), Herbert Levine says:

> . . . because the Psalms are rooted in conflict, they do indeed dramatize arguments with virtually every sacred postulate of Israel's religion. The conflictual drama of the Psalms is central to the life of every believer, for all wrestle with recurrent crises in the life of faith. The drama of the Psalms affirms doubt, but in the end transforms it. The questioning and petitioning in Psalms—all the urgent imperatives . . . — ultimately give way to acts of praise, as summed up in the Hebrew name of the book, *Tehillim*. (p. 107)

Exercise 6.1

1. Select five of the following psalms for careful study with the help of a reliable commentary such as the THP: 5, 7, 10, 12, 14, 17, 25, 31, 33, 35, 41, 44, 50, 55, 57, 60, 64, 66, 69, 71, 80, 85, 94, 118, 135, 139, 145, 147. Identify the various "dramatic roles" that are played throughout each psalm and their interaction. Tell how these relate, in turn, to the psalm's principal theme. Finally, make some suggestions with regard to the contemporary relevance of the psalm, that is, how one or more of its major communicative functions apply also to God's people today.

2. Look for the pronouns ("I," "you,", and "they") in Psalms 109 and 110. How does the interplay of these participants relate to the content and message of each psalm? Do you see any thematic connection between Psalm 109 and 110? (It will help you answer this if you observe the various associations with "hand" in these two psalms.)

3. Study the dramatic movement of Psalm 73. Summarize its "narrative plot," indicating the pertinent verses as you go along. Make a note of any surprises and points of strong emotion. How does this kind of analysis help you focus on the theme of the whole psalm? Read through Psalms 74–76 and suggest how they are related in form and function to Psalm 73. Notice that Psalm 73 is the beginning of Book III in the Psalter and the midpoint of the collection as a whole (cf. Psalms 1, 2, and 150; for a more detailed analysis of this pivotal psalm, see *Old Testament Essays* 11/1, 1998).

4. Sometimes a psalm's dramatic movement does not seem to follow a strictly chronological order. With time sequence in mind, examine Psalm 3 (easy) and Psalm 30 (more difficult) to plot the course of participant action, but allow for passages of repetition within them. Where, in these two psalms, do you find an action element that seems out of place that is, with respect to the overall temporal progression? Can you suggest any reason in relation to the psalm's total structural development that such skewing might have been done deliberately? Discuss your findings in class.

6.2 Topics and themes in the Psalter

When analyzing the topical content of the Psalter, the various subjects, themes, and motifs that appear throughout the whole book must be viewed as an integrated theological system. A "system" is an organization or arrangement in which diverse items are related so that they are seen to function as a whole. (The human body is an example of a living system.) A systemic perspective is appropriate to the Psalter, for, despite its rather diverse surface appearance in terms of form, content, and function, it gives evidence of a profound underlying unity. In fact, this unity provides a framework for interpreting individual psalms as well as the larger groupings of psalms. This framework, which is theologically based, also offers the present-day teacher, preacher, and translator a set of reference points for communicating more effectively the many similar as well as singular messages of the psalms in a coherent way.

In this section, then, we will survey some of the Psalter's primary topics (*topic* = what is being talked about) and themes (*theme* = a major topic plus something significant said about it). It will not be possible to treat the many different psalmic *motifs* (elements of a set of interrelated topics), but the same method of analysis is readily applicable to them as well.

6.2.1 Kingship

One comprehensive topic in the Psalter is that of kingship. This may be expressed thematically either as "Yahweh is King" (topic-comment, a relational view) or as "the LORD reigns" (subject-predicate, a dynamic view). Either one or both of these themes may be relevant in a given textual setting. The latter expression, *yhwh malak,* or a synonymous expression (e.g., with *ʾelohim,* "God"), occurs in six texts: Psalm 47:8; 93:1; 96:10; 97:1; 99:1; and 146:10. God is directly or indirectly addressed or referred to as "king" (*melek*) in at least another fifteen psalms scattered throughout the Psalter, from Psalm 9:4 to 149:2. The LORD's kingdom or royal rule is described as universal (Ps. 8:6), eternal (Ps. 9:7), holy (Ps. 22:3), powerful (Ps. 93:4), just (Ps. 94:15), and glorious (Ps. 24:7–8), always exercised for the good of his people (Ps. 2:12; 29:10–11) and to combat those who oppose or pervert his gracious purposes and righteous plans (Ps. 9:4–5; 10:17–18; 92:6–11). However, the "great King" will also exercise discipline and punish his covenant people when they rebel against him (Psalms 94 and 95). The divine kingship was intended to be prefigured in and symbolized by the throne of Israel, especially in the dynasty of David (Ps. 18:50 and Psalm 21), but it took God himself to make such a realization complete and effective in the person of David's great descendant, the promised Messiah (Psalms 2 and 110).

How this "divine-royal" theme interacts with some of the other key theological concepts of the Psalms (and the entire Old Testament) can be seen in Psalm 47. The universal scope of this short hymn is indicated in its very first line as "all peoples" (*ʿammim*) are called to worship, a most appropriate action in the presence of the "awesome LORD Most High (*ʿelyon*), the great King over all the earth" (v. 2). The almighty power of Yahweh, a victorious warrior fighting for his servants against all hostile peoples, is highlighted in verse 3 and is immediately contrasted with his gracious dealing with the chosen nation, "Jacob," in verse 4. The focal covenant that the LORD made with his people is alluded to under the concrete symbol of the land, their "inheritance" (*naḥala*). The incomparable glory of their "God the King" is praised in a joyous interlude (vv. 5–6; cf. Ps. 24:7–10). The final strophe of eight poetic lines (vv. 7–9) reiterates in more intensive fashion the main ideas of the first strophe, but with a slight, very significant, addition of great missiological import: here "the King of all the earth" is specifically said to "reign over the nations" (*goyim*), implying that they, too, are part of his righteous, covenantal rule (vv. 8–9; cf. Ps. 45:4, 7). The contrast between their former condition of wickedness and sin, which always requires punishment (v. 3), and their present state of blessed inclusion and fellowship (v. 9) is dramatic and unexpected. Truly, this gives us all a profound reason to exalt this God of Abraham, who is now our LORD too! This grand, royal vision is then reiterated, but in much more personal terms in the second half of Psalm 48.

6.2.2 Covenant

Another major topic of the Psalter is the covenant. The Great King of heaven and earth (Ps. 47:7; 48:2; 95:3-5) has wondrously deigned to dwell among his chosen people on Mount Zion, the royal city and stronghold of God, where his holy Temple is located (Psalm 48). The covenant he established with his people links all nations by grace to the LORD Most High, their Creator (Ps. 89:5-18), Provider (Ps. 132:15-16), and Protector (Ps. 59:1; 82:3). We might point out that the idea of the covenant is an even more basic notion than that of kingship, not only in the Psalms, but also in the Old Testament as a whole. "Covenant" (*bərit*) is explicitly referred to twelve times in the Psalter, especially in Psalms 89 and 132. Note that the Hebrew term does not mean an informal agreement between equals. It denotes a binding relationship of commitment more along the lines of an international treaty established by a powerful king (nation) and agreed to by a vassal king (nation). That is, the vassal agrees to obey the stipulated rules and requirements in return for a guarantee of peace and protection. This connection of the covenant with kingship is prominent in the psalms; Yahweh, the Supreme King, is praised for graciously establishing an eternal covenant with Israel's representative, the chosen human king David (Ps. 89:3-4, 28-29, 35-37).

The ancient covenant was to be a spiritual one based upon "loving loyalty" (*ḥesed*) and "faithfulness" (*ʾamuna*) (Ps. 89:1-2, 14, 33, 49), two key theological concepts which together with their correlates "righteousness" (*ṣedek*) and "justice" (*mišpaṭ*) recur throughout the Psalter (e.g., Ps. 89:14, 132:9). These four covenantal qualities are concentrated in some passages: In Psalm 86:5 and 15 they are mentioned from an individual perspective, and in Psalm 103:17 we see them in a communal context. Notice how, in Psalm 103, they are immediately linked with both the notions of covenant (Ps. 103:18) and kingship (Ps. 103:19). The problem throughout history was that the chosen nation of Israel and their kings, including the Davidic line, proved to be persistently unfaithful and rebellious. Therefore, severe punishment had to be meted out according to the stipulations of the covenant as explicitly stated in the *torah* (see Ps. 89:30-32, 38-51; 132:12). But God, in his mercy, "remembered his covenant" (Ps. 106:45) and promised to raise up the "Messiah," a new, eternal king from the descendants of David (Ps. 132:17). He would be divinely commissioned to renew and extend the blessings of the covenantal relationship with the LORD to people of all nations (Ps. 106:45-48).

Indeed, covenant and kingship can be said to be interconnected theological threads, along with their many related topics and motifs, forming the very warp and woof of the Psalter's thematic tapestry. The Psalter's didactic foundation has been firmly laid in Psalm 1, which speaks of God's covenant and law and then reinforced in Psalm 2, which speaks of divine kingship. This opening pair of psalms has a crucial structural and thematic discourse function: "Blessed" (*ʾashre*) by God is every person or community who accepts and lives in "righteousness" (*ṣ-d-q*) according to the divine covenant, which has been given expression verbally in "the law of the LORD" (*torat yhwh*, Ps. 1:2) and manifestation in a person as well, namely, "the anointed one" (*mešiaḥ*, Ps. 2:2). The "inheritance" (*naḥala*) now belongs to the Son, the LORD's chosen, consecrated "King" (*melek*) on the basis of both the Father's decree (Ps. 2:6-7) and also his regal deeds (Ps. 2:9). This covenant-kingdom is a diverse, living reality—a dynamic community which encompasses all the world's "nations" (*goyim*, Ps. 2:8). More specifically, it incorporates all those "who take refuge in" the anointed Messiah (Ps. 2:12) and who live in keeping with his revealed will (Ps. 1:1-2, 6). Their "way" of life is one of "blessed" fellowship with their King (*inclusio*).

6.2.3 Community

The theme of the fellowship of the godly—the community of "saints"—plays an important part in many psalms, both prayers and hymns, including the individual variety. In such psalms the role of the congregation is similar to that of the chorus in a Greek tragedy, which periodically interjects its incisive comments and pertinent reflections on the participants, their actions, and their life situations, good or bad. Often these comments take the form of a little *refrain*—whether personal (Ps. 58:9, 17) or corporate (Ps. 107:6, 13, 19, 28). This refrain may convey either a petition (Ps. 80:3, 7, 19) or an expression of solid trust in the LORD and a firm hope in his power to save (Ps.

62:1-2, 5-6). At other times (typically in the hymns but also in the laments), it is the psalmist who calls upon the religious assembly to respond in worship to something that their great God has done (Ps. 22:23; 136), or he may make a promise or vow that he intends to fulfill publicly in the presence of all God's people (Ps. 22:22, 25).

The notion of harmony and fellowship is of particular importance in the "psalms of ascent" (Psalms 120-134), which refer to experiences, both happy and sad, that affect the spiritual life of the faithful community. These psalms were probably sung or prayed in unison by groups of pilgrims making their way up to the worship center on the hill of Zion during one of the three great annual religious festivals, Passover, Pentecost, and Booths (see, e.g., Ps. 122:1-2).

The community of the godly comprise all those who have been chosen to enter into a covenant relationship with their glorious LORD (Ps. 33:12), those who worship him in truth (Psalm 26) and "walk in the light of his presence" (Ps. 89:14-18)—people of every age, class, race, and language (Ps.22:25-31). He is their God, and they are "the sheep of his pasture" (Ps. 95:7). God is ever near to help them in time of need (Ps. 65:5). Though ready to punish if they prove unfaithful to him (Ps. 81:11-16; 95:9-11), he is always willing to forgive when they turn to him in repentance (Ps. 65:3).

The Psalter is full of figurative and literal descriptions of the attributes, actions, words, and blessings of this divinely created and sustained covenant-community of believers who recognize their spiritual privilege (Ps. 16:2), mutual responsibilities (Ps. 16:3), and missionary vision (Ps. 67:5-7). Often we find such characterizations in conjunction with a depiction of their symbolic earthly locale, the royal city of Jerusalem (Psalms 46-48; 87; 122).

In vivid contrast to this joyful fellowship of the redeemed (Ps. 107:2-3) is the rebellious crowd of the wicked—an evil, destructive counter-assembly highlighted at the very beginning of the Psalter in Psalms 1 and 2 and referred to again and again throughout the corpus (e.g., Ps. 141:6-7; 142:3, 6). This diabolical community must be endured and opposed throughout this life (Ps. 26:4-5), but their shameful end is just as sure as the blessed future of the divinely honored inhabitants of Zion (Pss. 47-48; cf. 1:4-6; 2:9; 31:23; 77:15; 106:10; 149:6-9).

6.2.4 Peace

A theme less obvious but no less important than the previous three is that the LORD's covenant community experiences peace as a divine blessing, no matter what their external circumstances (Ps. 29:11). The mention of peace is often found in conjunction with an expression of the unshakable trust by which the faithful approach life and death (cf. sec. 6.2.7). This paradoxical but fundamental characteristic of the people of Zion (Ps. 122:6-9; 125:1-2, 4-5) is shown by the fact that the godly person can lie down and sleep at night (Ps. 4:3a, 8), happy and secure (Ps. 4:7-8) in the knowledge that Yahweh has heard his prayer for help (Ps. 4:3b) in a time of trouble and testing (Ps. 4:1, 2, 4, 6).

The best-known portrayal of living in the peace of God is, of course, Psalm 23. This lyric profession of trust makes the crucial point that divine peace does not mean "absence of war." Though the "deep-dark valley" be traversed, as it surely will be (Ps. 23:4a), the knowledge of the presence of God—and one's ultimate end (Ps. 23:5-6)—makes all the difference in one's overall attitude, outlook, and behavior (Ps. 23:4b).

In this connection, it is important to keep in mind that the Hebrew concept of peace (šalom) covers a considerably wider area of meaning than the corresponding English term; šalom encompasses one's total well-being—physical, psychological, and spiritual (in increasing order of importance in terms of one's relationship to Yahweh). It includes the idea of material prosperity in this life (Ps. 23:1-2; 72:3, 7), as well as the assurance one has by living in fellowship with God (Ps. 1:5; 23:6), in harmony with the LORD's principles (Ps. 23:3; Ps. 37:37; 119:165), and in the hope of his promised "inheritance" (Ps. 37:11). But the emphasis is on inner peace and rest, a salutary result of the purifying power of forgiven sin which then is manifested in a life full of personal joy (Ps. 51:7-12) and a zealous concern also for the spiritual welfare of others in relation to Yahweh (51:13-19).

6.2.5 Warfare

The sometimes shocking language of armies and battle present in many places in the Psalter might make us wonder how a God of love and a people of peace can be involved with so much fighting. It helps us understand this if we recognize that the nature of this warfare is essentially spiritual, though it does, of course, have significant social, physical, and psychological manifestations. We must also recognize that the military imagery frequently used to depict the battles in which believers are engaged with both Satanic and human forces of evil stems from the fundamental covenantal relationship that links the righteous with their faithful God. In other words, the upright community is waging war here on earth on behalf of their Sovereign LORD and under his leadership (cf. Deut. 7, 20). It is not that he needs their help; it is rather a privilege and a blessing for them to be allowed to participate in this aspect of divine dominion. It is both for their encouragement and their assurance that a reward is waiting when the victory is finally won. In contrast, what an awful experience awaits the wicked, especially those who have proven unfaithful to the divine covenant, when King Yahweh comes with his holy, heavenly armies to defend, as well as vindicate, his saints and to inflict a just punishment upon all impenitent sinners (Ps. 58). On the other hand, there often exists a stark contrast too in our present experience in life, which may be that of having to endure all sorts of oppression and persecution from those who hate God and his people (Ps. 59). (For an excellent study of the topic of *warfare* in the Psalter and its contemporary application, see James E. Adams, *War Psalms of the Prince of Peace*, Presbyterian and Reformed Publishing Co., 1991).

In the victory song of Psalm 18 some of these ideas are expressed in especially graphic imagery: The royal psalmist relies completely on the LORD—his fortress, deliverer, rock of refuge, shield, horn, and stronghold (vv. 2-3)—to defend him against the attacking enemies who have put his life in danger (vv. 3-5). In militant response to this cry for help (v. 6), God Most High comes to the rescue. This divine manifestation to do battle is described figuratively in terms of the forces of nature: a powerful earthquake, perhaps a volcanic eruption, a great thunderstorm, hail, lightning, and tempest (vv. 7-15). On the one hand, it is the LORD who guarantees the ultimate victory and deliverance from all adversaries (vv. 16-19), even death itself (vv. 4-6), for those who are righteous in his sight (vv. 20-24). But believers will still have their own little wars to wage in this life (vv. 37-45). They do this, however, secure in the knowledge that not only has God subdued every foe (vv. 46-50), but their celestial Warrior is geared up and at their side, ready to support, protect, guide, and empower them in the everyday battles in which they are engaged (vv. 25-36).

6.2.6 Sin

Closely related to the preceding is the subject of sin and sinfulness. The root cause of all types of warfare in the world according to the Psalter is the innate sinfulness of humanity, a perverted character and chronic condition that manifests itself in various forms of overt wickedness against both God and one's fellowman or woman (see the dramatic depiction of the evildoer Psalm 10). This internal and external state of affairs, which turns God into a formidable foe and an executor of judgment (Ps. 6:4-5), is expressed most forcefully in the seven penitential psalms (6, 32, 38, 51, 102, 130, 143). In these prayers the psalmist confesses and laments his evil, rebellious condition, which has alienated him from his holy and righteous LORD and frequently also from the community of faith (Ps. 51:13-15).

Perhaps the clearest example of the language of confession is found in Psalm 51. In this lament, the path of repentance and restoration is poetically outlined: It begins where every sinner must begin, with an appeal to the covenantally based "mercy" (*ḥesed*) of God (v. 1). The psalmist then honestly and openly confesses both his natural sinfulness and his persistent sins (vv. 2-5; cf. 19:12-13) in violation the LORD's standards of truth and wisdom (v. 6). This is followed by a passionate plea for forgiveness (vv. 7-9) and renewal (vv. 10-12). Then, in typical fashion for a lament petition, the psalmist suddenly makes a dramatic shift in content and tone, as he confidently expresses his trust that a positive answer to his prayer has already materialized. He further promises to proclaim the LORD's righteousness in personal testimony (v. 13), in public worship (vv. 14–15), and in consecrated devotion of the heart (vv. 16–17). He closes with a prayer that God would bless all his sacrifices and service dedicated towards the building up of the LORD's kingdom and the covenant community of Zion (vv. 18–19).

Most striking about these confessional psalms is the dramatic contrast between the pain and sense of separation that the psalmist experiences in his state of sinfulness, an aspect emphasized in Psalm 38 (vv. 3-5; cf. 102:1–11), and the righteous joy that he feels once he is assured of divine forgiveness (e.g., Ps. 22:22–31). This is typically manifested in a desire to praise God and to make a personal testimony of faith (Ps. 102:18-28).

Another good illustration of this sharp shift in perspective is found in Psalm 32. It begins with the psalmist's proclamation of "blessedness" in the sure knowledge that his "sins have been covered" (vv. 1–2). He then considers his pathetic former internal condition when he left certain transgressions unacknowledged before God (vv. 3–4). Next, in the thematic center of the prayer, he recalls his act of confession and sense of immediate forgiveness (v. 5). The appropriate response follows with a vivid profession of trust (vv. 6–7), a wise word of instruction for his audience (vv. 8–10), and a final call of joyous encouragement to all the righteous in heart (v. 11).

6.2.7 Faith and faithfulness

The opposite of sin and sinfulness is living a life characterized by unfailing faith in Yahweh and faithfulness to the covenantal ideals summarized in the *torah*. Faith is the basic requirement for initial entrance into the King's righteous community, and faithfulness the requirement for continued membership. These notions, which cannot really be separated in Old Testament theology, are expressed by the term *ḥesed*, a frequent topic in the Psalter. It may be translated in a variety of ways depending on the context, for example, as "loving loyalty," "steadfast love," "loving-kindness," "constant mercy." Since it is such a deep and complex concept, it has to be rendered in many languages by several words or an idiomatic phrase (e.g., Chichewa: "love that cannot change").

The *ḥesed* of God is central to the Psalter: it makes him the ultimate Source and Guarantee of a strong faith-life among his people. Indeed, *ḥesed* is always a dynamic, active principle—one that is ever manifested in deeds that demonstrate unshakable loyalty with regard to one's promises and commitments in life. Thus it is not surprising that virtually all acts of and appeals to *ḥesed* are defined in relation to the LORD (e.g., Ps. 17:7; 25:6; 36:7–10; 40:1–11). Though God's people are exhorted to manifest a corresponding sort of behavior, to the extent possible (Ps. 62:12; 119:88; 143:8–10), the usual term in the Psalter for the appropriate human response to divine *ḥesed* is "truth(fulness)" (*ʾemet*). These two terms are combined in 26:3: "for your *ḥesed* is ever before me, and I walk continually in your *ʾemet*." This word "truth," which is equivalent to "faith," refers to both internal (Ps. 51:6) and external trustworthiness (Ps. 86:11), and it is always described and defined in relation to Yahweh's revealed word (e.g., Psalm 119:43-44, 142-43, 151-52, 159-60).

The faith and faithfulness (or "faithful faith") of the psalmist are most clearly shown by his frequent words expressing consecrated dependence on the LORD. The LORD has spoken to his people in the *torah* and now they reply. As Psalm 1 suggests, God gave the *torah* to serve as a guide to the life of faith and the faithful life (a principle strongly reinforced in Psalm 119). The book of Psalms thus forms an ongoing divine-human dialogue that pertains to all aspects of this worldly pilgrimage—the ups, the downs, as well as the in-betweens of life, the periods of darkness and distress as well as those of rejoicing in the light/Light of life (Pss. 27:1-3, 36:9-12, 56:1-13). It is interesting to see how the central theme of *ḥesed* is worked out in the historical Psalm 107 (cf. the context of vv. 1, 8, 15, 21, 31, and 43; see also Ps. 89).

As his people express their trusting relationship with a trustworthy God, they sometimes give only a bare glimpse of their fundamental hope, for example, in that most pessimistic of psalms, 88.

On the other hand, there are psalms that are a complete prayer devoted to a profession of faith. Psalm 46 is an example. It lauds the ever-present LORD Almighty (vv. 7, 11), our refuge and strength anywhere on earth (v. 1 and v. 10). In fact, there are in the Psalter many such instances of confident anticipation and joyful optimism, some found even in the typical lament. In Psalm 22:22-31, 31:14-24, and 41:10-12, for example, we see expressions of a trust so deep and an assurance so strong that the once depressed and oppressed psalmist suddenly speaks as if his deliverance is immediately at hand or, indeed, has already taken place (e.g., Ps. 56:10-13).

6.2.8 Deliverance

Thus deliverance too is another of the prominent topics of the Psalter, one that is spoken of many times and with a variety of poetic images. Psalm 3 makes the first explicit mention of this subject: at the beginning the wicked say, "God will not deliver him" (v. 2), but at the end the psalmist's own words are, "From the LORD comes deliverance!" (v. 8). This boldness of the psalmist is based on the archetypal experience of Israel during the Exodus, and it continues throughout the Psalter—in the petitions by way of anticipation (Ps. 13:5), in the thanksgivings as a result of prior manifestation (Ps. 9:14), and in the hymns of praise as an eternal divine attribute (Ps. 149:4). The optimistic anticipation and assumption of divine deliverance is so strong that it colors the collection as a whole with a positive connotation that overcomes the negative in both the laments and the imprecations. Often the positive and negative are combined, as for example, in Psalm 69, where vv. 13-18 and 29-36 (+) contrast with vv. 1-12, 19-21, and 22-28 (-).

The trying situation from which the psalmist is delivered is often expressed in concrete natural images, such as deep waters (e.g., Ps. 32:6-7) or some debilitating disease or chronic physical affliction (e.g., Ps. 32:3-4). Nowhere is it more powerfully or plaintively pictured than in Psalm 22:6-21 with its graphic animal metaphors.

Whether the enemies from whom the psalmist seeks deliverance are human or spiritual, animate or inanimate, personal or social, physical or psychological (or some combination of these), is not always apparent (e.g., in Psalm 13 and 17:1-12). What is clear, however, is that the psalmist's experience, which is pushing him to the very brink of death and a fate from which God alone can save (Psalms 18, 25, 31), can be dealt with in no other way than by profound, heartfelt prayer (Ps. 31:22). No wonder that the exclamation of praise in response to a divine rescue that normally follows these bitter complaints is expressed in such triumphant and at times exaggerated language (e.g., in Psalms 9, 34, 47, 66).

A motif commonly associated with the theme of divine deliverance in the Psalter is that of "past performance": Yahweh is the LORD of human history and has already proven his complete dependability. God's covenant-based unchangeability is a strong argument in favor of his reliability and relevance to each succeeding generation, a theme that is highlighted in Psalm 81 (vv. 10, 16).

This time-related motif comes to the fore in the historical psalms, especially focusing, as they do, on the LORD's dealings with the people of Israel as an extended case study that stands for all of time. Psalm 78 is a good example here. It contrasts the record of Yahweh's gracious deeds of deliverance on behalf of Israel, performing wonders in Egypt and in the wilderness (vv. 12-16), with Israel's persistent and willful acts of rebellion against his covenantal principles, the two themes alternating back and forth throughout the psalm.

A similar sequence, divine rescue repaid with human wickedness, is found in Psalm 106. Here the focus is upon the LORD's ḥesed, shown to his people for the sake of his covenant despite their willful disobedience (vv. 43-45). Such acts of undeserved kindness, recorded also on the pages of world history, stand as a dynamic testimony to God's willingness and ability to do the same in the future. The righteous who ever rely solely upon him for their ultimate redemption will indeed be delivered (vv. 46-47). This is a dramatic salvation-history that calls out for joyful communal articulation and a reverent response: "Let all the people say, 'Amen'—Praise the LORD!"—for he is "the LORD, the God of Israel, from everlasting to everlasting" (v. 48).

6.2.9 Judgment

Judgment (š-p-ṭ), a major topic in the psalms, involves the righteously accurate distinguishing of one quality, person, utterance, action, or state from another and a consequent blessing or punishment being meted out, as appropriate (Ps. 1:6). The Judge is, of course, Yahweh (Ps. 7:11; 9:7; 50:6), who by virtue of his role as the almighty Creator (Ps. 19:1-6) has the authority, and indeed the responsibility, to establish a fixed norm or standard of judgment in the universe, namely, his covenantal law (Ps. 19:7-11). This "law" does not mean an oppressive set of rules and regulations, but a constant, unfailing guide for living a blessed life on earth in the confident hope of a certain blessed future (Psalm 119).

The LORD carries out his judicial activity with total righteousness (with respect to his person) and justice (in relation to others) (Ps. 9:4, 8). He judges the whole world, his own people (Ps. 135:14) as well as all outsiders (Ps. 110:6), on the basis of his everlasting covenant (Ps. 105:10; 72:2-3, 17-19). God's judgment is firmly founded upon God's free grace, as epitomized in his relationship with Abraham, the father of the faithful (Ps. 105:9; 72:17). The perfect, unbiased Arbiter of heaven and earth (Ps. 50:4-6) has a special interest in the needy and oppressed of society (Ps. 9:18; 10:14, 17-18; 12:5), and he expects his people, particularly the leaders, to manifest a similar righteous concern (Ps. 72:1-4, 12-14) and to act accordingly (Ps. 106:3). At all times and in every situation, the LORD stands as a last resort and final line of defense for the persecuted (Ps. 9:12-13; 11:2; 12:7; 17:1-2, 13-14). He will ultimately and unfailingly vindicate them and punish the wicked, whether individuals or nations (Ps. 9:4-6, 15-17; 11:5-6).

So strong is the psalmist's confidence in the righteousness of God and his just judgments that he occasionally gives expression to this certainty in a manner that may sound a little offensive today. His declaration of his own uprightness may seem somewhat boastful: "Judge me, O LORD, according to my righteousness . . ." (Ps. 7:8b; cf. 15:3-5; 18:20-24). And at times he expresses his desire to see the LORD execute judgment in words that appear rather harsh and unloving: "May [my enemies] be blotted out of the book of life and not be listed with the righteous" (Ps. 69:28; cf. vv. 22-27). Such statements are frequent in the so-called "imprecatory" psalms, for example, Psalms 58, 69, 83, 109, and 140 (cf. 2.2.3 and J. Adams *War Psalms*). But this type of prayer must first be understood in its total setting, both the wider literary context in which concentrated, conventional sayings, graphic imagery, and exaggeration abound, and the immediate textual context. Any questionable language must also be viewed from a divinely oriented perspective, for example, in relation to one's own complete unworthiness before God (see Ps. 25:7; 32:5; 40:12), the need for a complete dependence upon him as the source of all righteousness (e.g., Ps. 5:8; 7:17; 16:7-8), a willingness to leave all judging and punishment to the LORD (e.g., Ps. 7:7-8a; 11:4-6; 15:2), and a desire for the ultimate good of God's kingdom (e.g., Ps. 5:10-12; 7:9-11; 9:8-10; cf. Mt. 6:10). The psalmists may debate the justice of God, especially in view of the prevalent wickedness in the world, but they never doubted it. They knew by faith that the certain end of the dramatic conflict between right and wrong lay in the hands of a just and merciful LORD (Psalm 98), who will surely judge in their favor (cf. Ps. 96:13).

6.2.10 Worship

The nine topics already mentioned (and others could no doubt be added) have but one practical outcome, namely, our total worshipful service of Yahweh, in all of its functional aspects, such as petition, thanksgiving, praise, profession of trust, and acts of sacrificial devotion. Worship in the Scriptures, the Psalms in particular, always begins and ends with God—with his nature, presence, activities, and purposes. The holy and almighty LORD is "glorious" (k-b-d) and worthy of worship (Ps. 29:1-2, 9-10). It is he who stimulates and motivates the whole process of worshipping, for he does great things in so many different spheres, for example, in the wonders of creation (Ps. 19:1-4), in merciful love to rescue and sustain his people (Ps. 24:8; 84:11), in righteous wrath to punish the wicked (Ps. 63:2, 9-11), and in preparing an everlasting kingdom of glory for his saints (Ps. 45:2-4, 6-7, 13-17). The righteous community of faith then joyfully laud his deeds in a new song (Ps. 40:3), a skillfully composed song (Ps. 45:1), whether individually (Ps. 63:3-8) or corporately

(Psalm 96). They respond in praise to actual past performance (Ps. 40:1–5) and to anticipated future deliverance (Ps. 40:16–17).

A worshipful response, as many of the songs and prayers of the Psalter emphasize, is an essential part of a human being's personal relationship to the Supreme Being, not only in the good times, but also in the bad (e.g., Psalm 42). To glorify their Creator-King in both word (Ps. 50:15) and deed (Ps. 50:23) is, in fact, the primary purpose for which humanity was created (Psalm 48). His very name is glorious (Ps. 79:9). His glory is manifested everywhere in the world (Ps. 72:19), but especially in the place where his people worship him in faithful fellowship together (Psalm 24; 42:4).

Closely related to the theme of worshiping the LORD is the expectation that all those who would worship his name aright should display in their lives certain aspects of that same divine goodness, grace, and glory (Ps. 8:5–6; 40:8; 84:11; 96:8–9). Not just anyone can enter the sanctuary of his presence—only the person "whose walk is blameless and who does what is righteous" (Psalm 15) according to the *torah* (Ps. 43:3–4). Such perfect righteousness (Ps. 25:4–5, 8–10) is bestowed by the just Judge himself in response to sincere repentance and a personal faith in his willingness to forgive (Ps. 25:11, 16–18). This process of purification (Ps. 19:7–9) is manifested in a life of sacrificial commitment to serve the LORD (Ps. 66:13–15) and boldly testify to both God and man (Ps. 66:1–3) concerning all God's wondrous deeds (Ps. 66:5–7, 16–17), even in times of hard testing (Ps. 66:8–12).

6.2.11 Summary

To summarize the ten major topics of the Psalter, a diagram is presented below showing their interrelation as a theological chain, as it were, that begins with a covenantal faith-based relationship with God and culminates in the individual and corporate expression of dynamic, participatory worship focused completely upon him. Of course, this diagram is only an imperfect, two-dimensional attempt to visualize the multifaceted, tightly knit unity that the Bible student experiences when studying a given psalm within the context and from the perspective of the entire Psalter, whether for scholarly purposes or for personal devotion.

It is important to emphasize that the LORD is the crucial core of worship and the central topic of the Psalter, the one from which all other topics and themes derive their meaning and relevance. It is *YHWH*, the eternal I-AM and universal *King*, who has graciously established his chosen covenant *community*. He is the one who brings his perfect *peace* to those engaged in *warfare* with the forces of wickedness in this world, to those who daily repent of their *sin(fulness)* and receive the verdict of righteousness according to a *judgment* based upon the LORD's own perfect righteousness. These "blessed" people commit themselves, in turn, to a life of *faith(fulness)* as manifested in the constant attitude and activity of *worship* in keeping with the principles of his covenantal word ("law"). They thus live in ready preparation for the final *deliverance* to be realized when he brings about a total restoration of Zion and the complete renewal of his saints.

Virtually every verse of the Psalter reflects, and hence can be related to, at least one of the fundamental religious notions in this diagram. From a communicational point of view, this topical synopsis may also prove helpful to translators. These are the important interlocking ideas that they need to convey meaningfully, consistently, and cohesively in the diverse languages of the world.

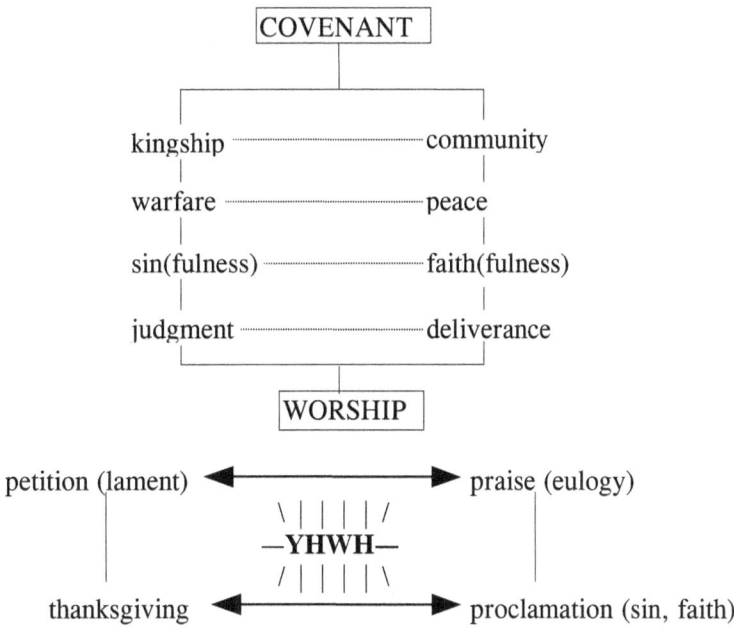

Exercise 6.2

1. Find one key passage in the Psalter (besides those mentioned in secs. 6.2.1–6.2.10) to illustrate each of the ten major topics: kingship, covenant, judgment, deliverance, warfare, sin(fulness), faith(fulness), community, and worship. Write each passage out and tell how the key concept relates to it and to the psalm as a whole.

2. Study Psalms 25, 50, 73, 86, 111–112. Identify the principal theological topics that appear in each. Describe how they are related to one another to form a unity. Propose a theme (with or without subparts) that summarizes each psalm's main point and purpose.

3. Which of the ten topics mentioned in assignment 1 are important in the sociocultural setting in which you live? Cite some examples to show how this is so. Which is the most important of all? Explain why it is important. Do any of them form the subject of songs or other poetic works in your language? If so, give an example.

4. If you have the Bible in your language, how is the Hebrew word bərit, "covenant," translated? Does this translation convey the sense of the original term adequately? Would any other word or phrase be more suitable? Explain with reference to a given passage.

5. Which of the ten central psalmic concepts is most difficult to render in your language? Why is this the case? Is the problem linguistic or cultural (or both)? Suggest how you can best solve this translation problem.

6. Choose one of the ten topics in sections 6.2.1–6.2.10. Look at the passages mentioned as examples in the section that discusses it. Do any of these references seem to you not to fit well? If so, explain why you think they don't. Then find three additional passages from the Psalms that *would* apply to various aspects this particular topic. Why are they relevant?

6.3 Key terms of the Psalter

Now that we have surveyed the major topics and themes of the Psalter, we turn to consider some of its individual vocabulary items in relation to a specific target language, namely, Chichewa. We want to overview several important words and phrases and observe how they interrelate to convey the author's intended message as a whole. We will not go into a detailed discussion of lexical analysis with respect to the original biblical text here. (A basic introduction to this type of study can be found in pp. 8–9 of Barnwell's 1986 *Bible Translation: An Introductory Course in Translation Principles*.) Bible translators who lack the skill to carry out a technical examination of Hebrew vocabulary must learn to use the available scholarly tools that give insight into their meaning, such as Bible dictionaries, encyclopedias, word-books, exegetical commentaries, especially the THP, and study Bibles. Scripture translations in other languages—major and minor, related or unrelated—are another helpful resource.

6.3.1 Learning to distinguish components of lexical meaning

After the specific sense of a given Hebrew word has been determined in relation to its context, it must be transferred to fit, as it were, within the framework of a totally different semantic system: the conceptual grid of the target language. This is never an easy process, even when two languages are closely related. In fact, it is the words that seem to correspond most closely that often give the most trouble; differences in *connotation* may be overlooked if the translator just assumes that they are the same. Thus, there may well be significant variations in the associations of an apparently equivalent TL word due to its usage in a very different sociocultural setting.

For example, if one asks for the Chewa equivalent of "sacrifice" (as in "You do not delight in sacrifice [*zebaḥ*]" in Ps. 51:16), just about any mother-tongue speaker person would quickly come up with the word *nsembe*. This was an important part of the ritual vocabulary of the traditional religious system. It was also the term adopted for use in the first Protestant and Catholic Bibles. Christians and non-Christians alike are very familiar with it. The term presents several problems, however. In the first place, the word's strong associations with ancient African indigenous religion—which is still being actively practiced in many places today—may give it a negative connotation for some people, in particular those Christians who wish to "purify" the Scripture from pagan ritualistic notions. But an even greater difficulty is presented by the precise referential aspects of *nsembe*. Traditional Chewa "sacrifices" for the purpose of worship only rarely, if ever (the issue is debated), involved the taking of life ("blood sacrifice"), which would have angered the ancestral spirits. Rather, they were offerings of some common domestic foodstuff, especially beer, meat, and maize meal, or agricultural produce which were brought to a rural ancestral shrine. This use of the term *nsembe* naturally results in a partial componential clash of meaning in those Bible passages where an animal sacrifice to God is explicitly referred to (e.g., Ps. 51:19).

A basic principle to keep in mind when dealing with the lexical aspect of translation is that the *meanings of words almost never correspond completely between any two languages*. The greater the historical and cultural distance between the languages, the greater this verbal gap will be. One cannot rely on a dictionary to solve this problem, for dictionaries are always incomplete or distorted by the perspective of the compiler(s). Therefore, Bible translators must learn to do their own research and carefully check out all the senses and usages that a dictionary cites for a particular term, even in the case of a special Scripture-related word list that the team itself has compiled. The same applies to the use of a closely related language version as a "model" during the translation process. Many seemingly corresponding terms will, on further investigation, turn out to be slightly different with regard to either denotation or connotation. A Tonga "village" (*munzi*), for example, tends to be much smaller in size than its Chewa counterpart (*mudzi*) due to socioeconomic as well as political reasons. Thus, while the latter could be used as a translation equivalent for "town" in the Bible, the former could not.

A related principle is this: Most words have several "meanings" or distinct senses. The analyst must aim to discover as many of them as possible, focusing on their use in specific sociocultural contexts and interpersonal situations. If a thorough study is not undertaken, serious mistakes can be made. Take, for example, the word selected to render "grace" (*ḥen*) in the early, missionary-translated Catholic and Protestant Chewa Bibles, for example, in Psalm 45:2: "grace was anointed on your lips" (or: "your lips were anointed with grace"). In the Protestant version "grace" is usually translated by the word *cisomo*. This interesting term does convey the notion of favor in some contexts, but this slight overlap in meaning with the Hebrew *ḥen* is relatively insignificant. In most cases, *cisomo* refers to the personal quality of affability or a certain attractiveness of disposition that makes other people like and admire you. In fact, a type of magical potion by the same name (*cisomo*) can be purchased at any local market to enable one to acquire or strengthen such a desirable characteristic! From a strictly secular Chewa perspective, the word *cisomo* is perfect for Psalm 45:2, which is speaking of a royal wedding scene. Certainly at such a time an amorous man would greatly long for the possibility of having his lips covered with *cisomo*!

The old Catholic Bible in Chewa used the term *kukongola*, "beauty," for "grace" in Psalm 45:2. Now this is an improvement on *cisomo*, but not by much. Here it would mean that the man being praised has "beautiful lips," rather than the intended meaning of "kind words" (CEV), "eloquent speaker" (TEV), or "fair speech" (NAB). The normal Catholic term for "grace" in Chewa was *caulere*, "a free gift," as in Psalm 84:11, but this does not fit at all in Psalm 45:2. It is not an accurate rendering either exegetically or culturally. And if it were to be used in Psalm 84:11, it could easily be misunderstood as referring to the most commonly presented "free gift" in traditional society, namely, a live chicken!

A literal, formally consistent type of translation only makes such problems of meaning-transfer worse. The use of Chewa *nyumba*, 'house/hut', for example, to render the Hebrew *bayit* is appropriate in *some* contexts, but cannot be used when *bayit* refers to "relatives" (Ps. 45:10), "nation" (Ps. 98:3), or "lineage" (Ps. 115:12). In this case, only *one* of the senses of the Hebrew term matches the corresponding TL word, and when the Hebrew term is used with a different sense, the same TL word cannot be used to convey it. The same difficulty presents itself in rendering the related Hebrew term *ʾohel* "tent": the Chewa equivalent *hema* is partially acceptable in a passage such as Psalm 15:1 with reference to the "tabernacle" (on its own it is too general). To use *hema* in Psalm 19:4, however, results in nonsense: "In [the heavens] he has set a tent for the sun" (RSV). No fabric dwelling could last long next to such fiery heat!

Translators must be on the lookout for the reverse situation as well. The TL term may be the one that encompasses a wider area of meaning than its apparent equivalent in the SL. For example in Tonga, *-yanda* can mean either "desire" as in Psalm 27:4 (Heb. *b-q-sh*), or it can mean "love" as in Psalm 31:23 (Heb. *ʾ-h-b*), or it can mean "want, will" as in Psalm 40:8 (Heb. *r-ṣ-h*).

The key term *ḥesed*, "mercy" is a more complex example: *ḥesed* is consistently rendered as *chifundo* in the old Protestant version of Chewa. The word *chifundo* denotes a strong desire for some person, usually to help him or her out in the time of trouble or need, though there is a latent, and troublesome, sexual component in certain settings. This term would fit well in Psalm 31:6, "Save me in your *ḥesed*," where the LORD is called upon to act against the pursuing enemies of the psalmist and to mercifully deliver him. The Catholic version employed a different word, *chisoni*, in this passage. While there is a considerable overlap in meaning between *chifundo* and *chisoni*, two crucial components are different: *chifundo* carries a much stronger implication of consequent action than *chisoni*. In other words, a person who feels *chifundo* not only observes someone who needs help, but is also strongly moved to give it. The person with *chisoni*, on the other hand, is not so deeply affected and might simply walk away and leave the situation for someone else to resolve. *Chisoni* is closer to the English "sorrow," especially since it may be applied in general, impersonal situations, whereas *chifundo* may not, for it must always have an animate object present in the context.

However, *chifundo* cannot be used as an equivalent for *ḥesed* in its every occurrence. If it were to be used consistently as the rendering for *ḥesed*, it would produce unnaturalness or it would distort the intended sense of the Hebrew text. In Psalm 33:5, for example, we read that "the earth is full of the *ḥesed* of Yahweh." The Protestant Chewa version has *chifundo* here, but the meaning is certainly not apparent: For one thing, a genitive ("of") construction is used here to convey what is essentially an activity on the part of Yahweh (i.e., "he is kind to everyone everywhere on earth" [CEV], though this may be a bit too general). Moreover, *chifundo* does not seem to fit the preceding context (vv. 1–4), which does not specifically mention anyone in need of the LORD's help. On the other hand, *chisoni*, "sorrow," would produce a collocational clash in this context with such terms as "celebrate," "praise," "sing," "make music," and "shout for joy" (vv. 1–4). For this reason the Catholic version instead employs *caulere* for "grace." But this then raises a valid question in the minds of most listeners: What sort of a divine "free-gift" fills the whole world? Perhaps the best solution in this situation is that of the new interconfessional version in Chewa, which is to utilize a compound expression, *chikondi chosasinthika* "unchanging/unfailing love." It conveys more of the richness of *ḥesed*, though certainly not in its full sense and theological significance.

The foregoing illustrates how important it is to analyze key words as related groups, not only in the SL, but also in the TL. How can this best be done? One way is with a procedure called *componential comparison*. The idea is to group the words of a given lexical field according to their "semantic components" of denotative (also called referential) meaning. This must be done with respect to the specific textual settings in which the word is used, for a word normally has its various senses defined according to particular contexts, and these will have to be fully determined first. For example, in Hebrew the verbs *gaʾal* and *pada* may both be translated either as "redeem," with an emphasis on the agent's beneficial action on behalf of someone (e.g., Ps. 44:26; 49:7–8, 5; 74:2; 77:15), or as "save/deliver" if the resultant state of the personal object seems to be in focus (e.g., Ps. 28:9; 72:13–14; 103:4; 109:31; 145:19). The second sense is covered by two other common verbs, *yašaʿ* and *naṣal*, both of which mean "deliver" or "rescue" (e.g., Ps. 34:6; 59:1–2; 72:12; 107:6). However, *naṣal* appears to cover a broader range of things that one may be rescued *from* (e.g., from "mud" and "water" as in Ps. 69:14), while the focus of *yašaʿ* is on some human enemy (e.g., Ps. 44:7). What distinguishes *gaʾal* from the other three verbs is that it carries an important additional component of meaning: an actual or symbolical *kinship* relation between the agent and object(s) concerned (see Ps. 107:2–3). This gives the word *gaʾal* a richer set of semantic associations since it appears in a wider variety of contexts (e.g., Ruth 2:20). It could also be said to have a deeper positive connotation, though this, of course, cannot be proved.

Now let us compare these four Hebrew terms with their closest Chewa equivalents: *-ombola* (*gaʾal*), *-sungitsa* (*pada*), *-pulumutsa* (*yašaʿ*), and *-landitsa* (*naṣal*). There is a rough correspondence here. But the favorable associations of the first Chewa word, which means "redeem," are a result of its connection with the practice of slavery, whether indigenous in nature or of foreign origin, not with blood relationship or legal obligation. As to the second Chewa word -*sungitsa*, it has the positive connotation of *pada*, generally speaking, although there is never any "ransom" involved, and it is normally used with inanimate objects. It is a causative form of the verb "keep, preserve, save up (something valuable)." The third and fourth Chewa terms should probably be reversed, from a strictly semantic perspective. However, the better-known and more widely used *-pulumutsa* was employed to translate *yašaʿ* because it has more important derivatives than *naṣal* (e.g., *yəšuʿa* "salvation" in Ps. 3:8; 14:7; 62:2).

An accurate, up-to-date dictionary in the target language can help to get one started in this comparative and contextualizing process of lexical study. But it will usually be necessary for the various individual "entries" to be tested and refined, supplemented, contextualized (with samples of actual usage), or even corrected on the basis of this investigation of a term's usage in natural discourse texts, whether oral or written, produced in diverse situations. The process of preparing and updating a biblical, key-term dictionary is one that needs to be carried out over the duration of a given translation project.

A componential analysis makes it possible to compare the sets of semantic components of a group of related words for their *similarities* with respect to one another and, even more important, for their various *differences* in meaning. Term X will be found to differ from Y with respect to component(s) such-and-such, and from Z with regard to some other focal component(s). After several words have been contrastively differentiated in relation to one another, then the complete *range* of usage and distribution for each term needs to be studied. This is to determine its supplementary features or associative aspects of meaning, especially those that restrict it to certain settings (e.g., traditional religion) or that give it a particular connotation, particularly if the latter is negative.

Once a given word group from the TL has been fully differentiated internally by cross-comparison and carefully plotted according to range of usage, one can turn to the closest related set in the biblical SL text (previously analyzed) to see how the respective terms match up and where any special problem areas lie. To resolve any points of mismatching (inequivalence), it will often be necessary to devise a concise phrase to convey the important components, for instance, a generic word (classifier) plus either a more specific term, a descriptive phrase, a loanword, or a cultural substitute (see Barnwell 1986, p. 9).

As a simplified example to illustrate the procedure just outlined, consider the Hebrew verbs that designate the general notion of "praise" in the Psalter. We will look at only four of them: *halal*, *zamar*, *yadah*, and *šabaḥ*, their most common context being "praise the LORD." An example of each can be seen, respectively, in Psalms 148:7, 9:11, 33:2, and 147:12. Their individual meanings can be distinguished as follows:

halal = laud, boast in the great attributes or activities of someone, especially of God (e.g., Ps. 10:3; 22:22; 44:8; 49:6; 64:10; 106:5; 115:17; 146:2; 150:1–6).

zamar = to joyfully praise someone with song or musical accompaniment (e.g., Ps. 9:11; 21:13; 33:2; 47:6–7; 71:22–23; 98:4; 101:1; 105:2; 149:3).

yadah = declare openly, confess, publicly acknowledge, often with an accompanying notion of gratitude (e.g., Ps. 6:5; 18:49; 32:5; 43:4; 71:22; 97:12; 100:4; 136:2).

šabaḥ = extol, exalt someone (always God) for his greatness/glory (e.g., Ps. 63:3; 106:47; 117:1; 145:4; 147:12). This is the most infrequent verb of the four.

A possible set of English equivalents for these four Hebrew words would be as follows: "praise" (or "acclaim") for *halal*, the most generic and frequent term; "exalt" (or "extol") for *šabaḥ*, a word that is roughly the same in denotation; "sing praises" for *zamar*, which has a more specific sense; and "thank" (or "laud") for *yadah*, which also has a specific sense.

The general lexical field of worship-praise is obviously an important one in Hebrew thought and culture, judging from the number of words in this grouping. In addition to the four just discussed, for example, a translator would also have to consider a number of others, somewhat less closely related: *rum*, "lift up/exalt"; *kabad*, "glorify"; *nagad*, "declare"; *šir*, "sing"; *barak*, "bless"; *ranan*, "sing/shout with joy"; and *gadal*, "magnify."

It may be difficult to find suitable equivalents for such closely related Hebrew words in another language. In Chewa, for instance, there is a somewhat smaller verbal inventory with regard to worship-praise to select from, though happily there are enough terms available that overuse can be avoided and the primary distinctions may be matched relatively closely. The Chewa verb *-tama*, for example, seems to be quite suitable to express the Hebrew *halal*: it denotes pure praise, the highest form of acclaim, such as would be given a paramount chief. A close synonym of *-tama* is *-tamanda*, which carries the additional notion of boasting in someone, and it is suitable to express *šabaḥ*. The Chewa word *yamika* expresses the Hebrew *yadah* well because it includes the component of thankfulness as part of the praise being offered. The most difficult among the four Hebrew terms to duplicate in Chewa is *zamar* with its additional feature of an associated musical accompaniment or setting. The closest single word equivalent in Chewa would be the verb *-imba*, "sing" with a suffixal extension (i.e., -*imbira*) making it "sing to/for (someone)" on account of something good that he or she did.

Hebrew words in the semantic field of "pray" and "petition" are an even more challenging semantic set to deal with. These verbs appear in the general context of praying to God: *palal* (Ps. 5:2), *qaraʾ* (Ps. 3:4), *ṣ/zaʾaq* (Ps. 77:1), and *šawaʿ* (Ps. 30:2). A survey of lexicons and Bible dictionaries suggests the following distinctions:

palal = apparently the most general and common word for prayer, appearing mainly in nominal form, with the possible overtone of intercession and/or a context of trouble (e.g., Ps. 4:1; 6:9; 32:6; 39:12; 69:13; 80:4; 88:13; 90 [title]; 102:17; 109:4; 141:5).

qaraʾ = to "call out" verbally in prayer to God (who is always named) in anticipation of his response at a time of need (e.g., Ps. 22:2; 27:7; 34:6; 79:6; 81:7; 116:2; 145:18; 147:9).

ṣ/zaʾaq = a loud outcry for deliverance in the time of trial or distress is implied, with a prominent vocal component (e.g., Ps. 9:12; 22:5; 34:17; 88:1; 107:6; 142:1; 142:5).

šawaʿ = only in verb form, the most infrequent and most formally restricted term (i.e., mainly 1st ps. sg.), suggesting a cry for help with a note of intensity, especially in a lament or a thanksgiving psalm (e.g., Ps. 18:41; 22:24; 28:2; 72:12; 88:13).

To illustrate the search for equivalents to "pray" in a receptor language, again we look at Chewa. Here the most general term for "pray," -*pemphera,* poses no problems. Related to the verb -*pempha* "ask (for)," it was frequent in the traditional religious system, directed either to the High God (*Mulungu, Chauta*) or to the ancestral spirits (*mizimu*). No special ritual associations are attached to this term; hence it has from the beginning of the Christian era been deemed suitable for use with respect to the God of the Bible. The word also implies speaking aloud, as is the case with the Hebrew *palal*. (In ancient times even when praying in private, silent speech was rare, if practiced at all.) The more intensive Hebrew word *šawaʿ* is adequately represented by the Chewa verb -*pembedza*, to "entreat, beseech," which has now been extended to refer to religious worship in general. The other two Hebrew terms, *qaraʾ* and *ṣ/zaʾaq* are more difficult to find equivalents for. Literal renderings following the KJV, RSV, or even the TEV turn out to be quite misleading in Chewa; for example, -*pfuula*, "shout out," for *qaraʾ* implies trying to get God's attention way up there in heaven! A better rendering would be -*pemba*, "beg (for)," even though it is not used very often in modern prayer contexts; but being related to the common word for worship, -*pembedza*, helps to convey the intended meaning. As for an equivalent for *ṣ/zaʾaq*, this too poses some problems. The Chewa word -*lira*, "cry (out)" has the sense of weeping in sadness, and it raises the question of why the psalmists always *cried* when they prayed to God. But if the intensifying lexical diversity of the original text is to be matched, the Hebrew "cry out" needs to be rendered some way, and it turns out that there *is* an idiom in Chewa which conveys the sense nicely, at least in certain contexts: -*gwira mwendo*, "grab the leg" (of the person being "entreated"). This idiom also brings out some of the strong emotive connotation of the Hebrew.

Precise distinctions in meaning may not always be intended, especially in poetry. The lexical diversity may have been introduced simply to beautify the language or to create a parallel poetic line, although the possible presence of the rhetorical strategy of "heightening" should always be kept in mind. Alternatively, it may be that the use of close synonyms is for some other literary purpose such as emphasis or to suggest the entire scope of a given subject. One of the clearest examples of the latter occurs with reference to the "law" (*torah*) in Psalm 119. Similarly, in Psalm 19:7–9, we find six Hebrew synonyms used to present a "complete" picture of the all-sufficient, ever-purposeful divine Word. They are as follows (with their renderings in both English and Chewa along with a literal back-translation):

torah "law": *ziphunzitso* = teachings (the kind given in schools and churches)

ʿedut   "instruction": *malangizo* = instructions (advice on moral behavior and correct living)

piqqud   "precepts": *zolamula zokhazikika* = established commands (a manufactured expression designed to bring out something of the original sense)

miṣwah   "commands": *malamulo* = laws (typical of any legal or judicial system)

yirʾah   "fear": *kulemekeza* = to-respect/honor (with "Yahweh" as direct object only in this instance)

mišpaṭ   "ordinances": *chiweruzo* = judgment (the singular form being more natural)

In Chewa this series is followed by a concluding summary expression, "all of these writings" (*zolembedwa zonsezi*). This is to show that they are to be considered together as closely related aspects of a single unit, a written corpus that is indeed "more precious than gold" (Ps. 19:10).

However, there is an important translation principle that should be mentioned here: the value of *consistency*. A central biblical concept such as *torah* ought to be rendered by the same expression in the target language whenever the context and natural TL usage allows. This pattern preserves semantic agreement and helps build the word's larger area of meaning, which accumulates with each occurrence and in every slightly different setting in which it is found. If synonyms were to be used interchangeably or indiscriminately, the key term's significance could be lost in translation; that is, its unique meaning and prominence would not be reproduced.

A particular word's meaning in a specific context can be determined by seeing what synonyms could replace it in the same context. But the word's overall *range* of meaning, that is, the various possible senses that it may designate, must also be fully explored. This is done by noting the distinctive senses (or sets of semantic components) that it carries in different contexts. Take the Hebrew word "glory" (*kabod*), for example. In a passage such as Psalm 24:7 ("that the king of glory may come in"), some awe-inspiring physical manifestation is evidently being referred to—something about the king that is visible for all to see (cf. Ps. 145:5, 12). This wonderful physical or visible component is made even more concrete in passages where God's "glorious" deeds are lauded (e.g., Ps. 111:13), especially in creation: "the heavens declare the glory of God" (Ps. 19:1; cf. Ps. 8:1). In Psalm 26:8 the term *kabod* designates the very presence of Yahweh himself; he is Glory personified, and the temple is "the place where [his] glory dwells." In other contexts, *kabod* designates the worship or praise that befits a glorious God: "Ascribe to the LORD . . . glory . . . in his temple all cry, 'Glory!'" (Ps. 29:1, 9). This is undoubtedly the most common usage (see also Ps. 34:3; 66:2; 69:30; 72:19; 86:12; 108:5; 149:1, 9). Related to this is the great honor and respect the LORD has because of his nature and attributes, and not only God but also his people and his place (i.e., the city of Jerusalem and the temple), for they too possess glory by virtue of their relationship with him (e.g., Ps. 3:3; 8:5; 16:3; 87:3). In a further, figurative use of the word (a metonymy), *kabod* may refer to that emotive-psychological component of a person that experiences glory and the great joy it inspires (Ps. 16:9), feelings that an enemy can extinguish (Ps. 7:5, perhaps also Ps. 4:2).

The principle of consistency that we referred to earlier is more difficult to maintain in translation with an abstract concept like *kabod*. In Chewa, for example, the component that involves some notion of visual splendor and magnificence must be rendered by the term *ulemerero* (related to the verb *-lemera*, 'to be wealthy,' which is, in turn, an applicative extension of the verb *-lema*, 'to be heavy' or 'weighty'). But the less concrete sense of possessing honor requires a different, but related word *ulemu*. Then for contexts where it is *verbal* honoring that is in focus (e.g., Ps. 29:9), there is yet another term: *M'lemekezeni!* (from the verb *kulemekeza*) meaning "Reverence him!" But none of these works for such idiomatic usage as occurs in Psalm 16:9 and Psalm 30:12; a term signifying the animating core of one's whole being is preferable, *moyo*, 'life (force)' (closely akin to *mtima*, 'heart', one's emotive-psychological center).

Finally, a word's *connotation* must be carefully considered, the emotive and attitudinal overtones that it carries. It is difficult to know for sure what this might have been in the case of a Hebrew expression, although a good guess can often be made based upon its context. For example, the words "glory" (*kabod*) and "Zion" (in Ps. 9:11) both probably evoked a very positive feeling in the minds of most Hebrew hearers. On the other hand, "evil" (*raʿ*, in Ps. 7:4), "enemy" (*ʾoyeb*, in Ps. 7:5), and "grave" (*šeʾol*, in Ps. 6:5) would obviously have had a negative connotation. Exclamations are almost completely connotative in their communicative force since they convey very little designative information. In Biblical Hebrew their connotation is usually negative, for example, "Aha!" (*heʾah*, in Ps. 70:3) or "woe" (*ʾoya*, in Ps. 120:5). But the connotation of most words is usually neutral in emotive effect and can be either positive or negative depending on their context. Many lexical items connote little or nothing at all: prepositions, conjunctions, demonstratives, relatives, and interrogatives as well as everyday terms such as "say" (Ps. 10:13) or "come" (Ps. 17:2). In any case, it is important for translators to be aware of the intended connotation of a biblical expression, especially where it is strong, and then to see that this gets communicated correctly in the TL. The term "nations" (*goyim*), for example, needs to be translated by one of two different terms in Chewa, depending on whether its connotation is negative (i.e., "heathen/pagans" *akunja* in Ps. 9:5, 17, 19, 20) or positive (i.e., "foreigners" *amitundu* in Ps. 67:2; 72:17; 105:1). The connotative component of words is an extremely important consideration in all poetry, which is designed to play on the various emotions of the hearer (or reader).

Exercise 6.3.1

1. Select three or more *related* key terms typical of the psalms, ones that you find difficult to distinguish in your own language. Try to define these terms according to their different shades of meaning in Hebrew. Then suggest words or phrases in your language that will best convey these different meanings, at least in most psalmic passages. Make a tentative componential analysis of each term as you carry out this assignment. (Refer to the THP for assistance.)

2. Which one of the key topical terms of the Psalter (6.2.1–10) is the most difficult to convey meaningfully in your language? Tell why this is so and what you have tried as possible solutions. Give several passages where one or another of the solutions works out satisfactorily and others where the sense does not get communicated very well, if at all.

3. Give a literal back-translation of Psalm 86:15 in your language (or another language that you are familiar with). Read the THP and/or some other reliable commentary on this passage. How do their insights bear on the original translation? Are any corrections or improvements needed? If so, comment on these.

4. List the various expressions in your language used to render the six terms for "law" in Psalm 19:7–9, and provide a back-translation of them into English. Is there a different TL term for each Hebrew term? Do the terms shed light on the overall concept of law? Can you suggest any improvements in the list? Now look at the TEV's renderings of these six terms. How would you evaluate them?

5. In the following passages the Hebrew word for "fear" (*y-r-ʾ*) has two distinct senses: Ps. 2:11; 19:9; 23:4; 33:8; 34:4, 9; 76:1; 91:5. What are these two senses? How would you differentiate them in your language? Look up these passages in the TEV and CEV, and make a chart showing how "fear" is rendered in each of them.

6. Do a componential analysis of the terms in each of the following sets both for Hebrew and for your language:

    (a) mercy, grace, love, kindness
    (b) trust, believe, hope, obey

To the extent that you are able, study the Hebrew terms in a commentary such as the THP, a concordance (Young's is good for this purpose, and from there move to *The New Englishman's Hebrew Concordance*), and a theological or exegetical dictionary. Also be sure to examine all the different contexts in which the word is used. Discuss the results of your investigation in class and try to come to some agreement as to how these words can best be distinguished in your language. (For a sample of more evaluations of key lexical sets in Chichewa, see *Buku Loyera*, ch. 4.)

7. Find three psalmic terms that you feel always (or normally) have the same strong connotation in every context—either positive or negative. Give an example of each such usage. Do the words that are used to translate these Hebrew terms in your language carry the same connotation as each of the Hebrew words? Describe any problems or possible exceptions that you encounter here with regard to either the SL or the TL analysis.

6.3.2 Idiomatic expressions

Hebrew idiomatic expressions present special difficulty when it comes to transferring them to another language with its own particular framework of meaning and lexical inventory shaped by a different sociocultural setting. Therefore they need special attention. The first problem is to recognize them where they occur in the biblical text. Often an unusual or difficult-to-understand group of words in a literal English version (e.g., NASB) is a clue that an idiom may be present in the Hebrew. This can be confirmed by a good commentary (e.g., THP).

An idiomatic expression consists of two or more words that together form a semantic unit. The constituent words are usually found in the same order every time the idiom occurs, and the meaning it conveys is something different from and more unified than the sum of the individual lexical items that make it up. For example, the expression "the one who lifts up my head" in Psalm 3:3 has nothing to do with lifting and nothing to do with somebody's head. Rather, it is about restoring confidence, courage, hope, honor, or dignity to a person who is discouraged or depressed. (In TEV it is rendered "restore my courage"; in CEV, "give me . . . great honor.") This idiom may initially have had some historical basis, such as a king telling a servant bowed down before him in humility or sorrow to look up, but if so, its origination is now unknown. The saying became conventionalized and was used by the psalmists without any thought of its literal relation to a real-life situation. The idiom may have added some additional impact to the utterance in which it occurs.

On the other hand, there are always a number of idioms in any language that are completely "worn out," that is, so frequently used that they carry no special impact in speech. Such expressions may be analyzed componentially just as if they were a single word, e.g., "lift yourself up against" means "oppose" in Psalm 7:6. Other idioms, however, are more forceful and thus contribute a degree of emphasis, intensity, or focus to the concepts they designate, e.g., "you dug/pierced ears for me" (= gave me the ability to hear/obey, Ps. 40:6), "he lifted his heel against me" (= betrayed me; Ps. 41:9) and "I have not restrained my lips" (= I have freely spoken about, Ps. 40:10). It is important to try to reproduce this rhetorical effect, if possible, in a translation. This can be done by using a functionally equivalent idiom in the TL or even some type of figurative usage. Some Hebrew idioms cannot be interpreted with certainty, for example, "with a killing in my bones" in Ps. 42:10 (cp. RSV: "As with a deadly wound in my body"; NIV: "My bones suffer mortal agony"; TEV: "I am crushed by their insults"). In such cases, translators can only refer to the commentaries or standard versions and select the interpretation that seems to fit the context best in their language.

In Psalm 4:6b the rather long Hebrew idiom "lift up the light of your face upon us" would be meaningless in most languages if rendered literally. Worse, it might convey a completely different meaning, one that is not correct. In Chewa, for example, a "shining/lightened face" refers to someone who is either very healthy or has an attractive facial expression. Thus to use it in Psalm

4:6 could mean something like "Make us all beautiful/handsome, O LORD!" This would seem to go right along with what is said in the first line of verse 6! Another complication here is the likelihood that in verse 6b there is an allusion to the Aaronic blessing of Numbers 6:25–26. Such an indirect reference, perhaps used in an ironic sense here, should not be ignored (see the THP). The original could be reflected partially as in TEV ("Look on us with kindness!") and in CEV ("Let your kindness . . . shine brightly on us") and in the Chewa (*mutiyang'anire ndi maso onse awiri*, "Look at/Watch over us with both eyes"). Even if that sort of rendering is possible, a footnote reference to Numbers 6:25–26 and a comment on its significance ought to be inserted.

There are a good number of idioms in Hebrew poetry that mention a certain part of the human body. Some examples are: "they have set their eyes" (Ps. 17:11), meaning to watch for a chance (TEV); "bend the ear towards" (Ps. 17:6), meaning to pay attention to (Chewa has *mundichere khutu* "set your ear like a trap [to catch what I have to say]"); "they shut tight their fat" (Ps. 17:10), meaning "they have no pity" (TEV) (Chewa has *alibe mtima*, "they have no heart"); "my kidneys instruct me" (Ps. 16:7), meaning "my conscience warns me" (TEV); "who does not lift up his breath to a lie" (Ps. 24:4), which TEV renders "who do not worship idols"; "my head shall be lifted up" (Ps. 27:6), which CEV renders "you will let me defeat all my enemies"; "they fell under my feet" (Ps. 18:38), which TEV renders "they lie defeated before me"; "he guards all his bones" (Ps. 34:20), which TEV renders "the LORD preserves him completely." A literal translation of these idioms is probably not possible in any language. For example, a formal reproduction of the last passage might well suggest the practice of divination, or even sorcery, in an African context.

A considerable number of Hebrew idioms are based upon verbs of motion and positional states. The following are some examples: "you gave a wide place for my steps under me" (Ps. 18:36), which TEV renders "you have kept me from being captured"; "my enemies you gave me [their] back" (Ps. 18:40), meaning "you make my enemies turn tail and run" (an equivalent idiom in English); "lead me on a level path" (Ps. 27:11), meaning "teach me to choose to do the right thing in life"; "nor stands in the way of sinners" (Ps. 1:1), which TEV renders as "do not follow the example of sinners" (the English expression "stand in the way of" means to oppose or block the progress of someone, just the opposite of the intended sense); "you established me a strong mountain" (Ps. 30:6), which CEV renders as "you made me strong as a mighty mountain"; "you set them in slippery places" (Ps. 73:18), meaning you trip them up (to use an English idiom); "I am cut off from your sight" (Ps. 31:22), which CEV renders as "they've chased me far away from you!" In Chewa if this last example were to be translated literally with the passive form of "cut," -*dulidwa*, it could imply that either witchcraft or the violation of a sexual taboo was the cause of the psalmist's misfortune!

It is not likely that these idiomatic expressions can be transferred word for word to any target language. However, the vernacular will have its own stock of idioms, and sometimes such idioms can be used to "compensate" for or replace those lost from the original text. For example, Chewa idioms that incorporate the word "heart" (*mtima*) have been employed for certain psalmic concepts that pertain to human feelings and attitudes: "to set one's heart upon" (= to trust, Ps. 9:10); "to lower the heart" (= to be patient, Ps. 40:1); "to burn in heart" (= to be angry, Ps. 78:21); "to die in the heart" (= to forget, Ps. 44:20); "to throw away the heart" (= to be troubled, Ps. 30:7); "to be good in heart toward" (= to show favor/kindness, Ps. 31:21); "to cause the heart to descend" (= to comfort, Ps. 119:76); "to be turned around in one's heart" (= to repent/change one's mind, Ps. 110:4); "to stir up the heart" (= to provoke, Ps. 78:58); "to make the heart strong" (= to strengthen/encourage, Ps. 27:14); "I had no heart" (= I was foolish, Ps. 73:22).

Biblical idioms need to be translated with great care. First, the intended meaning and impact of an idiom in the original context has to be accurately established. This requires the use of commentaries or a study Bible. Then, both the sense and the force should be conveyed with equal rhetorical power in the TL, whether by a functionally equivalent idiom, a figure of speech, an intensifier of some type, or perhaps an ideophone (in a Bantu language). Many times the biblical idiom will fall away during the process of meaningful translation. Therefore, as already suggested, it is important to try to compensate for this loss whenever possible, for example, by utilizing an idiom of the TL even where one is not present in the original text. This is a helpful thing to do especially when rendering some important theological concept or point of emphasis in poetic discourse, but only if it sounds natural and appropriate in the context of use.

Exercise 6.3.2

1. Pick three of the Hebrew idioms listed in section 6.3.2 and tell how they have been rendered in your language or English. Has the original sense been adequately conveyed? Is there a more dynamic expression available? Explain, with suggestions.

2. Look for three additional Hebrew idioms in the Psalms, using a literal English translation (e.g., NASB, RSV) or the THP. Give their references and intended meaning. How might the sense of these phrases be communicated idiomatically in your language? How have these expressions been handled in the REB, GW, TEV, CEV, and NJB?

6.3.3 Unknown concepts

Certain biblical words refer to concepts (plants, animals, instruments, roles, activities, events, customs, social institutions, situations, etc.) that are unknown or very unfamiliar in a contemporary world culture. The question for a translator is how to handle such foreign terms meaningfully in a translation.

In general, five basic strategies are available. (They are similar to those suggested for dealing with certain figures of speech in chapter 5 [see also *The Cultural Factor in Bible Translation*, UBS, 1987, chap. 4]). These five strategies are summarized here, each with an example from Chewa:

(1) Use a *loanword*. A good Chewa example is *golide*, "gold" used to render the Hebrew *zahab* (Ps. 19:10). Although this precious metal was not traditionally mined in Central Africa, it was an important resource and item of trade further south. Hence the concept of gold was known, and the word for it borrowed long ago. Its value was widely recognized throughout the region as befitting great chiefs and wealthy foreigners. But the problem with some loanwords is that their meaning may differ from that of their prototype. For example, the Chewa *sabata* is used to render the Hebrew *šabbat*, "Sabbath Day" (Ps. 92, title), but *sabata* simply means "Saturday" or a "week," and not "day of rest," as the Hebrew does. The danger of meaninglessness is even greater when the mere transliteration of an unknown term is used, as was done in the old Chewa Bible for "sulfur": *sulfure* (Ps. 11:6).

(2) Use a *generic term*. A Chewa example is *mbusa*, "herdsman," used to render "shepherd" (Ps. 23:1). In the Chewa culture, "sheep" (*nkhosa*), being less hardy and more foolish than goats, were not introduced or accepted as livestock on a large scale until much later than goats were. Therefore the word *nkhosa* does not carry the same positive connotation or emotive association as the word "sheep" in the Bible (e.g., Ps. 79:13). In this case, however, the more generic word *mbusa* is closer to the sense of the original term (*roʿeh*) than the specific "shepherd," though in recent years the central meaning has shifted to a great extent in the direction of Protestant "pastor," which it also designates.

(3) Use a *descriptive phrase*. A Chewa example is *malo a anthu akufa* "place of the dead people," used to render *šeʾol* (Ps. 16:10). This expression is a bit long for use in concise poetry, but in many instances it can be abbreviated (*malo a akufa*) and thus made to fit the pattern of rhythm without too much difficulty. In some contexts it may be condensed even more to *kwa akufa*, "to [the place of] the dead." The notion that this phrase conveys is probably closer to the original Hebrew idea than the English gloss suggests. In a traditional religious setting this phrase implies the rather nebulous abode of the ancestral spirits (*mizimu*). In any case it appears to be rather more precise than the old Chewa Bible's *manda*, "grave," though in some passages (Ps. 5:9) the latter might work.

(4) Use a *cultural substitute*. A Chewa example is *mphasa*, "sleeping mat" used to render the Hebrew word for "bed," *miṭṭa* (Ps. 6:6). A sleeping mat is the closest functional equivalent in the TL of "bed," which was originally a foreign term. The loanword *bedi*, though it is familiar, would sound anachronistic; however, in future, it will undoubtedly be thought of as the typical place where adults sleep at night. Cultural substitutes can be rhetorically very dynamic, often quite artistic and appealing as well. The problem is that they may lead to more or less cultural-historical skewing and a distortion of the biblical setting, especially if the terms are still closely associated with the traditional religious system and/or an indigenous way of life.

(5) Use any *combination* of the preceding. A Chewa example of a combination is *nsembe yootcha*, "offering for burning," which is a generic classifier plus a descriptive limiter. It is used to render the Hebrew term for "burnt-offering," ʿ*ola* (Ps. 40:6). Such a manufactured TL phrase, if it is compact and to the point, is usually readily accepted and may even sound quite natural. But sometimes, made-up combinations are less successful due to length, awkwardness, or ambiguity, or because they convey a different implication from what the original intended. In Chewa, for example, *chihema ca Mulungu*, "the big-tent of God," the rendering for "tabernacle," caused problems because it implies that God is a military deity. Only soldiers live in "tents," so perhaps he is a general, since he lives in a great *big* one! The phrase, *alonda a Mulungu*, "guards of God" used to render "cherubim," is misleading in another way. It suggests that God is so weak and fearful that he requires a security corps like so many other important social and government figures today!

The most "poetic" solution of these five is the cultural substitute since it denotes a concept familiar to people and often can easily fit into a given context as a single lexical item. It renders the unknown original term in a concrete, forceful manner and thus preserves or even heightens a psalm's associative meaning as well as its local relevance, impact, and appeal. The ideal, of course, is to find a term that closely matches the biblical expression with respect to pragmatic function and external referential appearance, but that is only rarely possible. However, this was done in Chewa on several occasions. For example, the dangerous and unpredictable Cape buffalo (*njati*) was substituted for the wild oxen of Psalm 22:21; and *cikopa*, "[animal skin] shield," was used for "horn" in Psalm 18:2. In this latter example, a literal rendering of the original *qeren*, which is combined with the notion of "salvation," would clearly have designated the practice of sorcery, a horn (*nyanga*) being commonly employed by a sorcerer in the preparation of black magic. In fact, a sorcerer is even called a *wanyanga*, "a person of the horn"!

But if the external formal appearance, the primary referent, of the cultural substitute is indeed very different from what is designated in the SL text, then the translator should reconsider its use at all. In such cases, a footnote or an illustration would be better, or one of the other strategies listed above. An example in Chewa is the word that was used to render "temple" in the old Protestant Bible: *kachisi*, "shrine-shelter." A *kachisi* is a small temporary hut made of grass and sticks and set under a large sacred tree out in the bush. When appealing for rain, people place offerings to the ancestral spirits at or inside the *kachisi*, accompanied by fervent prayers. What a small, insignificant god Yahweh must have been if a typical *kachisi* was his home, his only dwelling place! A *kachisi* and the Jerusalem temple are far different with regard to their external appearance. There is also a serious problem of connotative inequivalence here since *kachisi* is a word still too closely tied to the traditional religious worldview. Thus, in the new Chewa Bible, the generalized phrase *nyumba ya Mulungu* "house of God" is used to refer to the Temple. The term *kachisi* did find a place, however, in designating the pagan shrines known as the "high places" (e.g., Ps. 78:58).

To be sure, it sometimes happens that a borrowed term, a supposed equivalent, or a manufactured phrase becomes familiar and then acceptable to people through much church teaching and long liturgical usage. The question, however, is whether they really comprehend what they are reading (hearing) correctly, that is. Are pastors themselves aware of what people actually understand when they read or hear the text of Scripture? Have they carried out some systematic testing of these terms and concepts to find out for sure? Familiarity (with regard to lexical form) does not always mean intelligibility (with regard to the intended meaning in specific contexts). Just as a building is no stronger as a whole than the strength of its individual blocks or bricks, so also the Bible is only understandable when its constituent discourse has been accurately and meaningfully constructed. The text must be welded together to form a natural, comprehensible whole from bottom to top, from the individual items to a complete discourse unit, one that ideally resembles a functionally equivalent local genre.

Exercise 6.3.3

1. Tell how the following terms have been rendered in your language: "Holy Spirit" (Ps. 51:11), "soul" (Ps. 6:3–4), "sheol" (Ps. 6:5), "inheritance" (Ps. 37:18), "hyssop" (Ps. 51:7), "rahab" (Ps. 89:10), "leviathan" (Ps. 74:14), and "Yahweh." Can you suggest where some improvements might be made? Explain with some examples.

2. Which three psalmic terms that refer to unknown biblical concepts cause the greatest difficulty in your language? Why is this the case? In your opinion, what is the best way of handling these concepts so that their meaning is conveyed in the clearest possible way? Is a footnote advisable for either of these three terms? If so, how would you word it? Be concise, be poetic!

3. How have the following words pertaining to Jewish or pagan worship been translated in your language: "idols" (Ps. 78:58), "high places" (Ps. 78:58), "ark" (Ps. 78:61), "priests" (Ps. 78:64), "sanctuary" (Ps. 78:69), "temple" (Ps. 79:1), "demons" (Ps. 106:37), "altar" (Ps. 118:27), "sacrifice" (Ps. 40:6) and "offering" (Ps. 40:6)? If no translation has yet been done in your language, look up each of these terms in three recent English versions; compare and evaluate them critically and with a poetic ear.

7. A TEN-STEP METHOD FOR ANALYZING A COMPLETE PSALM

There are ten steps that we recommend for analyzing a psalm (see also Wendland 1994b, ch. 1; in fact, these procedures may be applied to any type of biblical text). They are based on the material of the preceding chapters. But before beginning to consider them, it would be appropriate to follow the example of the Psalter itself and start off with a prayer to the Spirit of God for inspiration and guidance in understanding the essential message that he wishes to communicate. This prayer is well expressed in the words of Psalm 119 (vv. 12, 15, 16, 18, 19, 27, 33, 34, 35, 105, 112):

> *Praise be to you, O LORD;*
>   *teach me your decrees.*
> *I meditate on your precepts*
>   *and consider your ways.*
> *I delight in your decrees;*
>   *I will not neglect your word.*
> *Open my eyes that I may see*
>   *wonderful things in your law.*
> *I am a stranger on earth;*
>   *do not hide your commands from me.*
> *Let me understand the teaching of your precepts;*
>   *then I will meditate on your wonders.*
> *Teach me, O LORD, to follow your decrees;*
>   *then I will keep them to the end.*
> *Give me understanding, and I will keep your law*
>   *and obey it with all my heart.*
> *Direct me in the path of your commands,*
>   *for there I find delight.*
> *Your word is a lamp to my feet*
>   *and a light for my path.*
> *My heart is set on keeping your decrees*
>   *to the very end.*

7.1 The ten steps

The following procedures may be followed more or less in the order given. They are only suggestions, however, and can easily be adjusted as needed to suit the particular situation in which a translation project is being carried out. Other exegetical techniques may also be added to extend the program of text study. Our goal is to thoroughly and systematically analyze a given psalm in preparation to translate it in an appropriate and acceptable manner—one that best fits the biblical text, its intended use in the target language, the primary audience concerned, and the abilities of the translators themselves.

7.1.1 Step one: Study the context

The first step of any complete analysis is to study the context. This is often overlooked in the rush to get into the text itself. The context includes everything that "surrounds" a text, whether a whole psalm, a verse, or a word. In relation to a complete psalm, the *textual context* (often called "cotext") refers, first of all, to the psalms that come immediately before and after the one being analyzed. Are there any noteworthy *inter*textual correspondences—or strong contrasts—among these three adjacent texts, either in their specific wording or just in their general theme? If so, is it possible that the similarities and/or differences exert some influence upon the interpretation of a specific part of the psalm under study? One should consider this same question in relation to the other psalms that comprise a related grouping, such as the "Asaphite" collection (50, 73–83).

If you are considering only a portion of a psalm, determine the larger discourse unit of which it forms a part. Is there a section heading or some indication of a paragraph (strophe) break for the passage in the standard English versions? Observe the flow of thoughts and emotions within the sequence of sections or strophes. Where are the points of special significance in terms of content, relevance, beauty, emphasis—or difficulty? How are these areas "marked" in the text? In other words, do you observe any special verbal forms or literary techniques?

The larger discourse context is important too. Are there any psalms found elsewhere in the Psalter similar to the one that you are examining? Carefully check out all cross-references to other psalms in any study Bible. You may discover individual passages that are similar, or a number of whole psalms that belong to the same genre. Scripture is its own best interpreter, and correspondences of form, content, or function in other texts can help you better understand certain difficult verses.

At the highest level, the larger context means the whole Old Testament. Are there any passages, in the Pentateuch or Deuteronomy in particular, that resemble or are somehow related to the text you are working on? Again, consult the cross-references and footnotes in a version such as the TEV or CEV or a good study Bible. If you find some related passages, ask yourself what the nature of their similarity is and how this helps in the process of interpretation, especially with reference to the key theological truths and moral injunctions. Such texts, if they are known to have been written earlier in time, may have influenced the psalmist, and they may shed some light on certain problematic expressions in the passage at hand.

Finally, the analyst should study the nonverbal, *extratextual* context of a psalm, that is, its historical situation and related sociological circumstances as they may have pertained to its composition. Many reference works, as well as the THP, tell something about the Ancient Near Eastern sociocultural setting of the times in which the Psalms were written: personal names, places, nations, historical events, geography, flora/fauna, customs, way of life, and religion. In this respect, it is important to distinguish, for example, the psalms written during or shortly after the Jews' period of exile in Babylon (Psalm 137 is one), for they will tend to reflect, among other things, a tone of national shame, sorrow, and perplexity that needs to be preserved in translation.

7.1.2 Step two: Read and internalize the psalm

It is very important to read the entire text *aloud* (in the Hebrew, if possible). Think of yourself as actually praying, reciting, chanting, or singing the psalm. Read it several times in this way, with a different emphasis, mood, or perspective on each occasion. One needs to actually *hear* and *feel* the text as well as to see it. This will help you to experience the psalm more fully—its various thoughts, values, purposes, attitudes, and emotions in relation to God and to your own particular circumstances. In the process you will get a general impression of the psalm: its major subject, primary motifs, principal genre, and overall movement. Write out a summary of the main topic(s) or theme(s) and their communicative motivation in a sentence or two. This may change after you have analyzed the text in more detail, but at least you will have a place to begin as you continue the study in more detail. Of course, one cannot simply read a psalm without also *meditating* upon its message and *applying* it to one's own life.

7.1.3 Step three: Determine the genre

Recognition of a psalm's genre, or topic-functional category, will guide you in a further analysis of its form and content. Start by reviewing the major categories (see chap. 2). Is the psalm mainly a *petition, thanksgiving,* or *praise* (or perhaps a mixture of all three)? Or does it involve strong *instruction* or a *profession of trust*? Perhaps it may then be specified as belonging to one of the minor categories: a psalm of *repentance, remembrance, retribution, royalty,* or *liturgy.* It will be easier to interpret (and re-communicate) the constituent parts of a given psalm once you have correctly determined the functional purpose(s) of the whole. In other words, ask yourself how the psalm may have been used in the public worship and/or the private devotional life of God's faithful people of old. Then its constituent verses can be seen as modifying or contributing to this overall aim.

7.1.4 Step four: Plot the patterns of repetition

An analysis of the various kinds of repetition present in the text will always give important insights into a psalm's structure and message. Thus the fourth step is a detailed examination and evaluation of any sort of recursion, whether of content or form. By reiteration of form we mean any words or phrases that are repeated, either exactly or synonymously. Make note of these repetitions and also their order or arrangement in the discourse. Obviously, it is best to do this while looking at the original Hebrew text or an interlinear. If this is not possible, a literal version like the RSV (better than the NRSV) or NASB in English will have to do.

Focus first on the different types of *parallelism*, whether near (connected) or far (separated). Note the ideas that occur more than once. Look not only for *similarities* (correspondences), but also for major *contrasts*. Join these recursive elements by arrows or underline them with ink or a felt marker of the same color. See if you can combine several similar thoughts together under a general topic, such as blessing, punishment, righteous/wicked, sin, good works, God's nature, promises, commands, and warnings. Your observations as you see certain topics being developed can be written down in related groups on separate pieces of paper. Working on a computer makes this job much easier and more reliable, especially when assisted by a Scripture text-analysis program like Bible Windows, Logos, or Paratext. After reading the psalm several times, you may decide to rearrange the categories, adding, deleting, combining, subdividing, or renaming them. As you do this, take note of any instances of separated parallelism that seem to mark an aperture, closure, inclusion, or topical overlap within the psalm's larger organization (cf. ch. 4). This is good preparation for the next step.

7.1.5 Step five: Locate the major breaks and peaks

Often separated parallel lines mark some sort of "break" between units such as a strophe or stanza. In other words, they may signal an initial or final discourse *boundary*. At other times nonadjacent parallel lines indicate a place of special importance *within* a given unit, especially if located at or near its center. Alternatively, the parallels may have some topical relation to the content of the psalm as a whole. Thus the repeated line may be a point of prominence in relation to the main theme (= *peak*), or it may serve to heighten the psalmist's primary emotion or emphasis (= *climax*). Lexical recursion by itself may not be enough evidence, however, that this is the case. But if such repetition is found to occur together with a major *shift* in certain aspects of content (e.g., time, place, speaker, topic) and/or a *concentration* of poetic features (e.g., figurative language, rhetorical question, direct speech, or hyperbole), it is indeed a good indication of a compositional peak. All proposed discourse breaks and potential peaks need to be related to the formal structure and thematic organization of the entire text. This forms the basis for doing the next step of the analysis.

7.1.6 Step six: Sketch out the compositional structure

On the basis of the information learned in steps 4-5, a provisional structure of the complete psalm can now be drawn up. First observe any *section headings*. Then look for the main units into which the text is divided by lines of space in the TEV, CEV, or NIV. (The introductory comments on structure in the THP and *NIV-SB* can help with this too.) You may decide later to disagree with some of these divisions, but at least they give you a guide to start with. More advanced students can prepare a propositional semantic outline of the psalm according to the method presented in chapter 3.

Next look more closely for some of the stylistic features that serve to mark borders. Do you see any manifested at the compositional boundaries you have proposed? In other words, do the strophe or stanza units each have a clearly marked aperture and closure? These are especially important for translators to note because they will have to find appropriate literary devices in their own language for marking such text divisions. The patterns of repetition you observed in step 4—especially aperture, closure, inclusion, and overlap—will help to confirm your first tentative "map" of a psalm's organization, or else lead you to decide to revise it now.

7.1.7 Step seven: Do a complete word study and a detailed thematic outline

Having examined the segmentation and macrostructure of the psalm, you are ready to give attention to the details of its microstructure. Begin by underlining, or in some other way marking, the primary theological concepts and expressions in the psalm, especially the repeated ones. These *key terms* will consist of both nouns and verbs, or to state these in semantic terms, "entities" and "events." The entities would include such things as persons or roles, geographical features, royal symbols, customs, and religious features (sacrifices, law, temple). A few prominent examples of events are deliverance, mercy, righteousness, judgment, praise, trust, fear, reverence, redemption, singing, confession, sin, and do evil. The analyst should next look for any important *word pairs*: "love/mercy," "grave/pit," "Zion/Jerusalem," "rock/fortress," "cry/call out" (to God). One may also list any larger related families of words within a given psalm (e.g., "law" in Ps. 119). Many of these lexical items may have already been examined in previous Bible studies. But a review of their distinct senses and range of meaning in the Psalms is necessary to ensure that one understands them correctly and fully, so that they may be rendered according to their specific religious and poetic context. In doing this step, the *NIV Study Bible* and the THP should be consulted. For the most difficult expressions, a more detailed investigation may need to be carried out, that is, with the help of Bible dictionaries, word books, commentaries, and so forth.

Once the significant concepts and word groups of a psalm have been studied, the analyst should now be able to summarize the principal idea of each of its larger sections (as determined in step 6). Try to organize these main thoughts into a *hierarchy* of theme and (sub)parts, for the discourse as a whole and each of its major portions. At first this may be stated in quite general terms, but as you continue to investigate the text, you should make the outline more specific to the particular psalm being analyzed. Further examination might also lead you to make some revisions in your thematic "map." The main thing is to recognize the *unity* of the psalm and how all of its parts fit together in *harmony* to convey its essential theological content and communicative purpose. Review any apparent gaps, obscurities, anomalies, and difficulties to see if your outline of the whole can assist in the interpretation of these problem areas.

7.1.8 Step eight: Analyze the poetic features of the individual verses

Study the constituent verses to make sure that you understand the full meaning (content plus intent) of each poetic couplet as well as the relation of one verse to another in the overall textual sequence. Identify all the major stylistic (artistic and rhetorical) features (see chap. 5), examining their usage in this particular context. Often, after discovering the *meaning* underlying these literary devices, you will be able to fit the ideas under one or another of the general topics that were specified in the thematic outline of step 7. As already noted, special concentrations of literary features normally combine with primary patterns of recursion to mark or reinforce discourse boundaries and points of emphasis.

In your study of the verses of a psalm, you may receive some assistance in places of difficulty from other translations or from analytical commentaries. Sometimes another passage from a different but related psalm can also shed some light on a difficult expression, so be sure to double-check all the main cross-references for any instances of such salient intertextuality.

7.1.9 Step nine: Determine the main "speech acts" and the personal interaction

The *meaning package* of a psalm includes not only its content (information) but also its varied expressions of emotion, attitude, preference, and purpose. The original poet carefully chose his structure and style in order to communicate these more subtle aspects of semantic and pragmatic significance too. Therefore they must all be considered, if the exegetical study is to be complete.

Though it is the psalm's principal religious objective that determines its "genre," some of its included sections may convey different communicative aims (known as *illocutions*). Also, these smaller sections may be *grouped* so that the higher-level unit has *its* own communicative intention as well. This is revealed in the succession of *speech acts* that the psalmist engages in with others—primarily God—during the course of his *main* speech event (*text-act*). For example, one frequently finds passages of encouragement, instruction, warning, rebuke, commitment, and condemnation, accompanied by personal feelings of joy, sorrow, anger, fear, pain, trust, despair, or hope. Such illocutionary purposes and their associated emotions are clearly a very important part of the total message, but they are not always fully recognized or correctly interpreted. All of these aspects of religious discourse and the rhetorical features that convey them need to be marked where they occur in the text to determine their individual and combined contribution to the overall expression of a particular psalm. Recording them will also help ensure that they get transmitted in the process of translation.

To help determine what the personal interaction in a psalm is, imagine it as being a *dramatic dialogue* or conversation between the psalmist and his God. Sometimes, of course, other participants may also be addressed or responded to, most notably the psalmist's enemies and the congregation of fellow worshipers in the house of the LORD. Ask yourself just how these different groups interact with one another, whether positively or negatively, during the course of the complete communication event. Is there an overall plan, or pattern, of speech acts? Who is speaking to whom and in what circumstances? What is the speaker saying and for what purpose? Are there any internal quotations? The more fully the analyst can psychologically enter into the intense dialogic situation, the better will be his or her grasp of the interpersonal dynamics of the psalm.

7.1.10 Step ten: Do a trial translation, comparing other versions

Once your analysis of a psalm has been completed according to the previous nine steps, it is important to *test* your results. One of the best ways of doing this is to prepare your own translation of the entire psalm. Translate from the Hebrew or an interlinear version, using this to get a picture of the original *form* and an overview of the *content*, namely, the basic lexical inventory. Then examine several meaning-oriented translations in major languages. Also look at a translation in a language related to your own, if there is one. All these versions, considered together with your own analysis carried out in steps 1–9, will enable you to prepare a meaningful rendering of the psalm in your mother tongue (or, alternatively, your own modified or "restructured" version in English).

As you work, remember the important communication principles of *efficiency* (ease and economy of expression) and *effect* (discourse impact and appeal) with the aim of achieving an acceptable measure of *accuracy* and *relevance* in relation to both form and content in the target language. The goal is to reproduce the *closest natural functional equivalent* of what you consider to be the essential message transmitted by the biblical text. If the circumstances allow, you might even be able to produce an appropriate *poetic* rendering in your language (see Zogbo and Wendland 2000).

Doing a close comparison of different versions helps the analyst to see how others have understood and expressed the various aspects of the text's meaning. It is especially important to pay attention to any outstanding *differences* among the versions. In many cases, such differences are simply a reflection of different styles of translation (e.g., literal vs. idiomatic vs. middle-of-the-road). But sometimes a variation will turn out to be more significant. It may indicate a failure to get the full, intended meaning across or maybe an addition to, or omission from, the original text. You will undoubtedly find such errors in your own rendering when you compare it to other versions. If you do, you may re-study the passages concerned according to the preceding steps and make any necessary revisions to your translation. Preparing one's own meaningful, perhaps even artful, "version" of a given biblical pericope requires the most intensive type of text study; it is therefore the best possible way of "analyzing the psalms."

Exercise 7.1

1. Summarize the ten steps for poetic (psalmic) analysis of section 7.1 in your own words (perhaps also in the local vernacular language that you will be translating into). Which of them do you feel is most important and why?

2. Are there any parts of this ten-step method that you don't understand or which you feel needs some more explanation? Please specify the areas that are especially difficult or unclear.

3. Which step is, to you, the most difficult to carry out correctly or completely, especially with respect to a meaningful translation into your language? Explain why.

4. Do you feel that any important steps for analyzing a psalm have been omitted or not explained fully enough? If so, briefly describe what you would add to the list of recommended procedures and why.

7.2 Sample analyses of selected psalms

The sample analyses of this section utilize the ten steps of section 7.1. The analyses are not as detailed as is required in "real life" translation; the first, however, an analysis of Psalm 1, is done more thoroughly than the others. Knowing what questions to ask in order to determine the meaning of a text is crucial. As you will see, skilled analysts go about their work by asking themselves questions—all kinds of questions. If you know what sort of information to look for, it is not quite so difficult to find the correct answers.

Although the way of working illustrated here is not the only possible method, it is a helpful model to follow when analyzing the Psalms and other poetic literature. It will facilitate an idiomatic, exegetically faithful and contextually relevant translation. In working through the sample analyses, the THP and the *NIV Study Bible* should be at hand to consult. Be aware that the questions listed under a given psalm are intended only as *representative* ones. Other questions will undoubtedly come to mind, and these should be jotted down for immediate or later consideration.

In doing psalmic *exegesis* there are five primary procedures, which summarize the ten steps outlined above:

1. Determine the psalm's overall communicative *purpose*, that is, its genre; then take note of the major speech functions plus any associated emotions within the various discourse parts.

2. Plot the psalm's compositional *structure*, that is, its major and minor divisions and how they fit together to form and convey the main message of the whole text.

3. Formulate a *thematic outline* which is, in effect, a summary of the main content units of the psalm and its constituent stanzas.

4. Interpret the verse-by-verse *meaning* as highlighted also by the text's rhetoric and artistry—all key terms, figures of speech, ellipses, rhetorical questions, allusions, points of emphasis, etc.

5. Make a *comparison* with similar passages in both the OT and NT (using several versions), noting any close correspondences in form and content.

In the sample analyses of sections 7.2.1–7.2.8, these five procedures are not compartmentalized in detail, but they are reflected more or less in all the suggested questions.

7.2.1 Psalm 1

The following are questions on the overall discourse structure:

(a) What genre is this psalm? Give reasons for your answer.

(b) Why is this a good kind of psalm to begin the Book of Psalms as a whole?

(c) Into how many poetic parts (strophes and stanzas) would you divide Psalm 1? What is your evidence for doing so? For instance, what are the textual markers for aperture or closure? An interlinear version and also THP (pp. 14–15) will help you here.

(d) This psalm contains two key concepts running throughout the psalm. Most of the important words fall into one or the other of these two general categories of content. Make a chart with two columns, and under each key concept list the words or phrases that express them.

(e) Outline the psalm, showing its major and minor parts and its overall symmetrical pattern of content. Summarize in one sentence the main thematic point of each of the segments that you propose.

(f) The TEV section heading is "True Happiness." Is this a good way to express the theme of the entire psalm (cf. CEV)? Explain your answer. Can you suggest a better alternative (in English)?

(g) Specify the rhetorical purpose of each of the main parts you proposed in e. What did the psalmist want to persuade listeners to think, feel, or do through his words addressed to God? What is the point of what he was saying? How did he try to reinforce or to modify their thoughts, attitudes, values, and behavior?

(h) Which outstanding poetic or literary devices did the psalmist use in order to communicate more effectively and powerfully with his God—as well as anyone else who happened to be listening to these words? How did he emphasize his main points? Mention several stylistic features and make note of the verse in which you find them.

(i) Finally, do a propositional analysis of Psalm 1. You may follow the outline below or construct your own. Fill in the blanks as in the exercises of chapter 3. First, divide each verse into its constituent propositions (i.e., simple clauses). For example, verse 1 contains four propositions, 1.1, 1.2, 1.3, and 1.4. Write them out on a separate sheet of paper. Then indicate the semantic relationship that links each pair. For example, the relation between 1.2 and 1.3 (a) is BASE-ADDITION.

A TEN-STEP METHOD FOR ANALYZING A COMPLETE PSALM 211

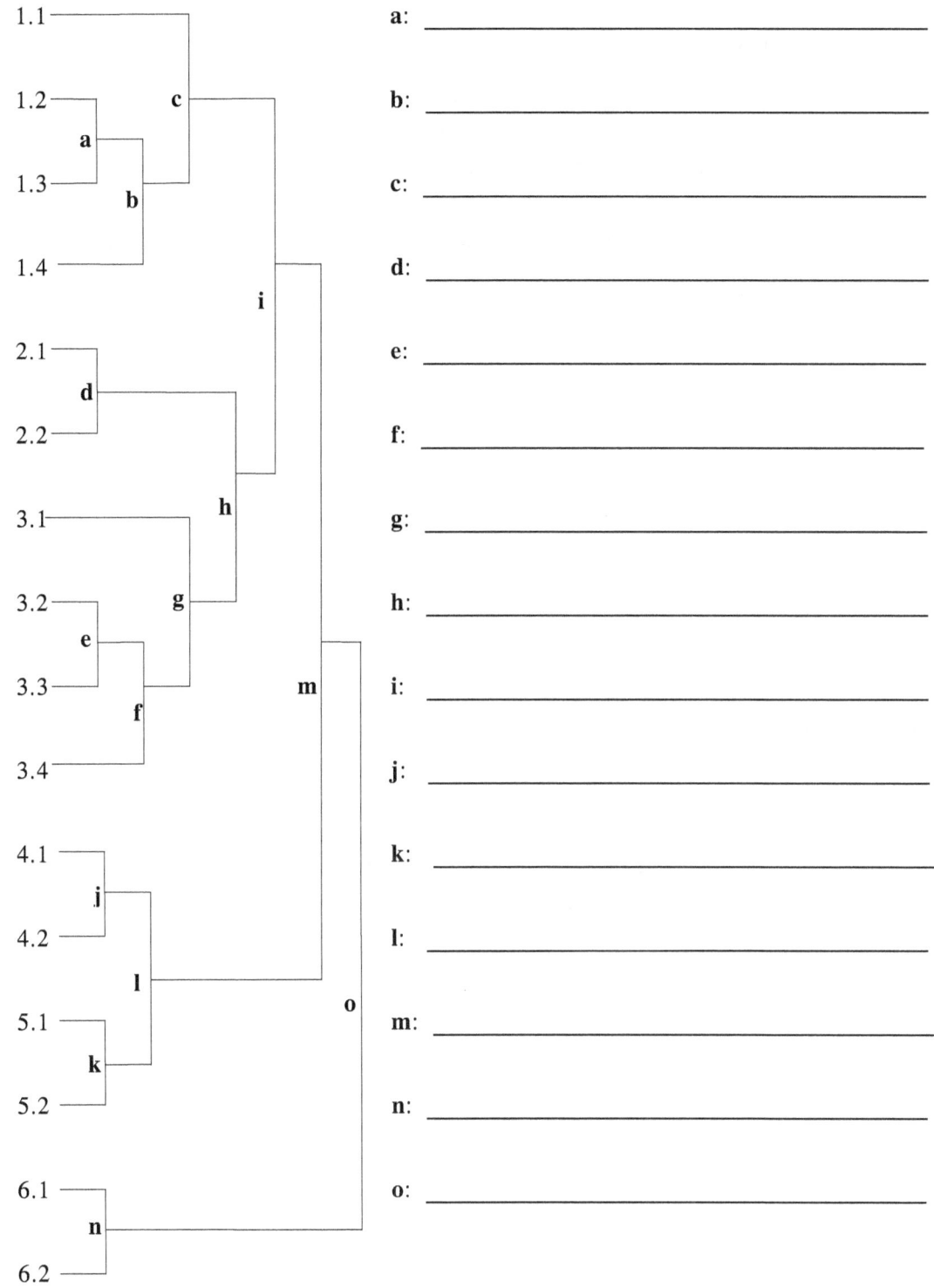

a: _____

b: _____

c: _____

d: _____

e: _____

f: _____

g: _____

h: _____

i: _____

j: _____

k: _____

l: _____

m: _____

n: _____

o: _____

The following are exegetical and translational questions on the individual verses of Psalm 1. Answer them as fully and clearly as you can.

Verse 1:

(a) What type of *parallelism* do you find in this verse?

(b) Do you see any significance in the fact that this verse has *three* poetic lines (a tricolon: A+B+C) instead of the usual two? Why should such a structure occur at this point in the text?

(c) Do you detect any difference in the meaning of each of the three parallel lines? Is there a *progression* or *intensification* of thought here? If so, describe it.

(d) What is the meaning of the word "blessed" (*ʾašrey*) in this context? Would the biblical/theological context affect your translation in any way? Explain.

(e) Why do you think TEV uses "those" instead of "man" in colon one (A)? Why then does it use "evil men" at the end of that same line?

(f) What is the general idea conveyed by the related *imagery* of "walking," "standing," and "sitting" in these three lines?

(g) Would any of these images transmit a similar notion in your language? Explain the problems, if any.

(h) Look at pp. 16–17 of THP and specify the semantic differences between the words "wicked," "sinners," and "scoffers" (RSV).

Verse 2:

(a) How is verse 2 related to verse 1 in terms of meaning? In view of this, what would you say is the significance of the emphatic double conjunction *ki ʾim* at the beginning of this verse?

(b) To whom does the pronoun "they" (TEV) or "he/his" (RSV) refer? Would this reference be clear if translated literally on its own in your language? Explain.

(c) What is the word for "law" in your language? Could it be used to render "*torah* of the LORD"? If not, what would you suggest as an alternative (cf. THP, pp. 17–18)?

(d) Why do you think TEV adds the word "obeying" in line A?

(e) Evaluate the CEV rendering "the Law of the LORD makes them happy"? Would there be any possibility of misunderstanding this in your language?

(f) How do you translate term "LORD"(YHWH–Yahweh) in your language? Carefully study the four approaches to the translation of this important word as outlined in THP (pp. 12, 18). Which of these are you currently using? Do you think some other term would be better in view of what THP says? Explain your decision in detail.

(g) The TEV uses "study" for the word rendered "meditate" by the RSV and NIV. Why is this? What does "meditate" mean (cf. the *NIV Study Bible* and the CEV)?

(h) What is the *hyperbole* in this verse? Do you have a similar figure of speech in your language? Could it be used here?

Verse 3:

(a) How is this verse related semantically to verse 2? What connection is there between the main ideas of verses 2 and 3?

(b) What type of figure of speech dominates this verse? What is its topic, image, and point of similarity? Which line gives the meaning of the figure? Is a figure like this meaningful in your language? If not, tell why.

(c) The TEV and CEV use the plural "tree*s*" instead of "tree" as in the RSV and NIV. What do you think is the reason for this?

(d) Why does the TEV omit "water"? Should this word be retained in your language (cf. THP, p. 19)?

(e) When is "the right time" (TEV) to bear fruit in your part of the world? How does the CEV render this?

(f) In keeping with the imagery of this verse, what is the significance of a tree's leaves "withering" (RSV) or "drying up" (TEV) (cf. CEV)? Which of these two expressions conveys the sense better in your language? Do you have another alternative?

(g) To whom does the pronoun "they" refer in TEV? Would that be clear enough in your language? If not, what would you suggest as an improvement?

Verse 4:

(a) How is this verse related in meaning to verse 3? Why does TEV begin with the conjunction "but"? (Note: *loʾ-ken* + *ki ʾim* is the A–B transitional sequence of the Hebrew text.)

(b) What type of figure of speech is used in this verse?

(c) What is the point of similarity between the topic and the image (cf. THP, p. 20)?

(d) What does the word "so" (RSV, NIV) refer to? The TEV has "like this." How is this idea expressed in the CEV? Do you need to clarify the reference in your language? Explain. (The translation principle involved here concerns the matter of making *implicit* information *explicit* in the TL text.)

(e) Can the image of "chaff" or "straw" being blown by the wind be used with the same impact in your language? Explain. If not, do you have a another figure, or an idiom, that would have the same meaning? For example, in Ila there is the idiom *tabapapulwa kapapa,* "no bark [can be] peeled off from them."

Verse 5:

(a) What is the semantic relation that links verses 4 and 5? This relation is marked in Hebrew by the conjunction *ʿal-ken*. What type of conjunction marks it naturally in your language?

(b) What type of parallelism is manifested by the terms "wicked" and "sinners" (RSV)? Do the two terms refer to one group or two different groups? Explain.

(c) Where else in the psalm do you find some ideas similar to the ones presented in this verse? Do you notice any difference in meaning between the earlier occurrence and this verse? If so, explain.

(d) What sort of "judgment" or "condemnation" is being referred to here (cf. THP, p. 21)? How can this be made clear in your language?

(e) In what way does line B of this verse emphasize what is said in line A?

(f) To what kind of people does "the congregation of the righteous" refer (RSV, NIV)? How can you convey this concept meaningfully and accurately in your language? What do you think of the TEV rendering (see THP, p. 21)? Compare it to the CEV translation.

Verse 6:

(a) What is the significance of the conjunction "for" in the RSV and NIV. (It is a rendering of *ki*.) What semantic relation does it indicate here (see THP, p. 22)?

(b) What type of parallelism is manifested in this verse? Why do you think that it is used at this particular point in the psalm?

(c) What is the meaning of the figure "way" in this context? Do you use the same or a similar image in your language? Explain. Notice that TEV uses "way" in a different sense here. What is that?

(d) What is the sense of the verb "know" (RSV) in this context (cf. TEV, NIV, CEV)?

(e) What is the meaning of "perish"? Can a "way perish" (NIV) in your language? Is the TEV rendering clearer: "are on the way to their doom"? How would you express the intended sense naturally in your language?

(f) Could the last line of verse 6 be stated more emphatically in your language? If so, explain how. Why is this a good place for special emphasis?

Now consider your translation of Psalm 1 as a whole. Look at it with this "check-list" in hand:

- Is your rendering *accurate*, faithful to the content, and representative of the communicative intention of the original?
- Is your rendering *natural*, in harmony with the normal poetic style of your language for such a genre?
- Is your rendering *dynamic*, reflective of the psalm's original beauty, impact, and rhetorical appeal?
- Is your rendering *appropriate*, suitable as a representation of the Word of God and fit for reproduction in a public worship service?

Seldom, if ever, can any version keep all of these factors in complete balance. A lot depends on targeting a particular audience and situation and then testing its use among those for whom it is designed. This is the way to find out the sort of translation (style and level of meaningfulness) that will work best.

The following is a back-translation of Psalm 1 in the Chewa language of South-Central Africa. It was written in the popular style of composition known as *ndakatulo*, which is characterized by a concentration of such rhetorical features as ideophones, figurative language, rhythmic diction, condensed expression, variations in syntactic order, grammatical flexibility, additional demonstrative-locative-pronominal suffixes, concrete and graphic vocabulary, exclamations and intensifiers, as well as elaborate alliteration, assonance, and punning. The abundance and diversity of these features that are found in a typical *secular* composition would not be appropriate for use in the Scriptures, certainly not a liturgical version. But a careful selection of such poetic devices is possible, and that is what was attempted in this text, which was specifically prepared for a public oral presentation. (The capitalized words are dramatic ideophones in Chewa.)

> *How very blessed is the "straight" person—*
> *to the wisdom of the wicked he pays no heed,*
> *in the way of sinners he does not walk,*
> *with the despisers of Yahweh he has no part.*
> *But his neck is MBEE! so clear, as he hears the words,*
> *yes, the laws of God, that's where he's at,*
> *day and night his heart is fixed there,*
> *deep meditation he never abandons.*
> *This sort of person resembles a tree—*
> *a tree growing along a drought-proof stream.*
> *Its fruits are PSYA! fully ripe at the right time,*
> *all its leaves are BILIWILIWILI! bright green.*
> *Herein lies the success of that one,*
> *everything will go just great for him!*

Now does the same thing happen for the wicked, do you think?
Ha! no, it's not the least bit similar.
As for them, they are like maize husks—
like a piece of chaff carried off by the wind,
they go up MWAA! and away—that's it, their fortune finished!
What they are going to "see" is quite shocking:
On that day an indictment God will serve them with,
judgment will befall them all toge... PSITI! burned up!
From the congregation of the righteous they will be expelled,
they will have no part in the assembly of the blessed.
So, there we have the righteous and sinners:
Those who do good are THI! clasped in the hands of Yahweh,
but those who do evil He will just cast them TAYU! completely away!
Thus people ought to realize that there is indeed a God!

Exercise 7.2.1

1. Pick out three especially effective poetic devices of those used in the Chewa version of Psalm 1. Why you think they are effective (even in the English back-translation)?

2. Did you observe any parts of Psalm 1 in Chewa where you feel that the vernacular rendering may have gone too far stylistically, or where something seemed to be added or omitted or was unclear? Describe any such problem that you noticed.

3. On a separate piece of paper do a *poetic* (rhetorically heightened) translation of Psalm 1 in your language. Also provide a literal back-translation into English. This may take some time and testing, but give it a try; that is the only way to find out what is really involved.

4. The following translation of Psalm 1 into English is from *The Message: Psalms* by Eugene H. Peterson (Colorado Springs: NavPress, 1994). If there are there any idiomatic English expressions in it that you do not understand, draw a circle around them. Have any important ideas of the original been left out or changed? Has there been any unacceptable distortion of the sociocultural and religious setting of the Hebrew? Underline any apparent instances of this nature that you find. Write out any other comments that you may have beside the line in question.

> *How well God must like you—*
>   *you don't hang out at Sin Saloon,*
>   *you don't slink along Dead-End Road,*
>   *you don't go to Smart-Mouth College.*
>
> *Instead you thrill to Yahweh's Word,*
>   *you chew on Scripture day and night.*
> *You're a tree replanted in Eden,*
>   *bearing fresh fruit every month,*
> *Never dropping a leaf,*
>   *always in blossom.*
>
> *You're not at all like the wicked,*
>   *who are mere windblown dust—*
> *Without defense in court*
>   *unfit company for innocent people.*
> *Yahweh charts the road you take.*
> *The road they take is Skid Row.*

5. Carefully compare the version above with the following one (Timothy Wilt, 2000). What are the main differences that you notice between these two versions (mention 3 in particular)?

Which version do you prefer and why (give specific reasons)? Also take note of the printed format of the version below; do you see any significance to the way in which the text is set out on the page? Does this help you to read and understand the psalm better? Explain.

Wonderful!

> *Not the walker in the way of the wicked,*
> *Not the bystander of slanderers,*
> *Not the sitter with the sinner, but*

The delighter in Yahweh's Torah,
meditating day and night on
the divine Torah,

Becoming like a
Spring-watered tree,
Bearing timely fruit,

> *No fading leaves*

Always thriving

> *Not like the wicked,*
> *husks scattered in the wind.*

> *Not like the wicked, the corrupt,*
> *who cannot stand at judgement time*
> *with those who have lived rightly.*

Yahweh knows the way of those who have done as they should.

> *The way of the wicked is being destroyed.*

7.2.2 Psalm 2

The following are questions on the overall discourse structure:

(a) What genre is this psalm? Give reasons for your answer.

(b) Into how many parts (strophes or stanzas) would you divide Psalm 2? Which verses belong in each stanza? Tell how each stanza is related in meaning to the next.

(c) Explain why you divided the psalm in this way. In other words, what are the markers in the text on which you are basing your divisions?

(d) Give a one-sentence summary of each stanza. Then suggest a general theme for Psalm 2 as a whole.

(e) How does the genre and content of this psalm relate to that of Psalm 1?

Verse 1:

(a) What type of question is found in verse 1? What is the expected answer to this question? Actually there are two questions here, but one has been "elided" in line B. What is the elided question?

(b) Who are the "nations" referred to in verse 1? How are they different from the "peoples"? How would you render the notion of "pagan" in your language?

(c) What do the words "to conspire" and "to plot in vain" mean? What slight aspect of meaning does line B add to line A?

Verse 2:

(a) In what sense is verse 2 more specific than verse 1?

(b) Are two groups of political leaders referred to here or just one? Explain.

(c) To whom does "the anointed (*mašiaḥ*) of the LORD" refer? There are two possibilities. Does one exclude the other? Explain. How can the concept of anointing be best expressed in your language?

Verse 3:

(a) What do the "kings of the earth" propose to do in their speech of verse 3? What attitude do they manifest in these words? The words "they say" are not present in the Hebrew. Why is it probably necessary to add them in a translation?

(b) The words "chains" and "fetters" are a figure of speech. What is such a figure called? What is its basic meaning?

Verse 4:

(a) Why is it reasonable to begin a new *strophe* or *stanza* at verse 4? List the various "markers" that indicate a break here.

(b) What is the figure of speech in verse 4 called?

(c) What does "God sits in the heavens" mean (RSV)? How is this expressed in the NIV and TEV? Which is easier to translate into your language? Is there some idiomatic way of saying this in your language? If so, what is it?

(d) Does God ever "laugh" according to the religious traditions of your culture? If so, what does it signify? Why, in this particular context, does God laugh? Does God ever make fun of people? Explain (see THP). If he does not, how can the notion of mocking people (i.e., viewing their actions as useless) be conveyed better than by saying God laughs at them?

Verse 5:

(a) How does verse 5 intensify the thought of verse 4? How does line B of verse 5 intensify the thought of line A?

(b) Why is the Lord so angry? Is this concept understood by most readers in your language? Is the expression of anger culturally appropriate in your society? If not, what could you do to clarify things in your translation?

Verse 6:

(a) Whose words are these? Does your translation make it clear who the speaker is? If not, how could this be made explicit without upsetting the poetic flow of the lines?

(b) How do you express the idea of installing a king in your language? What does God mean by saying "my king"? Does the semantic relationship implied by this possessive form have to be made explicit in your language? If so, tell how you would do it.

(c) To what does the proper name "Zion" refer (cf. THP, p. 28)? Why is this hill called "holy"? How is the concept of holiness expressed in your language? Is an explanatory footnote needed here in your translation? If so, how would you word it?

Verse 7:

(a) What indicators of a new stanza do you see at verse 7?

(b) What is a "decree" (NIV)? How would you express this notion in your language (see THP)?

(c) How many speakers appear to be saying something in this verse? Who are they? How can you make this clear in your translation (cf. TEV)?

(d) What does the word "begotten" mean in this context? How can you best get this idea across in your language?

(e) To which day, or time, does "today" refer? How would you make this clear in your translation?

(f) Is it natural in your language to say, "Today I have become your father"? Explain any difficulties (see the *NIV Study Bible* footnote).

Verse 8:

(a) Who is speaking the words of verses 8 and 9? To whom is he speaking? From the context give some evidence for your answer.

(b) What does the word "inheritance/heritage" mean here? What does it refer to? How would you express this concept in your language? Give a literal back-translation. What expression in line B corresponds to "heritage" (cf. THP, p. 29)?

(c) To what does the phrase "ends of the earth" refer? Do you have a figurative way of saying this in your language (e.g., in Chewa it is *ku mphepo zonse zinai*, "towards the four winds")?

Verse 9:

(a) What is the point of similarity of each of the two metaphors of verse 9? Evaluate the NIV's rendering of the verb as "rule" (cf. RSV, TEV).

(b) How does line B intensify what is said in line A? How can you convey this intensification in your language (cf. THP, p. 30)?

Verse 10:

(a) Why is it likely that a new stanza begins in verse 10? Is a special conjunction required in your language as in Hebrew (*wəʾattah*, "and now")? Explain. Who do you think is speaking here? Why do you think so?

(b) Why are the kings, the rulers, warned to "be wise"? What does it mean to be wise in this context? (The parallel in line B gives a definition.) Is it possible to indicate in your language that this is a warning? How would you do it? (In Chewa it is by the use of word order in the vocative phrase.)

Verse 11:

(a) Why are the rulers told to "tremble"?

(b) What does trembling signify in your culture? Can one rejoice and tremble at the same time, or does this sound like a contradiction or a paradox (cf. TEV)? How can you get the right sense across in your language (see THP)?

Verse 12:

(a) Why are the kings commanded to "kiss the Son" (NIV)? What was the cultural significance of kissing in this setting? What about in your own cultural context today? How is the first part of this verse rendered in the RSV, REB, TEV, and CEV? What is the problem here (see THP, p. 32)? What solution do you propose?

(b) What does "lest . . . you be destroyed in your way" mean?

(c) Why does the last line of the psalm seem out of place? Is it? Explain. What is the function of this line in terms of the discourse as a whole? How can this sharp contrast be conveyed in your language?

(d) What does it mean to "take refuge" in someone? Do you have an idiom for this in your language?

(e) The content of verse 12 is similar to two verses of Psalm 1. Which two verses? Note that 1:1 and 2:12 form an *inclusio*. (The similarity between 1:6 and 2:12 is the kind of unit-closing repetition known as *epiphora*.) Such repetition often functions to indicate compositional boundaries. In this case it also functions to tie Psalms 1 and 2 together. How so?

Many scholars believe that these psalms form a two-part theological introduction to the Psalter as a whole. Can you give some other reasons in support of this view, based on the two psalms' themes and content? Since the feature of repetition is so important, how would you draw attention to its significance in a translation?

7.2.3 Psalm 6

The following are questions on the overall discourse structure:

(a) What genre is this psalm? Give reasons for your answer

(b) Into how many stanzas would you divide Psalm 6? Give reasons for your divisions.

(c) CEV appears to have made a mistake in its structure of this psalm. Where is the error and why do you think so?

(d) Where is the major psychological turning point of Psalm 6? Describe this shift.

(e) What theme would you suggest for the psalm as a whole?

(f) Do a propositional-structural analysis of Psalm 6 as was done for Psalm 1 in section 7.2.1. First segment the psalm into its constituent poetic lines. Then determine the semantic relation between lines of each *bicolon* or *tricolon*. Finally, connect the related *clusters* of lines until the various parts of the entire psalm have been linked together.

Verse 1:

(a) What is the meaning of the word rendered "rebuke" in NIV (see THP)?

(b) Is the psalmist requesting two things in verse 1 or just one? Why do you think so?

(c) How does line B intensify what was said in line A?

(d) What does the CEV do with lines A and B? Would this be a good procedure for your language? Explain your preference.

Verse 2:

(a) How do you express the concept of "having mercy on" someone in your language? Is there a figurative way of saying this in your language (e.g., Chewa: "to be soft in the heart" for a person)? (A figure would give greater impact.)

(b) The psalmist is appealing for help. What was the reason for his desperate appeal to the Lord?

(c) What does "bones" in line B refer to? Describe how line B intensifies what was said in line A. What is the difference in interpretation between TEV and CEV? Are "bones" used figuratively in your language? With what meaning?

(d) How does the wording of RSV and NIV differ from that of TEV in this verse (see THP, p. 59)?

Verse 3:

(a) How is verse 3 related to verse 2? What do you think of the way these two verses are joined in CEV and TEV? Can you suggest a better way to do this?

(b) What does the word "soul" (*nepeš*) refer to in this context? How does this relate to the psalmist's "bones" in verse 2?

(c) In the Hebrew there is an interesting shift in word order to emphasize the point. What word has been shifted and why? (Consult an interlinear version.)

(d) What kind of question is "How long?" What thought is stressed here?

(e) Which key word is repeated throughout this stanza (vv. 1–5)? Why is this done?

Verse 4:

(a) Which stage of a petition psalm is expressed in this verse (see sec. 2.1.1)? How does this differ from what the psalmist said in verse 2?

(b) What does he mean by praying for the Lord to "turn" (*šub*)?

(c) The same word rendered by the NIV as "soul" in verse 3 is translated "me" here (*nepeš*). Why this different rendering? Is it necessary also in your language? Explain.

(d) Why does the psalmist ask the Lord to save him?

(e) Notice how the key term *ḥesed* is translated in the RSV, NIV, CEV, and TEV. Which of the different expressions do you prefer and why? Is there an appropriate idiomatic term, phrase, or figure of speech in your language to convey this important OT covenantal concept (see THP, p. 53)?

Verse 5:

(a) How is verse 5 related in meaning to verse 4?

(b) What belief about life after death is behind the psalmist's argument here? (Refer to the THP and the *NIV Study Bible*.)

(c) What does "remember" mean in such a context? Could a literal rendering here be misleading in your language? Explain.

(d) What is the difference between "death" in line A and "the grave" (NIV) or "Sheol" (RSV) in line B? How has TEV combined these ideas? What does the Hebrew term *šeʾol* refer to? How can this concept be conveyed meaningfully in your language?

Verse 6:

(a) Why do most versions begin a new stanza at this point? What features in the text would signal this change effectively in your language?

(b) The thought of which previous verse is continued here. What effect does this development have? How could the layout of the printed text be arranged to show the important connection between these verses?

(c) A striking figure of speech is found in verse 6, twice in fact. What is it? Describe the intensification of emotion in this verse. How are the images of this verse connected?

(d) Are hyperboles meaningful in your language? Explain. Can you convey an exaggeration with the forcefulness of a hyperbole in some other way?

Verse 7:

(a) What new thought is added to the psalmist's complaint in this verse?

(b) In your language do people speak of "sorrow" as having an effect on the eyes? Do they become "weak"? If not, what would be a natural way of conveying the same underlying meaning?

(c) In what way do you think the "foes" filled the psalmist with "sorrow" (cf. Ps. 5:9)? What may these foes have been saying about his relationship to the LORD?

Verse 8:

(a) There is a dramatic change in this verse marking the beginning of a new strophe. What is it? What do you think of the CEV's way of stating this (note the reversal in utterance order)? This sharp shift in tone is one of the key characteristics of a certain type of psalm. What type? How would you convey the strong emotion that is expressed here in your language?

(b) Who does the psalmist refer to when he says "those who do evil"? Is it necessary to make this explicit in your language?

(c) Note the difference between NIV and TEV in the *tense* of the verb in line B. (In Hebrew it is a completed-action tense/aspect.) Which rendering seems more appropriate in this context? Why do you think so?

Verse 9:

(a) How is verse 9a related to verse 8b in meaning?

(b) Notice the tense difference in English between the NIV ("has heard") and TEV ("will answer"). How does this variation affect the sense and significance of the whole psalm (see THP, p. 64)?

(c) What does it mean to "accept" someone's prayer? What is a more natural or forceful way of saying this in your language?

Verse 10:

(a) How does verse 10 relate to the two preceding verses and the psalm as a whole?

(b) What does the psalmist mean by saying that his enemies will "be ashamed"? What is so bad about that in terms of punishment? How is this idea emphasized in the verse? How would you express this idea naturally in your language?

(c) Who is it that will cause all this trouble for the foes? Is it helpful to make the divine agent explicit in your translation? Why or why not? How can this be done?

(d) What kind of "turning" is meant here (RSV, NIV)? Where else in the psalm was "turn" mentioned? What is the difference in meaning between the two occurrences?

(e) The word "sudden" is stressed in the Hebrew by means of its placement as the very last word. How may such emphasis be conveyed in your language? It was done in Chewa by the use of an ideophone (*mwadzidzidzi*).

7.2.4 Psalm 16

The following are questions on the overall discourse structure:

(a) What genre is Psalm 16? What are some of the major characteristics of this type of psalm?

(b) The overall structure of Psalm 16 is not very easy to discern. Identify the main differences among the NIV, RSV, GW, CEV, and TEV with regard to how they divide it. Which of these seems to make the most sense to you? How would you segment the psalm? What markers led you to your conclusions?

(c) Write a thematic summary outline of Psalm 16. Provide a title for each strophe and a theme statement for the psalm as a whole. Note how each strophe is linked semantically or rhetorically with the one that precedes and follows it.

(d) The CEV's title for this psalm is "The Best Choice." How could this be misleading as a summary the content of Psalm 16?

Verse 1–2:

(a) Verses 1 and 2 express the major petition in this psalm professing trust in Yahweh. What is the petition?

(b) What does it mean to "take refuge" in someone? Is there a figurative way of saying this in your language (e.g., Chewa: "to place/lean one's heart upon")? If so, what is it?

(c) What is the motivation for the psalmist's request?

(d) The words "LORD" (*yhwh*) and "Lord" (*ʾadonay*) both occur in verse 2. What is the difference in their meaning? Does this cause difficulties when translating into your language? Explain. How does the CEV solve this problem? Is this a good way of handling it?

(e) To say "You are my Lord" seems clear enough. But what does this really *mean*? Is the psalmist simply stating an obvious fact?

(f) Line B of verse 2 is "apart from you I have no good thing" (NIV). What does this mean? What does a "good thing" have to do with the Lord?

(g) What is the logical connection, or semantic relation, that joins verses 1 and 2?

Verse 3:

(a) Is there any reason to consider verse 3 as the beginning of a new stanza? Explain.

(b) The Hebrew of verse 3 is difficult. Do you see any differences of interpretation among these versions: NIV, TEV, RSV, and CEV? If so, point out the differences. Take note of the various footnotes giving alternative renderings for this verse. Which version do you prefer and why?

(c) Who are the "saints" (*qədošim*)? (Consult THP.) Why does the psalmist "delight" in them? Evaluate the CEV rendering, "Your people are *wonderful* . . ."

Verse 4:

(a) How is verse 4 logically related to verse 3 (see THP)?

(b) What does it mean to "run after" other gods? Do you have a similar figure of speech in your language? (In Chewa the same figure is used negatively for men "running after" other women.)

(c) The NIV grammar is unnatural in verse 4. Point out the problem here.

(d) What is the meaning of the second half of verse 4? Specifically, what does their "libations of blood" refer to, and what does it mean to "take up their names"? To whom does the pronoun "they" refer?

(d) Would a literal translation of verse 4 in your language be taken to refer to some rite of traditional ancestral worship? Explain any similarity that you notice and how you would avoid this by means of a different rendering.

Verse 5:

(a) Why is it natural to make a strophe break here? This verse seems to be a continuation of the direct speech of verse 2. In what way?

(b) To what does "portion" refer? What event in Israel's history is being alluded to here? The TEV rendering is "You, LORD, are all I have" (cf. also CEV). What does this mean?

(c) Explain the figures "cup" and "lot" (see THP). Do you have idiomatic ways of expressing these concepts in your language?

Verse 6:

(a) Just as in verse 5, the imagery of verse 6 is unfamiliar to most receptor audiences. What does the psalmist mean by "the boundary lines have fallen for me in pleasant places"? Would a footnote be needed here in your language? If so, how would you word it so as to be precise and concise?

(b) What sort of "inheritance" is in view here (see THP)? The CEV has "my future is bright." Could you translate this literally into your language? Why or why not?

(c) Notice how the common topic of the figurative language of verses 5–6 links them. The same sort of linkage should be evident in translation. What do you think about removing the imagery, as in TEV? If it is removed, what can be done in a translation to replace the beauty and impact of the original?

Verse 7:

(a) What marks the shift to a new strophe in verse 7?

(b) What are the two reasons the psalmist praises the Lord in verses 7–8?

(c) How can one's "heart" (literally, "kidneys") instruct a person, even at night? What does this figure of speech mean (see the *NIV Study Bible* note at 7:9)? CEV and TEV render this line differently. What is the difference? Which do you prefer and why?

Verse 8:

(a) What is it that links verses 7 and 8?

(b) Explain the idiom in verse 8a, "I have set the LORD always before me" (NIV), comparing its rendering in CEV and TEV.

(c) What does it mean to have the Lord "at my right hand" (verse 8b)?

(d) Do you have a figure of speech in your language that is similar in meaning to "I will not be shaken" (e.g., in Lenje it is "no one will poke a finger at me")?

Verse 9:

(a) Should verse 9 be joined to verses 7–8 as in CEV? Or does it start a new stanza as in TEV and NIV? Explain the reasons for your preference.

(b) What is the sense of "therefore" (*laken*) here? How does CEV render this? Is a deletion like this effective in your language? Explain.

(c) Why is the psalmist happy? What kind of figure is "my heart is glad" and "my tongue rejoices"? The Hebrew word rendered "tongue" in the NIV literally means "my glory." How does the RSV translate it? Which word seems to fit the context better? Why do you think so?

(d) What does the psalmist mean when he says that his "body will rest secure"? There is a serious translation problem in the TEV and CEV here. What is the problem, especially in view of what is said in verse 10?

Verse 10:

(a) What is the semantic relation linking verse 10 to verse 9? Notice the conjunction at the beginning of verse 10, "because" (*ki*) which could also be rendered "surely."

(b) Does the meaning of line A differ from that of line B? If so, in what way? What in line B is parallel to line A's "me"? What is line B is parallel to line A's "the grave"?

(c) What is the sense of the word *šeʾol* here (see THP)? How does TEV translate this word? How do NIV, RSV, and CEV express it?

(d) What does the term "pit" (*šaḥat*) mean? Compare its rendering in CEV, NIV, TEV, and RSV. Which do you prefer? Why?

(e) How would you render "holy one" (*ḥasid*) in your language? To whom does this name refer? Why do you think so? What possible interpretation have the TEV and CEV excluded by their translation of this? Is there a problem here (cf. Acts 2:27; 13:35)? Explain the issues involved and how they might be handled in a way that allows for difference of opinion.

Verse 11:

(a) How is the climactic verse 11 related to verses 9 and 10?

(b) What does "of" mean in "path of life"? In other words, what is the semantic relation between the two nouns that "of" links?

(c) What phrase in line C corresponds to the phrase "in your presence" in line B? Notice that there is a tricolon here. Can you propose any structural purpose for this?

(d) Do you have an idiom in your language similar in meaning to "at your right hand"? Does the sense of this expression differ from "at my right hand" in verse 8? In what way?

(e) How do you express the concept of "eternal" or "forever" in your language? Is the expression an idiom (e.g., Bemba: "always and always"; Chewa: "time and time")?

(f) How does the psalmist reinforce his expression of confidence in the LORD in this final strophe, verses 9–11?

(g) How does the close of Psalm 16 connect in thought and tone with its beginning?

7.2.5 Psalm 24

The following are questions on the overall discourse structure:

(a) What genre is Psalm 24? Give the reasons for your answer.

(b) There are some differences among the major English versions with regard to how they segment this psalm into stanzas. (They are not called "strophes" due to the presence of a refrain.) Which version do you prefer and why? Your reasons should be structurally based, specifying the *repetition* markers, major shifts in content or purpose, and any concentration of *poetic features,* as discussed in the THP.

(c) Describe how the stanzas that you have posited in b above are semantically related to one another. Note that this is a *liturgical* psalm in which the relation *BASE* (question/command/petition) + *RESPONSE* (proclamation) is a prominent structural feature. Are there songs in your language having such an alternating organization with the solo singer and the chorus taking turns? If so, give an example, religious or secular.

Verse 1:

(a) Identify the ellipsis in line B of this verse.

(b) What is the important word pair found in verse 1? Do you distinguish between "earth" and "world" in your language? If so, what two terms could be used? Which of them is more general and "non-poetic"; in which line should this term be placed, A or B, and why?

Verse 2:

(a) How is verse 2 related to verse 1? Should a new sentence begin here (cf. NIV)? Notice that the conclusion-grounds relationship is not very clearly expressed in the CEV and TEV. Why not? What seems to be the meaning of the CEV?

(b) What words in verse 2 correspond to "earth" and "world" in verse 1? What is the special meaning of this poetic pair of words (see THP)?

(c) What verse is the Bible does this one allude to? How can you show this connection?

(d) In the ancient creation stories of your culture are any ideas expressed that are similar to verses 1–2? If so, what are they? Are there ideas that conflict with verses 1–2? Perhaps your traditional homeland or country is far away from any large body of water; what can you do then to render this verse in a meaningful way?

Verse 3:

(a) How is verse 3 related to the rest of the stanza (vv. 4–6)? How do you think that this psalm was used during Israel's worship?

(b) What is the point of the two rhetorical questions of this verse? How can you express this idiomatically in your language?

(c) What place does "the hill of the LORD" refer to? Is an explanatory footnote needed here in your language? How would you word it?

(d) Does the expression "his holy place" in line B refer to the "hill" in line A? If so, how would you indicate this in your language? If not, to what place *does* it refer? Do you need to make the referents of these two expressions explicit in your language? Explain. What does it mean to "stand" (NIV, RSV) in this place?

(e) The verbs of this verse are expressed differently by RSV and TEV. Which rendering do you think is more accurate? Why?

(f) This verse may be the reason for the placement of Psalm 24 after Psalm 23. Compare verse 3 with 23:6. What is the connection? (Such thematic linkage between psalms is not uncommon.)

Verse 4:

(a) How does verse 4 relate in meaning to verse 3? Is this relationship clear in your translation?

(b) Should the personal referent of verse 4 be singular (NIV) or plural (TEV) in your language? Why so? If singular, should it be "he" or "she," or does it not make any difference? Explain your preference.

(c) What does it mean to have "clean hands" and a "pure heart"? Do you have any comparable idioms in your language?

(d) What kind of sin is referred to by the expression "who does not lift up his soul to what is false" (RSV)? What would a literal translation of this mean in your language?

(e) How does a person "swear by what is false" (NIV)?

(f) Identify the *ellipsis* in this verse (cf. v. 3).

Verse 5:

(a) The topical focus of verse 5 is upon which person(s)—the people referred to in verse 4 or God? How is this rendered in NIV? In TEV? What does THP have to say? Whatever is used, it should be the same as in verse 6. How would you translate this in your language?

(b) What is the meaning of the key term *ṣədaqah*, "vindication" (cf. THP)? How does the CEV express this important concept? Is this an accurate rendering? Explain.

(c) How is "vindication" related to "blessing" in line A? Is the conjunction "and" a good way to link the two lines of verse 5? Tell why (not).

Verse 6:

(a) What does "generation" mean in this context (see THP)?

(b) How does line B specify what is said in line A? Note another ellipsis here.

(c) What does it mean to "seek someone's face"? In some languages a literal rendering of this would refer to an attempt to bribe someone! What would a formal duplication of this expression mean in your language?

(d) For this verse the CEV has ". . . because they worship and serve the God of Jacob." The NIV renders it with a vocative : "O God of Jacob." Which wording seems to make the most sense in your language? Why? What is the precise meaning of "God *of* Jacob"?

Verse 7:

(a) Should there be a stanza break after verse 6? Why or why not (cf. NIV and CEV)?

(b) What kind of figure of speech do we find in line A of this verse? Would it sound natural to address a "gate" in your language? What do you think of CEV's restructuring to eliminate the vocative form here?

(c) What does it mean for gates to "lift up their heads"? What would a literal translation of this suggest in your language? What does it mean to describe these gates as being "ancient"? Is a footnote needed here? If so, how would you word it to provide a clear, concise explanation?

(d) Notice that line B repeats line A. Why is this repetition present? How has the CEV handled this? What would be the most natural way in your language to convey the same emphasis that in Hebrew was conveyed by repetition?

(e) To whom does "the King of glory" refer? Should the word "king" be capitalized? If it is not capitalized, should the referent be made explicit? Why or why not (cf. THP)? What exactly does "of" mean in "king *of* glory"?

Verse 8:

(a) Should there be a break between verses 7 and 8? Why or why not?

(b) How does line A of verse 8 relate to lines B and C? What is the purpose of this rhetorical question? Is it necessary to state B and C in the form of complete predications in your language (TEV)? Why or why not?

(c) Notice the repetition in lines B and C. How does this sound to you in English? In your language? Is it poetic, emphatic, or simply redundant? Explain.

(d) RSV has "mighty in battle." How do TEV and CEV render this? Which expression sounds more powerful in your language?

Verses 9–10:

(a) Why are verses 7–8 repeated in 9–10? What does this reveal about the genre of Psalm 24?

(b) Where are the differences between verses 7–8 and 9–10? This variation serves to emphasize something. What is emphasized? How would you highlight this in your language?

(c) What is the significance of the name "LORD of hosts" (*yhwh ṣəbaʾot*), according to THP? What would be a good way of conveying this in your language?

(d) How do you render the liturgical term *selah* in your language (cf. also v. 6)? What are your reasons for handling it this way?

7.2.6 Psalm 30

The following are questions on the overall discourse structure:

(a) What genre is Psalm 30? What is the characteristic feature of this genre?

(b) How would you divide this psalm into constituent strophes? What is the structural evidence for doing it in this way? How are these strophes related to one another? Which major English version(s) agree with you? Which do not (specify where the differences occur)?

(c) What theme would you give to the psalm as a whole? How does this compare to the actual Hebrew title? What connection (if any) does this title have with the contents of the psalm (see 1 Chron. 21:1–22:6)?

(d) Do a propositional-structural analysis and diagram of Psalm 30 (see the example in sec. 7.2.1).

Verse 1:

(a) How does the word "exalt" in the NIV differ from "praise," which is the TEV rendering (see THP)?

(b) What image is in view in verse 1 ("you lifted me out of the depths")? Read the *NIV Study Bible* note. TEV renders this "you have saved me." Is this an adequate translation?

(c) Are there 3 poetic lines (cola) in this verse or just two? Explain your preference in this respect and what difference it makes to one's understanding of this passage as a whole. If you posit 3 lines (as in NIV), how does line C relate to line B? How do B–C together relate to line A?

(d) What does "gloat" mean? Do you have an idiomatic expression for this action in your language?

Verse 2:

(a) How does verse 2 relate in terms of its meaning to verse 1?

(b) Do people "cry," "call," "shout," or "pray" for help in your language? Explain.

(c) Is the word "healed" to be taken literally or figuratively? Why do you think so? Would this make a difference for translation in your language?

Verse 3:

(a) How is verse 3 related to verse 2? Should these verses be joined as in the CEV? If not, how *should* they be connected to clearly show the relationship between them?

(b) How are the lines A and B of verse 3 related?

(c) What word pair do you find in verse 3?

(d) What does the word "pit" (*bor*) refer to? Read the *NIV Study Bible* note. (This is a different Hebrew word than the one RSV translates as "pit" in 16:10.) Is there an idiomatic way of expressing the meaning in your language?

Verse 4:

(a) What marker strongly indicates that a new strophe is to begin here?

(b) To whom does the word "saints" (*ḥasidim*) refer in this context (cf. 16:3)? How is this term rendered in your language? Is this expression meaningful or can you suggest something better (cf. TEV/CEV and the THP)?

(c) Observe the difference in how line B is translated in NIV and TEV, especially with regard to the word "name" (literally, "remembrance"). Note also the qualifier "holy." Which rendering do you think is more accurate (see THP)?

Verse 5:

(a) How does this verse relate in meaning to verse 4?

(b) Which pronouns does the CEV use here and in verse 4? Compare this with the other versions. Is the CEV rendering an improvement as far as the meaning is concerned?

(c) What does the word "anger" refer to in the context of this psalm? Is there an idiomatic expression for "anger" in your language? (It is "to burn in the heart" in Chewa.)

(d) There are four sets of contrasts in this verse. What are they? Which is the most difficult to express meaningfully in your language? Why?

(e) What do "weeping" and "rejoicing" have reference to here? How can you make the intended meaning clear in your language?

(f) The CEV has "we will celebrate." Could this be misleading? Explain.

Verse 6:

(a) What suggests to you that a new strophe begins here?

(b) Verses 6 and 7 seem to be a *flashback* to some earlier point of time. When was that, and how can such a shift back to a previous time be indicated clearly in your language?

(c) NIV and TEV have "I felt secure" here. How does CEV render the term "secure"? Which seems to fit the context better? Why do you think so?

(d) What does the psalmist mean when he says to himself, "I will never be shaken"? What sort of an *attitude* does he have? How would you express this in your language? In the poetry of your language does the speaker ever quote himself? If so, how can this be clearly, but concisely indicated in the text?

Verse 7:

(a) What "mountain" (NIV) is the psalmist referring to here? How would you express this notion meaningfully in your language? What do you think of the CEV rendering?

(b) What is the significance of God's "hiding his face" from someone? (In some Bantu languages a literal translation suggests that God himself was ashamed.) Do you have a figurative way of conveying the right meaning in your language?

(c) How is the NIV's "I was dismayed" rendered in TEV and CEV? Which of the three seems to fit the context best? Can you use direct discourse here in your language? Is it more dramatic?

Verse 8:

(a) Should a new strophe begin at verse 8? If so, why? And what is the relationship of the new strophe to the preceding one?

(b) The verb of line A is rendered in different ways in different versions: "cried" (RSV), "called" (TEV, NIV), and "prayed" (CEV). Which seems to fit best? Why do you think so (cf. the verb of line B)?

(c) How is God (*ʾadonay*) referred to in line B in the different versions? Note the error in RSV (retained in NRSV). What has been done in both TEV and CEV? Which solution is the most natural and dynamic in your language?

(d) Compare the rendering of verse 8 in the NIV and TEV. How are the references to God different with regard to person? Is the way the TEV adjusts the references necessary in your language?

Verse 9:

(a) What kind of questions are in this verse? What sort of feeling do they convey? How can the emotive emphasis created by these questions be retained in your language? Notice that in the TEV there are four questions instead of three? Why is that? Is it natural to speak four questions like this, one after the other, in your language (or even in English)?

(b) In your translation, has it been made clear as to who is speaking these questions?

(c) Two figures of speech are combined in the expression "Will the dust praise you?" What are they? How would you translate this question meaningfully—and with the same emphasis—in your language?

(d) NIV and RSV render the key term ʾ*emet* as "faithfulness." How is it rendered in TEV and CEV? What translation would sound best in your language?

(e) Is the psalmist's argument in verse 9 easy to follow in your language? If not, how could you make it clearer?

Verse 10:

(a) How is verse 10 related to verses 8 and 9?

(b) Notice where the two vocative phrases referring to the Lord are placed in the English versions. Is this the most natural position for them in your language? Does the repetition here sound natural in your language?

(c) CEV translates this verse "Have pity, LORD! Help!" Is this a good model to follow or not, especially with reference to the verb "help"? Would a noun form like "helper" (RSV) be more effective here? Why?

Verse 11:

(a) What sudden shift in content and feeling indicates that a new stanza begins here?

(b) Describe the figurative language you find here. How would you express the meaning (including any special emphasis) in your language? Would a footnote be necessary to convey the full sense of the funeral imagery of this verse? If so, how would you word it?

Verse 12:

(a) In RSV and NIV verse 12 is a continuation of the sentence begun in verse 11. What problem does this cause? Has it been solved in CEV and TEV? How so?

(b) The word rendered "heart" in NIV is literally "glory" in Hebrew (*kabod*). How is this word translated in RSV, NRSV, TEV, and CEV? Which would work out best in your language, or do you have an idiomatic expression that will sound even better in this final verse of the psalm (cf. THP)?

(c) How is the concept "forever" translated in CEV? Would this be a natural way of expressing it in your language? Why or why not?

(d) How is the initial emphatic vocative of line B expressed in CEV? Would such a rendering be forceful in your language? How has the TEV handled this? Do you think this is a good translation? Explain.

(e) How is line B related to line A in this verse?

7.2.7 Psalm 98

The following are questions on the overall discourse structure:

(a) What genre is Psalm 98? What are the typical characteristics of this genre?

(b) Psalm 98 is similar in many places to which preceding psalm in the Psalter? What is the literary—and theological—significance of each repetition? Why is this important to the Bible translator?

(c) What is the strophic structure of Psalm 98, and what are the main markers of the internal divisions?

(d) Is any sort of progression or heightening evident from one stanza to the next? If so, describe what you find (cf. the *NIV Study Bible*).

(e) Suggest a theme for the psalm as a whole.

(f) Prepare a structural diagram of Psalm 98 by listing the sequence of poetic lines and their semantic relation to one another in pairs and clusters.

Verse 1:

(a) What is meant by a "new song"; in what way is it "new" (cf. Ps. 33:3)? Read the note in the *NIV Study Bible* (see also THP, p. 311). What is the theme of this song?

(b) How is line B related to line A? How do you mark this relationship in your language?

(c) What do "right hand" and "holy arm" signify? What kind of figure are they? What is the point of this double figure? How can this concept be conveyed with equivalent impact in your language?

(d) How does CEV render the notion of "holy" (*qodeš*)? Is this satisfactory?

Verse 2:

(a) How does the TEV translate the word *yəšuʿah*, which is rendered "salvation" in the NIV? Do you prefer the TEV or the NIV rendering? Why? Would it make a difference in your language? Explain.

(b) How is line B related in meaning to line A? What is specified in line B?

(c) How is the term "righteousness" (*ṣedeq*) translated in TEV? Explain why this is not an adequate rendering (cf. THP).

(d) To whom does the word "nations" (*goyim*) refer? How do you convey the ethnic distinction between the Jews and *goyim* in your language, or between your ethnic group and other peoples?

Verse 3:

(a) In the NIV and RSV the meaning of line A of verse 3, which is a literal rendering, is not clear. Mention some of the problems that you see. What important theological word pair do you see here? How can these key concepts be transmitted in a meaningful way in your language?

(b) How is verse 3 related in meaning to verse 2? How does verse 3 expand upon or intensify the meaning of verse 2?

(c) To what or whom does the expression "all the ends of the earth" refer? Do you have an idiomatic way of saying this in your language?

(d) What exactly is it that all people "have seen" according to verse 3? What special sense does the verb "see" have in this context? Is it possible to "see" "salvation" in your language? If not, what would be a poetic way of expressing this concept?

Verse 4:

(a) Why is it natural to begin a new strophe here?

(b) What is a "joyful noise" (RSV)? How do people "make" it? Does "noise" have a good or bad connotation to you? How would you restructure this potentially unnatural expression in your language?

(c) How does CEV render "all the earth"?

(d) How does line B intensify line A? What does it mean to "burst" (NIV) or "break forth" (RSV) into song?

Verse 5:

(a) How is verse 5 related in meaning to verse 4? What additional emphasis is present?

(b) What is the general word for "music" in your language? Does it refer to instrumental music or vocal music or to both? How does one "make music to" God? Are words involved?

(c) What is your word for "harp"? Is this a common instrument? Is it ever used in the performance of religious music and song? If not, what would be a more appropriate instrument to use?

Verse 6:

(a) How is verse 6 related to verse 5?

(b) Do people distinguish between "trumpets" and "horns" in your language? Do they use any instrument like this at all to play music? Would these be used in worship at all? If not, do you have a close functional substitute?

(c) What thought occurs at both the opening and the close of this stanza, forming an inclusio? Does the closing line add to or specify the meaning of the opening line? If so, explain how.

(d) Does the expression "our LORD and King" (CEV) sound natural in your language? If not, is there a better way of saying it? Would a separate utterance (e.g., "He is our King!") be an improvement?

Verse 7:

(a) What indicates the start of a new strophe at verse 7?

(b) What type of figure is prominent in verses 7–8? Does this figure sound natural in your language? If not, how would you render this so as not to lose the dynamic power and poetic beauty of the figurative language?

(c) To whom is the "command" (CEV) of verse 7 given? What does this verse mean? Is there a problem of translation here? If so, what is it?

(d) What is the significance of the word pair "sea" and "world" in this context (see the *NIV Study Bible*)?

(e) The NIV line B of verse 7 contains an ellipsis. What has been left out? Can this be done meaningfully in your language? Explain.

Verse 8:

(a) In your language do "rivers clap their hands" (NIV)? How can you render this idiomatically?

(b) What figurative connection is there between the "rivers" and "mountains" (see the *NIV Study Bible*)? What parallel is there here with the word pair mentioned in verse 7? Do you have an idiomatic way of conveying the idea of a great expanse of space in your language?

Verse 9:

(a) The phrase "before the LORD" occurs at the beginning of verse 9, but in meaning it may fit better at the end of verse 8, as in TEV. What has the NIV done here (cf. CEV)?

(b) How does verse 9 relate in meaning to the preceding verses of this stanza?

(c) What does the word "judge" (*šopet*) connote in your language? Would this verse sound more like a blessing or a punishment? How has TEV solved this potential misunderstanding?

(d) How is the concept of "equity" (cf. Ps. 9:8) best expressed in your language?

(e) Is there any way in your language of marking verse 9 as the climax of the entire psalm? If so, describe how you would do this.

7.2.8 Psalm 19

The following are questions on the overall discourse structure:

(a) Which verses of Psalm 19 belong to each of its two main parts? What are the structural and semantic reasons for dividing the psalm like this?

(b) What psalm genre is part one? What psalm genre is part two?

(c) Suggest a title or theme for each part. Is it a good idea to combine these two as in CEV or to keep them separate as in TEV? What is the reason for your preference?

(d) Divide each of the two parts into its constituent strophes, giving reasons for your division. Notice the differences of division among the English versions. Which one seems the best? Can you suggest yet another structure, different from them all?

(e) Summarize the principal semantic relationships between the strophes in the structure you prefer. In other words, how is each strophe linked with the preceding and/or succeeding one and also to the main part in which it is found?

(f) Why do you think the two portions of Psalm 19, which seem so different, have been joined together to form a single psalm? Can you suggest a way of marking this connection in your language?

Verse 1:

(a) The two lines of verse 1 form a *chiasmus* in Hebrew. That is, they form an inverted parallel structure (A-B-C = C'-B'-A'). Refer to the Hebrew text or an interlinear version, and indicate how the three syntactic elements in lines A and B correspond to each other. What reason could there be for using such a construction at this point in the psalm (see THP)?

(b) Do "heavens" differ from "skies" in your language? Is any difference in meaning intended by the original text (see THP)?

(c) What sort of utterance does the TEV have as lines A and B of verse 1? Is there any reason for this? How would this sound in your language?

(d) What does the word "firmament" (RSV) refer to (see THP)?

(e) What is meant by the "glory" (*kabod*) of God in this context? What is the clearest way of expressing this concept in your language? A phrase may be better than a single word.

(f) What is meant by the "hands" of God? What sort of a figure of speech is this and how do you convey it poetically in your language?

Verse 2:

(a) How is verse 2 related to verse 1?

(b) What type of figurative language is found in both lines of verse 2? Is it possible to translate this literally in your language and at the same time preserve the intended meaning, or do some changes need to be made? Explain, with reference to your language.

(c) Exactly what is "it" (TEV) that the "day" and the "night" are announcing? Look at the CEV to see how unclear the referent is there.

(d) How has the concept of (*daʿat*), "knowledge" (RSV, NIV), been rendered in TEV and CEV? Have TEV and CEV handled this correctly? Explain (see THP).

Verse 3:

(a) What is the semantic relationship of verse 3 to verses 1–2?

(b) What is the meaning of verse 3 according to the RSV? How is this clarified in the TEV and CEV? What different sense is conveyed by the NIV?

(c) Does your language distinguish between "speech," "words," and "voice" (RSV)? If not, how can you best represent the intended meaning here?

Verse 4:

(a) How is verse 4 linked in meaning to verse 3?

(b) In this context what is the sense of "voice" (RSV, NIV)?

(c) How does line B intensify the meaning of line A? Is such intensification possible in your language? If so, tell how.

(d) What would suggest that the C line of verse 4 should really begin a new strophe? What kind of distortion in meaning might occur if this break is not clearly indicated?

(e) Explain the imagery in line C. Why is it applied to the "sun" (see the *NIV Study Bible* and THP)? Would the use of this imagery be meaningful in your language or might it be misunderstood?

Verse 5:

(a) The imagery of verse 4 is continued in verse 5. What are the two distinct images found in verse 5? What is the main point of these pictures? Do they make sense in the context of your culture? Point out any special problems that you see here.

(b) The RSV's rendering of "strong man" is quite literal. How is this translated in NIV, TEV, and CEV? Which expression seems to fit best in your language? Why?

Verse 6:

(a) To what does the pronoun "it" refer? Would it be necessary in your language to use a noun instead?

(b) What is the sense of the first two lines of verse 6? How does it fit as part of the description of the sun? Is the "sun" being praised literally in this verse? If not, what is the point (see the *NIV Study Bible* and THP)?

(c) What thought about God is expressed by the imagery of the final line of verse 6? Note how the end of the strophe is marked here with a *tricolon*. Also note the topical recursion between the two strophes (vv. 1–4 and 5–6) of part ("canto") one of the psalm: Verse 6 is similar to verse 1 and verse 4b opens (in Hebrew) with a phrase "to the end" that is found also in verse 6.

Verse 7:

(a) What is meant by the key term "law" (*torah*) (see THP, p. 192)? How has this word usually been translated in your language? Is this adequate? Explain. Why is it important to maintain consistency, if at all possible, in the rendering of this word (cf. Ps. 1:2)?

(b) The word "LORD" (*yhwh*) occurs in verse 7 for the first time in the psalm and then continues to be used throughout the rest of the psalm. But in verse 1 "God" (*ʾel*) was used. Is there any significance to this change? How do you represent *yhwh* in your language? Explain the translational options that you had and why you chose the term that you are now using.

(c) What does it mean to "revive the soul" (RSV, NIV)? How can you convey this notion idiomatically in your language?

(d) The word *ʿedut* is rendered "statutes" in NIV and "testimony" in RSV. What does this word mean? Does it refer to something different from "law" in line A? Explain.

(e) What kind of people are "the simple" (RSV, NIV)? (This could be taken as an insult in English!)

Verse 8:

(a) In verse 8 two more terms are used to refer to the Word of the LORD: "precepts" (*piqqudim*) and "commands" (*miṣwah*). What distinctions do these words add to the total description? Can they be expressed in your language? How?

(b) Why are all these different words in Hebrew used to describe the Word of God (cf. THP)?

(c) How can "precepts" cause one's heart to rejoice? What is the meaning here?

(d) Similarly, how can God's "commands" give "light to the eyes" (NIV)? If these expressions are translated literally into your language, is the intended meaning conveyed? If not, how can you clarify things? Is it possible to retain some of the imagery (or substitute local figures) for greater impact and poetic appeal? Explain.

Verse 9:

(a) In verse 9, line A, "fear of the LORD" (*yirʾah yhwh*) seems to be another reference to God's Word. Or is it to God himself? It is rather difficult to interpret. Consult several different versions and commentaries and propose what you think the intended meaning is here.

(b) In line B, "ordinances" (*mišpaṭ*) is rendered in different ways by different versions. (The related verb is usually translated as "to judge.") Which of the various translations of *mišpaṭ* sounds the most natural—and correct—in your language?

(c) What special emphasis seems to be present in both lines of verse 9?

(d) How would you convey lines A and B meaningfully in your language so that the central focus on God's Word is not lost?

(e) Notice that the CEV starts a new strophe at verse 9. Do you think that this is correct in view of the context? Compare this with the other versions. Why do all the versions keep verses 7–9 together as part of the same strophe?

Verse 10:

(a) To whom or what does the pronoun "they" refer? If a noun subject needs to be reintroduced here, which one would seem to fit best? Why?

(b) What figure of speech is used twice in verse 10? What is the point of similarity between the topic and each of the two figures? Are these figures natural ones in your language? If not, what adjustments or substitutions need to be made?

(c) How is the close of each of lines A and B intensified? Can this same intensification be conveyed in your language? Read the THP's explanation of this "double parallelism."

Verse 11:

(a) How will you handle the potentially ambiguous pronoun "them" (twice!) in this verse?

(b) Verse 11 is tied to verse 10 by the Hebrew conjunction *gam,* which the RSV renders "moreover." In this context, *gam* seems to mark some sort of a climactic conclusion. How would you indicate this in your language? What mistake has the CEV made here?

(c) To whom does "your servant" (NIV) refer? Is such third-person reference to oneself natural in your language? If not, how could you express this meaningfully?

(d) Which seems to fit the context better: "warn" (RSV, NIV, CEV) or "give knowledge" (TEV). The area of meaning of the Hebrew word includes both.

(e) What is a more natural way in English of saying "in keeping them there is great reward"? (Be careful not to allow the possibility of too much emphasis on a material reward as opposed to a spiritual reward.)

Verse 12:

(a) What would seem to indicate a break at verse 12, the beginning of a new strophe? What structural markers of a break do you find in CEV's rendering of the passage?

(b) How is verse 12 related in meaning to the preceding strophe?

(c) What kind of a question is here? What is the implied answer? In your language would a question form be as effective as an emphatic statement?

(d) What implicit element in line B does TEV make explicit? Why is this done? Would this be helpful also in your language?

(e) What is meant by "hidden faults"? Could the readers of your translation misinterpret this expression (e.g., as a reference to minor or unimportant sins)? If so, how might you clarify the intended meaning?

Verse 13:

(a) How is verse 13 related to verse 12?

(b) What are "willful sins (TEV)"? How do these differ from the "hidden faults" of verse 12?

(c) How do sins "rule over" a person? How would you express this personification in your language to make the intended meaning clear?

(d) What does the psalmist mean by saying that he will be "perfect" or "blameless"? Will a literal rendering of this lead to a possible misunderstanding in your language? Explain.

(e) How has "great transgression" been translated in TEV and CEV? What is the problem of meaning here (see THP, p. 195)? How can you convey the intended emphasis clearly in your language?

Verse 14:

(a) Why is it a good idea to set this verse off as a separate strophe on its own? Is there a way to mark the break with some kind of transitional expression in your language? If so, give an example. (Look at the verse's layout in the NIV and evaluate its suitability.)

(b) In what way is verse 14 a fitting conclusion to the psalm as a whole? What is the significance of a *tricolon* appearing at this point in the text?

(c) What kind of an utterance is line A? Does it need to be marked in a special way or reworded in your language? How may this be done?

(d) Which words of line A are omitted in TEV and CEV? Why do you think this was done? Should these words be left out of the translation in your language? Explain.

(e) How is line C related in meaning to lines A and B? Does CEV's "because" seem to fit well? If not, what connecting term would you prefer?

(f) What kind of a figure is "rock"? What are its image, topic, and ground? Does this image have the same meaning in your language? If not, is there some other image that would convey the desired meaning? Does the ground of this figure need to be made explicit?

(g) What is the full sense of "my Redeemer" (*goʾali*)? What would the lexical equivalent mean in the context of your culture? Would CEV's "protector" be more suitable here? How would you render this key term meaningfully in your language?

Exercise 7.2

1. As homework, each member of the class should select a psalm from among those studied in chapter 2 and prepare a complete set of exegetical and translational questions, along with suggested answers, like those illustrated in sections 7.2.1–7.2.8.

2. Later in class, participants will exchange the sets of questions (without the answers) and work them out. As they answer the questions, they should also keep a record of suggestions as to how the questions might be improved, whether by adding or deleting some, or by rewording those that are not clear enough. Each participant will then present his or her revised list of questions to the entire group. As time allows, the class can conduct a joint exercise in exegesis and translation, based on several of their corrected sets of questions and answers.

APPENDIX: ORGANIZING A BIBLICAL POETRY WORKSHOP

The dilemma of the translator is how to avoid becoming too much of a "traitor," as someone has so aptly put it. He or she must not betray the form *or* the content *or* the communicative intent of the original work. The problem is particularly acute where poetic discourse is concerned because the linguistic shape is so much a part of the total meaning of the message. In poetry, it seems, *something* has to be given way as it were in the transfer process, either the form and any special significance that it bears *or* the semantic content (thus the translator becomes a "trader" between texts).

This is the conclusion that many translators, and no doubt also a good number of translation consultants, have come to as they carry out their work on the poetic passages of Scripture. As a result, most choose to follow one of three principal options:

(1) A fairly *literal* rendering of the biblical form (e.g., RSV, NASB), hoping that perhaps its poetic flavor might be evident in the parallelisms and figurative imagery, at least.

(2) A *meaningful* prose rendering with the printed format arranged to look like poetry (e.g., TEV, CEV).

(3) A very *dynamic* rendering that ignores the Hebrew form and also to some extent also the strict referential content in order to reproduce the beauty, power, and emotions of the original by means of a dynamic paraphrase expressed in the form of some popular TL poetic genre (e.g., the free verse of *Psalms: The Message,* by Eugene Peterson).

Each one of these approaches is limited, or "unfaithful," in its own way, and it is up to the serious translator—or translation team—to evaluate each possibility in relation to their own language and literary tradition. They must then make a conscious decision as to which to adopt or adapt for their own particular situation.

To do this, some important questions need to be asked: How precisely or overtly do the translators wish to represent the essential meaning of the original communication event (as nearly as this can be determined)? How does one define "meaning" and its various aspects (i.e., formal, semantic, pragmatic)? Furthermore, which elements of the SL message are likely to be eliminated or distorted in the transfer process, and will any of this be transmitted implicitly? How important is a given poem's literary form to the overall meaning—its rhetorical significance, persuasive force, and aesthetic attraction, in particular? Then, having determined the answers to questions such as these, one must go on to ask which devices are available in the TL to either complement or compensate for the original devices that will be missing due to a literal transfer or a prosaic restatement.

The three options that have been mentioned are not necessarily the only ones. There is the possibility of a sort of combined approach, rendering the SL poetic composition by the closest functionally equivalent *genre*-form that is available in the TL. In this method, the informational content of Scripture is important, to be sure, but not to the exclusion of the socio-rhetorical objectives of the original, the so-called expressive and imperative aspects of discourse (see Nida and Taber's *Theory and Practice of Translation,* pp. 25–27; cf. Wendland 1985, ch.2). In many biblical texts, poetry in particular, these facets of "meaning" appear to be preeminent, and the literal content merely a vehicle for accomplishing these more basic objectives.

Given the importance of such *connotative*, or *associative* meaning (as distinct from *denotative* or *referential* meaning), one must pay special attention to it when translating poetry. A good way to do this is to seek to *recompose* the original text in the TL poetic genre that best corresponds to it. If this turns out to be too ambitious or controversial, then perhaps it can be done with some modification, that is, to transmit the conceptual core of a given psalm in a recognizable, rhetorically heightened style. Call it a "poetic" or "oratorical" adaptation, it makes no difference, as long it proves acceptable to a particular target audience and effectively duplicates the functional dynamics of a psalm/the Psalter in the target language concerned—in other words, the closest literary (*poetic*) equivalent. Thus the actual TL stylistic forms, especially those that affect the sound structure of the discourse, are of much greater importance in translating poetry than in translating prose. As signals of the chosen TL genre, they serve to highlight the thematic focus and communicative purpose of the original text.

This raises three questions of a practical nature:

(1) How does one go about stimulating an appreciation for indigenous verbal art and its relevance to Bible translation, not only among translators, but also among the target audience at large?

(2 How does one determine the pertinent stylistic features and functional characteristics of the various genres of poetry in the TL?

(3) Finally, how does one actually apply this knowledge in translator-training exercises, to begin with, and ultimately within the Bible translation itself?

A translator-training workshop that focuses on a translation of the Psalms might well be designed with these, and similar, questions or issues in mind.

1. The nature and purpose of a poetry translation workshop

A workshop is an intensive two to four week course designed to train translators for a specific project. The proposals of this appendix are directed to the organizers and instructors of a workshop that focuses upon a translation of the Book of Psalms. The workshop leaders should, however, expect to adapt the material of this textbook considerably (if it is to be used at all), that is, to fit their own time constraints and other variables. For example, depending on the workshop participants' educational-cultural background, knowledge of theology and Biblical Hebrew, and translational experience, a workshop might possibly include one or two less demanding, but related subjects. I would suggest a general introduction to the Hebrew language and literature for those not already acquainted with it, studies in the original Ancient Mediterranean setting (history, culture, ecology, geography, religion, etc.), the theory and practice of functional-equivalence translation, the base-model(s) method, and literary versus common-language renditions, as some possibilities.

Pre-planning is of paramount importance. But whichever plan is devised, the leaders must be flexible in implementing it. Whatever material is prepared in advance should be viewed merely as a guideline, or as a map with a number of different routes, any of which can be followed to reach the desired destination. The daily "lesson plan" may well have to be adapted in the middle of the course, depending on the resources at hand and the students' current needs, interests, or problems.

The planners should also be sure that all the participants in the workshop are *well prepared*, and experienced as translators. If they are not, this course of study will be too "heavy" for them, both conceptually and also assignment-wise. The instructors themselves also have to be *well prepared* for their manifold role as course organizers, subject presenters, and practical guides. They must know something substantial about oral and written poetry in the TL and have a considerable number of actual examples already analyzed before they begin the program. It is better if at least two instructors can be involved, including an experienced mother-tongue translator/exegete/poet, if possible.

The need for workshop leaders to be *flexible* in the methodology of presentation is paramount. What works in one situation may not succeed so well in another. Translators are individuals, especially where the rendering and evaluation of artistic works are concerned. Not all participants will have the same aptitude and ability in poetic composition, exegetical insight, critical text comparison, and compromise when finalizing a translation. Each of these skills is necessary, and the various strengths and weaknesses of all participants need to be recognized and supported as necessary during the workshop. Some aspects of the training may require more emphasis and practice than others, and therefore the schedule may have to be modified considerably, especially during the first week.

An *inductive, team-based, mutual teaching-learning* approach must be fostered at all times. This is a jointly applied methodology that seeks to draw out and build upon what the participants, translators and instructors alike, already know through previous experience. It demonstrates to all concerned what they are able to accomplish *together*, availing themselves of each one's respective skills and abilities. Instructors will learn a great deal about the target language, literature, and culture as well as certain things about some biblical psalmic texts that they never knew before. This essential *unity* of motivation, principle, program, and purpose must be maintained if the primary goal is to be achieved, namely, the accurate, re-composition of Scripture in a dynamic poetic mode of communication.

2. Choosing a poet to be part of the translation team

It has sometimes been suggested that it may be possible to find a renowned poet to do the actual TL re-creation, some individual apart from the regular translation team who would prepare the initial draft in recognizably poetic discourse without concern for exegetical details. This draft would then be corrected and modified later, as necessary. However, it is not very easy to find such an individual who is not already an active participant of the translation program. In my opinion, only a previously involved and committed person would be willing to put in the time and effort necessary to perfect the accuracy of content transmission as well as the poetic form of the text.

Even if such a specialist could be found, it will most likely be necessary for him or her to participate in a training workshop along with the rest of the translation team in order to learn the basic techniques of popular language Bible translation. Otherwise, the draft could end up as being an instance of excellent TL poetry but exegetically unacceptable or too difficult for readers to understand. Moreover, there is a definite limit on the extent to which real poetry, once actually composed, can be adjusted to remove significant content-related objections. Either the poet will become angry, frustrated, or discouraged and quit, or the adapter's task will simply be too great and a completely new composition will finally have to be undertaken.

It would, therefore, be beneficial for any specially selected poet to sit in on the translation workshop to learn some crucial exegetical skills as well as to serve as an inspiration, guide, or even instructor. It would help to establish him or her as an integral member of the team rather than to try to function as an outsider. But in most situations, I suspect, the lyrically gifted individual who is finally chosen to act as the principal drafter of the poetic portions of Scripture will eventually be selected from among the ranks of already existing translators or reviewers. This is because the activity of Bible translation is quite different from what a poet normally does. It is not very easy for artistically creative individuals either to limit their poetic freedom of expression or to consistently adhere to the major constraint of "faithfulness" to some pre-existent original text. Thus a workshop participant who is learning, practicing, erring, and receiving criticism and correction along with everyone else is generally the best sort of poet for this first-draft work. This presupposes, of course, that in the process he or she is found to possess the necessary literary-compositional gifts.

Instead of a poet's being the first drafter, there is another option: to start with, then poetically modify a draft that is a more or less literal one. This is the procedure that was followed in the 1995 Catholic translation, *The Psalter: A Faithful and Inclusive Rendering from the Hebrew into Contemporary English*, published by the International Commission on English in the Liturgy (Chicago: Liturgy Training Publications). Their objective was even more ambitious than to produce simply a poetic text. They aimed for one that would be "fitting for musical setting" (p. xxv). (Most translators do not have to worry about the musical aspect; the poetry being difficult enough.) To achieve their aim must have been very challenging, starting, as they did, with a literal text. Surely that was as hard as it would have been to "exegetize" a poetic version in order to render it semantically acceptable.

A better procedure, given the personnel, would be to fully train the original "drafter-poet" in the principles of fidelity to the SL message and naturalness in the TL to the point of being able to *intuitively* synthesize global form, content, emotion, and impact in constructing a poetic representation of the original text. This process would be greatly aided by having a good model version in a closely related language available to refer to, both for comparative purposes and as a source of possible new ideas. In this way a poetic version could be created right from the start, even though it would undoubtedly have to be corrected and refined later as to both form and meaning by artistically-sensitive fellow members of the team. But that would not be as difficult as beginning from a literal draft. (For further ideas on this subject, see Sterk 1997, Wendland 2000, and Holladay 1996: ch. 17.)

3. Form and function in poetic discourse

To begin a workshop, a general discussion of the participants' background, the daily procedures, and the workshop objectives is helpful. If several teams of translators and reviewers are involved, they first need to get acquainted and learn where each of the groups is in their translation progress and how each operates as a team. If only a single translation team is present, its members can share whatever experience they have had with poetry in the target language, whether as members of an audience or as actual performers. Perhaps some will have translated or even composed church hymns in the past, but have yet to apply this experience to Bible translation.

Sooner or later participants should be led to consider the subject of poetry. This investigation may be facilitated by discussing assigned readings from the manual by Zogbo and Wendland (2000). How does one define "poetry" in general? How is it defined with reference to the TL? Is there a term that means "poetry" as distinct from "prose" in their language? What are the features of various genres of poetic text in the TL? What are the differences between "oral" and "written" poetry, or between "sung/musical" and "nonmusical" poetry? What influence does the printed format have on a reader's perception of a text as being poetic? To further stimulate this preliminary discussion, a gifted individual may read or recite some good-quality vernacular poems aloud, after which the instructor can elicit the workshop participants' spontaneous opinions about them.

The following are a few thoughts that might be introduced into the discussion as time allows and interest develops: Both formal and functional criteria are important in defining poetry. As to the *form*, it is, in general, characterized by prominent linguistic and literary features such as repetition, balanced lineation, versification, rhythm, sound play, ellipsis and other types of condensation, word-order variation, figurative language, allusion, intensification, and frequently also a specialized vocabulary (e.g., the use of archaic, technical, proverbial, dialectal terms). The distinctive imagery (visual evocation) and phonology (aural stimulation) of a poetic text are especially important to consider. It would be helpful if the instructor, assisted by experienced translators, would illustrate these features (the relevant ones) with examples of poetry written in the major language of wider communication with which all workshop participants are familiar (e.g., Wendland 1993, ch.3). An *inductive* approach is probably the most effective. That is, the various stylistic and structural features of the selected examples would be identified first from actual poetic texts, then described in non-technical terms and related to one another in form-functional sets.

Depending on the students' educational background and aptitude, this exercise could be followed with a brief survey of Hebrew poetry (in anticipation of more detailed work later) including a few of the principal features of OT poetic discourse: parallelism, acrostic sequence, word-accent "meter," lexical pairs, key word/concept recursion, distinctive idioms and figures of speech, phonological consonance/dissonance, condensation, direct speech, aphorisms, refrains, merismus, hendiadys, hyperbole, rhetorical questions, irony and sarcasm, intertextual citation or allusion, exclamations, wordplay, and onomatopoeia (for biblical examples, see Watson's *Classical Hebrew Poetry*, Schoekel's *A Manual of Hebrew Poetics*, or Wendland 1993, ch. 2 and 1995, chs. 2-3). On the other hand, if the instructor feels that such an overview, even if abbreviated, would be too difficult to present at the beginning of the course, it can easily be postponed to a later time.

Along with this overview of formal features in both the TL and the SL, a preliminary discussion of literary *function* is essential. Remember, poetry involves the use of heightened and embellished language for the purpose of creating a special aesthetic and rhetorical effect (i.e., that which is attractive, persuasive, convincing, and/or compelling) over and above the purpose of conveying a message. The poetic forms are utilized to give the theological content of the psalmist's message an added impact and appeal as well as to enhance specific communicative objectives. To identify these functions, the participants need to adopt the perspective of an actual listening participant group, for most poetry is meant to be heard, experienced, felt, and responded to. In other words, for this exercise, the students do not engage in silent reading.

The major functions of religious poetry are *informative*, *expressive*, *evocative*, *imperative*, *mnemonic*, and *relational*. Biblical poetic discourse aims to reveal the heart and mind of the poet and also to influence the thoughts, feelings, desires, motives, attitudes, and actions of those who hear it. A well-done poetic text is highly appreciated (at least in most non-Western languages) and is generally easier to remember, hence also to transmit orally to others. More specific illocutionary purposes may be pointed as well; the sub-units of a given poem may have a particular function different from the objective of the whole. Thus a certain psalm may be intended by its author to praise, blame, encourage, console, warn, exhort, educate, or unify the audience—and, at the same time, to move them to experience such attitudes and emotions as anger, pity, sorrow, shame, joy, longing, penitence, awe, fear, reverence, comfort, courage, and many more. It should not take long to illustrate most of these psychological effects with actual examples from the Psalter.

Any of these stylistic features, or more often some harmonious combination of them, normally has a desired rhetorical purpose, if competently constructed and placed within a poetic text. Usually the skill and artful manner of composition involves some manner of discourse *foregrounding* (e.g., accenting, intensifying, reinforcing, highlighting, focusing, climaxing, specifying, etc.), especially in the second line of a parallel couplet. Such literary highlighting may also be demonstrated at key points within a given poem or psalm, for example, at its climax or conclusion. The instructor cannot, of course, go into too much detail at this juncture, but it is helpful to introduce students to the basic nature of poetic communication and the concept of message function as early as possible in the course. The diverse aspects of this principle may then be illustrated, at least in a general way, with reference to a well-known vernacular hymn or psalm (e.g., Psalm 23).

The functions of verbal style are, of course, both variable and relative. It depends very much on the particular language and culture as well as on the literary sophistication of its speakers. Every artistic tradition has its own esthetic standards and poetic structures, which are slowly developed over time in the establishment of a relatively fixed set of linguistic criteria and rhetorical conventions, even though they may not be set forth explicitly in a written text. Thus some independent research among the elders of the community—in particular, the gifted artists and respected commentators among them—will be necessary in order to discover this code of verbal esthetics and effects that we call *rhetoric*. Such principles of verbal persuasion serve to guide the composer as well as the critic in evaluating what is "good" or "mediocre" or "poor" oral and written literature. It is this natural and praiseworthy poetic style that we wish to reveal, describe, and then stimulate the translator-poet to emulate to a greater or lesser extent when rendering the Psalter, that is, to the degree that project-related circumstances allow, e.g., the primary target audience and principal use envisioned for the translation.

4. The presentation of Hebrew poetry and its features

After the preliminary overview outlined above, the workshop instructor is ready to begin teaching the details of poetic discourse in the Hebrew Scriptures. The Book of Psalms, with its wide variety of important Old Testament religious themes and diverse range of poetic styles, serves well as a source of poetic illustrations. And since it is often published either separately as a portion or in a special edition along with the New Testament, it is a good choice for a "one book workshop" with the definite goal in mind of giving translators a foundation for dealing with Hebrew poetry.

It is possible that selections from chapters 1–7 of *Analyzing the Psalms*, whether in English or in translated form, may be used as the workshop textbook. But this will depend on the needs of the translators in the class. For some, this might be too restrictive an approach to poetry or too "bookish" a method for translators accustomed to composing poetry orally. In any case, the textbook is intended as a workshop guide or resource tool, but it need not limit the participants' way of thinking or working. And even if the textbook is not followed closely, most of the same instructional material will have to be conveyed to translators, whether by topically oriented "lessons" or by some other means.

The textbook's *order* of presenting the different topics can easily be altered according to the preference of the instructor and the needs of a given group of students. The degree of *detail* on a given subject will also vary depending on the circumstances. Some sections may be too technical or extensive for use in an initial two to four week workshop. They can easily be modified or even omitted. Some can be reserved for the evening study of more advanced students. The more difficult topics might also be taken up in a subsequent workshop. A later workshop is often needed in any case, that is, once a team has actually had a chance to do an initial draft of the Psalms or a selection of them.

Similarly, it is not necessary that every part of every exercise be assigned. The teacher should select the study and practice questions that fall within the general competency of the class members, eliminating those which seem unclear or overly complex. Team-"assignments" are to be preferred over individual work. Furthermore, it may not be necessary for students to do all of the aspects of a particular exercise before they get the point, nor will it be always be productive for them to look up every specific reference. Once they have mastered the new concept, the remaining references may be skipped. The purpose of this textbook is simply to provide the instructor with some basic material of varying degrees of difficulty along with examples to help illustrate the points of discussion and their application to Bible translation.

The Hebrew poetry part of the workshop should include a treatment of the Psalter's background: its history, its five major divisions and smaller groupings, the two traditions of numbering, and a recognition of the "paired" psalms. Some time may also be devoted to the problems connected with psalm titles. Since most of these do not appear to have been a part of the original composition (though they must have been added shortly thereafter), the translation team will need to decide how such titles should be indicated in the TL version, for example, by smaller print or by a line of space separating the title from the psalm proper. It *is* recommended that these titles be translated and placed *somewhere* in the text, if only in a footnote, rather than simply be left out altogether (THP, p. 11). Perhaps it would be useful to include, at this point, an exercise or two that illustrates a number of the pertinent recommendations of THP with regard to the rendering of such information as it applies to some specific examples. (Workshop participants also need "hands-on" practice as to how to make the best use of the THP and related scholarly tools.)

The topic of "psalm types" (see chap. 2) seems to fit well after a basic introduction to the Psalter. The purpose is not to drill the students to the point of being able to classify every psalm or segment of one. There is too much overlapping and ambiguity to aim for such precision in analysis; besides, biblical scholars themselves are not agreed on what the relevant categories are and which psalms fall into each. Rather, the purpose here is to introduce students to the general notion of illocutionary force and communicative intention—what the psalmist is *doing* with his song in terms of interpersonal dynamics as distinct from what he is *saying* content-wise. Thus translators need to be able to identify utterances of thanksgiving, praise, complaint, sorrow, penitence, anger, imprecation, commitment-faith-hope, instruction, and other related objectives, attitudes, and emotions. The reason for this is that these associative aspects of meaning may need to be formally marked or stylistically shaded in some way in the TL.

The so-called messianic subgroup of psalms is not a separate functional category because normally it is not distinctive either in form or content. It is a classification based largely on theological interpretation. Hence it is not a problem for translation. However, the royal or messianic psalms are frequently referred to in the New Testament. Therefore, some time may be devoted to the subject of intertextual quotations and allusions in the Bible, along with the importance of maintaining contextual consistency (as opposed to artificial harmonization) between the OT and the NT citations of it.

Lessons on the SL discourse form and poetic style require the greatest amount of attention in a workshop on the Psalter. The present textbook material on this subject could be profitably supplemented by Katharine Barnwell's *Bible Translation*, Jacob Loewen's *Practice of Translation*, and Zogbo/Wendland's *Hebrew Poetry in the Bible*. However, it might be helpful, certainly in an initial workshop, to limit examples to the Psalter.

The topics of parallelism, recursion, figurative language, condensation, and phonological marking are particularly prominent features in the poetic discourse of Scripture, and thus they need to be dealt with in comparatively greater detail. The aim is to familiarize translators with these basic features so that they can be handled more successfully in the message transfer process. Another aim is to stimulate translators to start thinking about such features in their own literary tradition and to search for functional equivalents in the TL.

Parallelism (chaps. 3–4) may be treated in greater or lesser detail as the situation warrants. Some of the material in chapter 3 may be summarized without the exercises if they are too difficult for translators who have no knowledge of Hebrew. This may be the case for the discussion of the A–B relations of "similarity," "contrast," and "addition." On the other hand, the ability to isolate and compare the respective constituents of the A and B (and C) lines is basic, and the instructor may wish to spend more time on this point, especially in relation to the device of "heightening," as one moves from line A to line B of a parallel couplet. The "additive" category of linkage (sec. 3.3.3) will probably require special attention, breaking it down into different subtypes, for example, "temporal," "causal," and "completive," since these are the basis for a more or less standardized set of inter-propositional relations (e.g., base-temporal, reason-result, means-purpose, and condition-consequence). It may be necessary to give some supplemental instruction regarding these various semantic relations from ch. 30 of Beekman & Callow, chs. 25–27 of Larson, and ch. 4 of Nida (1985).

The analytical procedures of chapter 3 are to be practiced with respect to several complete psalms (e.g., Psalms 11 and 14). But it is recommended that one or more of these examples first be worked out in class by the instructor together with the students to make sure that they understand the method and how to apply it. Another short psalm or two can then be assigned as homework. It may take a while for students to get used to diagramming the psalms as shown in chapter 3, but once they grasp the idea, this often proves to be a popular exercise. At least it gets them to think more clearly about how the A–B cola and cola clusters are connected with each other to form a complete composition. Of course, one cannot be dogmatic in identifying the relations. Poetic condensation with its implicit information often allows for several relational possibilities in any given instance. But the exercise can help free translators from the shackles of literalism. Students need to be reminded from time to time to refer to the THP for guidance with regard to the range of exegetical possibility. As they become more familiar with it in class, their fears about consulting such a possibly imposing commentary can be allayed.

The next major topic for a workshop program is the notion of parallelism on the *macrolevel* of discourse (chap. 4). This is important for analyzing the overall organization and purpose of a poetic text, its structural boundaries in particular. In addition to *segmentation,* the related compositional attributes of *progression*, *cohesion,* and *prominence* can also be introduced and investigated here. This discussion, too, may be profitably supplemented by the material in the THP. Students could begin a "research" assignment of describing one or more of the discourse formats presented in THP. A more creative exercise would be for them to demarcate and outline the compositional organization of a complete psalm on their own, using the recommended procedures. On the other hand, some of this material on discourse structure may be too complicated for inexperienced groups to grasp in a short time. It may, therefore, be reserved for a follow-up workshop for more advanced teams.

The topic of lower-level stylistic devices (chap. 5) will probably be familiar to most translators. However, a review of this material would not hurt, especially in relation to psalmic examples. On the other hand, some of the subjects may not be so familiar, for example, expansion and condensation. These two devices might well be considered together as contrastive poetic techniques. Since the various types of patterned repetition were treated earlier, in relation to "adjacent" and "separated" parallelism, not much needs to be said about it at this stage, except to take the opportunity to explore reiteration of a non-structured nature as it relates to the TL (this will affect the use of key terms in particular): Does the indigenous tradition appreciate lexical recycling as a poetic device or not? If so, what are the forms that it most commonly takes (e.g., nominal or verbal) and how frequent is it? What functions does it perform? And what are the practical implications of the TL use of recursion for translating poetic texts of the Old Testament where both formal and semantic repetitions are frequent? If lexical iteration is *not* a prominent feature of literary texts in the TL, students need to consider here how to compensate for its various effects.

The importance of *condensation*, especially ellipsis and contraction, should not be ignored, although it is rather difficult to discern except in the original text. It is particularly important in relation to the sound qualities of poetic discourse, such as rhythm, proportion, and euphony. This is a distinctive feature of poetry in many languages, but one that is not always recognized and hence not applied either naturally or consistently in Bible translation. Thus a close examination some Hebrew examples (with the help of an interlinear, if necessary) may prove to be instructive. Translators should be asking themselves if TL poetic texts ever have such ellipses and shortened utterances. In this connection, it may be useful at this stage to re-emphasize the matter of Hebrew *word order* (normally, in prose, V-S-O in verbal clauses and topic-comment in non-verbal clauses) compared with TL syntactic patterns. Then variations of word order for special effect—topicalization, focus, impact, and rhythmic appeal—may be considered, both in Hebrew and in the TL. The reason for treating the two topics together is that condensation and syntactic rearrangement often co-occur in poetry. Some examples to illustrate this and a related exercise or two would probably be necessary; these can easily be found by working through a specific biblical text with an interlinear version at hand.

There are a number of other prominent stylistic features of Hebrew poetry—far too many for a single workshop. But they may be important enough to at least mention and illustrate. The matter of *free meter* (a variable accentual pattern), for example, is not really crucial for SL analysis, but it may be used to introduce translators to the related notions of poetic lineation, balance, and rhythm. These are qualities that may well characterize lyric discourse in the TL too. The frequently fluid use of pronouns in the Psalms, in conjunction with sudden shifts between direct and indirect speech, probably deserves a separate exercise just to increase the translators' awareness of this potentially confusing aspect of the original text.

The occurrence of various intensifiers, exclamations, and other instances of emphatic diction also needs to be pointed out with respect to both the effect of such devices on the overall associative meaning of the message and the obligation to find suitable TL equivalents. The resonantal, highly expressive sound structure of the original text is frequently an important factor in certain passages, but rather difficult to demonstrate for those who do not know Hebrew. Some reading aloud of texts may be helpful just for the sake of illustration, since similar devices are usually found in the poetry of other languages (e.g., alliteration, assonance, rhyme, and punning). Other interesting features that could be presented include parallel and crossed patterns of gender, irony, hendiadys, and enjambment. This is the time in the workshop also to look for poetic characteristics of the TL that are *not* found in Hebrew poetry in order to determine their corresponding rhetorical and discourse functions, e.g., the use of multiple deictic enclitics, alliterative concordial agreement patterns, or ideophones and exclamations in Bantu languages.

A discussion of some of the important psalmic themes, topics, and terms (chap. 6) may be introduced at any time for a change of pace. Can an overarching theological *theme* for the Psalter as a whole, such as "YHWH rules," be proposed? If so, how can this be demonstrated, for example, with respect to the frequency of prominent lexical sets? What are some of the other prominent *topics* in the Psalms and how are they related to one another (e.g., covenant, community, law, faithfulness, sin, and worship)? It is useful to allow students to arrive at answers to these questions inductively after reading through a representative selection of texts. In this connection, it may be helpful to point out the "dramatic" nature of the Psalms on the basis of the interaction among the primary "participants" (YHWH, the psalmist, and his "enemies"), with or without the secondary groups (the "nations" and the faithful "congregation"). As for an overview of psalmic *vocabulary*, the following all need to be analyzed componentially and the closest functional-conceptual equivalents in the TL determined: key terms (e.g., righteousness, mercy, sin, trust, hope, salvation, judgment, pray/cry/call), word pairs (e.g., answer–turn to, rejoice–exult, law–statutes), technical and culturally specific terms (e.g., Rahab, young lions, cedars, trumpets, *sheol*, tabernacle, deep waters), and key Hebrew idiomatic expressions.

Methodology (chap. 7) is another important issue to present for mutual consideration. The workshop participants need to get to the point of being able to undertake the complete analysis of an entire psalm on their own. A well-known example like Psalm 23 could be done together in class as a warm-up exercise. This brings up the question of whether or not to refer to commentaries while engaged in studying a text. This is debatable, but each approach can be justified. A first attempt at analyzing a text on its own terms without reference to commentaries has the advantage of teaching independence and how to think critically. It also encourages personal "immersion" in the text before the ideas of others are introduced. On the other hand, it takes much time and effort. Only a higher caliber student-translator can carry it out successfully. So perhaps it would be more practical to use commentaries and the THP to the degree recommended in the ten-step methodology of chapter 7.

If further application is felt necessary, some additional text analyses may undertaken, for completion either as a group or individually. Question-driven, exegetical-translational studies of selected psalms might be assigned for the students to prepare on their own and then present to the class for their correction and criticism. Doing this at least partially in the vernacular (for the sake of the instructor or TC) would allow for greater participation and freedom of expression. Formal exegetical (semantic, stylistic, structural) presentations may be too ambitious a goal to aim for, but it would be a good way of evaluating both the students' progress and the effectiveness of their tutor as this mainly instructional part of the workshop comes to a close.

5. Poetic composition in the workshop setting

The focus of the workshop's second half is *application*: working towards a poetic, yet essentially "faithful," re-creation of a psalmic composition in one or more target languages. It is assumed that the participants will have already begun a preliminary study of the forms, functions, settings, and occasions of TL poetry before they undertake the practical exercises of this segment of the progam. The instructor will frequently be asking the students to compare the principal structures, styles, and varieties of TL poetry to the Hebrew examples s/he presents. It is important to encourage translators to begin thinking seriously about oral and written poetic discourse in their own language.

We must remember that the objective of a poetry workshop is not to transform the participants into expert mother-tongue poets. Poets are born, not made. As Dr. Eugene Nida points out, "aesthetic sensitivity is essentially an aptitude or attitude, and though it can be developed, it is extremely difficult to really 'teach' " (personal correspondence, 1991). That has been my experience too over the years. Thus our general aim is, rather, to instill within the members of the translation team a sufficient poetic *sensibility* and *competence* so that they are able not only to recognize and appreciate, but also to capably evaluate poetic texts in their own language. It is hoped that at least one member of the team, whether a reviewer, a co-translator, or an "external" poet will be found to have the necessary lyric gift along with the ability and dedication to apply it skillfully in Bible translation. The other members, then, having been made aware of what good poetry is all about, should be in much better position to give the poet among them positive criticism in the form of possible alternative wordings, corrections, or revisions as needed, for exegetical or stylistic reasons.

I have found that most students have little initial conception of what "poetry" is in their language, even if they have a specific word for it. However, they are generally familiar with particular examples of poetic discourse. One way to begin to develop an artistic sensibility, coaxing it from mere intuition to perceptive awareness, is to study some popular hymns, especially those based on biblical texts. Traditional recited prayers to God/the ancestors, royal praise songs, and funeral dirges are other possible sources of potential poetic forms. But hymns, in particular, are useful because they are probably well known already and can thus be used to show the distinction between translation and paraphrase. However, if hymns or even secular songs are utilized by way of an introduction to poetry, the instructor must point out the need for conforming the poetic line to the melody in terms of rhythm, number of syllables, and lines per stanza. Such strict musical constraints do not apply to a spoken psalm unless, of course, a genre involving formal meter or stanzaic pattern is being used as the translation model. But the crucial oral-aural factor that is either explicitly or implicitly activated in any poetic performance must never be lost sight of.

If translators speaking different languages are participating in the same workshop, it may be possible to find familiar hymns in each of these languages that are based on the same biblical texts. These hymns may then be compared with respect to their stylistic similarities and differences, degree of literalness versus formal freedom, exegetical accuracy, and overall success in terms of rhetorical impact and appeal. At all times, a "discourse perspective" should be maintained during such text-comparative study: Participants must continually look at the "parts" within a framework of the "whole" composition. They may then try composing "improved" renditions of a given hymn in terms of both semantic or thematic fidelity and poetic naturalness.

My practice is to follow up the hymn survey with a careful study of a relatively modern genre of TL poetry. Depending on the language of the students, I usually use the Chewa genre called *ndakatulo* or the Tonga performing art termed *ciyabilo*. The former, originally an oral poetic type, is now widely written and published; the latter is only sung. First of all, I assign a reading of several brief introductions to collections of such poems in order to get an idea from the authors themselves as to how and why they went about creating their works. Several outstanding poems are then read and studied in class, mainly to start identifying their principal stylistic features, rhetorical techniques, and major themes. Later, these poems are compared with some poorer quality poems so that the differences in form, content, and effect become apparent.

The primary characteristics of the psalm genre under study are now compared with those of other poetic types and traditions. The aim is to develop an inventory of potential poetic "matches" in the TL that can later be employed in Bible translation to render the different genres and their associated artistic and rhetorical features. I have generally found oral texts to be more deficient in terms of the diversity of lexical and syntactic stylistic devices manifested than the written and published ones. Songs in particular, when reduced to writing, do pose a problem in that much of their "meaning," when sung, is conveyed by such variables as tone, stress, volume, tempo, and pause as well as by extralinguistic means (e.g., gestures, facial features, even dance). To begin with then, we use the written Chewa *ndakatulo* genre as our principal "model" and guide for poetic composition. This is a widely spoken lingua franca and so most workshop participants can understand, even if they do not speak, this language. Hence they can participate and start composing poetic texts following this pattern—until they have hit upon a style more in keeping with what would be regarded as natural, even if novel, in their mother tongue. A certain amount of trial and error may be necessary, but given the necessary skill, determination, and encouragement, it will not be too long before an acceptable—ultimately also a "beautiful"—result will be achieved (see Carl Harrison, "Poetry in Guajajara," *Notes on Translation*, 13(3), 50-51).

I continue this process of teaching by comparison with a study of a Chewa translation and a Tonga version of John 17:1–8 (see Wendland 1994a). The respective styles of these better-than-average poetic compositions are quite diverse. Thus they illustrate the formal *variation* that poetry allows with respect to the same basic content. Sample texts produced in former classes or workshops can also be examined and critiqued (I keep a corpus of student-produced psalm-poems, of varying quality, for this purpose). When student translators see what their peers have been able to do, they are usually ready, even eager, to give it a try themselves. The first assignment is limited to the first five verses of John 17, a section of praise. The main reason for starting with a NT passage is that it is well known. Many participants may have already worked on translating this pericope. They should be encouraged to refer to the earlier (or any available) translation of it, but not to follow this too closely since it will be a prose version. But John's repetitive style is also quite amenable to poetic composition, at least in a Bantu language. An adequate amount of time needs to be set aside for this exercise, perhaps an extra period in the afternoon for the initial composition and a free evening for testing, revising, and a mock "performance" before an invited audience. An even better idea, if it can be arranged, is to give the assignment over a weekend so the drafts can be tested in some local worship service or a Bible study class.

I generally have the workshop participants compose their versions individually at first, so as to identify the more gifted verbal artists among them. If they are speakers of one language, they can get together later and produce a combined version that incorporates the best features of all the individual efforts. But they should not to mix their TL genres, at least when first starting out. Alternatively, one text may be chosen at the outset to serve as a "base" to be modified and improved by input from all the participants. This is a good exercise, because it will no doubt be the method followed when the psalms are actually translated for publication. In this way translators can get a head start on experiencing "team revision" work and the essential compromises that this involves. The group must learn to foster among themselves an honest recognition and encouragement of the value of the recommendations of those persons who demonstrate a gift for combining an *accurate* translation of the SL text along with an *appropriate* stylistic restructuring of the original in an *artistic* TL text.

From this point on, the main focus of the workshop will be on poetic *recreation* (with periodic checks and additional instruction with regard to particular exegetical matters). Enough time must be left, though, for adequate discussion and the preparation of more sample texts. A free exchange of ideas and styles is encouraged at this stage. The nascent poets need to feel free to experiment with the full literary resources of the target language and to develop its expressive potential into a definable, reproducible poetic style. Once student/translators have mastered the mechanics of a natural compositional method, they can then concentrate on fine-tuning the text's content, modifying their drafts wherever some deficiency in meaning (addition, deletion, alteration) has been detected.

6. Final artistic touches

When participants reach this final stage of precision-work, they are each asked to prepare a *literal back-translation* of their compositions, with the individual "lines" demarcated according to parallel phrasing, syntactic completeness, characteristic transitional expressions, and/or major end pauses based on a tape-recorded performance. This literal back-translation is to be handed in for examination by the teaching staff. It serves several purposes. First, in cases where the workshop leader is not a mother-tongue speaker, it provides a means by which he or she can "enter" the text to some extent in order to understand what is going on with respect to form and content. It will also be the basis for pinpointing important areas for discussion in class—in particular, any possible distortions or divergencies in content from the SL text and, on the other hand, all noteworthy poetic devices utilized in the TL.

Doing a literal back-translation also helps the students learn how to check their own work for accuracy. The principle needs to be emphasized repeatedly here: formal *freedom* coupled with semantic *constraint*. The TL psalm should look and sound different from the original in various stylistic respects. But within the new verbal container, the biblical writer's essential content must be preserved. Of course, any real or perceived loss, gain, or shift in meaning is always debatable, especially when it comes to poetry; but such discussions should not be allowed to dominate the class time, for clearly, poetry is different from prose. Too much exegetical argument would dampen the budding poets' spirit of creativity or even cause them to regress into "safe" literalism, where they will be relatively free of criticism.

Again, as has been said before, poetry is more than referential "content," information per se. It involves attitude, intention, emotion, and verbal beauty as well, and the significance of these aspects of the overall message may well be greater than that of the pure content in certain passages. A literal approach can never arrive at those vital elements that give poetry its compelling attractiveness, sensory appeal, and persuasive power. But content is important, to be sure, and the drafts must always be carefully tested in order to make sure that a basic equivalence in designative meaning with respect to the original text has been achieved. But it is better to give a trained poet the benefit of the doubt rather than allow the compositional process become dominated by artistically insensitive exegetical critics! This particular issue cannot be emphasized enough.

After the warm-up assignment in John 17 or some similarly simple, non-psalmic passage, the group might turn next to a relatively short and straightforward example in the Psalter itself, such as Psalm 100. "Hymns," or praise-eulogies, tend to be easier to begin with than laments, although this may depend on the TL literary tradition. All participants work on the same text at this stage. This is to facilitate comparison in class and then, subsequently a joint revision exercise to produce a single "polished" composition. As already observed, this last activity is an important part of learning the essence of teamwork. The students may be divided into groups in order for each to compose (via all of the previously recommended steps) an exegetically corrected and stylistically perfected text. During this process students may use the base-model, or "comparative," method of analysis if some good TL-related Bible translations are available for use as models (cf. Wendland 2000).

Now the students' various versions are ready to be fine-tuned. Having carefully examined and revised the expression of content, they will work through their several drafts or, more likely, a selected "base" version, reading or reciting *aloud* with the aim of improving its audible poetic form. Revising the text as a team may include such things as reducing the amount of exact repetition, developing a more rhythmic and euphonious cadence, and introducing additional or substitute figures of speech. It may also involve adding praise names, ideophones, interjections, and rhetorical questions, whatever is appropriate in keeping with the prominent stylistic characteristics of the genre they are attempting either to reproduce or adapt. The draft at hand may be rendered in a *more or less* poetic form in keeping with the primary target audience envisioned. A less poetic rendition of a psalm would normally focus on artistically modifying the *sound* qualities of the text in particular, e.g., creating measured lines, symmetrical accent patterns, some alliteration, assonance, or even a little rhyme (if that is natural and expected in the TL).

After a relatively easy exercise or two to begin with, the participants may now be assigned a more difficult and complex psalm. But it should not contain more than twelve verses, or it will not be possible to translate it both accurately as well as artistically in the workshop time available. Psalm 1 may be a good choice because it is so crucial as an introduction to the Psalter. It could pose a problem, however, in terms of genre, if poetry in the TL is not normally used to present this kind of formal religious instruction. But even if TL poetry does not usually express didactic literature as poetry, it should not be too difficult, or foreign-sounding, to extend the use of the praise or petition genre to texts of a somewhat different content and purpose. Certain formal modifications of a minor sort may, of course, be necessary. For example, it may be necessary to restrict or suppress the use of devices of an expressive-emotive quality in a didactic poem. But most oral or literary traditions are flexible enough to allow such accommodation within the context of a larger composite work like the Psalter. It is the general poetic form, creating overall cohesion, that would bridge the Psalter's internal junctures and differences of topic, tone, technique, and communicative intent.

Psalms 2, 8, 16, 23, 43, 46, 53, 70, 100, 113, 138, and 142 are other good examples for workshop use, as time allows. The more practice that the students receive in poetic composition and in the experience of mutual compromise and criticism, the better. The fundamental steps of SL text-*analysis*, conceptual *transfer*, TL *restructuring*, text-*testing* and final *revising* need to be carried out consistently and in close conjunction with one another. The goal is to maintain an appropriate balance between the twofold objective of exegetical *fidelity* in relation to SL content, on the one hand, and lyric *fluency* in relation to TL form, on the other.

7. Follow-up

By the end of a three to four-week workshop, it should be possible to select and/or confirm a well-trained and integrated poetry translation team and review committee. (The reviewers chosen may well be different persons than the ones used to examine biblical prose texts.) Ideally, the translation team will consist of competent, cooperative, and committed individuals with a recognized expertise or aptitude in each of the essential areas of analysis, transfer, restructuring, testing, and revising.

Remember, the goal of a workshop of this nature is to teach translators how to produce a meaning-oriented, poetically phrased translation of the Psalter, one that will sound in specific audible respects like a "new song," an exhilarating, liberating song, to the receptor community for whom it is intended. This is the time, at the workshop's conclusion, to be sure the participants are imbued with and encouraged by this dynamic vision of the Word's aural potential.

Finally, plans must be laid for adequate *follow-up*. One workshop will neither a poet make—nor a poetically competent translation team. It is a good idea for them to begin (or resume) their translation of the Psalms *as soon as possible* after participating in an introductory workshop. This will preserve the momentum and build upon the enthusiasm and knowledge gained during the full days of working intensively on poetry together. It is important for the group (including all reviewers) to carry on with the basic method that was taught in the workshop. To this end, one of the instructors should make time to visit each translation team regularly, especially during the initial stages of their poetic endeavors.

It would also be useful, perhaps essential, to plan a subsequent workshop of at least two weeks no later than six months after the first. This would be a checking and revision session to review the exegetical and artistic quality of any draft translations the team has produced between the two workshops. Leading members of the review committees could be invited again at this time so that the nature and purpose of the poetic version under preparation can be more fully explained and practiced together. The differences and similarities between poetic and an ordinary prose translation need to be thoroughly understood—and experienced: namely, that a poetic rendering may be different from the Hebrew *formally*, but it is equivalent to it *semantically* and *pragmatically*. Workshop participants can then go out and explain what in the Word is going on to their constituency, both for their information and also to enlist their feedback and support for the program. Without such advance preparation, the leaders of the churches as well as the laity will probably not be very accepting of the new version.

Other preliminary efforts to prepare the receptor audience can be planned too, such as a public "reading" (a recital or even singing) of some polished drafts of a selection of well-known psalms. This gathering could serve as a gauge of popular reaction to the new poetic translation. On the basis of their response, the decision could then be made as to whether to publish the entire Book of Psalms as a portion or only some selected psalms, in textual form alone or also in a musical/choral rendition. This publication or cassette/CD production would be a further means of determining the degree of public acceptance a poetic version would meet with. Such testing and promotional work is an essential part of the translation process and must not be overlooked.

It should not be forgotten that poetry has a two-fold communicative purpose besides conveying religious content. The author of Psalm 45, at the close of his own inspired song, draws our attention to this:

My song will keep your fame alive forever,
and everyone will praise you for all time to come. (Ps. 45:17)

Do the Psalms as rendered (whether merely represented or fully transformed) in the languages that you know enhance the accomplishment of these important theological objectives—namely, to commemorate as well as to magnify the name of Yahweh? If they do not, what can be done about this significant loss of lyric form and rhetorical function, this vital beauty, mnemonic value, and potential motivational power? Future translators need to take up this vital challenge to "keep the LORD's fame alive" via the ageless praise-prayers of the Psalter.

8. A short case study

The following report from Roger Van Otterloo is an example of what might be done in the way of producing a more "poetic" translation of the Psalms in a given TL. In this case the goal was to produce a base TL text that was natural enough to be easily "sing-able" – paving the way for many Psalms to be adapted into Scripture songs. Altogether, 45 Psalms have been set to music for inclusion in the new Kifuliiru hymnbook. For further details on this exciting project, which is just now entering the final production stage, please contact roger_vanotterloo@sil.org.

The Bafuliiru people of the Democratic Republic of Congo love to sing. Local music styles include at least five indigenous song genres: group work songs, group recreational songs, "lonesome" songs sung by a solitary herder, funeral songs, and songs associated with African traditional religion. Some of those "natural" music styles are now being combined with natural language styles to produce powerful Scripture songs.

[Last year in the DRC] 35 highly educated Bafuliiru attended a three-day seminar focusing on Kifuliiru discourse grammar. The seminar focused on natural word order, which is so critical for easy-to-understand literature. Although the concepts were new, requiring many examples and lots of repetition, the participants made very nice progress. Some comments at the end of the seminar: "We never knew how rich our language was!...The seminar should have been a week long, not just three days. Please come and hold another one soon!"

The seminar concentrated on the discourse features of Topic/Comment/Focus. In a nutshell, we use the word "Topic" to refer to known information previously referred to, while "Comment" refers to new information. "Focus" is a subset of the Comment, featuring the "point" the sentence is driving at. After defining these terms for the seminar participants in a formal, academic way, I further explained the concepts by comparing Focus to "the king". Although the king may first listen to others, he's the one who always has the last word - after him no one speaks again. If anyone would dare to speak after he has, it would be a disgrace, reducing his honor.

By way of analogy, in Kifuliiru sentence final position is the "throne" for King Focus, reserved for the main new point of the sentence. No one else may sit on the king's throne. What shows the reader that we have reached the point of the sentence are final punctuation markers: periods, question marks, exclamation marks, and semi-colons. One of many important implications: When translating into Kifuliiru, if one sentence in the source language (English, French, Greek etc.) is making more than one point, one should cut up that long sentence into two or more short sentences in Kifuliiru. Each piece gets its own sentence final punctuation, in effect providing a "throne" for each important new point.

Based on these discourse features of Kifuliiru, when translating a Psalm, we carefully study each component of the sentence in the SL, asking the question: Is this known information, previously referred to, or new information, expressing the point of the sentence? We also give special attention to whatever is positioned on the throne at the end of the sentence, to see if the one sitting on it is really all that important! If the beginning of the sentence in the SL is NOT the topic (expressing previously referred to information) and if the end of the SL sentence is not the focus (expressing the point the sentence) then we need to figure out how to rearrange each sentence component into its proper place. In Kifuliiru that involves strategies typical of the Bantu language family: fronting the object, changing a verb into a noun and visa versa, utilizing passive, causative or applicative etc. extensions on the verb, etc. Once the topic, comment, and focus are properly positioned, the other sentence components usually fall into their places without too much effort.

After correctly ordering the sentence components, the translator must then look carefully at the verb phrase, finding just the right nuances relative to the complex Tense/Aspect/Mood system. Other important tasks include making sure that the participant references are natural and clear, pinpointing the appropriate vocabulary for the context etc. The Bafuliiru refer to all of this later work as "mafuta" (oil which helps the food go down smoothly.) But attention to the "oil" is basically a waste of time if the TCF backbone is not correctly ordered first.

At the three-day seminar in the DRCongo, we systematically followed the basic rules above, identifying old information, new information, and the point of each sentence. As one of the exercises we went through Psalm 92:1-4, without any of us having prepared for the activity. We spent considerable time and energy together reordering the sentence constituents. When the verses were read aloud, the participants were amazed at the result, exclaiming: "These verses sound just like music!" (even though they were <u>speaking</u> the verses and not <u>singing</u> them!) The flow of the passage was now crystal clear, with the point of each new sentence properly positioned.

The songs [that have already been produced] are very popular. People learn them quickly, and by default are actually memorizing Scripture! Especially encouraging is the fact that many preliterate people, the majority of them women and children, are singing the Scripture songs just as well as those who are able to read the words.

In addition, the Scripture songs afford opportunities for sharing appropriate Scripture in a non-threatening way. For example, when a death occurs among the Bafuliiru, everyone in the family and neighborhood is expected to attend the funeral – whether Christians or non-Christians. The whole funeral commonly lasts three or four days. After the wake and burial, people come back to the home of the deceased to play games and be sociable. While people are sitting around the fire at night, there's a golden opportunity to play the cassette tape featuring the Scripture songs on death and resurrection. With death still on their minds, all of the people gathered hear the words of I Corinthians, "Sown mortal, raised immortal..." Christians are comforted, and non-Christians who would never darken the door of a church are exposed to eternal realities.

In 2001 the Kifuliiru team completed the drafting of all 150 Psalms - of which 45 have been revised, polished, and set to music. These new songs from the Psalter, together with more than 200 other Kifuliiru Scripture songs, are now being compiled as the basis for a new Kifuliiru hymnbook. While that is being done, the songs are also being recorded onto audio-cassette and distributed to the local churches in the area. The plan is to produce a new audio-cassette tape of Scripture songs each month for a period of two and a half years - until the churches will have been exposed to more than 250 Scripture songs. For a long time to come, the Bafuliiru will "Sing to the Lord a new song" – hundreds of new ones!

RECOMMENDED READING

The following is not intended to be a complete bibliography on the Psalms and related literature. It consists of a selection of works that may prove to be helpful as one is working through this text, especially if this is being done in relation to a current or future poetic translation of the Psalter.

Alden, Robert. 1974. *Psalms: Songs of Devotion*. Chicago: Moody Press.
———. 1975. *Psalms: Songs of Dedication*. Chicago: Moody Press.
———. 1976. *Psalms: Songs of Discipleship*. Chicago: Moody Press.
Alter, Robert. 1985. *The Art of Biblical Poetry*. New York: Basic Books.
Barker, Kenneth (ed.) 1985. *The NIV Study Bible: New International Version*. Grand Rapids: Zondervan.
Barnwell, Katharine. 1986. *Bible Translation: An Introductory Course in Translation Principles*. Dallas: Summer Institute of Linguistics.
———. 1992. *Introduction to Semantics and Translation*. Dallas: Summer Institute of Linguistics.
Bellinger, W. H., Jr. 1990. *Psalms: Reading and Studying the Book of Praises*. Peabody, Mass.: Hendrickson.
Beekman, John, and John Callow. 1974. *Translating the Word of God*. Grand Rapids: Zondervan.
Berlin, Adele. 1985. *The Dynamics of Biblical Parallelism*. Bloomington: Indiana University Press.
Berry, Donald K. 1995. *An Introduction to Wisdom and Poetry of the Old Testament*. Nashville: Broadman & Holman.
Bratcher, Robert, and William Reyburn. 1991. *A Translator's Handbook on the Book of Psalms* [THP]. New York: United Bible Societies.
Broyles, Craig C. 1988. *The Conflict of Faith and Experience in the Psalms: A Form-Critical and Theological Study*. Sheffield: JSOT Press.
———. 1999. *Psalms* [New International Biblical Commentary 11]. Peabody MA: Hendrickson.
Brueggeman, Walter (P.D. Miller, ed.). 1995. *The Psalms in the Life of Faith*. Minneapolis: Fortress Press.
Bullock, C. Hassel. 1988. *An Introduction to the Old Testament Poetic Books*. Revised and expanded. Chicago: Moody Press.
Church of Scotland. 1995. *The Psalms in Verse*. Uhrichsville, OH: Barbour.
Day, John. 1992. *Psalms* (Old Testament Guides). Sheffield: Sheffield Academic Press.
Finnegan, Ruth. 1992. *Oral Poetry*. Bloomington: Indiana University Press.
Fisch, Harold. 1988. *Poetry with a Purpose: Biblical Poetics and Interpretation*. Bloomington: Indiana University Press.
Gerstenberger, Erhard S. 1988. *Psalms Part 1: With an Introduction to Cultic Poetry* [The Forms of the Old Testament Literature XIV]. Grand Rapids: Eerdmans.
Holladay, William L. 1996. *The Psalms through Three Thousand Years*. Minneapolis: Fortress.
Kugel, James L. 1981. *The Idea of Biblical Poetry: Parallelism and Its History*. New Haven: Yale University Press.
Larson, Mildred. 1984. *Meaning-Based Translation: A Guide to Cross-Language Equivalence*. Washington: University Press of America.
Levine, Herbert J. 1995. *Sing Unto God a New Song: A Contemporary Reading of the Psalms*. Bloomington: Indiana University Press.
Loewen, Jacob. 1981. *The Practice of Translation: Drills for Training Translators*. New York: United Bible Societies.
Longman, Tremper, III. 1988. *How to Read the Psalms*. Downers Grove, Ill.: InterVarsity Press.
Magonet, Jonathan. 1994. *A Rabbi reads the Psalms*. London: SCM Press.
Mays, James L. 1994. *Psalms*. Interpretation Commentary. Louisville: John Knox Press.
———. 1994. *The Lord Reigns: A Theological Handbook to the Psalms*. Louisville: Westminster/John Knox Press.

McCann, J. Clinton, Jr. 1993. *A Theological Introduction to the Book of Psalms*. Nashville: Abingdon Press.

Miller, Patrick D., Jr. 1986. *Interpreting the Psalms*. Philadelphia: Fortress Press.

———. 1994. *They Cried to the LORD: The Form and Theology of Biblical Prayer*. Minneapolis: Fortress Press.

Moomo, David. 1993. "Hebrew and Ebira Poetry." *Notes on Translation* 7(4): 9–25.

Newman, Barclay. 1993. "Biblical Poetry and English Style." *The Bible Translator* 29(2): 206–12.

Nida, Eugene A. 1985. *Exploring Semantic Structures*. Munich: Wilhelm Fink Verlag.

———. and Charles Taber. 1969. *The Theory and Practice of Translation*. Leiden: E. J. Brill.

Noss, Phillip. 1976. "The Psalms and Gbaya Literary Style." *The Bible Translator* 27(1): 110–18.

Ntuli, D. B. 1984. *The Poetry of B.W. Vilikazi*. Pretoria: J. L. van Schaik.

Petersen, David, and Kent Richards. 1992. *Interpreting Hebrew Poetry*. Minneapolis: Fortress Press.

Schoekel, Luis. 1988. *A Manual of Hebrew Poetics*. Rome: Editrice Pontificio Istituto Biblico.

Sterk, Jan. 1997. "Re-creating Isaiah's Poetry." *The Bible Translator* 48(3): 301–308.

de Waard, Jan, and Eugene A. Nida. 1986. *From One Language to Another: Functional Equivalence in Bible Translating*. Nashville: Thomas Nelson.

Watson, Wilfred. 1984. *Classical Hebrew Poetry: A Guide to Its Technique*. Sheffield: JSOT Press.

Wendland, Ernst R. 1985. *Language, Society, and Bible Translation*. Cape Town: Bible Society of South Africa.

———. 1993. *Comparative Discourse Analysis and the Translation of Psalm 22 in Chichewa*. Lewiston, N.Y.: Edwin Mellen Press.

———. 1994a. "Oral-Aural Dynamics of the Word: With special reference to John 17." *Notes on Translation* 8(1): 19–43.

———. 1994b. *Discourse Perspectives on Hebrew Poetry in the Scriptures*. New York: United Bible Societies.

———. 1995. *The Discourse Analysis of Hebrew Prophetic Literature*. Lewiston, N.Y.: Mellen Biblical Press.

———. 1998. *Buku Loyera: An Introduction to the New Chichewa Bible Translation*. Blantyre: Christian Literature Association in Malawi.

———. 2000. "A Form-Functional, Text-Comparative Method of Translation, Teaching, and Checking." *Notes on Translation* 14(1): 7-27.

Westermann, Claus. 1980. *The Psalms: Structure, Content and Message*. Translated by R. Gehrke. Minneapolis: Augsburg.

———. 1989. *The Living Psalms*. Grand Rapids: Eerdmans.

Wonderly, William. 1968. *Bible Translation for Popular Use*. New York: United Bible Societies.

Zogbo, Lynell, and Ernst Wendland. 2000. *Hebrew Poetry in the Bible: A Guide for Understanding and for Translating*. New York: United Bible Societies.

INDEX

–A–
A-B-A' ring construction, 116
abstract, 151
acrostic, 171
addition, 77
additive, 14
additive parallelism, 66, 77
adjunct, 63
Africa, 30
aim of analysis, 13, 36, 97, 122, 151
allusion, 162, 164
alphabet, 44
alternation, 95
ambiguity, 89, 160
anacrusis, 171
anadiplosis, 110, 122
anaphora, 111, 114, 122
anthropomorphic, 200
anthropomorphism, 152
antithetical parallelism, 66, 74
aperture, 14, 108, 111, 120, 122, 158, 173, 207
apostrophe, 153
appeal, 34
area of meaning, 193
artistic function, 177
aspect, 167
assonance, 171
asyndeton, 82, 120
attitude, 158
attribution, 91
ᶜal-ken, 81

–B–
back-translation, 25, 247
balance, 173
base, 67, 98
base addition, 94
base alternative, 95
base circumstance, 79
base comparison, 93
base-content, 72, 93
base–contrast, 74
base location, 92
base manner, 92
base-model, 248
base response, 93
base-addition, 71
base-amplification, 71
base-restatement, 71
beauty, 177
bicolon, 14, 64
blessed, 43
books, 21
boundary, 14, 108, 110, 118, 128, 135, 169, 206

–C–
case study, 250
causal addition, 81, 98
cause-effect, 81
center, 113
central core, 128, 134
characters, 180
chiasmus, 68, 125, 166, 232
Chichewa, 214
Chitonga, 246
ciyabilo, 246
climax, 14, 135, 206
closure, 14, 108, 113, 120, 122, 173, 207
cohesion, 136, 243, 248
cola, 62
collocational clash, 194
colometry, 95
colon, 62
communal, 34
community, 184, 185
compaction, 159, 162
comparative approach, 246
comparison, 107, 140, 208
compensation, 200
complementation, 66
completive addition, 91, 98
completive correlation, 97
componential analysis, 194
components of meaning, 192
compositional structure, 14
concentration, 206, 207
condensation, 159, 244
condition, 87, 88
condition-unexpected result, 88
confession, 30, 35, 187
conjunction, 79, 86
connected parallelism, 71
connotation, 55, 146, 153, 192, 197
connotative, 237
consonance, 171
construct, 63
content, 32, 180
context, 29, 97, 168, 204
continuity, 135, 139
contraction, 159
contra-expectation, 88
contrary to fact, 88
contrast, 74, 76
convergence, 118, 120, 121, 135, 174
conversation, 208
coordinate, 78
correspondence, 71, 121
cotext, 204
coupling, 62
covenant, 184, 189, 190

creation, 42, 247
cross-references, 205
cultural setting, 141, 205
cultural substitute, 201, 202

–D–
David, 18, 19, 24, 29, 51
defense, 35
deliverance, 188
denotative, 194, 237
diagram, 102, 115, 127
diagramming, 243
didactic psalm, 76
direct speech, 153, 179
discontinuity, 135, 139
discourse analysis, 13, 61
discourse parallelism, 23
discourse perspective, 246
discourse structure, 13, 61, 210, 216, 231
distribution, 244
doublet, 137
doxology, 21
dramatic movement, 182
dramatic roles, 182

–E–
ellipsis, 70, 75, 160
Elohim, 21
emic, 25
emotion, 54, 158, 162, 176, 177, 196, 208
emphasis, 66, 120, 131, 207
enallage, 169
enjambment, 171
epiphora, 114, 122, 145
essence of meaning, 237
etic, 25
eulogy, 38
euphony, 165
event, 96
expansion, 121
extended patterns, 123
external parallelism, 64
external structure, 62
extratextual, 205
Ezra, 19

–F–
faithfulness, 187
far parallelism, 62
fellowship, 184
figurative extention, 144
figurative language, 139, 229
figure of speech, 45
flashback, 228
flexibility, 168
footnote, 146, 164, 200

254

foregrounding, 241
form, 32
frequency, 140
front-shifting, 63, 167
function, 30, 32, 33, 36, 55, 63, 175
functional equivalent, 199, 208, 237
functional match, 202
functional matches, 214
functionally equivalent, 33
functions, 241

–G–
gapping, 69, 161
general-specific, 72
genre, 13, 25, 26, 32, 54, 57, 60, 175, 180, 205, 240, 246
grammar, 61
ground, 140, 142
ground-conclusion, 81

–H–
half-line, 64, 79
halleluyah, 41
heightened language, 135
heightening, 196
hendiadys, 138
ḥesed, 33, 186, 187, 220
hierarchy, 118, 207
historical psalms, 48, 188
hymn, 22, 41
hyperbole, 37, 50, 148, 154, 155

–I–
ideophone, 162
idiom, 199
idiomatic expression, 199, 200
illocution, 177, 208
illocutionary force, 129, 242
image, 140, 142, 147
imagery, 186, 233
implicit, 55, 70, 71, 141, 162, 164
imprecatory, 49, 155, 189
inclusio, 108, 122
inclusion, 108, 207
individual, 34
inductive, 239
inductive instruction, 239, 240
instruction, 42
internal parallelism, 65, 96
internal structure, 62
intertextual, 204
inversion, 126, 207
inverted pattern, 125
irony, 167
iteration, 136

–J–
judgment, 189
junction, 108, 110

–K–
key concepts, 192
key term, 22
key terms, 192, 207
kətubim, 21
Kifuliiru, 250
kingship, 183
kiy, 86

–L–
lament, 34, 166
law, 42
Law, 21
lexical analysis, 192
lexical equivalents, 195
lexical field, 195
literalism, 160, 193
literary devices, 61
literary functional equivalence, 13
liturgical, 28, 30, 53
liturgy, 33
loanword, 201

–M–
macrolevel, 243
major functions, 34
maqqeph, 63, 65, 174
marker, 118, 119, 123, 126, 140, 142
Masoretic Text, 20
meaning, 14, 55, 61, 135, 165, 192
meaning package, 208
means-purpose, 85
means-request, 83
means-result, 83
merismus, 148
Messiah, 43, 51, 184, 189
messianic, 243
Messianic, 52
metaphor, 142, 154
meter, 173, 244
methodology, 14, 73, 83, 84, 96, 99, 103, 118, 119, 121, 126, 141, 146, 193, 195, 201, 204, 209, 239, 245
metonym, 148
metonymy, 147
midpoint, 24
minor functions, 46
mizmor, 17, 25
mode, 118
model, 246
monocolon, 64, 173
mood, 118, 138
motif, 183
music, 26, 31, 251

–N–
natural equivalent, 146
ndakatulo, 214, 246
new topic, 158
nominal clause, 63

numbering, 20

–O–
onomatopoeia, 171
oracle, 55
oral presentation, 214
orality, 137

–P–
paragraph, 109
parallel passages, 19
parallel psalms, 23, 44
parallelism, 13, 62, 108, 135, 206, 243
paraphrase, 237, 246
Paratext, 206
participants, 180
part-whole, 148
pause, 62
peace, 185
peak, 14, 120, 135, 206
penitential, 46, 47
penitential psalms, 186
performative utterance, 176
personification, 150
petition, 22, 33, 34, 46
Pilgrimage Songs, 53
poet, 238, 239, 245
poetic, 165, 208, 238, 247
poetic lines, 62
poetry, 62, 89, 240
point of view, 182
popular language, 239
praise, 33, 35, 41
prayer, 34
preposition, 24, 84
printed format, 216
problem, 34
problem in analysis, 20, 21, 24, 25, 28, 37, 79, 84, 89, 93, 95, 145, 161, 168, 169
profession, 33, 35, 39, 45
prominence, 165, 243
promise, 39
pronoun, 153, 160, 169
pronoun shifting, 169
pronouns, 244
prophetic, 51
Prophets, 21
proposition, 98
propositional analysis, 133, 210
prosaic particles, 160
psalmoi, 17
psalms of ascent, 185
Psalter, 17
puns, 172

–Q–
qualification, 91
question, 157
questions, 209, 212, 228, 235
quotations, 52

–R–

range of meaning, 197
real condition-result, 87
reason-result, 81
receptor language, 13
recursion, 108, 135, 136
refrain, 23, 53, 54, 145
relevance, 163
religious setting, 163
remembrance, 33, 40, 48
repentance, 33, 47
repetition, 122, 136, 138, 175, 206, 219
request-purpose, 85
request-reason, 82
resonance, 197
retribution, 33, 49
rhetoric, 61, 241
rhetorical question, 157
rhyme, 172
rhythm, 165, 173
rhythmic unit, 173
righteousness, 189
ritual function, 140, 176
royal songs, 22, 52
royalty, 33

–S–
Salvation-History, 38
seconding, 67
segmentation, 243
selah, 28
semantic components, 194, 197
semantic field, 137
semantic relations, 98, 102
separated parallelism, 72
Septuagint, 18, 20, 28, 52
sequential time, 78
Sheol, 40
šir, 25
shift, 117, 118
shift in pattern, 170
sickness, 47
similarity, 67
simile, 140
simultaneous time, 78
sinfulness, 186
song, 30
Songs of Ascent, 53

sound effects, 172
sound qualities, 248
sound structure, 61, 171, 244
speech acts, 176, 208
speech event, 208
stages, 34
stanza, 14, 109, 224
strophe, 14, 109
structure, 55, 131, 181, 184
style, 13, 32, 33, 44, 55, 61, 241
stylistic features, 135, 171, 207, 240, 241, 244
superscriptions, 24
symmetrical pattern, 109, 123
symmetry, 64, 120
synecdoche, 148, 150
synonymous correlation, 98
synonymous parallelism, 66, 67
synonymy, 69, 71
syntactic elements, 69
synthetic parallelism, 77
system, 183

–T–
target language, 32
temporal addition, 98
temporal correlation, 77
tense, 167
terrace pattern, 123
test, 208
testing, 202, 249
tetracolon, 64
textual criticism, 20
təhillim, 17
təpillot, 17
thanksgiving, 33, 38, 39, 48
thematic movement, 102
thematic outline, 207
theme, 183, 204, 245
theological, 30
theophany, 40, 153
THP, 17
titles, 24, 242
TL poetry, 245
TL substitute, 146
tone, 118

topic, 118, 140, 142, 147, 183, 190, 205
Topic/Comment/Focus, 250
torah, 22, 42, 44, 187, 196, 233
training, 240
translation, 112, 143, 197, 200, 208, 214, 237
transliteration, 201
tricolon, 64, 173
trust, 33
truth, 187
type, 33

–U–
unity, 68, 70, 183, 207
unknown concept, 201
unreal condition-result, 88

–V–
variation, 68, 165, 247
variety, 165
verbless, 75, 121
vocative, 34, 119, 153, 229
Vulgate, 20

–W–
warfare, 186
Warrior, 186
wayyiqtol, 167
wisdom, 42, 43
wisdom question, 158
word order, 63, 68, 120, 244, 250
word pairs, 130, 137, 207, 245
word unit, 68
word-unit, 65
workshop, 14, 238, 240, 249
worship, 53, 189
Writings, 21

–Y–
Yahweh, 21

–Z–
Zion, 42, 51, 53, 185

www.ingramcontent.com/pod-product-compliance
Lightning Source LLC
Chambersburg PA
CBHW080409300426
44113CB00015B/2453